MEN IN FAMILIES
When Do They Get Involved?
What Difference Does It Make?

MEN IN FAMILIES
When Do They Get Involved?
What Difference Does It Make?

Edited by

Alan Booth
Ann C. Crouter
The Pennsylvania State University

LEA LAWRENCE ERLBAUM ASSOCIATES, PUBLISHERS
1998 Mahwah, New Jersey   London

Lawrence Erlbaum Associates, Inc., Publishers
10 Industrial Avenue
Mahwah, New Jersey 07430

Cover design by Kathryn Houghtaling Lacey

Library of Congress Cataloging-in-Publication-Data

Men in families : when do they get involved? : what
    difference does it make? / edited by Alan Booth,
    Ann C. Crouter.
        p. cm.
    Based on presentations from a national sympo-
sium on men in families, held at Pennsylvania State
University, 1996.
    Includes bibliographical references and index.
    ISBN 0-8058-2539-8 (cloth : alk. paper)
    1. Fathers—Congresses. 2. Father and
child—Congresses. 3. Family—Congresses. 4. Sex
role—Congresses. I. Booth, Alan. II. Crouter, Ann
C.
HQ756.M453 1997
305.31—dc21   97-12617
                                                     CIP

Books published by Lawrence Erlbaum Associates are
printed on acid-free paper, and their bindings are
chosen for strength and durability.

Printed in the United States of America
10   9   8   7   6   5   4   3   2   1

Contents

Preface

The role of fathers and husbands in families has come to the fore as an important issue. It shows up in legislation aimed at deadbeat dads, social movements such as the Million Man March and Promise Keepers, in the development of advocacy groups, and in think tanks. Contemporary research on men in family relationships has very mixed results. Some studies show small effects of fathers on child development and their role in preventing antisocial behavior; others suggest no effects. Still other research suggests the primary importance of men in families is in their role as provider. Others suggest husbands and fathers do their most vital work in new families, while others indicate that it is when offspring reach adolescence. Labor market trends would suggest that men's family roles may diminish. The time seems appropriate to bring scholars together to try to define men's current family roles, as well as estimate what the future portends for fathers and husbands. The chapters in this book address these issues; they are based on the presentations and discussions from a national symposium on men in families held at The Pennsylvania State University, October 31–November 1, 1996, as the fourth in a series of annual symposia focused on family issues.

ACKNOWLEDGMENTS

There are many to thank for assistance with the symposium. We are indebted to The Pennsylvania State University Population Research Institute, College of the Liberal Arts, College of Health and Human Development, Department of Sociology, Department of Psychology, Department of Human Development and Family Studies, Department of History, and Women's Studies Program for funding the symposium. We also are indebted to Patricia Book, Associate Vice President for Continuing Education, for her role in awarding the symposium a grant from the Continuing Education Program Innovation Fund. We appreciate the advice and encouragement of members of the Population Research Institute throughout the process of planning and conducting the symposium. The contributions of Chuck Herd, Ramona King, Kris McNeel, Sheri Miller, Sondra Morrison, Pat Thomas, Sherry Yocum, and Laura Zimmerman in assisting with the administration of the symposium were invaluable. Special thanks to professors William Axinn, Catherine Cohan, Daniel Lichter, and Susan McHale for their excellent work in presiding over the four sessions, and for their contributions to the flow of ideas during the sessions.

Part I

MEN'S ROLES IN FAMILIES:
A LOOK BACK,
A LOOK FORWARD

From Patriarchy to Androgyny and Other Myths: Placing Men's Family Roles in Historical Perspective

Steven Mintz
University of Houston

It is not a historical accident that Father's Day only became a national holiday in 1972, 58 years after Mother's Day received national recognition. Nor is it accidental that although Mother's Day is the busiest day of the year for telephone calls, Father's Day is just another Sunday (although it is the largest day for collect calls). Since the 1920s, Americans have held curiously ambivalent attitudes toward men's roles in families. Although sometimes admiring the family man as nurturer, protector, mentor, adviser, role model, authority figure, romantic partner, or big pal, popular culture has more often depicted such men in much more negative ways—as aloof and distant, inept and ineffectual, philandering or violent, neglectful and irresponsible, self-absorbed and emotionally insensitive, or simply super-fluous. Lovable but pitiful bumblers, like Dagwood and Homer Simpson; henpecked louts like Ralph Kramden or Fred Flintstone; or fantasy-driven schemers like Al Bundy have been more common representations of fathers and husbands than the stammering but understanding Ozzie Nelson, the wacky but romantic Ricky Ricardo, or the authoritative and responsible Jim Anderson, Mike Brady, Ward Cleaver, and Cliff Huxtable.

Until very recently, it was quite properly said that the history of women was *terra incognita*. Twenty-five years of intensive research by women's historians has begun to correct this omission, as women's historians have struggled to recover women's past cultural, domestic, economic, and political roles. What remains less charted, even today, is men's history. To be sure, historical research has always focused on men's public achievements. But it largely ignored men's private lives, especially their roles in families as fathers and husbands.

By shattering the assumption that gender roles are natural, ahistorical, and unchanging, and revealing that gender roles are cultural and ideological constructs, the products of particular historical circumstances, women's history has inspired a wide-ranging effort to understand how and why men's roles within the family have changed over time (Carnes, 1989; Carnes & Griffen, 1990; Danahay, 1993; Gerson, 1993; Griswold, 1993; Kimmel, 1987; Kimmel, 1996; Pugh, 1983; Rotundo, 1993; Stearns, 1990). One of women's historians' great accomplishments has been to demonstrate that women's relationship to work and production has structured their status, roles, and self-image. In the pages that follow, I argue that men's historians must not shy away from understanding how men's work relationships shape their status and roles in the family.

It is only across the past decade and a half that historians have begun the intensive archival research necessary to reconstruct men's familial roles. Scholarship, however, abhors a vacuum, and a lack of historical data did not prevent historians, psychologists, and sociologists from speculating about the hidden history of men's domestic roles. Drawing on a limited number of historical examples, scholars devised a variety of stage theories and functionalist models describing long-term trends in the history of fatherhood. These frameworks tended to either romanticize or demonize men's familial roles in the past, depicting the preindustrial era as a time when men were intensely and actively involved in family life, especially in childrearing, or, conversely, as a period when men were domestic patriarchs who dominated their children and tyrannized their wives.

Much of this theorizing focused on men as fathers. Demos (1986), J. Pleck (1987), and Rotundo (1985), for example, advanced multistaged models of historical change, which described shifts from the image of father as moral overseer and pedagogue, to father as disciplinarian and breadwinner, father as sex role model, and the "androgynous" male mother and nurturer. Popenoe (1996) and Blankenhorn (1995), in contrast, described the history of fathers as a long-term movement from the center toward the periphery of family life, whereas Griswold (1993) argued that throughout the 20th century, men's breadwinning role served as a rationalization for a persistent unwillingness to assume an equal role in childrearing and housework. These and many other models of change tend to identify industrialization as the critical turning point in the history of men's familial roles, as the defining moment when men's position in the family became marginalized, and economic ties with his wife and children began to outweigh his emotional connections.

This essay draws on the latest historical research to reconstruct the shifting contours of men's roles within families throughout U.S. history. Given the incompleteness of historical knowledge, any conclusions must necessarily be tentative and subject to revision. Furthermore, because much of the research deals exclusively with White middle-class families, it is difficult to generalize beyond this particular group. Nevertheless, recent historical findings raise profound questions about earlier models that describe unilinear patterns of change, argue that industrialization fundamentally weakened men's familial roles, or homogenize men's experience across class, ethnic, or geographical lines. Above all, this body of research throws into question binary modes of thinking that contrast patriarchal conceptions of men's roles in the past with egalitarian definitions in the present, and underscores the theme that men's roles within the family cannot be understood apart from changes in the organization in the economy or such major historical events as mass immigration, depression, and war.

MEN'S ROLES IN COLONIAL FAMILIES

There are two contrasting views of men's familial roles in the colonial era. One view is that the conditions of colonial life encouraged intense male involvement in family life. Because there was no sharp split between home and work or between productive and reproductive activities, men supposedly interacted with family members much more frequently and actively than they have done later in U.S. history. Fathers, according to this view, were responsible for instructing their children in basic literacy, craft skills, and religion, whereas mothers, and even children, participated directly in their husband or father's livelihood. Historians who stress paternal involvement in family life during the colonial era point to a variety of striking examples: Childrearing manuals were addressed to fathers, not mothers; in cases of divorce, fathers were almost automatically awarded custody; and young men, when they corresponded with their family from school or an apprenticeship, wrote to their fathers (Demos, 1986).

It would be a mistake, however, to exaggerate colonial men's involvement in family life. Although there is evidence of paternal attachment to, and indulgence of, very young children, there is no evidence to suggest that men engaged in the daily care of infants or toddlers. Diapering, feeding, bathing, cooking, and the general tasks of childrearing were left to women, the wives, older daughters, or servants. By our standards, childhood was quite brief, and consequently direct paternal oversight over children was similarly brief. Many children, as early as the age of 7, lived apart from their parents for a period of time, with other families as apprentices or servants under the authority of another master. Finally, many of the examples cited to demonstrate male involvement—drawn from a handful of leading New England ministers and merchants—may be unrepresentative of the much larger number of men who made their livelihood as farmers, artisans, traders, or sailors (Stearns, 1991).

A second viewpoint defines men's roles in colonial families in terms of patriarchy. Colonial America was a hierarchical society, and paternal and husbandly authority was part of the "Great Chain of Being" that bound every being in a line of authority and subordination extending from God. Both the tenets of Protestant religion and the dictates of colonial law stressed wifely submission to her husband's will and children's dependent and subordinate status (Amussen, 1988; Morgan, 1965; Norton, 1996; Schochet, 1975).

This stress on patriarchal authority was itself a product of specific historical circumstances. The Protestant Reformation augmented paternal authority within the home, giving fathers, for example, a legal right to determine which men could court his daughters and a legal responsibility to give or withhold consent from a child's marriage. Throughout the English-speaking world, certain basic patriarchal principles were taken for granted: hierarchy was essential to successful household functioning, fathers and husbands were responsible for directing family activities, and wives and children were subject to men's authority. Because husbands and fathers were thought to play a crucial role in the maintenance of social order, local government extended them explicit and far-reaching responsibility to oversee all aspects of their dependents' lives (e.g., colonial law required fathers to lead their families in prayer; teach children and servants the catechism; report runaway servants; place children in a lawful calling or occupation; oversee children's choice of a spouse; and, above all, discipline wayward or disorderly household members). In exchange for his support, education, and training, a man's children's services and earnings were his property, as were his wife's property and earnings. In addition, authorities required household heads to correct and punish abusive or insubordinate wives, disruptive children, and unruly servants in order to maintain orderly households (Mintz, 1992; Norton, 1996; Ozment, 1983).

Surviving artifacts reinforce the impression of a patriarchal society. A prime symbol of male dominance lay in the fact that he sat in an armchair, whereas other family members sat on benches or stools. In letters, husbands seldom asked their wives for advice; they generally addressed their wives in their correspondence with condescending terms such as "Dear Child," whereas women addressed their husbands as "Mister" and signed their letters "your faithful and obedient Wife." Patriarchy characterized relations with children, too. In Connecticut and Rhode Island, a rebellious son could be confined in a house of correction, and a 1646 Massachusetts law made it a capital offence for "a stubborn or rebellious son . . . to not obey the voice of his Father" (Mintz, 1992, p. 640). Native Americans were shocked by the harsh way that colonial fathers disciplined their children.

Many documents record fathers' intervention in children's marital decisions, on such issues of timing, financial considerations, and religious concerns (Greven, 1977, 1991; Koehler, 1980; Morgan, 1965; Norton, 1996).

Yet, to characterize the male family role simply as patriarchal without qualification would be misleading. Although religion and law prescribed a hierarchical ordering of family relations—summed up in the Biblical command to Eve "Thy desire shall be to thy husband and he shall rule over thee"—actual familial realities were much more complicated. The Protestant Reformation gave expression to a radical reevaluation of marriage and family life. Although most Protestants, unlike Catholics, did not consider marriage a sacrament, they did extend to marriage a new spiritual significance and value (summed up in the phrase "holy matrimony") and considered the companionship and intimacy of marriage as one of the elements that gave life meaning (a far cry from an older view that the best thing that could be said about marriage is that it is better to marry than to burn). Colonial law required husbands to live with their wives, support them financially, assume any debts that their wives contracted before marriage, and pay fines for their wives' criminal behavior (Norton, 1996; Ozment, 1983).

In addition, the concept of patriarchy is somewhat misleading in that women shouldered many duties that would subsequently be monopolized by men, including trade and home manufacturing, and, at times, supervising planting or even administering estates. Furthermore, community pressures and law circumscribed men's familial authority. For example, Puritan Connecticut and Massachusetts instituted the first laws in U.S. history against wife beating, adultery, and fornication; these colonies also recognized a right to divorce with remarriage in cases of abandonment, adultery, and extreme physical cruelty and prohibited "any unnatural severitie" toward children (Mintz, 1992; J. Pleck, 1987).

A thorough understanding of men's roles in families during the colonial era must begin by understanding the economic and demographic circumstances that shaped family life in various geographical regions. There were significant regional variations in the direction of change. In New England, a patriarchal conception of men's familial roles began to break down as early as the 1670s, whereas in the Chesapeake colonies of Maryland and Virginia, a more patriarchal structure of relationships did not truly emerge until the late 17th and 18th centuries (Greene, 1988).

There can be little doubt that many Puritan men in the first and second generations aspired to become family patriarchs (although they specifically eschewed use of the term). Likening their "errand in the wilderness" to the ancient Hebrews' 40 years of wandering in the desert, the first generation sought to recreate a hierarchical form of family life that was disintegrating in England itself. These men tended to conceive of the family in dynastic and corporate terms. They wanted to keep their children near by and pass on their patrimony from one generation to the next. These men placed great stress on family continuity, an emphasis that was apparent in their naming patterns, their economic strategies, and their inheritance practices. Compared to other English-speaking people, they were more likely to name their first-born sons after themselves. Viewing the family as a cooperative economic enterprise, men exercised strict control over their children, particularly their sons. They closely supervised apprenticeships, offered explicit instructions to their children (even when they reached adulthood), monitored sexual contacts, and took an active role in courtship and marriage. To a remarkable extent, sons accommodated themselves to paternal authority. Precisely because sons were fearful of losing their paternal inheritance, few publicly challenged their father's authority (Ditz, 1986; Fischer, 1989; Greven, 1970; Norton, 1996; Shammas, Samlon, & Dahlin, 1987).

Demographic circumstances that were truly unique made this patriarchal role attainable. Because of its cold winters and low population density, 17th-century New England was perhaps the most healthful region in the world at the time. After an initial period of high mortality, life expectancy quickly rose to levels comparable to our own. Prolonged life expectancy allowed a clearly delineated age structure to emerge (Mintz & Kellogg, 1988).

Other demographic circumstances also contributed to a more patriarchal conception of men's roles. Husbands tended to be significantly older than their wives—4 or 5 years on average—and sought to look older still by wearing white wigs and elaborate waistcoats. Because virtually all women married (between 95% and 98%), it was a nearly universal experience for a woman to transfer subordination to a father to subordination to a husband (without the interruption of a period of relative freedom, which antebellum Americans called *girlhood*, when women worked temporarily outside a home; Ulrich, 1982).

The organization of the economy further reinforced patriarchy. A central unit of production was the family farm, which functioned as a corporate unit. Wives and children were expected to contribute to the family's economic well-being under men's direction. Control of landed property and craft skills further buttressed men's authority (Mintz & Kellogg, 1988).

Few institutions competed with a father's authority. Despite laws requiring the establishment of schools, most children were educated informally, and although older children were temporarily put out as servants or apprentices between 7 and 12 years of age, most adolescents lived at home under their father's watchful eye. Available evidence suggests that fathers did indeed play an active role in decisions involving choice of an occupation, courtship, and marriage. To maintain control, fathers usually refused to pass legal title to land to their sons until death, keeping them dependent for years, delaying full adulthood autonomy until sons reached middle age (Ditz, 1986; Greven, 1970; Shammas et al., 1987).

Yet, it is striking how quickly this patriarchal blueprint frayed. As early as the second or third generation, high rates of fertility and increased geographical mobility began to undermine the patriarchal order. Fathers no longer had sufficient land to keep sons at home and sons lacked sufficient incentives to stay. Increased occupational choice and new economic opportunities in seaports and commercial towns drew many young men away from the parental home, undermining patriarchal authority. A separate adolescent subculture, free from adult control, began to emerge, as young men joined militia companies, voluntary associations, and religious groups. The external controls imposed by churches, courts, and parents on children's sexual behavior all lost effectiveness, a development apparent in a sharp increase in illegitimate births and prenuptial pregnancies. Fathers also increasingly lost the ability to control the timing of their children's marriages (Mintz & Kellogg, 1988).

Class, regional, ethnic, and religious differences characterized men's familial roles and relationships during the colonial era. The families created by Quakers in Pennsylvania, New Jersey, and Delaware, were far less authoritarian and patriarchal than those in New England. Far less anxious than the Puritans about "infant depravity" or original sin, Quakers sought to protect childhood innocence by raising their children within nurturing families. Unlike the New England Puritans, Quakers also emphasized early autonomy for children and companionship between wives and husbands. They provided daughters with an early dowry and sons with sufficient land to provide a basis for early independence. In addition, the Quakers' stress on conjugal love and companionship contributed to the fact that they were the first U.S. group to self-consciously reduce birth rates (Fischer, 1989; Levy, 1988).

The portrait of a patriarchal order giving way to diminished paternal authority and increased autonomy for children may have been true in New England, but it fails to describe trends elsewhere. A very different pattern of change took place in the Chesapeake colonies of Maryland and Virginia. Here, the trend was toward increased paternal authority, not its diminishment (Moran, 1991).

A key reason for this shift was demographic. The further south one looks, the more unbalanced the sex ratio and the higher the death rate. In New England, the sex ratio was relatively even, with men outnumbering women 3 to 2 in the first generation. But in New Netherlands, there were 2 men for every 1 female and the ratio was 6 to 1 in the Chesapeake. Whereas the New England population became self-sustaining as early as the 1630s, New Jersey and Pennsylvania did not achieve this until the 1660s to the 1680s, and Virginia until after 1700 (Kulikoff, 1986; Rutman & Rutman, 1984).

During the 17th century, a high death rate and an unbalanced sex ratio made it impossible to establish the kind of the stable, patriarchal family that took root in New England. In the Chesapeake region, half of all marriages were broken by death within 7 or 8 years and half of all children lost their fathers before marrying. Death rates were so high that a parent's remarriage was often dissolved by death before a child reached adulthood. Under these circumstances, most families in the Chesapeake were highly complex units consisting of a complicated assortment of step-parents, step-children, wards, and half-brothers and sisters. The high death rate contributed to a society that attached relatively more importance to the extended kinship network and less to the nuclear family. As late as the American Revolution, few men in the southern colonies could be confident of directly passing property to their sons. And even in the 20th century, southern families have been much more likely than their northern counterparts to use surnames as first names, underscoring the continuing importance of extended family identity (Rutman & Rutman, 1984).

Between 1690 and 1760, as the death rate declined, the sex ratio grew more balanced, and marriages survived longer, a more stable set of patriarchal family relationships began to emerge. Yet the nature of patriarchy was quite different in the Chesapeake than in New England. Outwardly, relations between fathers and children were even more hierarchical than in New England, with many southern sons addressing their father in letters as "Sir" or "Dear Sir." And certainly many planters tried to mold their sons into gentlemen and influence their offspring's education and marriage decisions. But it is also clear that parental indulgence, lax discipline, and early independence characterized many planters' relationships with their offspring. It seems likely that the more indulgent patriarchy of the Chesapeake region was an ironic by-product of slavery, because social control energies were diverted away from their own children to racial control (Greven, 1977; Moran, 1991).

Marital relations, too, appear to have blended together an odd mixture of patriarchy and wifely independence. The age difference between husbands and wives was far greater in the southern colonies than elsewhere. Prior to 1700, a man would usually marry in his mid-20s, whereas most women married by 17. The female age of first marriage rose during the 18th century, but remained far lower than in the northern colonies (Fischer, 1989).

Yet, if the age gap discouraged close companionship between spouses, the law extended greater legal and property rights to women than was true in New England. Puritan lawmakers considered marital unity under the husband a prerequisite of social stability, and eliminated English common-law protections that assumed that husbands and wives had separate interests such as separate estates for women, dower interest, prenuptial contracts, and suits in equity. In contrast, in Maryland, South Carolina, and Virginia, where the death rate was higher and widows were more likely to be left with young children, women received greater protections for personal and real property (Mintz, 1992). It is not a surprise, given these circumstances, that southern marital relations seem to have been more strife-ridden. In a famous incident in Virginia in 1687, Sarah Harrison disrupted her wedding to Dr. James Blair, the future founder of William and Mary College, by refusing to promise to obey her husband (Fischer, 1989).

Yet for all the regional differences in men's familial roles, one striking characteristic that emerges from the historical record is the importance of father figures in young men's lives. As a result of the nature of the economy, the father–son (or fictive father–son) axis appears to have been much more important than it today. Although 18th-century America was not as highly stratified as 18th-century Britain, it was, nevertheless, a patronage society organized around vertical bonds of patronage and kinship. Society was conceived in terms of a succession of patron-dependent relationships: God to man, king to subject, husband to wife, master to servant, parent to child. Indeed, one of the primary objectives of socialization of boys was to teach them to accommodate themselves to hierarchical authority and to forge vertical connections (Wood, 1992).

When one looks at the biographies of many influential 18th-century figures, such as Benjamin Franklin, George Washington, Alexander Hamilton, or Thomas Jefferson, one is struck by the pivotal importance of relationships with certain patrons or kinsmen. Take the example of Alexander Hamilton, who was born out of wedlock in the West Indies. It was only through the generosity of wealthy benefactors that he was able to go to New York to study. Or take Franklin, whose apprenticeship with an older brother provided the training in the printing trade, which would make the young man wealthy enough to retire at an early age and begin a new career in science and politics. Or take Washington, whose father died when he was 11. After his father's death, George went to live with his half-brother Lawrence, 14 years his senior, who secured him an appointment as a surveyor through connections with the wealthy British Fairfax family. When Lawrence's only child died in 1752, George inherited his half-brother's estate. Standing out in each of these examples is the critical role that older males served in training or placing younger men (Alden, 1984; Brodie, 1974; Emery, 1982; Ferling, 1988; Lopez & Herbert, 1975; McDonald, 1979).

The essential point is that ideologically and economically, colonial America attached greater symbolic significance to the father–son dyad (or to the fictive father–son relationship) than to spousal relationships or the mother–child dyad. How and why this changed—and how this transformation was connected to broader economic, religious, and social transformations—is one of the major themes in the history of U.S. family life.

REVOLT AGAINST PATRIARCHY

The years preceding the American Revolution witnessed repeated attacks on the principle of patriarchy. The most popular books in the American colonies on the eve of the revolution dealt not with politics, like John Locke's *Second Treatise on Liberty,* but with childrearing, like Locke's *Essay Concerning Human Understanding* or Rousseau's *Emile,* or marriage, like Oliver Goldsmith's *The Vicar of Wakefield.* Novels, plays, and poems by the writers Samuel Richardson, Oliver Goldsmith, Henry Fielding, and Laurence Sterne attacked patriarchy and hierarchy as unduly repressive and out of step with the times. Readers learned that love was superior to property as a basis for marriage; marriage should be based on sympathy, affection, and friendship; parental example was more effective than coercion in governing children; and the ideal parent sought to cultivate children's natural talents and abilities through love (Fliegelman, 1982).

A key component of the late 18th century revolt against patriarchy was a profound shift in sensibility. An older classical ideal of formality, emotional restraint, self-mastery, and rational control gave way to a growing idealization of marriage based on companionship, affinity, and affection and emotional concern for children. This romantic revolution placed a much higher value on emotions and feelings. It viewed the family not as a productive unit embedded in a broader community, but as a "walled garden" of loving and caring in an inhospitable world. The older view that individuals should strive to moderate their affections and remember that marriage ceases with death gave way to a new emphasis on emotional expression and a conception of heaven as a place where family members will be reunited (Lewis, 1983).

The revolt against patriarchal authority cannot be understood apart from broader changes in society. In part, condemnation of patriarchy was rooted in shifting generational relations. The older ideal of a patriarch controlling the details of his children's lives gave way to a very different ideal: the father as benefactor, who sought to promote his children's success and found fulfillment in their lives. This new view, in turn, was rooted in fathers' diminishing ability to transmit their status position to their children. In a shifting economy, the young found increasing opportunities outside of agriculture, and partible inheritance practices produced plots too small to viably support a family (Fliegelman, 1982).

The condemnation of patriarchy also reflected the growing importance of choice of a husband in a woman's life. No longer was marriage a virtually universal experience for women; instead, it became a conscious choice, and a more important one at that. To a much stronger degree than in the past, a woman's economic well-being was linked to the identity of her future husband. It is not an historical accident that for the first time many women went through a "marriage crisis" before entering or rejecting a marriage proposal (Cott, 1977).

Finally, the attack on patriarchy was part of a larger assault against a patronage society, the vertical bonds of dependence that limited men's freedom. Much as the contractualist philosopher John Locke scathingly attacked the organic and patriarchal philosophy of Filmer, the attack on patriarchy was part of a broader condemnation of outmoded restraints restraining individual mobility and opportunity. Indeed, in the wake of the American revolution, many vestiges of a patriarchal patronage society were outlawed, including plural officeholding, nepotism, and laws requiring parental consent for their children's marriages (Mintz & Kellogg, 1988).

The essential point is that the assault on patriarchal authority did not undermine mens' position in the family. Although it delegitimized one particular conception of men's familial roles, it simultaneously promoted an alternate vision, emphasizing sentimentality toward children and a more companionate relationship with one's wife. Instead of emphasizing docility and obedience, a new view of fatherhood sought to encourage sons' initiative and independence. And instead of stressing hierarchy, a new view of marriage stressed companionship and emotional closeness. If the decline of the corporate family economy weakened the material basis of paternal authority, a new romantic sensibility urged greater masculine involvement in the lives of their family (Mintz & Kellogg, 1988).

Three developments underscore these changes. In naming practices, fewer children are named after their father or mother. Instead they receive more individualized names (and middle names as well). Second, men's letters to their wives exhibit a marked change in tone. Husbands use a variety of terms of endearment (e.g., "dear," "honey," "sweetest") in their correspondence, seek their wives' advice, and tell them how much they love them (Mintz & Kellogg, 1988).

The third development is a reduction of the birth rate, which began in the United States at the end of the 18th century. The methods couples employed—coitus interruptus and periodic abstinence—required male cooperation. Although limitations on the birth rate partly reflect economic changes—especially rising standards of living and the fact that children were no longer economic assets—this development also reflects an ideological shift: An increasing number of husbands no longer regard wives as childbearing machines (Degler, 1980).

MEN IN 19TH-CENTURY FAMILIES

It is a commonplace of historical commentary that the decline in the
household economy of the colonial era marginalized men's role in the
family. The colonial home, according to this view, was not only a center
of production, but a system of authority, and with the rise of a commercial
economy, men moved to the periphery of family life, their contribution
becoming essentially economic. Is this view justified? Did industrialization
thrust fathers to the emotional and psychological periphery of family life?
Or is this simply an example of nostalgia for a mythical golden age?

Certainly a number of contemporary observers were convinced that
social change sharply altered the nature of men's family involvement. In
1851, Horace Bushnell (cited in Thernstrom, 1984), a Presbyterian minister, declared that over his lifetime he had witnessed a "complete revolution in domestic life" (pp. 207–208). He lamented the breakup of the
"organic" household economy and especially men's declining influence
on their children's lives. The most famous statement about the weakness
of paternal authority was made by the French visitor Alexis de Tocqueville.
He observed that in the United States, bonds of affection between fathers
and sons were stronger than in Europe, but that these emotional ties were
premised on their offspring's early independence and mobility (Mintz &
Kellogg, 1988).

Yet, if in many cases the shift toward a more commercial and industrial
economy weakened paternal authority and reduced paternal involvement
in the family, this was not an automatic or inevitable consequence of social
change. One can point to many counter-examples, like the financier J. P.
Morgan, who wrote letters to his father virtually every day (Frank, 1992;
Mintz, 1983).

One cannot understand men's roles in the early 19th century apart
from two fundamental developments: The evangelical religious revivals
that shaped the moral atmosphere of pre-Civil War America, and the
emerging separation of home and work. During the decades before the
Civil War, a series of religious revivals known as the Second Great Awakening swept across U.S. society. The revivalists placed a new emphasis on
domesticity and especially on men's role as the family's moral overseer.
The revivalists depicted the family as a repository of moral values and a
school of character and promoted a new definition of masculinity: A truly
Christian family man who would serve as his family's religious leader,
educate his children, restrain their impulsive behavior, and take a loving
interest in his wife and children's lives. He was supposed to lead daily
family prayers, start his sons in a career, make decisions about schooling,
and enforce discipline. With many activities that might have competed
with an intense family life denied on religious grounds—such as dancing,

drinking, or the theater—and with relatively few dining groups or sporting activities targeted at adult men, many evangelical fathers found their closest companionship with their families (Davidoff & Hall, 1987).

During the 19th century, men tended to define themselves either in terms of this religiously rooted conception of domesticity or in opposition to it. Even in the early 19th century, family involvement for men was a matter of choice. Although many men embraced the evangelical conception of the father's role, many others rejected it. A variety of pieces of evidence suggest that desertion and abandonment as well as divorce increased sharply in the early nineteenth century (Stearns, 1991). Among the factors that may have led to the proliferation of "bad" husbands and fathers are an increase in geographical mobility as well as heightened economic stress and productive responsibilities that gave men new opportunities and incentives to leave unhappy families.

The physical separation of the household and the workplace also contributed to a new conception of the family and of men's familial roles. According to an emerging middle-class ideology, the family was an oasis or haven set apart from the pressures of business world, and the husband and father was his family's protector and provider. During the early 19th century, family roles were reorganized around the idea of sexual difference, with men and women increasingly occupying separate spheres. Prior to the 19th century, women had been active participants in commerce, farming, and many business pursuits, assisting their husbands, keeping books, overseeing apprentices and journeymen, and manufacturing many goods for sale. Not only artisans but even lawyers and doctors practiced in a room in their house, so women tended to have a direct relationship with their husband's business affairs.

During the first decades of the 19th century, however, the workplace moved some distance from the home. Increasingly men left home each day to go to work, whereas their wives stayed home. The midday meal, when an entire family gathered together, was now replaced by the evening meal. Apprentices, who previously had lived with their masters, were expelled from middle-class homes and began to live in distinct working-class neighborhoods. Even farm families adopted a sharper sexual division of labor, erecting separate structures for productive activities apart from the farmhouse and replacing the wife's productive labor with paid farm laborers (Mintz & Kellogg, 1988).

A new heavily gendered language emerged to describe familial relationships, which identified the husband as provider and his wife, children, and servants as his dependents. Indeed, a key component of middle-class status was a man who could dispense with his woman's productive labor. A shift in vocabulary underscores this change: Instead of calling a wife "mistress," a word descriptive of a woman's responsibilities over servants, apprentices, and journeymen, she was called "Mrs.," usually with her husband's name appended. In a wholly new way, a woman's identity was absorbed by her husband's (Davidoff & Hall, 1987).

A much more rigid demarcation of male and female spheres gradually emerged. Many middle-class women began to define themselves self-consciously as nurturers and full-time mothers, whereas the father was viewed as protector, provider, and the representative of public authority. Unlike the mother, whose position in the family was rooted in child care and household work, the middle-class father's authority within the home ultimately rested on material conditions outside the home—property, proprietorship, and connections to networks outside the family. The early years of the 19th century witnessed the emergence of a self-conscious middle class. Although a growing number of middle-class men worked temporarily as salaried employees, clerks, agents, copyists, and brokers, most middle-class men still worked or aspired to work as individual proprietors or professionals. This economic role exerted a strong impact on men's identity as husbands and fathers (Davidoff & Hall, 1987; Mintz, 1983).

Here, it is important to note a contrast between the early 19th century, wherein evidence of active male involvement in families remains strong, and the last 50 years of the century, wherein such evidence weakens. Many factors contributed to this shift. Masculine identity became increasingly identified with a man's occupation or career. Informal and formal systems of apprenticeship declined, replaced by modern forms of educational credentialing. The separation of home and workplace widened, a gulf that was apparent in the spatial restructuring of cities, with the middle class living further from business districts, and in the rise of single-sex clubs and fraternal orders. Male-only forms of recreation offered an increasingly attractive alternative to domesticity (Griswold, 1993).

To be a middle-class father and husband during the 19th century was to shoulder a heavily demanding role. A man was responsible for supporting his family at a much higher standard of living than in the past; he was also responsible for respectably educating and placing his offspring and caring for the increasing number of extended relatives who lived with his family—aging grandparents, aunts and uncles, younger unmarried siblings, and children of deceased relatives. Middle-class men, clad in black trousers and coats, began to dress in ways that underscored their maturity and weighty responsibilities (Davidoff & Hall, 1987). Nothing better symbolizes such fathers' important role in their family's psychic life than the host of 19th-century biographies—such as Harriet Beecher Stowe's, William and Henry James's, or Louisa May Alcott's—in which the father is a dominant presence, whereas the mother or stepmother is a shadowy figure (Mintz, 1983).

Many men were unable to meet the pressures of an emerging market economy. In a changing economy, lacking modern bankruptcy and limited liability laws, life insurance, and secure forms of investment, a man's economic position was much less stable than in the past. Technological displacement, mounting economic competition, economic vacillations, and opportunities for success or failure—all increased in frequency. If economic change increased opportunities for success and advancement, it also heightened the chances of failure. Not surprisingly, per capita consumption of alcohol doubled or tripled in the first decades of the 19th century, offering men a way to cope with increasing economic and social stresses (Rorabaugh, 1979).

The expanding market economy demanded new character traits. Obtaining credit in a society without modern credit bureaus required a man to offer tangible evidence of one's respectability through such symbols as church membership (after its founding, R. G. Dun, the prototype for the modern credit bureau, used church membership and sobriety as measures of a man's creditworthiness). Those who failed to adapt were doomed to failure (Davidoff & Hall, 1987).

Even a superficial survey of the biographies of significant early 19th century politicians, intellectuals, reformers, and religious leaders reveals a woe-filled litany of failed, abusive, or absent fathers and husbands. The fathers of Ralph Waldo Emerson, Nathaniel Hawthorne, and Andrew Jackson died prematurely when their sons were young boys. Herman Melville's father suffered insanity before dying when his son was 6. William Lloyd Garrison's father was an alcoholic; Thomas Wentworth Higginson's went bankrupt. Sam Houston left his wife and moved to Texas. The fathers of Abraham Lincoln and Joseph Smith were among the many economic failures who moved repeatedly in search of financial success. In cases like these, the early 19th century adage, "all that I am I owe to my mother," was at least in part an accurate description of reality (Reynolds, 1995, pp. 22–23).

Although a minority of youth began to spend a prolonged period in the parental home, often into their 20s—a period often characterized by intense intergenerational conflict with a father—an increasing number of young men and women left home in their early or midteens, often to move to a growing city. Distant from a father's influence, these young people had to socialize themselves for adulthood. Many young men joined sports clubs, fire companies, temperance societies, debating clubs, and other organizations that created provided a surrogate family, a network of connections, and an opportunity to develop speaking skills that would be useful in later life (Rotundo, 1993).

The urban working class developed a very different family configuration than the middle class. At a time when the middle class believed that the husband should be the sole breadwinner, very few working-class families were able to meet that cultural ideal. An older notion of a cooperative family economy persisted. Older children were expected to defer marriage, remain at home, and contribute to the family's income. Young men and women were frequently unable to establish households of their own until their early 30s (Mintz & Kellogg, 1988).

Despite the fact that few men could support a working-class family on their own wages, paternal authority was reinforced by the nature of employment. In factories and other workplaces, foremen, until the 1920s, did their own hiring, allowing fathers and kinsmen to find work for young relatives, or simply use their relatives as assistants. For the working class, the importance of the father–son dyad maintained its significance after the middle-class family had begun to stress spousal ties and mother–child bonds (Hareven, 1982).

It is important not to romanticize the working-class family life. Although ties to the immediate family and wider kin network tended to be strong, family cohesion stemmed in large measure from the marginal economic existence of many working-class families. The frequency of premature death, irregular employment, disabling accidents, and wages at or below the subsistence line, coupled with the inadequacy of public welfare mechanisms required individuals to rely on the family and kinship network for assistance and support (Griswold, 1993; Tentler, 1979).

The stresses produced by work and financial marginality clearly took a toll on 19th-century working-class family life. Many wives fed their husbands apart from the rest of the family and pressured children to play in the streets so as not to disturb their fathers' rest. The kinds of work available to working-class men produced high rates of geographic mobility and meant that many fathers were away from their homes for prolonged periods of time. Indeed, it was a common pattern for immigrant fathers, who were sometimes called "birds of passage," to work in the United States for an extended period before returning home to their families (Griswold, 1993; Piore, 1979).

It would not be until the mid-1910s that the cooperative working-class family economy began to give way to the "family wage" economy, which allowed a working-class male breadwinner to support his family on his wages alone. Increased real wages, particularly after the beginning of World War I in 1914, reduced the number of working-class children in the workforce. Contributing to this new family formation were the establishment of the first seniority systems governing promotion, layoffs, and rehiring. The New Deal further solidified this father-centered family economy by prohibiting child labor, expanding workmen's compensation, and targeting jobs programs at male workers (Mintz & Kellogg, 1988).

MEN'S FAMILIAL ROLES SINCE THE 1870s

Since the 1870s, public anxiety over men's familial roles has generated controversies strikingly similar to those that rage today. Men's roles as fathers and husbands first became recognized social problems in the decade following the Civil War, when "family preservationists" and "child protectors" denounced the lazy, dissolute working-class father who violated every standard of manly decency by deserting or beating his wife and economically exploiting or abusing his children. In response, 11 states made desertion and nonsupport of destitute families a felony and three states instituted the whipping post where wife-beaters were punished with floggings (Gordon, 1988; Griswold, 1993; E. H. Pleck, 1987).

To combat the economic exploitation of children, reformers pressed for compulsory school attendance laws, child labor restrictions, orphanages, and "orphan trains" to place abused and neglected children (many of whom had one or two living parents) with farm families in the Midwest. Meanwhile, there were concerted campaigns to reduce the divorce rate (which an 1880 report had revealed to be the world's highest) by reducing the grounds for divorce, extending waiting periods, and establishing family courts, along with efforts to eliminate segregated male-only forms of recreation, campaigns that achieved ultimate success with the destruction of red-light districts throughout the country during the 1910s and of saloons following adoption of Prohibition in 1918 (Cohen, 1990; Peiss, 1986; Rosenzweig, 1983).

Around the turn of the century, the way that the problem of men in families was socially and culturally constructed underwent radical redefinition. Alongside heightened efforts to promote the male family wage, to allow a man to support his family without the contribution of wives and children, there was a growing concern about the immigrant father, who seemed to symbolize "Old World" values and obstruct efforts to Americanize his children. To promote assimilation, self-conscious efforts were made to use schools, settlement houses, and peer relationships to help first-generation wives and children break free from traditional cultural values, often symbolized by the bearded, unassimilated, foreign language-speaking adult man (Griswold, 1993).

During the 1920s, public concern shifted away from working class and immigrant men to the "new" middle class of salaried employees. Between 1880 and 1920, a fundamental shift occurred in the way that urban middle-class men earned a living, as individual proprietors, professionals, or artisans rapidly gave way to wage earners with far fewer opportunities for economic autonomy and independence. As older sources of male identity in independent work, sex-segregated politics, and community leadership disappeared, a host of educators, psychologists, sociologists, and advertisers argued that in a changing society men would find their greatest satisfaction in private life, especially relations with their wives and children (Griswold, 1993).

The new cultural ideal was the *companionate* family, in which husbands and wives would be "friends and lovers" and fathers and children would be "pals." Proponents of this new ideal argued that in a modern society it was imperative that a family based on male authority and hierarchy give way to new family relationships emphasizing sexual fulfillment, mutual respect, and emotional satisfaction. Fearful that wives were growing increasingly discontented and that men were becoming increasingly estranged from their families, advocates of the companionate ideal promoted courses in family education, a more active fatherly role in children's development, and, above all, participation in a host of leisure activities (such as car excursions, board games, hobbies, and attendance at sporting events) that would bring family members closer together (Griswold, 1993).

A source of particular concern was that boys, raised almost exclusively by women, were becoming overly feminized. In response, family professionals called on fathers to become buddies with their sons, share sports and hobbies with them, provide them with sex education, and serve as a model of masculine maturity. And yet, as Robert Griswold showed, this advice was not accompanied by sustained efforts to involve fathers in childrearing. Experts addressed their advice almost exclusively to mothers, and organizations, like the Parent–Teachers Association, which might have involved men in child development, limited their membership almost exclusively to women. The sole exceptions to this pattern of male exclusion were the Boy Scouts and the 4-H Clubs (and beginning in the late 1930s, the Little Leagues). Sports and outdoor activities became defined as the primary link between men and their children (Griswold, 1993).

The Great Depression and World War II elevated public concern about men's familial roles and reinforced an older ideal of man as protector, provider, and disciplinarian. Many observers were convinced that the depression drastically altered family roles. Many unemployed fathers saw their status lowered by the Great Depression. With no wages to punctuate their authority, they lost status as primary decision makers. In fact, large numbers of men who could not fulfill their role as breadwinners lost self-respect, became immobilized, and stopped looking for work, whereas others turned to alcohol and became self-destructive or abusive to their families. Still others walked out the door, never to return. A survey in 1940 revealed that more than 1.5 million married women had been deserted by their husbands. Convinced that preserving men's breadwinning role was a special national priority, government job programs focused largely on putting the male jobless to work. A major goal of New Deal policy was to restore the male breadwinner ideal (Griswold, 1993; Mintz & Kellogg, 1988).

World War II also thrust men's familial roles into the public spotlight. Intense fears flourished during the war years that father absence produced a host of social problems, including an upsurge in juvenile delinquency among boys and sexual promiscuity among teenage girls. A particular source of concern was that father absence resulted in maternal oversolicitousness toward children, producing boys who were spoiled sissies (Blanken-horn, 1995; Griswold, 1993).

As a result of the Great Depression and World War II, many postwar social analysts argued that fathers had a critically important role to play in children's personality development—not so much as playmate but as sex role model and disciplinarian. The lack of a proper male role model was blamed for a wide range of social problems. Rigid, distant, overbearing fathers, it was argued, produced authoritarian personalities in their children, whereas weak, ineffectual fathers produced schizophrenia or homosexuality. Absent or uninvolved fathers resulted in delinquency in boys or in an overcompensated hypermasculinity. Yet, although experts called on fathers to guide and befriend their children and play sports with them, they did not expect fathers to change diapers or take an active role in child care or housework, arguing that this would make it difficult for boys and girls to develop a clearly defined sex role identity (Griswold, 1993).

Since 1960, there has been heightened cultural and political focus on men's familial roles. The Moynihan Report (see United States Department of Labor, Office of Policy Planning and Research, 1965), "The Negro Family: The Case for National Action," raised the issue of absentee African American husbands and fathers—a specter that has haunted discussions of poverty until today. The rapid rise in the divorce rate during the late 1960s and 1970s touched off a mounting anxiety about the impact of the loss of men's economic, psychological, and emotional contributions to the family, and also ignited a father's rights movement calling for increased legal rights to custody and visitation. To an unprecedented degree, men's roles as fathers and husbands became politicized (Griswold, 1993; Mintz & Kellogg, 1988).

NEW AGE MEN IN TROUBLED TIMES

Janus-like, recent media images of men in families reveal two very different faces. On one side is the "new" father and husband, far more involved, nurturing, and emotionally sensitive than the distant, disengaged dad of a generation ago. This image first reaching a broad audience in the 1979 film *Kramer vs. Kramer,* in which Dustin Hoffman was transformed from a workaholic absentee parent into a caring, nurturing, French-toast-making father. But it was *The Cosby Show,* which featured the comedian Bill Cosby as an obstetrician who refused to allow his professional responsibilities to stand in the way of his commitment to his family, that did the most effective job of popularizing the engaged, emotionally sensitive new man. Popular films like *Mr. Mom,* a gender-role-reversal film featuring a subtext highly critical of maternal employment, and *Mrs. Doubtfire,* the story of a divorced father who disguises himself as a maid and nanny in order to remain near his children, suggested that men could be even more nurturant than women (Furstenberg, 1988).

Yet, alongside of the Cosby image of the involved, sensitive new man, there were also disturbing images of deadbeat dads and abusive husbands, who fail to meet the most basic responsibilities of the masculine family role: to provide their children with emotional and financial support and to treat their wives and children in a civil, if not a loving, manner. One of the most profound social changes in recent years is the increasing absence of biological fathers from their children's home. Today, more than one third of the nation's children live apart from their biological father. White children have just a 50% chance of living with their father through age 18. A Black child has roughly 1 chance in 12. Yet, such figures only touch the surface of public concern. There is a widespread sense that even men who live in intact families are profoundly alienated from their children, that even "daddy trackers" are mere helpers and secondary caretakers who leave ultimate responsibility for housework and child care to their wives; and that men's primary connection with other family members is essentially economic, not emotional (Furstenberg, 1988).

In recent years, an older consensus about men's familial obligations has been thrown into question as the place of men in families has become highly politicized. The perception that American men are in a sea of confused identities, emasculated egos, and misplaced priorities has elicited a wide variety of responses. These include the "Promise Keepers" movement, the all-male Christian renewal movement that tells men to become the "spiritual leaders" of their homes; and the proliferation of mytho-poetic groups, whose members, inspired by the poet Robert Bly's 1990 book *Iron John,* explore their inner masculinity to the beating of drums. Other responses were evident in the 1995 "Million Man March," led by Louis Farrakhan, seeking to promote family responsibility among African American men; or in various grassroots movements to assert father's rights, which call for joint custody arrangements and expanded visitation rights after divorce (Griswold, 1993).

The "flight from fatherhood" and the "breakdown of the family" have elicited a variety of explanations that tend to break down along political lines, with liberals emphasizing economic forces and conservatives pointing to changes in cultural and moral standards. In his 1995 bestseller *Fatherless America: Confronting Our Most Urgent Social Problem,* Blankenhorn (1995), a prominent neo-traditionalist, attributed the retreat from fatherhood to changes in the dominant "cultural script" that tells men what society expects of them. He linked the growing confusion about men's familial responsibilities to the ascendancy of a set of values destructive of commitment, obligation, responsibility, and sacrifice. In a sharply contrasting explanation, Griswold (1993), author of the first full-length history of fatherhood, stressed the reorganization of the household economy, which undermined the male breadwinning role that had undergirded male authority and defined male identity, and the reemergence of feminism, the first mass movement to directly challenge the gender division of labor in the family. Other authors emphasized the erosion of well-paying, low-skill entry level jobs, which made men without high school or college degrees less attractive as marriage partners, whereas the influx of women into the workforce gave them greater economic independence (Blankenhorn, 1995; Griswold, 1993; Wilson, 1987).

A lack of comparative perspective has exaggerated the novelty of current debates over men's familial roles. A fundamental paradox of our time is that the celebration of male involvement in families has been accompanied by a decline in actual amount of time that men spend in families. Men today are at once more and less involved in family life than a generation ago. On the one hand, many men are more prepared than in the past to play an active, nurturing role in the lives of their children and to participate more equally in child care and domestic chores. Although it is easy to exaggerate the extent of change, men are more likely than their predecessors to accompany their wives to prenatal examinations, attend their children's birth, change diapers, drop off children and pick them up at day-care centers, assume some day-to-day responsibilities for their children's well-being, and perform some housework. On the other hand, as a result of delayed marriage, unmarried cohabitation, and divorce, men also spend a declining proportion of their adult lives as fathers and husbands. Since the 1950s, the share of children living in mother-only families has quadrupled, from 6% to 24% of the nation's children. Which trend, one is eager to know, is stronger: The impulse toward engagement or toward disengagement? (Furstenberg, 1988).

The history that we reviewed offers some clues. Although the nature of men's familial roles has changed profoundly across the past 300 years, one fact has remained constant: The authority and respect that men receive inside the home have been inextricably connected to their authority and status outside the home. I would like to suggest, by way of conclusion, that both the fragility of men's familial involvement and the indicators of greater engagement are connected to broader economic and cultural shifts.

In discussing the changes in men's familial roles, it is possible to point to many factors: The sexual revolution, which undermined the monogamy-for-sexual access bargain implicit in traditional marriage; the influx of women into the workforce, which diminished men's role as sole breadwinner; the legalization of abortion, which led many men to shed moral responsibility for a child's birth; the growth in divorce and nonmarital cohabitation, which have made families somewhat less stable than in the

past. Here, however, I would draw attention to the impact of two long-term
historical developments that have strongly shaped men's familial roles in
recent years: The erosion of the family wage and its replacement by the
individual wage; and the increasing emphasis attached to the mother–child
dyad. The effect of both trends has been to weaken the necessity of male
involvement in the family, making male involvement more voluntary and
elective (Griswold, 1993; Taylor, 1992).

Throughout the 20th century, breadwinning has been a defining characteristic of men's familial roles, helping to define men's identity, providing
their feelings of self-worth, and structuring the amount of time available
for their family. The very language that men have used to describe their
family roles since the 19th century—terms like *duty, responsibility, obligation,
investment,* and *commitment*—are words drawn from the economic sphere,
a pattern that underscores the way that men's economic life has tended
to interpenetrate their emotional and psychological life (Griswold, 1993;
Weiss, 1990).

The nature of men's jobs, in turn, has had profound implications for
their family orientations. Since the mid-20th century, middle-class men
typically responded to the demands of work in certain characteristic ways.
Some became careerists, focusing their energies almost exclusively on their
jobs at the expense of their family ties. Others, who felt intense alienation
from work, responded by becoming hobbyists, puttering in the basement,
tinkering in the garage, tending the yard, coaching Little League, or leading a Scout troop. Still others coped with workplace tensions by rigidly
compartmentalizing their family and work lives. Men's jobs often demanded socializing after work hours, either with their spouses or with
other employees. Now that an earlier system in which men regarded themselves as the sole or primary breadwinner is eroding, it has become easier
to assess the high psychic and emotional costs that each of these modes
of adaptation exacted (Mintz & Kellogg, 1988).

Today we are in the midst of a profound and wrenching economic
transformation, a shift from the family wage economy to an individual
wage economy, echoing the earlier transition from family labor to the
family wage economy. The individual wage economy differs in fundamental
ways from the economy that preceded it: Based on the ideal of totally
frictionless, mobile labor, the new economy has been characterized by the
growth of temporary work, a declining assumption of lifetime employment
by a single firm, and a movement away from benefit packages for entire
families. Although often represented as a liberation from stifling, unpro-
ductive older forms of corporate organization, the shift to the individual
wage economy has been accompanied by the stagnation or actual decline
in real male wages and an increase in job instability. Despite limited growth
in telecommuting and part-time work, which held out the promise of a

more family-friendly work environment, for many employees, the tensions between the demands of work and family life have grown more intense in recent years, with an increase in evening and night work, longer work hours, and increasing demands for travel. Although many women increasingly define their identities around their job or career, the growing diversity of the workplace may have made the job less of a "club" or "community" for many White men (Schor, 1991).

Entry into the paid workforce has given women an unprecedented degree of economic independence, including the freedom to leave loveless and abusive marriages and the power to demand greater participation in housework from their husbands. Meanwhile, the stagnation or decline in average male real wages has apparently led some middle-class men to emphasize intense family ties as a class marker or as compensation for their inability to achieve greater success in the workplace. For some men, a conviction that traditional measures of success are inadequate has led to a greater investment in domestic life (Griswold, 1993).

One might suppose that the shift to the individual wage would have intensified spousal interdependence because two incomes are much higher than one. That this has not been the case is the result of many factors, including a growing unhappiness with what many women see as the unfairness of marriage, with its advantages flowing primarily to men while its burdens fall largely on their shoulders. Here, however, I stress a long-term historical trend that I believe has played a critical role in making male family commitment more optional and voluntary: The increasing cultural emphasis placed on the mother–child dyad.

During the 19th century, many middle-class women began to self-consciously define their identity in terms of motherhood. Yet compared to the 20th century, women's childrearing roles remained extensive rather than intensive. That is, intensive childrearing responsibilities were confined to a relatively limited number of years, a period that contemporaries referred to as infancy, which generally involved the period from birth to 3 to 6 years of age, and childrearing advice remained largely unsystematic. Furthermore, large families and other demands on women's energies sharply limited the amount of time mothers could devote to the care of individual children. Mothers typically shared day-to-day child care responsibilities with others, especially older daughters and, in the early part of the century, female neighbors who ran "dame schools," which provided care for very young children (often as young as 2 or 3 years old; Sklar, 1973; see also Hoffert, 1989; McMillen, 1990).

Even in the early 20th century, childrearing advice literature recommended a degree of maternal detachment that we find surprising today. Childrearing experts advised mothers to establish strict schedules for their children and avoid picking them up or caressing them. But during the

1930s, the mother–child axis began to stand at the very heart of family relationships, as children overwhelmingly identified the mother as the family's source of emotional sustenance. Since the Great Depression, the emphasis on the mother–child bond has intensified. The attachment theories of John Bowlby and the advice of such childrearing gurus as Benjamin Spock, Selma Fraiberg, T. Berry Brazelton, and Penelope Leach contributed to a belief that mothers were almost wholly responsible for their children's emotional, psychological, and social development and well-being. The rapid increase in the divorce rate further reinforced the impression that mothers are the only parents that children can count on in a pinch (Genevie & Margolies, 1987; Griswold, 1993; Parke, 1996).

Up until the 1960s, the increasing weight attached to the mother–child bond remained partially counterbalanced by the concept of gender complementarity: that husbands and wives each played distinctive roles in raising children. But during the 1960s and 1970s, feminism leveled two devastating criticisms against the idea of complementarity. The first was that complementary suggested a false equivalence between men and women's familial contributions. The concept obscured the fact that women were responsible for a wildly disproportionate share of child care and housework—and that the kinds of household labor that men performed, such as shoppping or playing with children or mowing the lawn, were far less onerous than the demands placed on women. The other criticism was that insofar as men did convey certain gender-specific values to their children, these values had profoundly negative social consequences. The lessons that men transmitted to sons were overly masculine; they emphasized toughness, competitiveness, and emotional self-control, and encouraged sexism, aggression, and emotional repression (Miedzian, 1991).

The rapid entry of mothers into the workforce has not weakened the mother–child dyad. Although its form has changed somewhat, an ideal of intense mothering persists. Although mothers work in wholly unprecedented numbers, they also are now expected to breast feed their newborns, be familiar with the stages of child development, keep close tabs on their children during the day, and help them with their homework at night. The essential point is that over the course of the 20th century, mothers have become the primary parent, the key conduits and gatekeepers through which fathers relate to their children.

What possible messages can the history that we have examined offer to contemporary social scientists? Looking to the past for present-day lessons is always a risky business, but if the discipline of history is to offer more than mere antiquarianism, it is essential that historians spell out with some specificity how their findings challenge current assumptions, which, I believe, tend to be profoundly ahistorical. By way of conclusion, I would suggest that the history we studied makes three essential points.

The first is that the history of men's roles in the family has not moved in a unlinear direction. As we have seen, models of historical change that emphasize a long-term drift from patriarchy to androgyny and egalitarianism are wholly inadequate to capture the complexity of transformations that we have traced. Thus, I suggest that it would be a grave mistake for contemporary social scientists to assume that men's roles in the family are converging on a single destination or shifting in a uniform direction.

A second historical generalization is that at any particular point in time there has never been a single, unitary family role for men. Rather, we have seen profound variation along and across lines of race, ethnicity, class, and religion. Hence, we should not expect there to be a single characteristic or normative male role today. I suggest to you that the diversity that characterizes men's roles today—enshrined in such images as the wife beater, the "male mommy," the co-parent, the deadbeat dad, and countless others—is no greater than the range of behavior that we have witnessed in the past.

A third and perhaps a key lesson involves the historical roots of the contemporary crisis of men's authority in the family. Historically, men's family authority was rooted in certain concrete material conditions—ownership of property, control of craft skills, or men's role as the family's chief wage earner. If anything, the rise of the family wage that accompanied industrialization actually enhanced men's familial authority. A father's love could always be more conditional than a mother's precisely because other family members were in tangible respects dependent on him.

Across the past generation, however, the material bases of male familial authority have measurably declined. With the erosion of the family wage and its replacement by the individual wage, a central component of male identity, a critical factor in defining men's time commitments and roles in the family, has given way.

Men have adopted a host of adaptive strategies as they wrestle with the consequences of this historical shift. Very few men have responded by becoming co-parents and truly egalitarian husbands. Others have responded by attempting to assert a patriarchal authority grounded in religion. Still others have tried to function as noncustodial fathers. Most men have tried to muddle through—making greater, but still modest, contributions to housework and child care, but remaining secondary parents and continuing to define their spousal and parental identity largely as family breadwinner, despite the growing disjunction between this self-image and social realities. When the demands made on them become too great, many resolve this tension by disengaging or severing their family ties. Thus, 400 years of history of American men in families end not with a bang, but a whimper, an outcome particularly appropriate to a postmodernist age: fragmentation and splintering into diverse, indeed highly polarized adaptations.

REFERENCES

Alden, J. R. (1984). *George Washington: A biography.* Baton Rouge: Louisiana State University Press.

Amussen, S. D. (1988). *An ordered society: Gender and class in early modern England.* Oxford, England: Basil Blackwell.

Blankenhorn, D. (1995). *Fatherless America: Confronting our most urgent social problem.* New York: Basic Books.

Brodie, F. (1974). *Thomas Jefferson: An intimate history.* New York: Norton.

Carnes, M. C. (1989). *Secret ritual and manhood in Victorian America.* New Haven, CT: Yale University Press.

Carnes, M. C., & Griffen, C. (Eds.). (1990). *Meanings for manhood: Constructions of masculinity in Victorian America.* Chicago: University of Chicago Press.

Cohen, L. (1990). *Making a new deal: Industrial workers in Chicago, 1919–1939.* Cambridge, England: Cambridge University Press.

Cott, N. F. (1977). *The bonds of womanhood: "Woman's sphere" in New England, 1780–1835.* New Haven, CT: Yale University Press.

Danahay, M. A. (1993). *A community of one: Masculine autobiography and autonomy in nineteenth-century Britain.* Albany, NY: SUNY Press.

Davidoff, L., & Hall, C. (1987). *Family fortunes: Men and women of the English middle class.* Chicago: University of Chicago Press.

Degler, C. N. (1980). *At odds: Women and the family in America from the revolution to the present.* New York: Oxford University Press.

Demos, J. (1986). The changing faces of fatherhood. In J. Demos (Ed.), *Past, present, and personal: The family and the life course in American history.* New York: Oxford University Press.

Ditz, T. L. (1986). *Property and kinship: Inheritance in early Connecticut, 1750–1820.* Princeton, NJ: Princeton University Press.

Emery, N. (1982). *Alexander Hamilton: An intimate portrait.* New York: Putnam.

Ferling, J. E. (1988). *The first of men: A life of George Washington.* Knoxville: University of Tennessee Press.

Fischer, D. H. (1989). *Albion's seed: Four British folkways in America.* New York: Oxford University Press.

Fliegelman, J. (1982). *Prodigals and pilgrims: The American revolution against patriarchal authority, 1750–1800.* Cambridge, England: Cambridge University Press.

Frank, S. M. (1992). Rendering aid and comfort: Images of fatherhood in the letters of Civil War soldiers from Massachusetts and Michigan. *Journal of Social History, 26,* 5–31.

Furstenberg, F. F., Jr. (1988). "Good dads—bad dads: Two faces of fatherhood. In A. J. Cherlin (Ed.), *The changing American family and public policy* (pp. 193–218). Washington, DC: Urban Institute Press.

Genevie, L., & Margolies, E. (1987). *The motherhood report.* New York: Macmillan.

Gerson, K. (1993). *No man's land: Men's changing commitments to family and work.* New York: Basic Books.

Gordon, L. (1988). *Heroes of their own lives: The politics and history of family violence, Boston, 1880–1960.* New York: Viking.

Greene, J. P. (1988). *Pursuits of happiness: The social development of early modern British colonies and the formation of American culture.* Chapel Hill: University of North Carolina Press.

Greven, P. J. (1970). *Four generations: Population, land, and family in colonial Andover, Massachusetts.* Ithaca, NY: Cornell University Press.

Greven, P. J. (1977). *The Protestant temperament: Patterns of child-rearing, religious experience, and the self in early America.* New York: Knopf.

Greven, P. J. (1991). *Spare the child: The religious roots of punishment and the psychological impact of physical abuse.* New York: Knopf.

Griswold, R. L. (1993). *Fatherhood in America: A history.* New York: Basic Books.

Hareven, T. K. (1982). *Family time and industrial time: The relationship between the family and work in a New England industrial community.* Cambridge, England: Cambridge University Press.

Hoffert, S. D. (1989). *Private matters: American attitudes toward childbearing and infant nurture in the urban North, 1800–1960.* Urbana: University of Illinois Press.

Kimmel, M. S. (Ed.). (1987). *Changing men: New directions in research on men and masculinity.* Newbury Park, CA: Sage.

Kimmel, M. S. (1996). *Manhood in America: A history.* New York: Free Press.

Koehler, L. (1980). *A search for power: The "weaker" sex in seventeenth-century New England.* Urbana, IL: University of Illinois Press.

Kulikoff, A. (1986). *Tobacco and slaves: The development of southern cultures in the Chesapeake, 1680–1800.* Chapel Hill: University of North Carolina Press.

Levy, B. (1988). *Quakers and the American family: British settlement in the Delaware Valley.* New York: Oxford University Press.

Lewis, J. (1983). *The pursuit of happiness: Family and values in Jefferson's Virginia.* Cambridge, England: Cambridge University Press.

Lopez, C.-A., & Herbert, E. W. (1975). *The private Franklin: The man and his family.* New York: Norton.

McDonald, F. (1979). *Alexander Hamilton: A biography.* New York: Norton.

McMillen, S. G. (1990). *Motherhood in the old south: Pregnancy, childbirth, and infant rearing.* Baton Rouge: Louisiana State University Press.

Miedzian, M. (1991). *Boys will be boys: Breaking the link between masculinity and violence.* New York: Doubleday.

Mintz, S. (1983). *A prison of expectations: The family in Victorian culture.* New York: University Press.

Mintz, S. (1992). Children, families, and the state: American family law in historical perspective. *Denver University Law Review, 69,* 639–640.

Mintz, S., & Kellogg, S. (1988). *Domestic revolutions: A social history of American family life.* New York: Free Press.

Moran, G. F. (1991). Adolescence in Colonial America. In R. Lerner, A. C. Petersen, & J. Brooks-Gunn, (Eds.), *Encyclopedia of adolescence* (pp. 164–167). New York: Garland.

Morgan, E. S. (1965). *The Puritan family* (rev. ed.). New York: Harper & Row.

Norton, M. B. (1996). *Founding mothers and fathers: Gendered power and the forming of American society.* New York: Knopf.

Ozment, S. E. (1983). *When fathers ruled: Family life in reformation Europe.* Cambridge, MA: Harvard University Press.

Parke, R. D. (1996). *Fatherhood.* Cambridge, MA: Harvard University Press.

Parke, R. D., & Stearns, P. N. (1993). Father and childrearing. In G. Elder, J. Modell, & R. D. Parke, (Eds.), *Children in time and place* (pp. 147–150). New York: Cambridge University Press.

Peiss, K. L. (1986). *Cheap amusements: Working women and leisure in turn-of-the-century New York.* Philadelphia: Temple University Press.

Piore, M. J. (1979). *Birds of passage: Migrant labor, industrial societies.* Cambridge, England: Cambridge University Press.

Pleck, E. H. (1987). *Domestic tyranny: The making of social policy against family violence from colonial times to the present.* New York: Oxford University Press.

Pleck, J. (1987). American fathering in historical perspective. In M. Kimmel (Ed.), *Changing men* (pp. 83–97). Newbury Park, CA: Sage.

Popenoe, D. (1996). *Life without father.* New York: Free Press.

Pugh, D. G. (1983). *Sons of liberty: The masculine mind in nineteenth-century America.* Westport, CT: Greenwood Press.

Reynolds, D. (1995). *Walt Whitman's America.* New York: Knopf.

Rorabaugh, W. J. (1979). *The alcoholic republic: An American tradition.* New York: Oxford University Press.

Rosenzweig, R. (1983). *Eight hours for what we will: Workers and leisure in an industrial city, 1870–1920.* Cambridge, England: Cambridge University Press.

Rotundo, A. (1985). American fatherhood: A historical perspective. *American Behavioral Scientist, XXIX,* 7–25.

Rotundo, A. (1993). *American manhood: Transformations in masculinity from the revolution to the modern era.* New York: Basic Books.

Rutman, D. B., & Rutman, A. H. (1984). *A place in time: Middlesex County, Virginia, 1650–1750.* New York: Norton.

Schochet, G. J. (1975). *Patriarchalism in political thought: The authoritarian family and political speculation and attitudes especially in seventeenth-century England.* New York: Basic Books.

Schor, J. (1991). *The overworked American: The unexpected decline of leisure.* New York: Basic Books.

Shammas, C., Samlon, M., & Dahlin, M. (Eds.). (1987). *Inheritance in America: From colonial times to the present.* New Brunswick, NJ: Rutgers University Press.

Sklar, K. K. (1973). *Catharine Beecher: A study in American domesticity.* New Haven, CT: Yale University Press.

Stearns, P. N. (1990). *Be a man!: Males in modern society* (2nd ed.). New York: Holmes & Meier.

Stearns, P. N. (1991). Fatherhood in historical perspective: The role of social change. In F. W. Bozett & S. M. H. Hanson (Eds.), *Fatherhood and families in cultural context* (pp. 28–52). New York: Springer.

Taylor, P. (1992, June 7). Life without father. *Washington Post,* p. C1.

Tentler, L. W. (1979). *Wage-earning women: Industrial work and family life in the United States, 1900–1930.* New York: Oxford University Press.

Thernstrom, S. (1984). *A history of the American people.* San Diego: Harcourt Brace Jovanovich.

Ulrich, L. T. (1982). *Good wives: Image and reality in the lives of women in northern New England, 1650–1750.* New York: Knopf.

U.S. Department of Labor, Office of Policy Planning and Research. (1965). *The Negro family: The case for national action.* Washington, DC: U.S. Government Printing Office.

Weiss, R. S. (1990). *Staying the course: The emotional and social lives of men who do well at work.* New York: Free Press.

Wilson, W. J. (1987). *The truly disadvantaged: The inner city, the underclass, and public policy.* Chicago: University of Chicago Press.

Wood, G. S. (1992). *The radicalism of the American Revolution.* New York: Knopf.

Chapter 2

The Invisible Man Revisited: Comments on the Life Course, History, and Men's Roles in American Families

Linda M. Burton
Anastasia R. Snyder
The Pennsylvania State University

> *I am an invisible man. No, I am not a spook like those who haunted Edgar Allan Poe; nor am I one of your Hollywood-movie ectoplasms. I am a man of substance, of flesh and bone, fiber, and liquids—and I might even be said to possess a mind. I am invisible, understand, simply because people refuse to see me . . . That invisibility to which I refer occurs because of a peculiar disposition of the eyes of those with whom I come in contact. A matter of the construction of their* inner *eyes, those eyes with which they look through their physical eyes upon reality.*
>
> —Ellison, 1952, p. 3

More than 40 years ago, Ralph Ellison, in his classic novel *Invisible Man*, challenged us to consider the influences of social forces on the work and family lives of African American men. In this novel, Ellison artfully chronicled the impact of nested contradictions in history, political ideologies, work, kinship relations, and personal development on one man's life. This man, who remained nameless throughout the novel, was African American and two generations removed from slavery. Through his eyes, we witness one male's struggle to define, acquire, and maintain work and family roles during an era in U.S. history characterized by social and personal paradoxes concerning the place of non-White males in the larger social order. This nameless man's work and family roles implicitly reflected the interplay between visible and invisible social forces of the time. These forces included, but were not limited to, overt and covert institutional racism and restrictive U.S. labor markets opportunities for non-White males. In addition, these forces were indicative of historically based economic and political linkages that bound the lives and livelihoods of African American men to the lives of men from other ethnic or racial groups.

Ellison's *Invisible Man* offers an intriguing backdrop for our commentary on Steven Mintz's chapter, "From Patriarchy to Androgyny and Other Myths: Placing Men's Family Roles in Historical Perspective." Much like the literary work of Ellison, Mintz's chapter provokes consideration of the effects of visible social forces, such as the Industrial Revolution, on the lives of men. Using an historical analytic approach, Mintz chronicles the impact of prevailing social, economic, and demographic forces on White men's work and family roles in U.S. society from the colonial era to the early 1990s. Unlike Ellison, however, Mintz prods us to consider social paradoxes and the invisible forces that influence men's lives *not* because of the story he tells about White male roles in work and family, but rather, because of the story he *doesn't* tell. Mintz's chapter does not discuss how the work and family roles of White American males were historically shaped and shaped by the work and family lives of ethnic or racial minority males. Such a discussion seems important for understanding the impact that visible and invisible forces have had on the lives of men similar to Ellison's nameless character in *Invisible Man.*

Drawing the parallel between Ellison's literary work and Mintz's historical analysis on men's roles raised a challenging question for us: How does one build on Mintz's analysis of White men's lives to enhance our understanding of the visible and invisible social and historical connections between the work and family roles of American White men and the roles of men in other ethnic or racial groups? Posing this question guides our comments on Mintz's chapter.

Overall, we view Mintz's work as an historically grounded starting point from which we can generate and explore questions concerning the complex relationship between history, social forces, and White men's work and family roles. To move beyond this starting point requires the application of a theoretical perspective to his analysis. Although there are a number of theoretical perspectives that are useful in exploring these issues, one that is particularly relevant for framing our comments is the life course perspective (Bengtson & Allen, 1993; Elder, 1995; Hareven, 1978).

Using the life-course perspective as the conceptual anchor for our discussion, the goal of our comments is to suggest ways in which Mintz might expand his analysis to reflect the social and historical connections of White men's work and family roles to those of non-White males. We contend that the social forces and historical connections that Ellison wrote about in his fictional account of a nameless African American man's life are, indeed, invisible in Mintz's historical analysis of White males' work and family roles. By framing Mintz's analysis within a life-course perspective these invisible forces become central to the interpretation of White males' work and family roles across historical time.

In presenting our commentary, we provide an overview of the life-course perspective and its importance for understanding men's work and family roles across historical time. Three interrelated life-course themes are discussed relative to Mintz's work: (a) individuals as agents and mediators of social change, (b) social interdependence, and (c) the temporal context of lives. We conclude our comments with a brief discussion of the implications of the life course perspective for acknowledging the role of invisible social forces in emerging histories on men's roles in families.

THE LIFE-COURSE PARADIGM, HISTORICAL PERSPECTIVES, AND MEN'S ROLES

The life-course perspective is a particularly appropriate conceptual framework for the historical analysis of men's work and family roles. This perspective provides a "contextual, processual, and dynamic approach" to the study of role transitions and change in the lives of individuals across historical time (Bengtson & Allen, 1993, p. 492). A core premise of the perspective asserts that an individual's role acquisitions, transitions, and outcomes are shaped by the social trajectories they follow. These trajectories represent the "interplay between human lives and historical time and place" (Elder, 1995, p. 107).

Elder (1995) indicated that the life-course paradigm draws on a broad array of intellectual traditions including life-span development theory (Baltes, 1987), social age systems (Riley, Johnson, & Foner, 1972), life history studies (Elder, 1974), intergenerational research (Burton & Bengtson, 1985; Kertzer & Keith, 1984), and role theory (Riley, 1996). Through the integration of these various intellectual streams, the life-course paradigm comprises multiple interrelated themes, three of which are directly relevant to our discussion of Mintz's chapter (see Bengtson & Allen, 1993, or Elder, 1995, for a detailed review of the life-course perspective). These themes include: Individuals as agents and mediators of social change, social interdependence, and the timing of lives.

Men as Agents and Mediators of Social Change

The first theme concerns individuals as agents and mediators of social change or what Elder, (1994) terms *reciprocal continuity*. This theme suggests that individuals are "not passive recipients of social change, but rather, are active agents in negotiating social-historical events, taking charge of their destinies and lives" by creating change as well as "reacting to events and circumstances external to them" (Bengtson & Allen, 1993, p. 489; Hareven, 1982).

In contrast to the notion of reciprocal continuity, Mintz employs a unidirectional approach in describing the relationship between social change and men's roles across historical time. Essentially, Mintz portrays White working and middle-class men over historical time as being acted on by social change rather than as actors who create and implement social change. Mintz's use of this unidirectional approach constraints his ability to explore how White males shaped social events (i.e., restructuring labor markets) that influenced their roles in families. Moreover, it precludes an assessment of the reciprocal influences of White males on the family and work roles of males in diverse ethnic or racial groups (Billingsley, 1988; Franklin, 1993; Kalmijn, 1993; Stewart & Scott, 1978). Using Ellison's metaphor, *Invisible Man*, the unidirectional approach employed by Mintz reduces the visibility of the impact reciprocal influences have on shaping history and the work and family roles of White men.

Integrating a life-course perspective in his analysis would allow Mintz to broaden his interpretation of social change and men's work and family roles. As illustrated in Fig. 2.1, a reciprocal continuity approach would draw attention to the process by which sociohistorical events influenced and are shaped by the roles of White and non-White men in families. In addition, the influence of White males' work and family male roles on those of non-White men could also be assessed. Using a life-course approach, Mintz could more fully explore how the lives of White working- and middle-class men are linked to the lives of other men and how this linkage impacts the work and family roles of men across ethnic or racial groups.

Social Interdependence

The second life-course theme that is important to our discussion is social interdependence or "linked lives" (Elder, 1995; Plath, 1980). This concept,

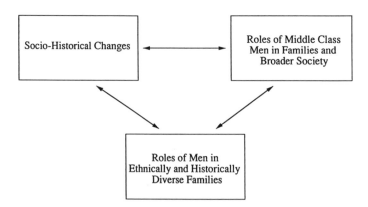

FIG. 2.1. Reciprocal influences on the roles of men in families.

which is an extension of reciprocal continuity, reflects the embeddedness of human beings in each others' actions and reactions. Specifically, social interdependence suggests that social changes, role transitions, and personal choices concerning work and family that occur in one group are related to and have implications for social changes, role transitions, and personal choices around work and family for other groups. Thus, adopting a social interdependence perspective facilitates explorations of the interconnections between the work–family interface over historical time across different ethnic or racial groups.

Exploring the social interdependence dimension of White males' lives seems essential to interpreting the meaning of their family roles over historical time. Consider, for example, the linked lives perspectives relative to the roles White males have played in African American families. One historical reality, not mentioned by Mintz, speaks quite poignantly to this issue. The reality involved the sexual victimization of African American females by White males during slavery and reconstruction.

Historians such as Genovese (1976), Gutman (1979), White (1985), and Franklin (1993) informed us that during slavery and reconstruction, White males, often through subjugation and force, created "other families" with African American females. It is quite probable that the creation of these other families influenced White males' relationships and roles in their primary families (Genovese, 1976). However, this practice also impacted the role of African American men in their families. Jones (1985) wrote:

> Slave holders used sexual violation of women and separation of families via sale as a primary means of disrupting black families. Often wives were raped by slave owners and there was nothing that they or their husbands could do about it. This adversely affected the relationships between husbands and wives. Slave women often lived in fear of giving birth to a bi-racial child because of the reaction of their husbands and the damage it would do to their relationship. (p. 113)

A second example of the impact of social interdependence is witnessed in economic and labor systems created primarily by White middle-class men and the implications of those systems for the employment opportunities for males from diverse ethnic or racial groups. In his chapter, Mintz gives no attention to how the White middle-class men he describes controlled the economy and influenced the employment opportunities and subsequent family roles of poor White and non-White males. For example, the institutional decimation of African American males at the hand of White males has occurred in our society since the time of slavery in the form of economic oppression, racial discrimination, and incarceration (Scott & Stewart, 1978). Institutional decimation has influenced African American males' abilities to assume economic support roles in their families for centuries (Billingsley, 1988; Franklin, 1993). Consequently, using these examples, I argue that an historical perspective of White men's roles in work and families is not complete without some attention being given to how their lives and behaviors are linked to the familial situations and economic opportunities of others.

The Temporal Context of Lives

The third life-course theme pertinent to our discussion is the timing of lives. *The timing of lives* refers to the multiple temporal contexts in which an individual acquires work and family roles. The dimension of time most central to our discussion is historical time (Bengtson & Allen, 1993; Elder, 1995). Historical time concerns temporal periods marking events that occur in the broader social context and alter the roles and values of individuals. The depression era is example of such a temporal period (Elder, 1974).

Mintz's chapter, in part, reflects the historical time dimension of the life course perspective. His analysis comprises specific historical periods that he defines as relevant to the work and family roles of White working- and middle-class men. The historical periods he examined included colonialism in the 1600s and 1700s, the "Great Awakening," the Civil War, the Industrial Revolution, the Great Depression, World War II, and the "New Age." Although these historical periods may be important for understanding the work and family roles of White working- and middle-class men, they may have had a different impact on men's roles in other ethnic or minority groups. The life-course perspective posits that historically based social changes are not uniformly experienced or interpreted similarly across all segments of American society (Elder, 1995). As such, if Mintz were to develop a more integrated analysis of men's roles across historical time, he would need to include historical anchors that were also relevant to other ethnic groups (Harley, 1995).

Consider, for example what historical anchors would be relevant if one were to examine the linked historical lives of White and African American males. Table 2.1 illustrates a parallel stream of historical events relevant to an informed historical portrait of White and African American men's family roles. These streams suggests that distinct, yet, related historical events influenced White and African American men's work and families over time. For example, although White Americans were experiencing colonialism, African people forcibly brought to this land were experiencing enslavement. Mintz notes that during this period, White male roles were dictated by a patriarchal family structure. In contrast, when we examine the lives of African American slaves during colonialism–slavery, we find that patriarchy was not a defining feature of African American men's family roles (Genovese, 1976). Families in slavery needed to rely on the strength

TABLE 2.1
Historical Eras in the Family

Mintz		Burton and Snyder	
Historical Events	Year	Historical Events	Year
Colonialism	1607–1776	Slavery	1619–1865
		The Jamestown Boat	1619
Nineteenth Century	1800s	Civil War/Reconstruction	1861–1877
		Birth of the KKK	1866
Second Great Awakening	1820s–1850s		
Civil War	1861–1865	Jim Crow Laws	
		Plessy vs. Ferguson	1898
Industrial Revolution	1880–1910	(separate but equal)	
"New" Middle Class			
		Depression/Word War II	1930–1945
Depression/Word War II	1930–1945	Northern Migrations	1933–1936
			1941–1945
1960s and 1970s	1960–1979	Civil Rights Movement	1960s
		Men's Movement begins	1960s
"New Age" Men	1980s–present		
		Post-1970s/Reaganomics	1980–1992
		Million Man March	1995

of both men and women to survive. Thus, in contrast to the patriarchy in White families, a more equalitarian relationship between the sexes emerged among African Americans (Meacham, 1983).

Another example of the differential effects of unique, yet, linked histories is apparent in 19th century America. During the 19th century, both Whites and African American males experienced the post-Civil War period. However, this historical period had very different meanings for both groups. During this time, newly emancipated African Americans were struggling with issues of family cohesion and sustainable employment while simultaneously facing new racial oppression in the form of Jim Crow laws. On the other hand, according to Mintz, many White males during this historical period were dealing with the decline of patriarchy and a new market economy.

What is important to note about the impact of historical time on men's roles is that, as the life course perspective suggests, men from different ethnic or racial groups have unique historical experiences, but these experiences do not occur in isolation of one another. In comparing the histories of White and African American men, we see that their experiences, although unique, are linked in very important ways. Thus, we submit that it is the interconnectedness and reciprocal continuity of these histories that produced men's work and family roles across historical time. These social forces, however, are invisible in Mintz's historical analysis of men's roles.

CONCLUSION: WRITING CONTEMPORARY
HISTORIES OF MEN'S ROLES

Drawing on the metaphors in Ellison's novel, *Invisible Man*, and the life-course perspective, we addressed a specific issue concerning Mintz's chapter: How does one build on Mintz's historical analysis of White men's lives to enhance our understanding of the visible and invisible social and historical connections between the work and family roles of U.S. White men and the roles of men in other ethnic or racial groups? We suggested that there are three issues that must be considered in subsequent historical analysis of men's work and family roles: (a) men are agents and mediators as well as receptacles of social change; (b) men's lives are interconnected such that the actions of one has implications for the actions of another; and (c) men of different ethnic or racial groups may have unique historical experiences, but it is the unique combinations of these experiences across race and ethnicity that produce the outcomes we see in their work and family roles.

In concluding our commentary, we have one final thought. As we approach the 21st century and write the emerging histories of men's lives we can no longer afford to be myopic, unidirectional, or ignore the connectedness of men's lives across ethnic or racial groups in our discussions of how family and work roles emerge for men. Contemporary social forces, such as recent increases in ethnic or racial diversity in the U.S. population, suggests that the *Invisible Man* Ellison wrote about some 40 years ago is truly a metaphor for the past. Consequently, we must write contemporary history accordingly.

ACKNOWLEDGMENTS

The authors research reported in this paper was supported by grants to Linda M. Burton for the William T. Grant Foundation, A FIRST Award from the National Institute on Mental Health (No. R29MH 4605-01), and support services provided by the Population Research Institute, The Pennsylvania State University which has core support from NICHD Grant 1-HD28263.

REFERENCES

Baltes, P. B. (1987). Theoretical propositions of life-span developmental psychology: On the dyamics between growth and decline. *Developmental Psychology, 23*, 611–626.
Bengtson, V. L., & Allen, K. (1993). The life course perspective applied to families over time. In P. G. Boss, W. J. Doherty, R. LaRossa, W. R. Schumm, & S. K. Steinmetz (Eds.), *Sourcebook of family theories and methods* (pp. 469–498). New York: Plenum Press.

Burton, L. M., & Bengtson, V. L. (1985). Black grandmothers: Issues of timing and continuity of roles. In V. L. Bengtson & J. F. Robertson (Eds.), *Grandparenthood* (pp. 61–77). Beverly Hills, CA: Sage.

Billingsley, A. (1988). The impact of technology on Afro-American families. *Family Relations, 37,* 420–425.

Elder, G. H. (1974). *Children of the Great Depression: Social change in life experience.* Chicago: University of Chicago Press.

Elder, G. H. (1994). Time, human agency, and social change: Perspectives on the life course. *Social Psychology Quarterly, 57,* 4–15.

Elder, G. H. (1995). The life course paradigm: Social change and individual development. In P. Moen, G. H. Elder Jr., & K. Luscher (Eds.), *Examining lives in context* (pp. 101–139). Washington, DC: American Psychological Association.

Ellison, R. (1952). *Invisible man.* New York: Vintage Books.

Franklin, J. H. (1993). *The color line: Legacy for the twenty-first century.* Columbia: University of Missouri Press.

Genovese, E. D. (1976). *Roll, Jordan, roll.* New York: Vintage Books

Gutman, H. (1979). *The Black family in slavery and freedom: 1750–1925.* New York: Pantheon.

Hareven, T. K. (1978). *Transitions: The family and the life course in historical perspective.* New York: Academic.

Hareven, T. K. (1982). *Family time and industrial time.* New York: Cambridge University Press.

Harley, S. (1995). *The timetable of African-American history.* New York: Simon & Schuster.

Jones, J. (1985). *Labor of love, labor of sorrow: Black women, work, and the family from slavery to the present.* New York: Basic Books.

Kalmijn, M. (1993). Trends in Black/White intermarriage. *Social Forces, 72,* 119–146.

Kertzer, D. I., & Keith, J. (Eds.). (1984). *Age and anthropological theory.* Ithaca, NY: Cornell University Press.

Meacham, M. (1983). The myth of the Black matriarchy under slavery. *Mid-American Review of Sociology, 2,* 23–41.

Plath, D. (1980). *Long engagements.* Stanford, CA: Stanford University Press.

Riley, M. W. (1996). Age Stratification. In J. E. Birren (Ed.), *Encyclopedia of gerontology* (Vol. 1, pp. 81–92). New York: Academic Press.

Riley, M. W., Johnson, M. E., & Foner, A. (Eds.). (1972). *Aging and society: A sociology of age stratification* (Vol. 3). New York: Sage.

Stewart, J. B., & Scott, S. W. (1978). The institutional decimation of Black American males. *Western Journal of Black Studies, 2,* 82–92.

White, D. (1985). *Ar'n't I a woman: Female slaves in the plantation south.* New York: W. W. Norton & Company.

Chapter 3

On the Flexibility of Fatherhood

Andrew J. Cherlin
Johns Hopkins University

When I started writing about the family in the late 1970s, the phrase "traditional family" referred to the 1950s. Although the field of family history had already produced its early masterpieces, such as Ariès' (1962) *Centuries of Childhood,* Demos' (1970) *A Little Commonwealth,* and Greven's (1970) *Four Generations,* the great flood of studies that we now take for granted had hardly begun. People's recent memories tended to take them back to the 1950s, either as parents or as children. One particular family form, the one-earner, two-parent household, had been a cultural ideal since the late 19th century and had reached its zenith in the 1950s. These facts help to explain why, in a collective act of hubris, Americans defined the breadwinner–homemaker family as "traditional."

We now know better. Figure 3.1, taken from the work of demographer Donald Hernandez (1993), shows changes in the living arrangements of children from 1790 to 1989. At the beginning of this period, the vast majority of children were living in two-parent farm families. As commercialization and then industrialization of the economy proceeded in the 19th and early 20th centuries, the percentage of children in breadwinner–homemaker families increased steadily and then peaked in the 1950s and early 1960s at more than 50%. However, since then it has plummeted, replaced by the rapidly growing percentage of children who are in dual-earner two-parent families or single-parent families. These latter family forms are not traditional either, for the chart shows that few children lived in dual-earner or single-parent families until the mid-20th century. More-

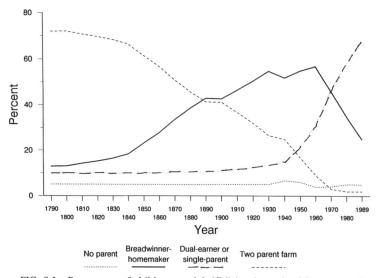

FIG. 3.1. Percentage of children aged 0–17 living in each of four types of families, 1790–1989 (from *America's Children: Resources from Family, Government and the Economy,* by Donald J. Hernandez, © 1993 Russell Sage Foundation, New York, NY; reprinted with permission).

over, the chart glosses over important differences according to race and class, which I will leave to other contributors.

Clearly, then, there is little that is traditional about any of the nonfarm family forms of the 20th century. The more historians have searched for the traditional family, the more elusive it has become. Family structure in the western nations has continually evolved over the past several centuries as economic, cultural, and political changes have occurred. To be sure, there were some constants: Compared with our era, there were relatively few divorces and births outside of marriage. Children did, of course, live with a single parent as a result of the death of their other parent. But the remaining parent often remarried quickly because it was too hard to sustain a household without two parents. It was so hard, in fact, the when the remaining parent did not remarry, children were sometimes sent to foster families or to group homes called *half-orphanages*; the theory being that it was too difficult for one parent to raise a child without help.

Steven Mintz's chapter amply demonstrates that there is no single traditional form of fatherhood in the history of the United States either. He argues that a simple progression from patriarchy to androgyny does not fit the facts. For example, it is a mistake to think of the authority of fathers as lessening continually from colonial times to the present. It is true that colonial fathers had far more authority than did fathers in subsequent eras. It's also true that the movement of production out of the home and off the farm reduced fathers' authority considerably. For example, fathers could no longer could threaten to withhold the family farm from rebellious children. Their legal rights to their wives' property also eroded. But as Mintz notes, the rise of the breadwinner–homemaker family in the late 19th and early 20th century probably increased fathers' authority once again. As rising wages allowed more and more fathers to earn enough to support their families, their wives and children withdrew from paid work. By doing so, wives and children became increasing dependent on fathers economically. That dependency created bargaining power that fathers could use to impose their will over their wives and children.

The historical record also suggests that fathers have been important figures in their children's daily lives; until the mid-19th century, they were considered the primary parent. Childrearing manuals were addressed to them, not to mothers; and in the case of a divorce, the father typically retained custody.

So the historical record shows that fathers' roles have varied from being the parent with primary responsibility to being a relatively uninvolved, secondary parent. Moreover, there is no simple historical path along which fathers are marching. Their role is variable and socially constructed in whole or part. By implication, then, their role could change further in the future. I suspect this is welcome news to most of the readers of this volume. The readers, I am sure, would like fathers to play a larger role in their children's lives. Some are concerned primarily with nonresident and noncustodial fathers; others are concerned with having fathers share more of the childrearing and household tasks with their wives; still others want fathers to provide more guidance and stewardship to the children they live with.

I, too, am pleased to know that fathers' roles, in principle, could grow in importance in a number of ways. But without disputing that point, let me suggest that, in our enthusiasm at discovering great historical variation in fatherhood, we could commit the error of overstating it. We could mistakenly take the historical record as showing that fathers' roles have been almost completely flexible—and that, by implication, we could easily change fathers' behavior in most every aspect. Mintz does not make that mistake, but others may are close to doing so.

For instance, well-respected family historian John R. Gillis (1996) recently published *A World of Their Own Making: Myth, Ritual, and the Quest for Family Values.* The thesis of the book is that we should be reluctant to take the midcentury, middle-class family as the standard from which to compare other kinds of families because of the great variations in family patterns in the western historical record. The 1950s family, Gillis argued (as do Mintz and others), was not the culmination of a linear process of social change; rather it was the dominant form only at a particular historical moment. In other words, Gillis added his voice to the chorus who proclaim that the breadwinner–homemaker family was not traditional.

As should be clear, I agree with this position. But Gillis went further: Concerning fathers, he seems intent on showing that fathers have, at one time or another, commonly done most every set of important childrearing and household task. In the period from the 1500s to the 1800s, he stated, "patriarchal figures took on nurturing as well as protective qualities" (p. 182). In fact, "Fathers were active in all the major nurturing and educational functions we now associate with motherhood. They oversaw the wetnursing of infants and knew how to clothe and doctor children" (p. 182). Furthermore:

> They were as comfortable in the kitchen as women, for they were responsible for provisioning and managing the house. Until the nineteenth century, cookbooks and domestic conduct books were directed primarily to them, and they were as devoted to decor as they were to hospitality. (p. 183)

As for the kitchen, men may have provided the provisions, but I am not familiar with any studies suggesting that men usually did the cooking. But let us leave the kitchen and turn to the broader issue of nurturing. How nurturing were fathers? It is true that childrearing manuals were addressed to them until the 1800s. But the content of these manuals reveals little encouragement for behaviors that we would consider the essence of nurturing in our era. Consider the well-known words of advice to fathers in a childrearing essay by John Robinson, the minister of the Puritan group that sailed across the Atlantic on the Mayflower:

> And surely there is in all children, though not alike, a stubbornness, and stoutness of mind arising from natural pride, which must, in the first place, be broken and beaten down; that so the foundation of their education being laid in humility and tractableness, other virtues may, in time, be built thereon. (cited in Greven, 1973, p. 13)

The key task for the father was to break the young children's will before it became part of the child's character. It was preferable to do so without physical force, but hitting was allowed if necessary.

If the question is who did the emotionally supportive care that we would today associate with the word *nurturing*, the answer is no one. The idea that love, encouragement, support and the like were at the core of childrearing would have been foreign to parents during that period. Life was hard and children were valuable sources of labor. The task for parents was to prepare their children to survive by working hard and cooperating with others. The fundamental reason that fathers were the primary parents was that fathers legally owned all of the household property and children were a form of property.

By the middle of the 19th century, this view of the young child as inherently corrupt had given way to the view that she or he was inherently good. Infants and toddlers, it was now thought, mainly needed emotional support, gentle guidance, and love. In *Christian Nurture*, an essay on childrearing in the first 3 years of life, well-known minister Horace Bushnell shifted the emphasis to mothers. Although he thought that fathers were still important, he viewed mothers as more nurturing:

> First the mother has us, at her bosom, as a kind of nursing Providence. Perused by touch and by eyes, her soul of maternity, watching for that look and bending ever to it, raises the initial sense of a divine something in the world; and when she begins to speak her soft imperative, putting a little decision into the tones of her love, she makes the first and gentlest possible beginning of authority. (Greven, 1973, p. 177)

The father's influence comes later: "And then the stiffer tension of the masculine word, connected with the wider, rougher providence of a father's masculine force, follows in a stouter mode of authority" (p. 177).

Bushnell's writings show that as the idea of emotionally supportive nurturing took hold in the 1800s, it came to be associated primarily with mothers, not fathers. Fathers were never expected to be nurturing in the same sense as mothers were, and even mothers were not expected to be as nurturing as parents are today. Mintz tells us in his chapter that until the 1930s, childrearing manuals encouraged a greater degree of maternal detachment than would be expected now. Since then, he argues, the mother–child bond has become even more imbued with significance.

I am not arguing that fathers cannot be nurturing, nor that they cannot help out more in the kitchen. All I am suggesting is that in our desire for social change we not exaggerate the important and hopeful lessons that historians such as Steven Mintz have provided for us. Fatherhood is a role with great flexibility and wide variations. We can expect change and, in the name of equity and even demand it. In fact, as mothers have entered the labor force in large numbers, fathers have been asked to increase their contribution. They have done so, however, only modestly. Thus, Hochschild (1989), in her book, *The Second Shift: Working Parents and the Revolution at Home*, writes of a "stalled revolution" as husbands refuse to fill the child care and housework gaps left by wives' greater time commitment outside the home. My point is that we should not interpret the historical flexibility of fatherhood to mean that it will be easy to further increase fathers' nurturing behavior toward young children. It is not a role they have been socialized for and not one they have historical experience with. They may also have inherited, on average, a weaker set of skills for caring for infants and toddlers. This does not mean we should not attempt to increase fathers' contributions to early child care, only that, in our rush to announce the historical variability in fatherhood, we shouldn't underestimate the difficulty of doing so.

REFERENCES

Ariès, P. (1962). *Centuries of childhood: A social history of family life.* New York: Vintage.
Demos, J. (1970). *A little commonwealth: Family life in Plymouth Colony.* Oxford: Oxford University Press.
Gillis, J. R. (1996). *A world of their own making: Myth, ritual, and the quest for family values.* New York: Basic Books.
Greven, P. J., Jr. (1970). *Four generations: Population, family, and land in colonial Massachusetts.* Ithaca, NY: Cornell University Press.
Greven, P. J., Jr. (1983). *Childrearing concepts, 1628–1861: Historical sources.* Ithaca, NY: F. E. Peacock.
Hernandez, D. J. (1993). *America children: Resources from family, government, and the economy.* New York: Russell Sage Foundation.
Hochschild, A. (1989). *The second shift: Working parents and the revolution at home.* New York: Viking.

Chapter 4

Fatherhood Then and Now

Michael E. Lamb
National Institute of Child Health and Human Development

For more than 20 years, fatherhood has become an increasingly fashionable topic of study for social scientists from diverse backgrounds, and social historians have been drawn into the fray as well. Nonhistorians like myself have surely benefited from the breadth of focus and perspective offered and brought to bear by historians such as Mintz (chap. 1, this volume; Mintz & Kellogg, 1988), Stearns (1991), Griswold (1993), Elizabeth Pleck (Pleck & Pleck, 1997), Demos (1986), Vinovskis (1986), and Rotundo (1993) as well as the historically sensitive analyses offered by nonhistorians such as LaRossa (1988; LaRossa, Gordon, Wilson, Bairan, & Jaret, 1991) and Joseph Pleck (1987). Many of their thoughtful and engaging accounts are cited by Mintz in his own interesting focal chapter. The interdisciplinary communication fostered and represented by these efforts has provided a welcome and much-needed antidote to the increasingly narrow and specialized analyses that bedevil scientific and academic inquiry at the end of the 20th century.

OVERSIMPLIFICATION AND ITS COSTS

Multidisciplinary exchanges are not without risk, however. One inherent disadvantage of multidisciplinary communication is the pressure toward oversimplification. However complementary their focus, colleagues in other disciplines demand the broad outlines, not the excruciating detail, the areas of consensus, not the parameters of endless debates about arcane details. As a result, it is rare to satisfy the demands and expectations of both intra- and interdisciplinary audiences. At the very least, writers must hope that colleagues within their own disciplines understand the need to accept one another's abbreviated statements as personalized theses prepared with the needs of a particular interdisciplinary discourse in mind. The same standards of critical evaluation should obviously not be afforded to such position papers and to extended specialized analyses written for professional colleagues.

The dangers of oversimplification and overgeneralization are exacerbated when the available evidence is scanty, selective, and perhaps open to contradictory interpretations. The historical record, even when it pertains to the recent past, is especially problematic when social historians seek to describe changing patterns of family life. First, those who compiled the raw materials relied on by today's scholars did not have the needs and interests of later researchers in mind, and their documents are often obliquely relevant to the interests of contemporary humanists and social scientists. Second, literacy was far from universal in earlier times, and even those who wrote letters and documents were not all equivalently likely to save and preserve these records or have descendants who were equally prescient. Third, both official documents and informal materials like letters and diaries are often written from subjective and judgmental perspectives, frequently with persuasion or self-justification in mind. As such, they are best viewed as idiosyncratic and individual testaments, seldom representative of the writers' social and economic peers, let alone the masses of contemporaries from different ethnic, racial, cultural, and economic backgrounds. For these reasons, the evidentiary basis for many assertions is often both ambiguous and open to diverse interpretations.

These caveats are not new, of course. They surely haunt family historians and all social scientists whose scholarship involves the secondary analysis of unusual forms of data and who are inclined to commune with those of different disciplinary bents. It is worth recalling these issues, however, if only to underscore how much agreement exists among those who have sought to describe the recent history of fatherhood in the United States, despite the inevitable differences in emphasis and interpretation. Such differences notwithstanding, all seem to describe evolutionary rather than revolutionary change along the same general trajectory whether or not they choose to refer to stages or phases as rhetorical cues to help clarify their descriptions. There are, of course, differences in terminology and interpretive frameworks, although outsiders may view these as differences in emphasis rather than as fundamental disagreements. In his chapter, Mintz criticizes some of his fellow historians for overemphasizing the role of industrialization, for example, even though his own account clearly documents the effects of industrialization on family processes and roles. Indeed, Mintz's thoughtful discussion repeatedly underscores the likelihood that historical change is unlikely to be propelled by singular events, trends, or causes, just as it is unlikely to change in a unilinear direction. In certain scholarly contexts, however, it may be appropriate, and even valuable, to analyze historical development along a single dimension, even when the writer recognizes the oversimplification represented by such analyses.

Although these realities bedevil the efforts of social historians striving to find organizing themes to give direction to their contributions, especially when they are also hampered by the need to be brief and to speak to the interests of disparate social scientists, the latter face problems of their own. Sociologists tend to demand analysis of distinct groups defined by contrasting economic, cultural, ethnic, religious, and gendered backgrounds, whereas psychologists may be drawn so strongly to recognize the myriad variations on the human experience that the generalizable lessons are lost or those offered are misguided and unrepresentative. In the course of interdisciplinary discourse, as a result, the expectations, assumptions and perspectives of these adjacent disciplines can misdirect each other's efforts, pushing historians to make finer distinctions than the data are suited to support, for example, and forcing sociologists, psychologists and historians to represent personal hunches and predilections as though they were the products of disciplinary consensus.

DIVERSE PATERNAL ROLES

It is perhaps worth emphasizing that the diverse perspectives of various disciplines do not simply reflect a rather superficial and banal relativism but contain important and concrete lessons for contemporary students of families in general and fatherhood in particular. For one thing, the realization that fathers have filled and continue to fill a diverse variety of roles in their families and in society is an essential prerequisite for understanding both contemporary debates about the meaning and nature of fatherhood, as well as more narrow attempts to explore paternal influences on family functioning and child development. We cannot hope to elucidate paternal influences without recognizing the contrasting conceptions of fatherhood guiding the behavior and expectations of the specific fathers, mothers, and children being studied. By the same token, we cannot elucidate the changing family in the United States and its diverse functions without recognizing its diverse and divergent representations (Lamb, 1982, in press). Mintz's warnings about the simplistic portrayal of the father's role in recent historical epochs apply with equivalent impact and import to the writings of contemporary social scientists and commentators of various disciplinary backgrounds, whatever their scholarly or sociopolitical goals.

When used to enrich the evaluation of fatherhood in the present context, Mintz's conclusions have important cautionary relevance. The diversity of family roles in the past and present should warn those who would develop prescriptive rules regarding the appropriate or acceptable roles of men and women, or mothers and fathers, in contemporary society. As many social scientists have emphasized for more than 10 years, it is potentially dangerous, as well as counterproductive to offer universal prescriptions of this sort, or to attribute major social problems to singular secular changes such as the ascent of fatherlessness (Blankenhorn, 1995; Lamb, 1996). Successful fatherhood must surely be defined relative to the specific socioeconomic, cultural, ethnic, and historical niches in which individual men and women together define their needs and roles, whether in or out of enduring relationships. In such a context, knowledge of alternative solutions, such as those developed in other historical epochs or cultural circumstances, can be of tremendous heuristic value, just as it may be helpful to understand or at least become cognizant of the many factors influencing the contemporary definition of parental roles and responsibilities.

Although students of contemporary fatherhood and its implications for child development have shifted focus many times during the last 20 years, most would now agree that fathers play multiple roles in contemporary families, with the relative importance of the various components varying from family to family and from subgroup to subgroup, just as the relative prominence of these different responsibilities appeared to rise and fall historically (Lamb, 1986; Pleck, 1987). Clearly, breadwinning remains a key component of the father's roles in many, if not most, segments of society today, with the economic support of children and family representing an important way in which American fathers contribute to the rearing and emotional health of their children, whether they do or do not live together. A second important but indirect source of influence stems from the fathers' roles as sources of emotional support or stress for their partners and former partners, their children's mothers (Parke, Power, & Gottman, 1979). The father's functioning as a source of emotional support for the mother and others in the family tends to enhance the quality of the mother–child relationship and thus facilitates positive adjustment. By contrast, children may suffer when fathers are unsupportive and relationships between the parents are hostile (Cummings & O'Reilly, 1997). Fathers can also affect the quality of family dynamics by being involved in child-related housework, thus reducing the mother's workload (Pleck, 1983, 1984) and modeling such participation for their children. Fathers further influence their children by interacting with them directly, and much of the early research conducted by psychologists was concerned with paternal influences attributable to paternal caretaking, teaching, play, and one-on-one interaction with particular children (Lamb, 1997).

For more than 20 years, however, social scientists, particularly psychologists, have shifted their focus from the narrow study of fathers, father–child dyads, and direct father-to-child influences to a broader focus on fathers in the context of family systems and subsystems. Researchers have also come to emphasize the diverse rather than the restricted number of roles played by fathers, with the relative salience of these roles varying across time and subcultural context. Instead of emphasizing solely the formative impact of paternal interaction with their children, for example, contemporary researchers are much more likely to emphasize the importance of marital and family harmony—itself a product of diverse paternal and maternal behavior, attitudes, expectations, personalities, and circumstances—as a determinant of child development. Even a cursory review of the first and third editions of *The Role of the Father in Child Development* (Lamb, 1976, 1997) amply illustrated these changing conceptions and approaches and makes clear that contemporary fatherhood is at least as fluid a concept as fatherhood in historical perspective.

REFERENCES

Blakenhorn, D. (1995). *Fatherless America.* New York: Basic Books.

Cummings, E. M., & O'Reilly, A. W. (1997). Fatherhood in family context: Effects of marital quality on child adjustment. In M. E. Lamb (Ed.), *The role of the father in child development* (3rd ed., pp. 49–65). New York: Wiley.

Demos, J. (1986). The changing faces of fatherhood. In J. Demos (Ed.), *Past, present, and personal: The family and the life course in American history* (pp. 41–67). New York: Oxford University Press.

Griswold, R. L. (1993). *Fatherhood in America: A history.* New York: Basic Books.

Lamb, M. E. (1976). *The role of the father in child development.* New York: Wiley.

Lamb, M. E. (Ed.). (1982). *Nontraditonal families: Parenting and child development.* Hillsdale, NJ: Lawrence Erlbaum Associates.

Lamb, M. E. (1986). The changing roles of fathers. In M. E. Lamb (Ed.), *The father's role: Applied prospectives* (pp. 3–27). New York: Wiley.

Lamb, M. E. (1996). Review of "Fatherless America" by David Blankenhorn. *Journal of Marriage and the Family, 58,* 526–527.

Lamb, M. E. (Ed.). (1997). *The role of the father in child development* (3rd ed.). New York: Wiley.

Lamb, M. E. (Ed.). (in press). *Nontraditional families: Parenting and child development* (2nd ed.). Mahwah, NJ: Lawrence Erlbaum Associates.

LaRossa, R. (1988). Fatherhood and social change. *Family Relations, 36,* 451–458.

LaRossa, R., Gordon, B. A., Wilson, R. J., Bairan, A., & Jaret, G. (1991). The fluctuating image of the 20th century American father. *Journal of Marriage and the Family, 53,* 987–997.

Mintz, S., & Kellogg, S. (1988). *Domestic revolutions: A social history of American family life.* New York: Free Press.

Parke, R. D., Power, T. G., & Gottman, J. (1979). Conceptualizing and quantifying influence patterns in the family triad. In M. E. Lamb, S. J. Suomi, & G. R. Stephenson (Eds.), *Social interaction analysis: Methodological issues* (pp. 231–252). Madison: University of Wisconsin Press.

Pleck, E. H., & Pleck, J. H. (1997). Fatherhood ideals in the United States: Historical dimensions. In M. E. Lamb (Ed.), *The role of the father in child development* (3rd ed. pp. 33–48). New York: Wiley.

Pleck, J. H. (1983). Husbands' paid work and family roles: Current research issues. In H. Lopata & J. H. Pleck (Eds.), *Research in the interweave of social roles (Vol. 3), Familes and jobs.* Greenwich, CT: JAI Press.

Pleck, J. H. (1984). *Working wives and family well-being.* Beverly Hills, CA: Sage.

Pleck, J. H. (1987). American fathering in historical perspective. In M. Kimmel (Ed.), *Changing men* (pp. 83–97). Newbury Park, CA: Sage.

Rotundo, E. A. (1993). *American manhood: Transformations in masculinity from the revolution to the modern era.* New York: Basic Books.

Stearns, P. N. (1991). Fatherhood in historical perspective: The role of social change. In F. W. Bozett & S. M. H. Hanson (Eds.), *Fatherhood and families in cultural context* (pp. 28–52). New York: Springer.

Vinovskis, M. A. (1986). Young fathers and their children: Some historical and policy perspectives. In A. B. Elster & M. E. Lamb (Eds.), *Adolescent fatherhood* (pp. 171–190). Hillsdale, NJ: Lawrence Erlbaum Associates.

Part II

MEN'S INVESTMENT
IN PARENTHOOD

Human Parental Investment and Fertility: The Life Histories of Men in Albuquerque

Hillard S. Kaplan
Jane B. Lancaster
Kermyt G. Anderson
University of New Mexico

The reduction in fertility accompanying modernization poses a scientific puzzle yet to be solved. The problem has received wide attention by economists, sociologists, demographers, anthropologists and biologists, yet no discipline in the social or biological sciences has offered a full and coherent theory to explain the timing and pattern of fertility reduction in the developed or developing world. The inability to offer an adequate theory raises fundamental questions about the theoretical foundations of those disciplines. For example, although economics has made great strides in explaining consumer behavior, time allocation, and labor force participation through the recognition that the household is a fundamental organizational unit of human action, there is no adequate explanation of why households are mostly composed of men and women who marry and have children, why reproductive partnerships form such a fundamental organizational principle in human societies, nor why people have and want children in the first place. The very modest progress of economists in explaining long, medium, and short term trends in fertility highlights this weakness.

Evolutionary biology in its application to human fertility has fared no better. The core theoretical foundation of modern evolutionary biology is that differential reproductive success is the principal driving force determining evolutionary change and stability. A corollary proposition is that competition for the resources for reproduction is the primary determinant of differential reproductive success. Thus, the fact that people in modern industrial societies obtain access to and utilize more resources than ever before in human history and yet evidence the lowest fertility rates ever recorded presents a particularly critical challenge to evolutionary biology, at least in its application to humans (Vining, 1986).

This chapter presents the results of an in-depth study of fertility and parental investment using a representative sample of men from Albuquerque, New Mexico. Our goal is to develop and test a general theory of human fertility and parental investment, with a specific focus on explaining recent historical trends in family behavior within developed nations. We present a theoretical framework that unifies life-history theory, developed in biology, with human capital and household allocation theories, developed in economics. We then offer a specific theory of modern fertility reduction based on the emergence of skills-based competitive labor markets. This theory generates a set of empirical predictions that are tested with data derived from the sample of Albuquerque men. The empirical analysis focuses on age at first reproduction, completed fertility, the formation and dissolution of marital and quasi-marital relationships, investment in children, and child outcomes. The analysis examines both historical trends and variation among men within cohorts and time periods.

LIFE-HISTORY THEORY AND THE ECONOMICS
OF THE FAMILY

Biological and economic theories of life histories and fertility decisions developed independently, yet they share some formal properties and substantive conclusions. They both assume that individuals act to optimize the allocation of limited resources through the life course so as to maximize some currency. Biological models assume that *fitness*, defined in terms of quantity of descendants or the instantaneous growth rate of genes, is the ultimate currency that individuals are designed to maximize. Economic models assume that utility or satisfaction is the ultimate currency. We consider first models of life history developed in biology and then compare them to economic models of investment in human capital and fertility.

Life-history theory grew out of the recognition that all organisms face two fundamental reproductive trade-offs (see Charnov, 1993; Kozlowski, 1992; Lessells, 1991; Roff, 1992; and Stearns, 1992, for general reviews; see Hill, 1993, for a review of the application of life-history theory to humans). The first trade-off is between current and future reproduction. The second is between quantity and quality of offspring. With respect to the former trade-off, early reproduction is favored by natural selection, holding all else constant. This is due to two factors. First, the production of offspring will be a positive function of the length of the reproductive span. Because the probability of death in any time period is always nonzero, earlier reproduction tends to increase the length of the reproductive period. Second, shortening generation length by early reproduction increases the total reproductive output of the lineage in growing populations.

These forces favoring early reproduction are balanced by benefits derived from investments in future reproduction. Those investments, referred to as *somatic effort*, include growth and maintenance. The allocation of time and energy to growth has three major benefits. Larger organisms often suffer lower rates of mortality. Therefore, growth can increase the length of the life span. Growth also can increase the efficiency of energy capture per unit of time allocated to food production or acquisition. Therefore, allocation of resources to growth can increase the total energy available for reproduction over the life course. Finally, larger body size can increase success in intra- and intersexual competition for mates, ultimately affecting reproductive rate. These three benefits to growth also accrue to investments in maintenance, because physical condition will depreciate through time if no effort is allocated to maintenance.

For each unit of energy acquired, the organism is assumed to face a choice between investing it in growth and maintenance, which increases future rates of surplus production, and investing it in reproduction. Natural selection is expected to shape the life history of those allocations so as to maximize the time-discounted surplus energy for reproduction over the life course (Charnov, 1993; Hill & Hurtado, 1996; Kozlowski, 1992; Kozlowski & Wiegert, 1986, 1987; Roff, 1986; Stearns & Koella, 1986). Because the costs and benefits associated with alternative allocations are likely to vary with phylogenetic history, local ecology, and individual condition, optimal distributions of effort to current versus future reproduction are likely to vary as well.

The second major life-history trade-off concerns the allocation of resources for reproduction between quantity and quality of offspring, given a specific solution to the allocation problem regarding current versus future reproduction. This trade-off is presumed to result from the fact that parents have limited resources to invest in offspring and that each additional offspring necessarily reduces average investment per offspring. Most biological models operationalize this trade-off as number versus survival of offspring (e.g., Lack, 1954, 1968; Lloyd, 1987; McGinley & Charnov, 1988; Rogers & Blurton Jones, 1992; Smith & Fretwell, 1974). Natural selection is expected to shape investment per offspring and offspring number so as to maximize offspring number times their survival. Optimal fertility and parental investment are also expected to vary with phylogenetic history, local ecology, and individual condition.

These two allocation problems have direct analogues in human capital theory and the theory of the family in economics. The first, intertemporal problem can be divided into two parts. One is the trade-off between present and future consumption and the other is the trade-off between present and future income. Given perfect lending markets, it is possible to separate the consumption problem from the income problem. If people can borrow and lend (or, save) at going interest rates, they can adjust consumption over time to maximize utility as long as the present value of total consumption equals the present value of total income. Therefore, the first problem that must be solved is the optimal investment in human capital to maximize the present value of lifetime income.

Human capital may be defined as a stock of attributes embodied in an individual, such as skills and education, that affect the value of time allocated to productive labor, and hence affect earnings. There are two kinds of costs associated with investment in human capital. There are the direct costs, such as school fees and books, and the indirect costs associated with time spent in training during which income is foregone. As in biological models, the same relationship exists between timing and rate of payoff, the sooner one enters the labor force the more years of earning will occur; however, the longer one trains, the higher the wage rate will be when one enters the workforce. The work of Ben-Porath (1967), Mincer (1974), and Becker (1975) showed that investment in human capital is at an optimum when the net rate of increase in earnings due to a unit of time invested in capital accrual (i.e., after direct costs of investment have been subtracted) is equal to the prevailing interest rate. Given that the present value of the lifetime income stream is maximized, consumption allocations through the life course may be shifted through borrowing and lending to maximize utility or satisfaction.[1] Thus, there is a direct equivalence between somatic effort and investment in human capital. Both are expected to maximize the effective resources available to the individual over the life course. The principal difference is that in biological models, those resources are utilized for reproduction to maximize fitness and in economic models resources are used for consumption to maximize utility. As a result of this equivalence, biological and economic models of investment in growth and human capital share many features. For example, both focus on the rate of return on investment and both recognize that the length of time over which the investment yields a return will be positively correlated with investments in the future. The third shared feature is analysis of the effect of timing on the value of the return. In biological models, the population growth rate is the primary determinant of temporal effects

---

[1]Although most economists would argue that the utility derived from investments in human capital probably includes such nonmonetary rewards as increased status and on-the-job satisfaction, most theoretical developments and empirical applications focus on income effects.

on the value of reproduction (Charlesworth, 1980; Rogers, 1993, 1994). If populations are growing, later reproduction has a smaller impact on relative gene frequencies than earlier reproduction, and vice versa if populations are shrinking. Thus, the payoff to investment in growth decreases with population growth rate. In economic models, the overall interest rate on investments determines the temporal effects of the earnings stream on the value of real income (i.e., adjusted for inflation). Again, the higher the interest rate, the lower the payoff to investment in human capital.

Becker (1975) also showed that under most conditions, the costs of human capital investment increase as capital is acquired. Human capital acquisition generally requires time inputs from the individual acquiring the capital. If investment extends over many time periods, then the time spent in capital acquisition becomes increasingly expensive as capital is acquired. This is also true of the biological growth models. As organisms grow, the opportunity cost of each unit of time dedicated to growth increases.

With respect to fertility regulation, the problem is also viewed as a quantity–quality trade-off by economists (Becker & Lewis, 1973; de Tray, 1973; Willis, 1973). Quality is considered to be an index of the human capital embodied in children. Thus, parents are expected to derive satisfaction from both child quality and child quantity, and to chose the combination of offspring number and offspring quality to maximize the satisfaction derived from children and other forms of consumption. Later models (e.g., Becker, 1991; Becker & Barro, 1988; Becker, Murphy, & Tamura, 1990; Becker & Tomes, 1986) explicitly treat fertility decisions in terms of an intergenerational utility function. The individual's optimization problem is to maximize satisfaction derived from the intergenerational consumption stream through the allocation of earnings to own consumption and investment in children.

These two approaches can be usefully unified to build on the strengths of each. A major strength of biological models is the causal closure provided by the theory of natural selection and the use of fitness as the currency to be maximized. The theory of evolution by natural selection specifies the causal processes by which the characteristics of organisms change and a justification for why organisms should be designed to maximize fitness. In contrast, the economic assumption that people maximize utility is not derived from a known causal process, but rather is maintained as a working heuristic because it seems to characterize human behavior. Thus, economic models are less specific about the nature of interpersonal utility functions. However, the theory of human capital in economics is much more developed than the corresponding theory of investment in somatic effort in biology.

Figure 5.1 unifies biological and economic approaches to life-history decisions by extending the economic concept of human capital to organisms in general (with the term, *embodied capital*) and by utilizing biological

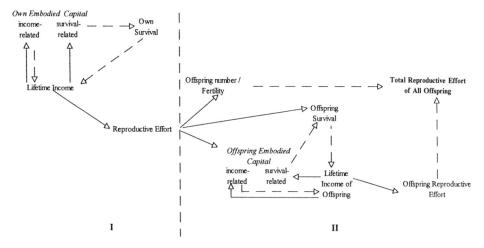

FIG. 5.1. Decision model for life history of investments.

fitness as the ultimate currency. Development can be seen as a process in which individuals and their parents invest in a stock of embodied capital. In a physical sense, embodied capital is organized somatic tissue. In a functional sense, embodied capital includes strength, immune competence, coordination, skill, and knowledge, all of which affect the profitability of allocating time and other resources to alternative activities such as resource acquisition, defense from predators and parasites, mating competition, parenting and social dominance. Because such stocks tend to depreciate with time due to physical entropic forces and to direct assaults by parasites, predators, and conspecifics, allocations to maintenance such as feeding, cell repair, and vigilance can also be seen as investments in embodied capital. Individuals may invest not only in capital embodied in their own soma, but in the capital embodied in offspring, other relatives, and in other individuals with whom they interact.

In the first part of Fig. 5.1, we begin with lifetime income. Income is defined here in the general sense of the total value of time allocated to alternative activities, such as resource acquisition, child care, rest, and so on. At each age, an individual's income will be a function of his or her embodied capital. Income can be invested directly in reproductive effort, or in embodied capital. Embodied capital, in turn, can be divided into stocks affecting the ability to acquire the resources for reproduction and stocks affecting the probability of survival.

The solid arrows depict investment options. The dotted arrows depict the impacts of investments. Investments in income-related capital, such as in growth, physical coordination, skills, and knowledge, affect lifetime income through the value or productivity of time in the future. Investments in survival-related capital, such as immune-function, predator defense, and tissue repair, affect lifetime income through increasing the expected life span of earnings. However, an organism that does not reproduce leaves no descendants. Thus, the first optimization problem acted on by natural selection is to allocate lifetime income among investments in future income, survival and reproduction at each age so as to maximize the time-discounted surplus energy for reproduction over the life course.

The second part of the figure shows the relationships between investments and outcomes for two generations. Here, both the parent and the offspring can invest in the offspring's survival- and income-related capital. For parents, the optimal allocation between fertility and investments in embodied capital of offspring should maximize the total lifetime allocations by offspring to their own reproduction (summed over all offspring). This requires consideration not only of the effects of parental investment on offspring survival, but also on the adult income of offspring as well. If individuals in each generation allocate investments in their own and their offspring's embodied capital optimally, then the "dynastic" or multigenerational fitness of the lineage is maximized.

In this model the diversity of life histories is due to the fact that the shape of the relationships between investments and outcomes varies ecologically. For each major class of mortality (predation, disease, intraspecific violence, accidents, starvation), there will be variable relationships between the probability of dying from it and investments by the organism. There is also ecological variability in the benefits to investment in income-related capital. The relationships between body size and productivity depend on the feeding niche. The value of knowledge, skill, and information-processing ability depends on the type of foods exploited.

FERTILITY AND PARENTAL INVESTMENT
IN TRADITIONAL HUMAN SOCIETIES:
AN ECOLOGICAL MODEL

One of the most important problems in understanding contemporary demographic processes is that the proximate physiological and psychological mechanisms underlying fertility, parental investment, and family formation evolved primarily in the context of a hunting and gathering lifestyle. All but the last 10,000 years of evolution in the hominid line occurred among foraging populations. An understanding of the hunting and gathering lifestyle is essential to understand the evolved physiology and psychology governing fertility and parental investment. Because most people now live in environments radically different from our ancestral environment, we also require an understanding of what our minds and bodies are designed to do and how our evolved physiology and psychology respond to modern environments.

Compared to other primates and mammals, there are three distinctive characteristics of human life histories: (a) an exceptionally long life span with older nonreproductive individuals supporting their offspring's reproduction, (b) an extended period of juvenile nutritional dependence coupled with the provisioning of young of different ages, and (c) marriage and the involvement of men in the care and provisioning of children (Kaplan, 1996a; Lancaster & Lancaster, 1987). Because all well-studied hunting and gathering groups exhibit these three characteristics, it is likely that some fundamental features of the traditional human lifeway account for their evolution. We have proposed that those three features of the human life course are interrelated outcomes of a feeding strategy that emphasized nutrient-dense, difficult-to-acquire foods (Kaplan, 1996a, 1996b). The logic underlying this proposal is that effective adult foraging requires an extended training period during which production at young ages is sacrificed for increased productivity later in life. The returns to investment in training depend positively on adult survival rates, favoring increased investment in mortality reduction. An extended postreproductive, yet productive, period supports both earlier onset of reproduction by next-generation individuals and the ability to provision multiple dependent young at different stages of development.

There are two principal proximate determinants of fertility—age at weaning and net energy flow to women. They correspond to the constraints imposed by the different phases of the parental investment. Because humans almost never customarily nurse two infants at the same time, the intensity and length of infant investment is a critical decision variable determining fertility. The net energy flow to women represents the available energy for reproduction and investment, after accounting for the net productivity of children, postreproductive individuals, and adult men. Exposure to sex, a third proximate determinant, is probably most relevant to the onset of fertility in late-marrying populations, which, for reasons of length, is not treated here. With respect to the survival during the infancy period, there are two critical forms of parental investment, breast milk and direct care. It is useful to think of infancy in terms of a gradual transition from complete dependence on breast milk to complete dependence on other foods. The provision of breast milk increases during the first few months of life as the baby grows and then supplemental foods are introduced at about 4 to 6 months of age, providing an increasing proportion of food in the child's diet as his or her caloric needs increasingly exceed the energy its mother can provide with breast milk (Oftedal, 1984; Vitzthum, 1994; Whitehead & Paul, 1981). Ecological factors affect the relationship between the rate of those transitions and offspring survival (Lee, Majluf, & Gordon, 1991; Vitzthum, 1994). The digestibility of available foods is one factor. The maturation of the child's digestive system will interact with the kinds of weaning foods available to eat in determining the optimal age to introduce new foods and the optimal proportion of milk to other foods in the child's diet at each age (Sheard & Walker, 1988). Disease organisms are another factor. The density and intensity of diseases that infect individuals through ingestion should be related to length of the breast-feeding period for two reasons. First, breast milk increases the child's immunocompetence (Hanson, 1982; Howie, Forsyth, Ogston, Clark, & du Florey, 1990). Second, babies that are sickly require the high-quality nutrition provided by breast milk (Sheard & Walker, 1988). On the other hand, the relative importance of diseases that are unaffected by diet should be related to acceleration in the rate of weaning, because breast milk will account for less of the variance in survival (Borgerhoff Mulder, 1992; Harpending, Draper, & Pennington, 1990; Pennington & Harpending, 1988). Because infancy and early childhood is also the period during which offspring require the most direct care, maternal food production, and hence her budget for reproduction, should be affected by ecological factors affecting the relationship between direct care and survival. The availability of safe spaces for children, which should be negatively associated with mobility, and the dangers in the environment should both affect the age-specific benefits of direct maternal care.

The age-specific productivity of children is also likely to depend on ecological factors. The dangers associated with acquisition of different food types should affect whether and how much children forage. This issue has received extensive treatment in a series of papers contrasting the foraging behavior of !Kung and Hadza children (Blurton Jones, Hawkes, & O'Connell, 1989; Blurton Jones, Hawkes, & Draper, 1994a, 1994b; Hawkes et al., 1995). In addition, as just discussed, the suite of resources available and the impacts of skill and strength on foraging return rates should determine both children's time allocation to productive labor and the total amount they produce (cf. Bock, 1995; Draper & Harpending, 1987; Hawkes, O'Connell, & Blurton Jones, 1995). Children also face a potential trade-off between early productivity and later adult production. Thus, the impacts of both productive labor and nonproductive practice on later adult productivity should also affect children's food production. For example, boys in many societies spend a good deal of time in nonproductive hunting practice. Among the Machiguenga, boys spend much time hunting small lizards and in target practice. They sacrifice the more immediately productive activities of helping their mothers in the garden and collecting wild foods, activities that their sisters perform.

The characteristics of potential food resources also affect the productivity of adults. Rates of return from hunting are likely to impact on men's food production (see Lancaster & Kaplan, 1992, for a discussion). The productivity of older people may also depend on the availability of foods that may require skill to extract, but do not require great strength or stamina. The productivity of the environment, relative to population density, is also likely to determine the net energy flow to women.

These two main constraints on reproduction, the length of the infancy period and the net energy flow to women, may vary in their importance in different ecological contexts. When food is abundant, the main constraint on fertility may be the health impacts of weaning. This would likely correspond to periods of maximum population growth rates (cf. Hill & Hurtado, 1996). When population density is high relative to the productivity of the environment, the net energy flow to women may be most important.

MECHANISMS UNDERLYING HUMAN RESPONSES TO ECOLOGICAL VARIATION

In order to adjust parental investment and fertility optimally in relation to ecological variation, humans must possess a set of mechanisms that translate environmental inputs into behavioral outputs. Many of these adjustments, especially those involving parental investment, may be accomplished through psychological processes that direct attention to functional relationships, aided by a store of cultural knowledge. Other adjustments, such as those governing fertility, may be accomplished by the physiological mechanisms discussed earlier.

The optimality conditions specified by the quantitative analysis of the model (Kaplan, 1996a) suggest that these psychological mechanisms must be able to detect diminishing returns to investments. It is the shape of the relationship between investments and outcomes that determines the optimal amount to invest. When returns to an extra unit of investment in offspring income or survival produces a smaller fitness improvement than a comparable investment in fertility, it no longer pays to invest more in the offspring, even if the investment is beneficial. Compared to observed investments, a slightly longer nursing period, a slightly lower work requirement for children, and slightly more food given to children would probably increase their survival or adult income. However, people should be selected to possess psychological mechanisms that detect diminishing returns and to adjust investment accordingly (Borgerhoff Mulder, 1992; Harpending et al., 1990; Pennington & Harpending, 1988).

To summarize, the proposal here is that selection acts on the coordinated outcome of mechanisms that both regulate parental investment and fertility. Investment may be regulated by psychological mechanisms that direct attention to fundamental relationships between investments and outcomes, and that detect diminishing returns to investment. Actual decisions will be the product of those mechanisms and some reliance of cultural norms that benefit from accumulated experience. The regulation of fertility, on the other hand, may involve little or no direct cognition, and be wholly regulated by physiological mechanisms responsive to breast-feeding regimes and net energy flow. This makes sense in the context of the theoretical model insofar as fertility is the passive result of optimal parental investment and an income budget for reproduction. If, after allocating investments to existing children, there is enough time and energy to support the next offspring, it should be produced.

PARENTAL INVESTMENT AND FERTILITY REDUCTION IN INDUSTRIAL SOCIETIES: THE COMPETITIVE LABOR MARKET THEORY

The Empirical Relationship Between Fertility and Fitness, and the Requirements for a Theory

There is mounting evidence that people in modern state societies in the developed world do not maximize fitness through their fertility decisions (e.g., Irons, 1983, 1990, 1993, 1995; Kaplan, Lancaster, Bock, & Johnson, 1995; Lam, 1986; Perusse, 1993; Retherford, 1993; Vining, 1986; but see Simons, 1974, for data suggesting a positive correlation among wealth and fertility within socioeconomic groups). Observed fertility behavior deviates from the predictions of fitness maximization in two ways. First, and most important, observed fertility is lower than would be predicted based on models of fitness maximization. For example, we showed that among men in Albuquerque, New Mexico, the number of third-generation descendants (i.e., grandchildren) is highest among those who produced the most (i.e., >12) children (Kaplan et al., 1995). This contrasts sharply with the observed modal fertility of 2 (Fig. 5.2). Higher parental fertility in modern developed societies is associated with lower achieved educational and economic status of offspring (Kaplan et al., 1995; see also Blake, 1989, and Downey, 1995, for reviews), but the lower earning capacity of children from large families does not decrease their fertility and so there is no apparent fitness reduction associated with lowered parental investment per child.

The second way in which modern behavior deviates from the predictions of simple budget constraint models of quantity–quality trade-offs is that higher earning adults produce no more children than their lesser earning counterparts, even in well-controlled studies. Whereas available data on

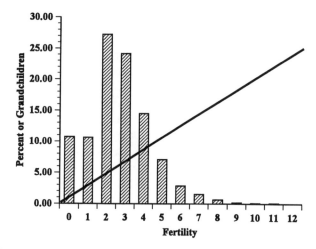

FIG. 5.2. Fertility and grandchildren. (The bars show the frequency distribution of fertility in percents for Anglo men born between 1920 and 1939. The solid line plots the OLS estimate of the relationship between number of children and number of grandchildren among Anglo men whose children have completed reproduction. Modal fertility is 2 children, but number of grandchildren is maximized with the highest number observed, 12.)

pre-industrial societies consistently exhibit a positive relationship between resources or power and reproductive success (Barkow, 1989; Betzig, 1986; Boone, 1986; Borgerhoff Mulder, 1987, 1988; Chagnon, 1988; Cronk, 1991a, 1991b; Flinn, 1986; Hughes, 1986; Irons, 1979, 1993, 1995; Kaplan & Hill, 1985; Low, 1990; Mealey, 1985; Turke & Betzig, 1985; Voland, 1990), studies of postdemographic transition societies either find no relationship or a negative one (Kaplan et al., 1995; Perusse, 1993; Retherford, 1993; Vining, 1986; as we found in this study, see Fig. 5.4).[2] The models presented here predict that under most conditions, fertility should be a monotonically increasing function of resources for investment in reproduction, and when wealth does not affect the value of parental investment, fertility should increase linearly with resources.

An adequate theory of the demographic transition must accomplish two things. First, it must specify the conditions that changed, leading to a reduction of fertility and the observed relationship between wealth and

---

[2]Studies of traditional small-scale societies suggest that fertility may be optimized to maximize the production of descendants over the long run (e.g., Blurton Jones, 1986, 1987, for the !Kung in Botswana; Blurton Jones & Sibly, 1978; also see Hill & Hurtado, 1996, for disconfirmation among the Ache). The abrupt change in the association between wealth and fertility that occurs at the same time fertility is reduced historically (Retherford, 1993) requires explanation.

fitness. Second, it must account for why those changes produced the observed responses within a larger theory of the determinants of fertility in general. In the context of the theory proposed here, it is necessary to specify the critical differences in the relationship between parental investment and child outcomes in pre- and postdemographic transition societies and to show why the suite of evolved, proximate mechanisms just discussed might produce the fertility and parental investment behavior observed in modern, post-industrial revolution labor markets.

In order for the theoretical models to explain the reduction in fertility, especially in the face of growing wealth, exogenous changes in the value of parental investment are required. The transition from high to low fertility requires that the marginal returns from parental investment decrease more slowly in modern societies than in traditional and peasant societies. In fact, the difference in the rates at which returns to parental investment must be great enough to more than compensate for the higher real wealth in post-transition contexts. We present an analysis (building on Becker's [1975] analysis of investment in human capital) that implies that, for a large part of the range of investments, investments in offspring income in skills-based competitive market economies exhibit either constant returns to scale or, with growing technology, increasing returns to scale (see Fig. 5.3).

Similarly, to account for the fact that, within modern societies, wealth is uncorrelated with fertility, the model requires that the shape of the functions relating parental investment to offspring income or survival must differ systematically with wealth. In particular, it requires that higher earning parents must be more effective at producing embodied capital in children than lower earning parents. This part of the analysis relies on the idea that the skills affecting productivity with modern technology are cu-

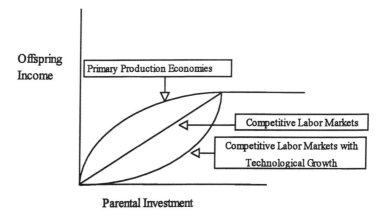

FIG. 5.3. Relationship between parental investment and offspring income as a function of the economy.

mulatively acquired and that the production of embodied capital in children depends on the capital embodied in parents (see Becker, Murphy, & Tamura, 1990, for a related argument in the analysis of macropatterns in economic growth and fertility). For these conditions to predict low modern fertility, the sum of age-specific investments in offspring must constitute a greater proportion of adult income in modern contexts than in high fertility regimes. To predict the lack of a positive association between income and fertility, age-specific parental investments must increase proportionally with wealth. Our theory is that skills-based competitive labor markets produce just such conditions. In response to those conditions, the evolved proximate mechanisms governing fertility and parental investment produce a fertility much lower than the fitness-maximizing output. The psychological processes regulating desired investment per child and other expenditures produce a budget that does not permit more than two to three children. There is a conflict between the fertility schedule that our physiological response system would produce and consciously desired fertility. This has stimulated the demand for effective birth control technology. The interaction of those processes with current socioeconomic conditions is discussed following the analysis of investment in embodied capital in competitive labor markets.

Investment in Embodied Capital in Skills-Based, Competitive Labor Markets

There are qualitative differences between subsistence production and modern competitive labor markets in the relationship between investments in human capital and productivity. In subsistence-based economies, the relationship between skills and productivity depends on the activity. For example, successful agricultural production requires knowledge of weather, soil, and pests in differing degrees depending on the local ecology. Some function with eventually diminishing returns will likely characterize the relationship between productivity and human capital. In those economies, optimal levels of investment will be determined by the diminishing impacts of further investments on productivity. However, competitive labor markets will tend to produce wage structures that equalize the present value of costs of investments with the earnings (see Becker, 1975, for a detailed presentation of this argument).

   This section begins with a basic summary of some of the principal results from the economic analysis of labor markets. It then applies those results to parental investment in the embodied capital of offspring. It also models the case in which parents with higher levels of skill are able to produce embodied capital in offspring at a higher rate per unit of investment. This model is designed to specify the conditions that would have to be met in order for the models of fitness-maximizing investments in offspring number and offspring quality to predict the empirical pattern of results found in modern society.

This analysis is a form of reverse optimality. We already know much about the basic empirical patterning of modern fertility and parental investment behavior. The goal here is to develop an optimality framework for analyzing optimal fertility and parental investment behavior in the context of a labor market economy, and then to determine the assumptions that would have to be met for the model to predict the observed behavior. Once those conditions are specified, empirical research can be conducted to determine if they hold in modern society.

The economic analysis of labor markets examines wage structures in terms of the supply and demand for labor. Firms are expected to hire labor and combine it with physical capital in an optimal mix to produce goods at the lowest cost. The firm's demand for labor is depicted as a function of the wages paid per unit of labor. The demand curve slopes downward, because as wages decrease, profit-maximizing firms will wish to hire more workers (see, for example, Varian, 1992). The basic assumption underlying the downward sloping demand curve is that, if all other inputs into the production process are held constant, each extra unit of labor will have a diminishing marginal product. Thus, if there are 1,000 laborers employed in the labor market, the 1,001th worker will increase total production (and hence sales revenues) less than the 1,000th worker. A profit maximizing firm will wish to employ units of labor as long as the revenues derived from adding the next worker are greater than the wages that must be paid (i.e., until a quantity is reached such that the marginal revenue derived from a unit of labor is equal to the cost). Thus, the demand curve represents the marginal revenue of a worker as a function of the total quantity employed.

Fitness-maximizing or, in economic usage, utility-maximizing individuals will attempt to get the highest possible return for their labor. The supply curve represents the amount of labor that workers would be willing to supply as a function of wages. In general, supply curves are upward sloping because higher wages will entice more workers to join the labor force. The market is cleared at the point of intersection between the demand and supply curves, and the wage level defined by this intersection is the equilibrium wage paid to workers. One important result obtained from the analysis of wage structures is that at equilibrium, the difference in wages paid for jobs requiring differing levels of human capital will exactly compensate for the increased costs of acquiring the capital (Becker, 1975).

This result can be extended to parental investment in offspring embodied capital. According to the model in Fig. 5.1, fitness-maximizing parents will be willing to pay those costs if the increase in the adult income of their offspring would offset the loss in fertility. Define the total parental investment in the traditional and unskilled labor sectors at equilibrium as $p*$ with an associated fertility rate,

$$b* \ (= \frac{I_0}{p*}).$$

The fertility of parents producing skilled offspring, b', would be

$$b' = \frac{I_0}{p* + c} = b* \ \frac{p*}{p* + c}.$$

Fitness-maximizing parents would be indifferent to raising skilled workers if

$$b*I_0 = b'I', \text{ or } I' = \frac{p* + c}{p*} I_0$$

where I' is the income of skilled workers. This leads to the prediction that forces of supply and demand will automatically generate an equilibrium in which parents are indifferent to alternative levels of fertility and offspring income. Fitness gains from increased income per child will exactly equal the fitness costs of lost fertility.

In addition, variation in fertility will also reflect changes in other investments due to increased investment in skill. The initial model of investment trade-offs among fertility, survival, and income of children implies that increased investment in one component of offspring reproductive value leads to increases in other components (Kaplan, 1996b). Thus, anyone investing in more skilled children will also invest more in their health and survival. This would engender even greater fertility differences among parents investing in differing skill levels for their children. In fact, one might argue the increased investment in public health at the end of the 19th century was as much a consequence of fertility reduction as a cause.

This simple analysis is potentially capable of explaining several aspects of the empirical pattern just discussed. It explains why competitive labor markets with skill-differentials linearize the relationship between parental investment and offspring income for a large part of the observed range. It also predicts variation in fertility levels within income classes, because parents will be indifferent to alternative choices of fertility and income. In addition, the children of higher investing parents will earn more, but will not necessarily have more children than the children of lesser investing parents. Because optimal investment in this model does not depend on income, skilled workers will be indifferent to producing skilled or unskilled offspring. If they produce unskilled offspring, they will have more children than unskilled workers. If they produce skilled offspring, they will have the same fertility as unskilled workers who produce unskilled offspring. If both skilled and unskilled workers invest in skilled offspring, then skilled workers will again have higher fertility due to their higher income. It also predicts investments in health will reflect investments in income-producing skills, both historically and across skill levels.

Still, several major problems remain unresolved. First the model, as it stands, predicts that there will be a mean difference in the fertility of skilled and unskilled workers. Although both types of workers will be indifferent to raising skilled and unskilled children, skilled workers, on average, should be more fertile due to their higher income. Second, the model can not account for sustained fertility reduction because initial decreases in fertility in one generation will be matched by increases in some future generation. Third, the model does not predict an intergenerational correlation in income (i.e., wealthier parents producing wealthier children), as is found empirically.

To explain the equality of fertility across income classes and the intergenerational correlation in fertility, higher-earning parents must invest more in children than lesser-earning parents. Here we follow Becker et al.'s (1990) suggestion that the production of human capital is human-capital intensive. If the qualities that increase productive output are knowledge, reading, writing, logic, and mathematical skills, the production of those qualities are likely to require inputs of a similar nature. The value of many inputs, in terms of the embodied capital produced, should depend on the capital embodied in those inputs. First, consider inputs of parents' time. There is significant evidence that the nature of parent–child interaction varies with the educational level of parents (Hart & Risley, 1995; Hoff-Ginsberg & Tardif, 1995). This probably means the skills and behavior patterns that result from parental time inputs are associated with the capital embodied in parents. By the time children enter the public education system, there are clear differences among them in school-related skills, and those differences are related to socioeconomic status. Second, the rate at which a child learns may depend on the knowledge and skills she already possesses. Much of the education offered in schools is based on the premise that knowledge is cumulative (Cromer, 1993). Basic skills are acquired first, and those skills are used as a foundation for the acquisition of the next set of skills. This would imply that the impact of the child's time inputs would depend on skills already in place.

This would mean that the net increase in embodied capital at each age would be functions of both the quality of inputs, and the capital acquired at younger ages. Define E_x as the total amount of embodied capital at age x, and e_x as the net increase in embodied capital at age x. We can think of E_x as a stock and e_x as a flow where

$$E_x = \sum_{y=0}^{x-1} e_y.$$

Next define for a given age of the child, $t_{c,x}$ as the child's time, $t_{p,x}$ as parent's time, $t_{o,x}$ as other's time (such as teachers'), $E_{c,x}$ as the child's existing stock of capital, $E_{p,x}$ as the embodied capital of parents, $E_{o,x}$ as the embodied capital of the others giving time to the child, and i_x as resources spent on all other inputs. Then e can be written as a funciton of inputs:

$$e(x) = e(t_{c,x}, t_{p,x}, t_{o,x}; E_{c,x}, E_{p,x}, E_{o,x}, i_x, x, t),$$

where

$$\frac{\partial^2 e_x}{\partial t_{c,x}\, \partial E_{c,x}}, \frac{\partial^2 e_x}{\partial t_{p,x}\, \partial E_{c,x}}, \frac{\partial^2 e_x}{\partial t_{o,x}\, \partial E_{c,x}}, \frac{\partial^2 e_x}{\partial i_x\, \partial E_{c,x}}, \frac{\partial^2 e_x}{\partial t_{p,x}\, \partial E_{p,x}}, \text{ and } \frac{\partial^2 e_x}{\partial t_{o,x}\, \partial E_{o,x}} \gg 0.$$

The first four cross-derivatives or interaction terms are written to indicate that the effect of each input will be greater as the recipient's (i.e., the child's) stock of embodied capital increases. This is important because it means that at each age, optimum investment in the child will be a positive function of the skills the child already possesses and that variance in investment will increase with age. The last two terms indicate the expectations, that the value of parents' and other's time inputs will also be an increasing function of their own stock of embodied capital. This means that more skilled parents should invest more and that parents should also invest more in children who are receiving inputs from higher quality schools. The rate of capital embodiment is also a function of time, t. This is meant to indicate that the overall level of technology and knowledge in the society will impact the rate of capital acquisition and optimal levels of investment.

If this is true, it has important implications for the supply and demand for embodied capital in the labor force. Now, the optimal level of investment in children may vary with income. It is easy to imagine a positive covariance between income of parents and the child's stock of human capital in early childhood, due to the positive covariance between income and the value of parental time inputs to children's development. Even if there are diminishing returns to parental time inputs, parents with more embodied capital may actually spend more time with children if the impact of their time is greater at each level than that of the time parents with less capital have to spend.

If the value of later inputs, such as resources and time dedicated to education, is an increasing function of the child's stock of embodied capital, then the stock of capital in children will become increasingly divergent with age. This will also mean that the total costs of embodying a given amount of capital will be a decreasing function of the parents' stock of capital. Although the cost of the time parents invest in children will be greater as parental income increases, the increased efficiency of later inputs will compensate for the greater expense of time by higher earning parents.

Total investment in embodied capital at the optimum will therefore be positively related, both directly and indirectly, to the stock of capital embodied in parents.

The significant implication of this reasoning is that the population distribution of fertility, parental investment, and incomes in competitive labor markets will be determined by both demand and supply functions. The demand curves will reflect technologies of production and the attendant demands for workers with varying levels of skill. The shape of the supply curves will reflect population variance in rates of return to investment in embodied capital. The values of the cross-derivatives just discussed are critical for determining whether the model predicts a positive association between parental stocks of embodied capital and parental investments in children's stocks, and a corresponding association between children's incomes and parents' incomes. The lack of income differences in fertility requires that optimal investments increase linearly with income. If we denote optimal parental investment for the ith and jth parents as $\tilde{p}_i^0$ and $\tilde{p}_j^0$, respectively, then equal numbers of children for all income levels requires that

$$\frac{\tilde{p}_i^0}{\tilde{p}_j^0} = \frac{I_i^0}{I_j^0} = \frac{I_i^1}{I_j^1}$$

with superscripts 0 and 1 representing the parental and offspring generations. However, if embodied capital decreases, the costs of embodying capital in offspring increases as well, the increased income necessary to motivate people to invest in higher levels of skills for offspring need not be as great as the fitness costs of obtaining those skills.

This within-population heterogeneity in the costs of embodying capital in children means that diminishing returns to parental investment are not determined by the environment as they would be in primary production economies, but rather by the population distribution of embodied-capital production functions. First, consider the highest skilled jobs in the economy. Those jobs would be filled by individuals with the lowest costs of skill acquisition in decreasing rank order until the point is reached when the next cheapest worker is more expensive than the product he or she produces. His or her parents would therefore invest less in him or her than would be necessary to obtain the highest skilled jobs, and he or she would find employment in the next tier of skill. That tier would then be occupied by individuals in decreasing rank order until the next cheapest worker would not be paid enough to compensate for skill embodiment. This process would continue through the lowest skilled jobs in the economy.

Next, consider the related proposition that technological change in production will be positively related to the stock of embodied capital at the population level (Becker et al., 1990). If higher levels of general education of the population are associated with more rapid technical progress, the demand for more skilled workers will increase as more investment is made in education. Through time then, the demand for new levels of skill will grow. For the simple model, this would imply that skilled parents would not only have the option of producing children of equal or lesser skill, but will have the opportunity to reinvest the dividend from their own educational investments in even higher levels of skill for their children. As long as technology is constantly growing and generating demand for new levels of skill, sustained fertility reduction over many generations is possible.

Although the continual intergenerational reinvestment of dividends from investments in embodied capital seems hard to sustain indefinitely, it does seem consistent with the last century of technological growth and increasing investment in education (see, e.g., Denison, 1985, Lesthaeghe & Wilson, 1986; and Lindert, 1986). In fact, there may be some excess return to education, especially at high levels, if there is a significant lag between increases in demand for skilled labor and corresponding increases in supply (see Fig. 5.3). Because the embodiment of skills takes time, some lags between demand and supply are likely. This would lead to higher rates of return to investments than would be expected at equilibrium. Such excess returns could drive fertility to a minimum level.

So far, we considered only fertility reduction and not the quantitative level of fertility. We also neglected the integer constraints on fertility and have treated fertility as if it were continuous. However, we know that minimum fertility greater than zero is one. If there were excess returns to investments in embodied capital, one might expect most people to have one child. Yet evidence suggests most people consider an only child to be undesirable and have a target fertility of two or three children (see Fig. 5.2). There is also evidence, however, that only children do not differ in education and achievement from children raised in two-child families (Blake, 1989). Yet, families with more than two children do show reductions in educational and income achievement (e.g., Blake, 1989; Kaplan et al., 1995). This suggests that decreases in family size below two children does not increase the total capital embodied by children.

This lack of effect may be due to several factors. Some of the costs of investment in embodied capital may be fixed (see Becker, 1991, for an analytical treatment of fixed and variable costs). The choice of a neighborhood to live in and the taxes paid for social services, including public education, are obvious examples of fixed costs. Thus the non-impact of a reduction from two children to one child may reflect diminishing marginal returns to variable costs, as they represent an increasing proportion of total costs. This would be true if the two types of costs were not perfectly substitutable. Also, men in focus-group discussions in Albuquerque expressed the opinion that interactions with siblings were an important contribution to development, and that mutual assistance among siblings was helpful in attaining life goals. Regardless of the reasons for this lack of impact, there seems little positive incentive to reduce fertility below two children. Moreover, because the number of children is not continuous, a reduction of fertility below two children requires a 50% change in fertility. This fact, coupled with the risk associated with the possible loss of an only child, creates a large disincentive. Increasing returns to scale for increases in embodied capital, combined with a lack of increase in embodied capital with a reduction to one child, may be sufficient to account for the two-child family.

Empirical Predictions Derived from the Skills-Based, Competitive Labor Market Model

To summarize, we propose that two characteristics of modern economies might be sufficient to account for a period of sustained fertility reduction and for a corresponding lack of income variation in fertility. The first characteristic is the direct link between costs of investment and wage rates due to the forces of supply and demand for labor in competitive economies. The second is the increasing emphasis on cumulative knowledge, skills, and technologies in the production of resources. These two characteristics may together produce the historically novel conditions that (a) investments in offspring income have nondecreasing (i.e., constant or increasing) returns to scale at the population level, and (b) embodied capital of parents is positively associated with returns to investment in embodied capital of children with diminishing returns at the individual level set by the within-population distribution of costs of skill embodiment.

These propositions generate a series of predictions with respect to fertility, parental investment, and child outcomes. Patterns of fertility should reflect investments in embodied capital and efficiency in the production of embodied capital. First, the observed relationship between income and fertility (i.e., no effect; see Fig. 5.4) should be the result of two opposing causal processes. Increased resources should be associated with higher fertility, but increased efficiency in the production of human capital should decrease fertility. However, because education and training affect both income and efficiency in the production of human capital in the same direction, the two opposing effects cancel each other out. Second, two kinds of fertility effects of embodied capital should be discernible. One effect is due to investments in own embodied capital. Men who invest more in training and education are expected to delay fertility. Another effect is due to increased investment in offspring embodied capital. Holding income constant, more educated men are expected to stop reproducing at

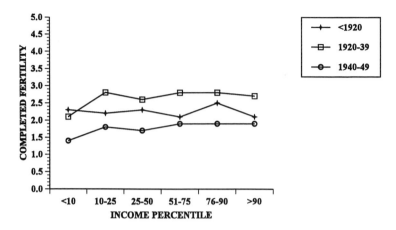

FIG. 5.4a. Anglo completed fertility by income and birth period.

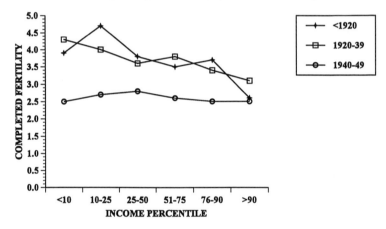

FIG. 5.4b. Hispanic completed fertility by income and birth period.

lower parities. Third, education has become increasingly important in determining economic outcomes during the course of this century (Burck,
1976; Herrnstein & Murray, 1994; Newcomer, 1955; Vinovskis, 1994), so
that we should find a pattern of increasing importance of education in
determining fertility.

A similar series of predictions are generated with respect to parental
investment. First, within economic strata, more educated parents should
invest more time and resources in each child as well as having lower fertility.
This should be especially true of investments in the child's education.
Second, parental education should be negatively related to the probability
of ceasing to live with an offspring, because the negative effect of lowered
parental investment will be greater for children of more educated parents.

Third, more academically able children should receive higher levels of investment (especially, school-related investment) than less able children, even within families, because there are higher returns to investment in their human capital (see Becker & Tomes, 1976, for a similar argument). Fourth, levels of investment at different stages of the child's development should be positively correlated with one another, contingent on the child's progress. The quantity and quality of early investments should positively affect early educational performance, which should, in turn, positively affect later investments. The loss of parental investment due to marital or relationship dissolution should also negatively impact child outcomes.

METHODS

The specific aims of the project were to test alternative theories of fertility, mating and parenting among men, using a representative sample from Albuquerque, New Mexico. The research design for the Albuquerque men sample consisted of two complementary interviews, a short interview administered to a large representative sample and a longer interview administered to a subset of the men in the short interview sample. Approximately 7,100 short interviews and 1,250 long interviews were conducted.

Potential respondents for the short interview were contacted at the Bernalillo County Motor Vehicle Division (MVD) as they received their driver's license photograph. The Bernalillo County MVD serves all of Albuquerque. All men who appeared to be over 18 years of age were considered eligible for initial contact. If they agreed to the short interview, which took about 7 minutes to administer, the interview was conducted in a private area at that time. On the basis of the answers to the short interview questions, eligibility for inclusion in the long interview sample was determined. The criteria for eligibility were (a) being age 25 or over and (b) having come to the MVD for the purpose of license origination, renewal, or for a photo ID. The purposes of the study were then explained to eligible men in more detail and they were offered the opportunity to participate in the long interview, for which they received a $30 payment. An appointment was then made to conduct the long interview in either a mobile office vehicle, an office at the University of New Mexico, or at their homes.

Albuquerque is the largest city in New Mexico with a population of 455,000; approximately 35% of the state's population lives in greater Albuquerque. More than 95% of all New Mexican males over 20 years of age have a current driver's license (U.S. Department of Transportation, 1993), compared to an estimated 92% telephone availability (of which 30% are unlisted numbers) for the Albuquerque area (U.S. Department of Commerce, 1992). Individuals who do not drive use the MVD to obtain valid photo IDs, and drivers' licenses and photo IDs must each be renewed every 4 years. By law in New Mexico, drivers' licenses and IDs cannot be renewed by mail or by phone. Thus, sampling licensed drivers and individuals obtaining photo ID's at the MVD provided a highly representative sample of the male population.

This approach has several advantages over standard sampling techniques, such as random digit telephone numbers, city directory listings, or housing units. The long interview requests sensitive information about illegitimate children, sexual affairs during marriage, family violence, homosexual experiences, and variation in male parental investment in children of different wives or of different sexes. Our ability to guarantee privacy, confidentiality, and anonymity was essential to the gathering of such intimate data from a large sample of men.

Evaluation of Sample Bias

We compared the demographic characteristics of our sample with data from other sources such as the census. We examined the age and ethnic distributions of our sample compared to licensed drivers and to census population data for males. There were no significant differences in any of these comparisons. In fact, the ethnic breakdown of the MVD sample is almost identical to the one obtained from the 1990 Census.

The Short Interview

This instrument was designed to obtain information on place and year of birth of the respondent and his parents, years in Albuquerque, ethnic, educational, religious, and economic background of the respondent and his parents, number of years he lived with each parent, number of half- and full-siblings, the fertility and age of siblings, number and age of biological children, years lived with biological children, number of spouses and women with whom the respondent had children, number of nonbiological offspring (step and foster) that the respondent parented, and income of the respondent and his current partner.

The Long Interview

The long interview collected information on the life history of the respondent, including his family history, rearing background, the parental investment he and his siblings received, employment history, major sexual and marital relationships, investment in children, and child outcomes. The form began by establishing the composition of the respondent's current household and then asked about the respondent's childhood and about the people who raised him. It focused on parental and extraparental investment the respondent received, and the stability of caretaking relationships. This information provided us with a socioeconomic and educational context for the respondent's upbringing, as well as a measure of the stability of his parents' major sexual relationships. The next section of the interview focused on resources in the life course such as the financial investment made in the respondent by the previous generation or by his caretakers, and at what age he established financial independence. It recorded the respondent's employment history with occupation, industry, and income data collected in a life-history format. The subsequent section gathered data on each of the respondent's full and half-siblings. This section was designed to provide data on each of the respondent's siblings, which was comparable to data regarding the respondent himself. This allowed us to extend our data set by one generation. The next section concerned reproductive relationships. It elicited data regarding the interviewee's sexual unions, marital relationships, and any relationship that produced a pregnancy. Data in this section was also collected to follow a life-history format for integration with employment, reproductive and parenting data. The following section covered parental investment, reproductive decision making, and parenting behavior. The initial portion was a history of all pregnancies and outcomes, which the respondent believed or suspected he fathered or someone claimed he fathered. The next part collected data regarding parenting of children, both biological and nonbiological. If the man did not live with the child until age 18, a special series of questions were asked as to why they were separated and what investment the man made in the child. Questions were also asked about financial investment in all children after the age of 18 that parallel the questions in the sibship portion of the interview. The last section of the interview focused on life-course strategies. We asked about reproductive or family composition preferences, reasons for not having more children, reasons for not reproducing at all, and financial strategies during the life course such as changes in being a borrower, saver, and spender, and current financial status. The interview concluded with a brief self-report questionnaire that allowed us to ask some personal questions, such as attitudes about women, relationships and commitment, engagement in behaviors used to get women to have sex with them, total numbers of sexual partners during stages of the life course, and risk-taking behaviors that affect morbidity and mortality.

RESULTS

Fertility

Figures 5.4a and 5.4b show the effects of year of birth, ethnicity, and income on the completed fertility of men. Parallel to national statistics on the fertility of women, the results show that Anglo men(non-Hispanic

Whites) men born prior to 1920 and after 1940 have lower completed fertility than men born between 1920 and 1939, who accomplished most of their reproduction during the Baby Boom years.[3] New Mexican Hispanics evidence higher fertility than Anglos in each cohort. However, there is no indication of a baby boom; instead there is a trend toward lower fertility through time, approaching Anglo norms. There is no net effect of current income on completed fertility among Anglos, and a slight negative effect among the earlier cohorts of Hispanics.

Although the lifetime data show no net effects of income on completed fertility, the relationship between fertility and income is, in fact, complex and bidirectional. Education is a major pathway to higher income, and education clearly depresses fertility at young ages. Table 5.1 summarizes the results of a set of logistic regression analyses, designed to determine the impacts of education on the probability of having a child during a year at risk, using data from the short interview sample. All years from age of 15 to 49 are in the risk set. One regression analysis was conducted for each age class and ethnicity. Income was controlled for in each analysis. The column labeled N is the sample size in risk years. The education parameter is the maximum likelihood estimator of the impact of an additional year of education on the log-odds of a birth occurring. The odds-ratio can be interpreted as approximating the relative risk due to a unit change in the independent variable when event probabilities are close to zero. The partial p is the standard probability that the education parameter is actually zero for the population as a whole, given the estimated value of the sample statistic.

The results show that for both Anglos and Hispanics, education has a very strong negative effect on reproduction during the late teens and even through the 20s. It gets gradually weaker with age, and in fact, is mildly positive among Anglos in the age classes of 35 to 39 and 45 to 49, suggesting differential scheduling of births. In these analyses, income at the time of the interview either has a small positive effect on fertility or no effect on fertility, after education is controlled for (results not shown—see analyses based on year-by-year income data from the following long interview).

The data presented in Fig. 5.5 clearly demonstrate, however, that for most men, there is a long delay between the completion of education and first reproduction, suggesting that the inhibitory effects of early reproduction on subsequent education are not great. Panels A and B of the figure show the hazard of first reproduction for Anglos and Hispanics, respec-

---

[3]Men born after 1945 are omitted from this analysis because many of them had not completed their fertility by the time of the interview. Results published previously (Kaplan et al., 1995) show that most men complete their reproduction by age 45, and including years past the age of 45 does not alter results appreciably.

TABLE 5.1

Effect of Each Additional Year of Education on Male Fertility by Age-Class and Ethnicity

Age Class	Anglo				Hispanic				All			
	N	Education Parameter	Education Odds-Ratio	Partial p	N	Education Parameter	Education Odds-Ratio	Partial p	N	Education Parameter	Education Odds-Ratio	Partial p
15–19	17878	-0.24	0.79	0.0001	12495	-0.17	0.85	0.0001	29873	-0.19	0.83	0.0001
20–24	17373	-0.15	0.86	0.0001	12495	-0.10	0.90	0.0001	29868	-0.12	0.89	0.0001
25–29	17347	-0.03	0.97	0.0003	12465	-0.06	0.94	0.0001	29812	-0.05	0.96	0.0001
30–34	15960	0.01	1.01	0.2228	10744	-0.02	0.98	0.0489	26704	-0.00	1.00	0.5120
35–39	13435	0.05	1.06	0.0001	8192	0.00	1.00	0.8054	21627	0.03	1.03	0.0014
40–44	10602	0.03	1.03	0.1902	5872	-0.03	0.98	0.2155	16474	-0.01	0.99	0.6947
45–49	8028	0.08	1.08	0.0289	4000	-0.00	1.00	0.9366	12028	0.03	1.03	0.2792

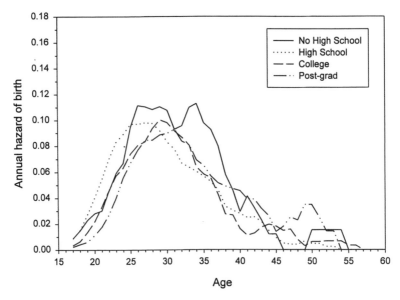

FIG. 5.5a. Hazards curves (5-year running average) for first birth of Anglo men by education level.

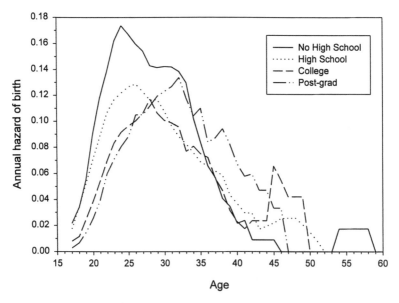

FIG. 5.5b. Hazards curves (5-year running average) for first birth of Hispanic men by education level.

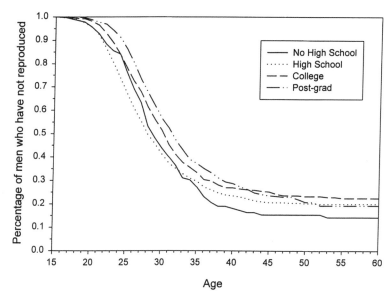

FIG. 5.5c. Survival curves for first birth of Anglo men.

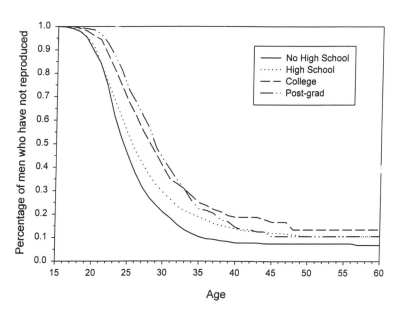

FIG. 5.5d. Survival curves for first birth of Hispanic men.

tively; panels C and D show the corresponding survival curves (the figures were generated using the life-table method with the Lifetest procedure in Statistical Analysis Software). The hazard of first reproduction is very low for all education levels prior to the age of 20. Even for those who did not complete high school, the peak hazard of first reproduction does not occur until about ages 25 and 22 for Anglos and Hispanics, respectively. In fact, for Anglos, the hazard of first birth is actually higher among those who completed high school than among dropouts during the late teens and early 20s. For college graduates and those with postgraduate degrees, the peak hazards of first birth do not occur until 29 and 31, respectively, among Anglos and 28 and 32, respectively, among Hispanics. The survival curves that correspond to these hazards distributions reflect these trends, and also show that almost twice as many Anglos fail to reproduce as do Hispanics.

The impact of education on reproduction has increased through time. Table 5.2 presents the result of logistic models in which the log-odds of a birth occurring in a year at risk prior to the age of 30 are regressed on education by decade of birth and ethnicity. For both Anglos and Hispanics, the negative effect of education increases dramatically for men born after 1940.

There are also period-parity interactions in fertility. Table 5.3 shows the results of logistic models in which the probability of a birth is regressed on period by parity. The baseline period is all years of risk prior to 1946 (i.e., prior to the Baby Boom period). The Boom period denotes the years between 1946 and 1962, and the post-Boom period denotes the years after 1962. For both Anglos and Hispanics, the probability of first reproduction (i.e., at parity zero) is about twice as high during the Boom period (see the odds-ratio column) and about 75% higher during the post Boom period than it is prior to the Baby Boom. This reflects the much later ages at first reproduction during the depression and war years (cf. Table 5.5). The progression from one child to two children also occurs more rapidly during the Boom period for both Anglos and Hispanics, but is not significantly different between the pre- and post-Boom periods. The higher parity progressions show a very different trend. There is no significant difference between the Boom and pre-Boom periods in the progressions from two or more children to the next higher parity; however, after the Baby Boom, men are less than half as likely to progress from two or more children to the next higher parity.

Table 5.4 examines the period-parity-education interactions. For Anglos, education has a strong negative effect on first reproduction for all periods. However, during the Baby Boom period, it increases the rate for all parity progressions after the first child. During the pre- and post-Boom periods, education has no significant effect on higher parity progressions. For His-

TABLE 5.2
Effect of Each Additional Year of Education on Fertility for Men Under 30, by Decade of Birth

Decade of Birth	Anglo				Hispanic				All			
	N	Education Parameter	Education Odds-Ratio	Partial p	N	Education Parameter	Education Odds-Ratio	Partial p	N	Education Parameter	Education Odds-Ratio	Partial p
< 1920	6585	−0.05	0.95	0.0148	1500	−0.02	0.98	0.5796	8085	−0.10	0.96	0.0033
1920–1929	5100	−0.02	0.98	0.1828	2310	−0.03	0.97	0.1782	7410	−0.03	0.97	0.0244
1930–1939	7350	−0.05	0.95	0.0001	4560	−0.05	0.95	0.0003	11910	−0.05	0.95	0.0106
1940–1949	14400	−0.11	0.90	0.0001	10275	−0.09	0.91	0.0001	24675	−0.10	0.91	0.0001
1950–1959	15960	−0.14	0.87	0.0001	14805	−0.10	0.91	0.0001	30765	−0.12	0.89	0.0001
1960+	2700	−0.15	0.86	0.0005	4005	−0.09	0.92	0.0001	6705	−0.10	0.90	0.0001

TABLE 5.3
Effect of Period on Male Fertility, by Previous Parity

Parity		Anglo					Hispanic					All			
	N	Period	Period Parameter	Odds-Ratio	Partial p	N	Period	Period Parameter	Odds-Ratio	Partial p	N	Period	Period Parameter	Odds-Ratio	Partial p
0	56652	Boom	0.73	2.08	0.0001	31662	Boom	0.95	2.60	0.0001	88314	Boom	0.75	2.12	0.0001
	56652	Post	0.56	1.76	0.0001	31662	Post	1.08	2.96	0.0001	88314	Post	0.71	2.04	0.0001
1	13565	Boom	0.43	1.54	0.0001	9476	Boom	0.47	1.60	0.0167	23014	Boom	0.44	1.55	0.0001
	13565	Post	-0.11	0.90	0.2861	9476	Post	0.00	1.00	0.9912	23014	Post	-0.08	0.93	0.3682
2	15995	Boom	0.10	1.11	0.5671	10809	Boom	-0.01	0.99	0.9696	26804	Boom	0.07	1.07	0.6263
	15995	Post	-0.67	0.51	0.0002	10809	Post	-1.00	0.37	0.0001	26804	Post	-0.79	0.45	0.0001
3	8277	Boom	0.06	1.07	0.8544	7248	Boom	-0.56	0.57	0.0820	15525	Boom	-0.24	0.79	0.2915
	8277	Post	-1.00	0.37	0.0034	7248	Post	-1.79	0.17	0.0001	15525	Post	-1.39	0.25	0.0001
4 or more	5634	Boom	-0.04	0.97	0.9597	7068	Boom	-0.00	1.00	0.9981	12702	Boom	-0.08	0.93	0.7916
	5634	Post	-0.83	0.43	0.2631	7068	Post	-1.15	0.32	0.0003	12702	Post	-1.11	0.33	0.0001

TABLE 5.4

Effect of Each Additional Year of Education on Male Fertility, by Previous Parity. Results Shown by Period of the 20th Century (i.e., Pre-Baby Boom, Baby Boom, Post-Baby Boom, and Overall) and by Ethnicity

			Anglo					Hispanic					All		
Parity	N	Period	Education Parameter	Odds-Ratio	Partial p	N	Period	Education Parameter	Odds-Ratio	Partial p	N	Period	Education Parameter	Odds-Ratio	Partial p
0	8665	Pre	-0.05	0.95	0.0088	2207	Pre	-0.03	0.97	0.4341	10872	Pre	-0.05	0.95	0.0034
	12412	Boom	-0.07	0.93	0.0001	6472	Boom	-0.08	0.93	0.0001	18884	Boom	-0.07	0.93	0.0001
	35575	Post	-0.07	0.93	0.0001	22983	Post	-0.07	0.94	0.0001	58558	Post	-0.07	0.93	0.0001
	56652	All	-0.06	0.94	0.0001	31662	All	-0.07	0.93	0.0001	88314	All	-0.07	0.94	0.0001
1	993	Pre	0.02	1.02	0.4946	203	Pre	0.04	1.04	0.3713	1196	Pre	0.02	1.03	0.3245
	3099	Boom	0.08	1.08	0.0001	1185	Boom	0.04	1.04	0.0516	4284	Boom	0.07	1.07	0.0001
	9473	Post	0.01	1.01	0.3637	8088	Post	-0.03	0.97	0.0070	17561	Post	-0.01	0.99	0.2218
	13565	All	0.04	1.04	0.0001	9476	All	-0.01	0.99	0.2431	23014	All	0.02	1.02	0.0119
2	419	Pre	0.00	1.00	0.9535	119	Pre	-0.03	0.97	0.6810	538	Pre	-0.02	0.98	0.6720
	3621	Boom	0.04	1.04	0.0350	978	Boom	0.02	1.02	0.4925	4599	Boom	0.02	1.02	0.1183
	11955	Post	-0.03	0.98	0.1276	9712	Post	-0.06	0.94	0.0001	21667	Post	-0.05	0.95	0.0001
	15995	All	0.00	1.00	0.8628	10809	All	-0.04	0.96	0.0005	26804	All	-0.03	0.98	0.0032
3	112	Pre	0.03	1.03	0.7826	54	Pre	0.20	1.22	0.0643	166	Pre	0.09	1.09	0.2012
	1698	Boom	0.06	1.06	0.0281	707	Boom	0.03	1.03	0.2475	2405	Boom	0.05	1.05	0.0143
	6467	Post	0.01	1.01	0.6864	6487	Post	-0.03	0.97	0.0837	12954	Post	-0.02	0.98	0.1862
	8277	All	0.03	1.03	0.0640	7248	All	-0.01	0.99	0.6325	15525	All	0.01	1.01	0.5976
4 or more	23	Pre	—	—	—	64	Pre	0.02	1.02	0.8022	87	Pre	0.01	1.01	0.8711
	998	Boom	0.11	1.12	0.0029	872	Boom	-0.04	0.96	0.1359	1870	Boom	0.02	1.02	0.4667
	4613	Post	-0.02	0.98	0.4076	6132	Post	-0.07	0.93	0.0003	10745	Post	-0.06	0.94	0.0001
	5634	All	0.02	1.02	0.3066	7068	All	-0.06	0.94	0.0002	12702	All	-0.04	0.97	0.0044

TABLE 5.5
Median Age at First Reproduction by
Birth Cohort, Ethnicity, and Education

| | Cohort | No High School | | High School | | College | | Post-Graduate | |
		Age	N	Age	N	Age	N	Age	N
	< 1920	30	54	30	264	31	115	33	80
	1920–1929	29	24	27	148	29	114	27	89
Anglo	1930–1939	26	21	25	221	26	137	27	139
	1940–1949	30	13	26	374	28	303	31	323
	1950–1959	28	21	30	531	33	306	34	265
	< 1920	27	56	28	39	34	8	29	113
	1920–1929	25	62	26	90	27	22	27	9
Hispanic	1930–1939	24	80	25	181	26	44	26	32
	1940–1949	23	97	24	473	26	102	27	75
	1950–1959	24	127	25	738	30	137	31	66

panics, there is no effect of education during the pre-Boom period. During the Boom period, there is a negative effect on first reproduction, a small positive effect on the progression from one to two children and no effect on higher progressions. During the post-Boom period, education has a negative effect on all parity progressions.

Table 5.5 examines the ethnicity-education-cohort interactions for first birth in greater detail. It shows the median age at first birth for men by decade of their birth, educational attainment and ethnicity. For Anglos, two effects are readily apparent. First, median age of first reproduction is high for the oldest men, decreases steadily to a minimum age for the men born between 1930 and 1939, and then increases steadily for men born later in the century. The effect of education changes through time. There is a small positive effect for men prior to 1920, no effect for men born between 1920 and 1939, and a very large positive effect on age at first reproduction for the 1950 to 1959 cohort. For the 1940to 1949 cohort, there is a positive effect for men who have at least completed high school, but high-school dropouts have a high median age at first reproduction. For Hispanics, there is little effect until the 1940 to 1949 cohort. The positive effect of education on age at first reproduction is also greatest for men born in the 1950 to 1959 cohort.

Table 5.6 examines marital and cohabiting fertility with the smaller, but more detailed, long interview sample. It displays the results of a logistic model of the predictors of the probability of a first birth. With respect to ethnicity, it shows that overall Anglos are only 93% as likely to reproduce in a given year as are Hispanics. The period effects on marital/cohabiting

TABLE 5.6

Logistic Regression Model for the Probability of Birth for Married and Cohabiting Couples*

Variable	DF	Parameter Estimate	Standard Error	Wald χ^2	Partial p	Standardized Parameter Estimate	Odds-Ratio
Intercept	1	-4.65	0.81	33.24	0.0001	—	0.01
Anglo	1	-0.08	0.02	12.70	0.0004	-0.07	0.93
During Boom	1	0.49	0.17	7.68	0.0056	0.10	1.62
Post-Boom	1	-0.59	0.17	12.48	0.0004	-0.13	0.55
Parity of 1	1	1.08	0.09	130.41	0.0001	0.24	2.94
Parity of 2	1	0.23	0.12	3.75	0.0528	0.05	1.25
Parity of 3	1	0.20	0.17	1.49	0.2224	0.04	1.22
Parity of 4	1	0.95	0.19	25.57	0.0001	0.14	2.59
Presence of youngest child age 1–2	1	-5.45	0.71	58.64	0.0001	-0.87	0.00
Presence of youngest child age 2–3	1	-4.51	0.59	59.97	0.0001	-0.63	0.01
Her education (years)	1	-0.05	0.02	11.44	0.0007	-0.08	0.95
His education (years)	1	0.01	0.01	0.40	0.5277	0.02	1.01
Number of her kids from previous relationships	1	-0.17	0.08	4.94	0.0262	-0.08	0.84
Number of his kids from previous relationships	1	-0.07	0.08	0.93	0.3343	-0.03	0.93
Income (in thousands of 1990 dollars)	1	0.00	0.00	7.15	0.0075	0.06	1.00
Her age	1	0.43	0.06	54.25	0.0001	1.87	1.54
Her age (squared)	1	-0.01	0.00	96.63	0.0001	-2.93	0.99

*$N = 10,210$ $\chi^2 = 1661.1$, $p < 0.0001$.

fertility reveal the different causal processes at work in determining total fertility for the different periods. The pre-Boom period is the baseline. The probability of a birth is about 62% higher during the Boom period, and only half as high during the post-Boom period relative to the pre-Boom baseline. Although for Anglos, total fertility rates are almost the same for cohorts reproducing prior to the Baby Boom as for those reproducing after the Baby Boom (Fig. 4.4a), marital fertility is much higher prior to the Baby Boom. This shows that the low completed fertility prior to the Baby Boom is due primarily to delay in marriage, whereas the low completed fertility after the Baby Boom is due to decreased marital fertility. To examine the parity effects, a parity of zero is used as the baseline. Because all years from the age of 15 to 49 define the risk set, the lowest probability of reproduction occurs before the first birth. After the first birth, men are more than 3 times as likely to have a second child in a given year. The progressions to higher parities, although higher than the probability of first birth, are much lower than the progression probability from first to second birth. Birth spacing effects are evident as well. The baseline is no child under the age of 3. Not surprisingly, if there is a child of 1 year or less of age, the probability of the next birth is only 5% as likely. If the child is between 1 and 2 years of age, a birth is 10% as likely. The data also show that the characteristics of a man's mate are highly determinate of fertility rates. The effects of a man's education on fertility appear to operate solely through his mate's education (the Pearson correlation between the two is .6). When both a man and his mate's education are in the regression model, the woman's education has a strong negative effect on fertility (the odds-ratio is .95 for each additional year of education), but the man's education is not significant. In addition, if his mate has children from a previous marriage, they are also less likely to reproduce (see below). If a man has children from a previous relationship, on the other hand, there is no significant decrease in the likelihood of having a child. Because the long interview sample contains data on income earned during each year of a man's life, we can also assess the impact of income on fertility. A man's income in a given year is positively associated with the probability of having a child. This reduces the negative effect of education on fertility.

Investment

Parental investment in children is multidimensional and difficult to measure. Men can spend time with their children, take an active interest in their development, spend money on them directly, and attempt to influence their well-being through the choice of a partner, residential location, and school system. To begin the analysis, we examine physical co-presence, and the likelihood of ceasing to live with a child before he or she reaches given ages. We then proceed to time investments and monetary expenditures.

Table 5.7 presents the results of a logistic model in which the log-odds of divorce/relationship dissolution for each year of the relationship are regressed on a vector of predictor variables using the long interview sample of Hispanic and Anglo men. Ethnicity has no apparent effect on relationship dissolution. As found in other samples, there is a distinctive time trend in divorce. Years at risk after 1980 are the baseline for the analysis. During the 1940s and 1950s, the hazard of dissolution was much lower. The hazard increases significantly in the 1960s, but it is still lower than in the years after 1980. The 1970s are not statistically different from the period after 1980. The log-odds of divorce decreases linearly with time in the relationship (a second-order polynomial term is not significant—not shown in the table). Marriages are much less likely to end than are cohabiting relationships (note the odds-ratio of 0.16). As found in other studies, the woman's age at the beginning of the relationship is a strong predictor of dissolution, with the likelihood of dissolution decreasing with age. The conditional probability of dissolution increases with each successive relationship (i.e., with each prior dissolution).

The effect of children's presence depends on their biological relationship to the men. Children who are the genetic offspring of men inhibit dissolution. The log-odds of dissolution increase almost linearly with each additional biological child (the linearity of this effect can be seen when number of children is treated as a vector of indicator or dummy variables—not shown here). The presence of a child under the age of 4 also has an additional negative effect on the likelihood of dissolution. The presence of a child from a previous union of the woman (i.e., her child, but not his) increases the likelihood of divorce, whereas if the man has children from a previous relationship, there is no discernible effect.

As in the case of fertility, the effect of education on dissolution operates through the woman. Although in an uncontrolled analysis, male education is negatively associated with the likelihood of dissolution, it has no effect once the negative effect of the woman's education is controlled for. Male income has no effect on dissolution, but the proportion of total family income contributed by the man is positively associated with the likelihood of divorce.

Figure 5.6 examines separation from children per se. Using the data from the short interview sample, Fig. 5.6a shows the changing likelihood of ceasing to live with a child under the age of 6 as a function of the child's year of birth and the man's education. A very small percentage of children (about 5%) born before 1960 cease to live with their father before the age of 6, regardless of parental education. However, as separation

TABLE 5.7
Logistic Regression Model of the Annual Probability of
Divorce/Relationship Dissolution for Married and Cohabiting Couples.*

Variable	DF	Parameter Estimate	Standard Error	Wald χ^2	Partial p	Standardized Parameter Estimate	Odds-Ratio
Intercept	1	1.62	0.44	13.77	0.0002	—	5.04
Anglos	1	0.02	0.03	0.51	0.4775	0.02	1.02
During 1940s	1	-1.13	0.40	7.84	0.0051	-0.13	0.32
During 1950s	1	-1.42	0.37	14.48	0.0001	-0.22	0.24
During 1960s	1	-0.51	0.19	7.08	0.0078	-0.10	0.60
During 1970s	1	-0.04	0.12	0.08	0.7755	-0.01	0.97
Duration of the relationship so far	1	-0.03	0.01	13.18	0.0003	-0.19	0.97
Married	1	-1.81	0.13	187.50	0.0001	-0.24	0.16
Her age when the relationship began	1	-0.08	0.01	47.37	0.0001	-0.27	0.93
His number of previous relationships	1	0.21	0.06	10.93	0.0009	0.08	1.23
Number of children they have together	1	-0.23	0.06	13.55	0.0002	-0.21	0.79
Presence of youngest child under age 4	1	-0.83	0.17	23.16	0.0001	-0.20	0.44
Number of her kids from previous relationships	1	0.14	0.06	5.20	0.0226	0.07	1.15
Number of his kids from previous relationships	1	-0.08	0.07	1.15	0.2846	-0.03	0.92
Her education (years)	1	-0.09	0.02	17.87	0.0001	-0.14	0.92
Income (in thousands of 1990 dollars)	1	-0.00	0.00	0.56	0.4533	-0.03	1.00
Percentage of family income he provides	1	0.49	0.22	5.11	0.0238	0.07	1.63

*$N = 12{,}191$, $\chi^2 = 654.4$, $p < 0.0001$.

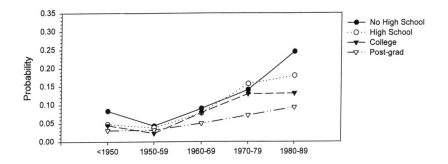

FIG. 5.6a. Effects of father's education on the probability of ceasing to live with a child before the age of 6.

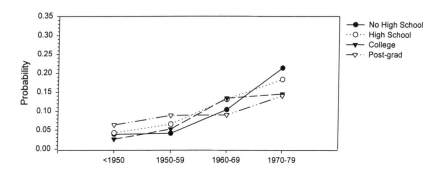

FIG. 5.6b. Effects of father's education on the probability of ceasing to live with a child between the ages of 6 and 15.

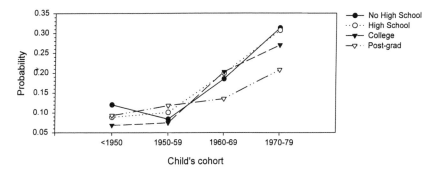

FIG. 5.6c. Effects of father's education on the probability of ceasing to live with a child before the age of 15.

becomes increasingly likely through time, the effects of education become readily apparent. For the cohort born in the 1980s, the probability of separating from the father before the age of 6 increases to about 25% for children whose father has less than a high school diploma, 18% for those whose father has only a high school diploma, 12% for children of men with a Bachelor's degree, and only 8% for children of men with a post-graduate degrees (this graphical presentation is supported by regression analyses, not shown). A similar, but less dramatic, pattern of effects can be seen for the probabilities of ceasing to live with the father between the ages of 6 and 15 (Fig. 5.6b) and for all children prior to age 15 (Fig. 5.6c).

Table 5.8 presents the analysis of men's time investments in children during their elementary school years. The dependent variable is an index of time involvement, derived from summing time spent alone with the child between the ages of 5 and 12 (in 5 levels, for ranges of average number of hours per week) and involvement in the child's education (low = 1, mid = 3, and high = 5). Hispanic men report higher time in-volvement with children than Anglos. Neither sex nor income appear to have any effect, although there is a nonsignificant trend toward slightly more involvement with both. Men report much lower time involvement with children who are not their biological offspring. Similarly, the number of siblings within 2 years of the focal child is negatively associated with time involvement. Men's time involvement has increased through time, as the child's year of birth is positively associated with it. Both the respondent's education and assessment of the child's scholastic intelligence are positively related to time involvement. Only 11.5% of the variance in the dependent variable, however, is accounted for by the independent variables in the model.

Analyses of monetary expenditures on children during the year prior to the interview are reported in Tables 5.9a and 5.9b. They cover all monetary expenditures on children (the sum of expenditures on the child including food and housing, education, clothing, lessons and hobbies, pocket money, medical expenses, room and board [if away], and gifts). A tobit model was run to account for the truncation in the distribution associated with reports of zero expenditures, especially for children be-tween 18 and 23 years of age. It is possible that some children actually contributed to their parents, and that some men would have taken money from children they parented if they could. In any case, the results of the tobit analyses were very similar to the Ordinary Least Squares (OLS) re-gressions, which we omit for the sake of brevity.

For children under the age of 18 (Table 5.9a), total expenditures do not vary by sex. The respondent's year of birth and ethnicity affect expen-ditures, indicating a trend toward increased expenditure with age and lower expenditures by Anglos, respectively. Expenditures increase with age

TABLE 5.8
Least Squares Regression Model of Men's Time
Investment in Elementary School-Aged Children*

Variable	DF	Parameter Estimate	Standard Error	T	Partial p
Intercept	1	−30.55	9.97	−3.06	0.0022
Anglo	1	−0.70	0.14	−4.96	0.0001
Child's sex	1	−0.18	0.12	−1.55	0.1219
Income when child was 5	1	0.00	0.00	−0.60	0.5469
Unrelated child	1	−0.58	0.16	−3.69	0.0002
Number of siblings 2 years older or younger	1	−0.39	0.09	−4.60	0.0001
Child's year of birth	1	0.02	0.01	3.63	0.0003
His education (years)	1	0.07	0.02	3.53	0.0004
His assessment of child's intelligence	1	0.46	0.07	6.33	0.0001

*$N = 1173$, $F = 18.91$, $p < 0.0001$, $R^2 = 0.115$.

of the child. Not surprisingly, both the respondent's and his mate's income (measured in thousands of dollars) are strong positive predictors of expenditures. However, years of education of both the respondent and his mate have independent positive effects. The parameter estimate for number of children in the family is negative, but the standard error of the estimate is so high that it is not significantly different from zero. The effects of genetic relatedness and cohabitation with the child's mother are interesting. Children are divided into four groups. Children who are the

TABLE 5.9a
Tobit Maximum Likelihood Regression Model of Men's
Monetary Expenditures on Offspring Ages 0 Through 17*

Variable	Parameter Estimate	Standard Error	Z	Partial p
Intercept	9925.60	2286.60	4.34	0.0000
Offspring's sex	−210.27	226.34	−0.93	0.3529
Man's year of Birth	−48.50	21.15	−2.29	0.0219
Anglo	−574.95	254.69	−2.26	0.0240
Offspring's year of birth	−107.10	26.76	−4.00	0.0001
Man's income (in thousands of dollars)	8.33	2.31	3.60	0.0003
Wife's income (in thousands of dollars)	14.69	6.42	2.29	0.0222
Man's education (years)	114.11	52.90	2.16	0.0310
Mother's education (years)	157.43	60.90	2.59	0.0097
Total number of offspring	−89.21	90.40	−0.99	0.3237
Unrelated child living with him	−478.34	468.73	−1.02	0.3075
Genetic offspring not living with him	−1008.90	272.27	−3.71	0.0002
Unrelated child not living with him	−1910.40	471.17	−4.06	0.0001

*$N = 500$, log likelihood = −4308.07, $p < 0.0001$.

TABLE 5.9b
Tobit Maximum Likelihood Regression Model of Men's
Monetary Expenditures on Offspring Ages 18 Through 23*

Variable	Parameter Estimate	Standard Error	Z	Partial p
Intercept	−1917.80	11089.00	−0.17	0.8627
Sex	−405.67	543.58	−0.75	0.4555
Offspring's year of birth	39.52	160.31	0.25	0.8053
Anglo	−766.65	662.40	−1.16	0.2471
Total number of siblings	−169.96	209.05	−0.81	0.4162
Man's year of birth	−95.81	46.56	−2.06	0.0396
Man's income (in thousands of dollars)	54.79	8.58	6.39	0.0000
Wife's income (in thousands of dollars)	12.22	13.27	0.92	0.3572
Man's education (years)	39.61	118.05	0.34	0.7372
Mother's education (years)	394.34	122.93	3.21	0.0013
Unrelated child, man living with the mother	−2686.10	912.54	−2.94	0.0033
Genetic offspring, man not living with the mother	−2362.50	699.11	−3.38	0.0007
Unrelated child, man not living with the mother	−4600.80	920.10	−5.00	0.0000

*$N = 195$, log likelihood = −1623.76, $p < 0.0001$.

genetic offspring of the respondent and who are still living with the respondent are the baseline. They receive the most monetary investment. The next highest level of investment is given to nongenetic offspring (i.e., usually the mate's child) who are living with the respondent (in fact, those children do not differ significantly from genetic offspring). Genetic offspring who are not living with the respondent receive less investment, approximately $1,000 less. Children who are not the genetic offspring of the respondent and who no longer live with respondent receive the very least investment, $1,900 less.

Expenditures during the college years (ages 18 to 23; Table 5.9b) do not vary by the child's sex, age, ethnicity or number of siblings. Father's gross income is the strongest predictor of expenditures, whereas mother's income is nonsignificant. Mother's years of education has a strong positive effect (again, father's education has a positive effect when mother's education is omitted from the model, suggesting that father's education may operate through mother's education). In this case, genetic relatedness and the respondent's relationship to the child's mother both have large effects. Children who are the genetic offspring of the respondent and whose mother is still living with the respondent are the baseline; they receive the most monetary investment.[4] The next highest level of investment is given to genetic offspring whose mothers are separated from the respondent

[4]Because many children over the age of 18 reside away from their parents and we are particularly interested in the effects of marital dissolution on children, we use the respondent's coresidence with the child's mother as the baseline.

and to unrelated children whose mothers are living with the respondent; they receive $2,000 less investment. The very least investment is given to children who are not the genetic offspring of the respondent and whose mothers no longer live with the respondent, a decrease of $4,600.

Finally, Table 5.10 examines financial support for higher education by the respondent. The cause and effect relationship between educational attainment and support for education is difficult to disentangle. If a child decides not to attend college, it is not possible to provide support for college; however, it is also possible that a lack of support is the cause of nonattendance. For this reason, we restrict our analysis to only those children of the respondent who attended college, about 50% of whom received some support. A logistic regression analysis was conducted. Hispanics are less likely to provide support. Number of siblings is negatively associated with support, and the effect is strong. The respondent's income is also associated with the probability of support, although his mate's is not. The education of both mother and father are significant with small effect sizes, as is the father's prior time involvement with the child (i.e., when he or she was in elementary school—see previous definition). Again, we find strong effects of biological paternity and the respondent's relationship to the child's mother. Support is reduced when the father does not live with the child's mother and is not the child's biological parent. Children who are not the respondent's biological offspring and whose mother is no longer living with him do not receive support from him.

Outcomes

In a previous paper (Kaplan et al., 1995), we reported that both the respondent's education and income were negatively associated with number of siblings, positively associated with father's income and number years prior to the respondent's 18th birthday that he lived with his father. Those analyses were based on the short interview data set. Here, we examine outcomes for the respondents' children using the long interview data set. An OLS regression analysis of the child's years of education is presented in Table 5.11. Only individuals older than 22 years of age are included in the analysis. The child's sex, year of birth, and number of siblings apparently have no effect, once the other predictors are controlled for (even though in uncontrolled analyses, individuals with more siblings have lower educational attainment). Anglos have about .6 years more education on average. The respondent's income when the child was 18 is positively associated with educational attainment, although his mate's income is not. Both the respondent's and the child's mother's years of education are positively associated with the child's education, although mother's effect is greater. The respondent's time involvement has an additional positive

TABLE 5.10
Logistic Regression Model of the Probability of a Man Providing Financial Support for an Offspring's Higher Education*

Variable	Parameter Estimate	Standard Error	Z	Partial p	Odds-Ratio
Intercept	-5.09	1.45	-3.50	0.0005	0.01
Offspring's year of birth	0.05	0.03	1.87	0.0615	1.05
Man's year of birth	-0.03	0.02	-1.36	0.1739	0.97
Sex	0.18	0.25	0.73	0.4648	1.20
Anglo	0.62	0.33	1.86	0.0628	1.85
Total number of siblings when offspring was 18	-0.33	0.07	-4.39	0.0000	0.72
Man's income (in thousands of 1990 dollars) when offspring was 18	0.01	0.00	2.88	0.0039	1.01
Wife's income (in thousands of 1990 dollars) when offspring was 18	-0.01	0.01	-1.39	0.1638	0.99
Man's education (years)	0.10	0.05	2.03	0.0426	1.10
Mother's education	0.11	0.06	1.80	0.0714	1.11
Man's time involvement with offspring when offspring was young	0.15	0.07	2.13	0.0333	1.16
Unrelated offspring, man lived with the mother when child was 18	-0.99	0.50	-1.97	0.0492	0.37
Genetic offspring, man not living with the mother when child was 18	-1.35	0.40	-3.36	0.0008	0.26
Unrelated offspring, man not living with the mother when child was 18	-3.34	0.94	-3.56	0.0004	0.04

*$N = 387$, $\chi^2 = 84.2$, $p < 0.0001$.

TABLE 5.11
Least Square Regression Model of the Number of Years of Education Obtained by Respondents' Children Age 23 and Older*

Variable	Parameter Estimate	Standard Error	Z	Partial p
Constant	11.46	1.06	10.86	0.0000
Sex	0.01	0.19	0.04	0.9721
Offspring's year of birth	-0.01	0.02	-0.28	0.7765
Man's year of birth	-0.02	0.02	-1.27	0.2041
Total number of siblings when offspring was 18	-0.05	0.05	-0.99	0.3214
Anglo	0.64	0.26	2.50	0.0126
Man's income (in thousands of 1990 dollars) when offspring was 18	0.01	0.00	2.62	0.0087
Wife's income (in thousands of 1990 dollars) when offspring was 18	0.00	0.01	-0.26	0.7958
Man's education (years)	0.07	0.03	2.12	0.0338
Mother's education (years)	0.21	0.04	5.42	0.0000
Man's time involvement with offspring when offspring was young	0.11	0.05	2.05	0.0403
Unrelated offspring, man lived with the mother when child was 18	-0.74	0.36	-2.07	0.0383
Genetic offspring, man not living with the mother when child was 18	-1.28	0.30	-4.33	0.0000
Unrelated offspring, man not living with the mother when child was 18	-2.65	0.59	-4.52	0.0000

*$N = 559$, F = 16.30, $p < 0.0001$, adjusted $R^2 = 0.263$.

effect (a separate analysis, not discussed here, indicates that this effect of time involvement operates through the child's school years, during elementary and secondary school). Children who are not biologically related to the respondent but whose mothers were living with him when they were 18 years of age achieve about .7 years less education than biological offspring whose mothers were living with him when they were 18 years of age. Biological offspring whose mothers ceased to live with the respondent before the child turned 18 achieve about 1.3 years less education, whereas children who are not biological offspring and whose mothers ceased to live with the respondent before the child turned 18 achieved 2.6 years less education.

DISCUSSION OF THE RESULTS

The data on male fertility indicate that both the onset of reproduction and parity progressions have changed through the course of the century. Age at first reproduction is high for men born early in the century, decreases for men born during 1920 to 1939, and then increases for men born after 1940. The effect of investment in human capital, as measured by years of education, on fertility is greatest before the age of 30. This reflects its greater impact on the onset of fertility than on parity progressions after the first child. However, the impact of investment in own human capital on the onset of fertility appears to have changed through time. For men born during the early part of the century, years of education have little effect on age at first reproduction. The delaying effect of education on fertility has increased through time.

One interpretation of these results is that the Great Depression of the 1930s and World Wars I and II delayed fertility for all men. During the postwar Baby Boom, low-cost loans for affordable housing and the GI bill allowed men to reproduce at earlier ages, even though investment in education was increasing. Following the Baby Boom, the onset of fertility is again delayed for everybody, but especially for men investing more in human capital. This may reflect increasing costs of education, as well as increasing importance of education in the determination of wages (Burck, 1976; Herrnstein & Murray, 1994; Newcomer, 1955; Vinovskis, 1994).

The onset of reproduction is probably determined by many factors. In addition to investment in human capital, men must obtain a partner and acquire the resources necessary for reproduction. This is probably why there is a significant delay (as much as 10 years, on average) between completion of schooling and first reproduction. Examination of fertility onset among men without high school education suggests that those other factors were more important during the early part of this century. Perhaps

the earlier onset of reproduction among less-educated men in recent cohorts is due to the fact that acquiring the resources for reproduction is
less of a constraint now that there are social welfare supports for poor
families. It is also possible that now more educated men are also engaging
in more postgraduate, on-the-job training. In both national samples (U.S.
Bureau of the Census, 1985) and the Albuquerque sample, men with higher
education exhibit greater increases in wages with increasing employment
experience than do men with fewer years of education. This may also
account for an increasing delay in the onset of fertility with education.

There has also been major historical change in the higher parity progressions. For Anglos, the hazard of progressing from one parity to the
next is greater at all parities during the Baby Boom than either prior to
or after the Boom. There appear to be different causal processes underlying
the low completed fertility prior to, and after the Baby Boom. The principal
cause of low fertility prior to the Boom is the low hazard of progression
from zero children to the first child. Following the Boom, the low fertility
is due to the low hazard of progressing from two to more children. Perhaps,
this change reflects an increasing trend toward investing in the human
capital of children and increasing costs of educating them. Men today are
much more likely to stop reproducing at the second or third child. Focus
groups' discussions with men in Albuquerque suggest that men are consciously deciding to stop reproducing at low parities so that they can invest
more time in their children and provide them with funding for education.

The analysis of the long interview data on marital fertility suggests that
once a union is established, it is the man's partner's level of education,
rather than his education, that significantly lowers marital fertility. One
way men may opt into a parental investment strategy is through the selection of a partner. Men who choose educated women may be selecting a
low-fertility, high-investment strategy. It is also interesting that after controlling for partner's education, male income positively affects fertility.
This result runs counter to conventional wisdom.

The predictions of the competitive labor market model just discussed
were supported by the analysis of the data on investment in children and
on child outcomes. Consistent with the idea that human capital of parents
is positively associated with rates of return to investment in offspring human
capital, men's education is associated with higher levels of investment in
children, including time involvement, monetary investments, and the probability of living with the child throughout the period of parental investment.
Also, as predicted by the model, men's time involvement with children is
positively associated with their assessment of the child's scholastic intelligence, although the direction of causality may be unclear. A third prediction of the model is that investments in children be positively correlated
over the child's life course. This prediction is supported by the fact that

financial support for college is positively correlated with the man's earlier time involvement with the child during elementary school years.

The impact of fertility on parental investment appears to be greater for time involvement than for monetary investments. The number of siblings within 2 years of the focal child is negatively correlated with time involvement, but we find no effects on expenditures. The effect of income is just the opposite. There is no effect of income on time involvement, but it is by far the strongest predictor of monetary expenditures.

The data on outcomes suggest that those investments do increase the educational achievement of children. It is interesting to note that even after the effects of investments are taken into account, there is still a residual effect of both mother's and father's education on children's educational achievement. This result is consistent with the idea that the rate of return to investments in human capital of offspring increases with the level of parental human capital. However, it is also possible that the effect is due to genetically mediated parent–offspring correlations in academic ability or motivation. Another possibility is that more educated parents instill more positive attitudes toward education and greater expectations of educational achievement in their children.

Taken together, these results provide substantial indirect support for the embodied capital approach to fertility and parental investment, and for the specific model of investment in embodied capital in skills-based labor markets. However, the support is based largely on qualitative predictions, each of which is potentially consistent with some other theoretical model. An adequate assessment of the model will require more rigorous tests of quantitative predictions.

Two major difficulties must be overcome. First, the model's theoretical constructs are very difficult to measure. Years of education is only a proxy for embodied capital. Measuring the embodied capital of both parents and children is especially challenging, given that it is multidimensional and heterogeneous. Similarly, parental investment is only poorly approximated by our recall-based measures of expenditures of time and money. The effect sizes we obtained are probably smaller than the true effect sizes as a result of measurement error. In order to determine the quantitative relationship between parental embodied capital and the rate of return on investments in children's embodied capital, a prospective study that overcomes those measurement problems will be necessary.

Second, selection bias produces another difficulty. Educational achievement, fertility, parental investment, and mate selection are endogenous choices. This means that men are not randomly assigned to educational achievement levels, parities, and so on. As a result, it is difficult to assess the impacts of those characteristics on child outcomes. For example, the association between parental education and the child's education could be due partially to unobserved characteristics that affected the parents choices about how many years of education to pursue as well as to the effect of education, per se. Because the theory presented here implies an intricate causal pathway relates endogenous choices to one another and ultimately, to child outcomes, the problem of selection bias must be solved so that an accurate quantitative assessment of those relationships can be obtained.

As a final point, there is clear evidence that biological paternity is relevant to male parental investment. Men invest less in children from previous unions of their mate. Although expenditures on young children are not affected by biological paternity, both time investment and support during the college years is greater for genetic offspring than for a mate's child. In addition, the investment in a mate's child is contingent on a continuing relationship with that partner. Men cease to invest in a child after they stop living with the child's mother, unless the child is also the biological offspring of the man, and even then support is reduced significantly (see Weiss & Willis, 1985, for a theoretical treatment of this effect). The effect of those reduced investments is also seen in child outcomes, with children who are raised by men other than their biological father or who are not fully raised by their father achieving lower educational outcomes (even after parental income and education are controlled for).

SUMMARY

The fundamental features of the human life course, clearly exhibited by all extant hunter-gatherers and in contrast to other nonhuman primates and mammals, are prolonged postweaning juvenile dependence on parents, the simultaneous support and provisioning of multiple, dependent young of different ages, marriage, and the involvement of men in the care and provisioning of children, and a long life span with older, nonreproductive individuals supporting their offspring's reproduction (Kaplan, 1996a; Lancaster & Lancaster, 1987). In other words, the critical human life-history adaptations are all features that focus on the investment in offspring by parents over much of the life course, particularly after infancy, and not simply on greater numbers of children produced.

Selection must have acted on the coordinated outcome of mechanisms that both regulate parental investment and fertility. Investment may be regulated by psychological mechanisms that direct attention to fundamental relationships between investments and outcomes, and that detect diminishing returns to investment. Actual decisions will be the product of those mechanisms and some reliance on cultural norms that benefit from accumulated experience. The regulation of fertility, on the other hand, may involve little or no direct cognition, and be wholly regulated by physiological mechanisms responsive to breastfeeding regimes and net energy flow. This makes sense in the context of the theoretical model insofar as fertility is the passive result of optimal parental investment and an income budget for reproduction. If, after allocating investments to existing children, there is enough time and energy to support the next offspring, it should be produced.

This complex set of mechanisms that regulated parental investment and fertility in time past, one that appreciates relationships between investments and outcomes and diminishing returns to effort, is now expressed in the context of modern economies and is associated with major reductions in fertility and increases in parental investment. We proposed that two characteristics of modern economies might be sufficient to account for a period of sustained fertility reduction and to a corresponding lack of income variation in fertility. The first characteristic is the direct link between costs of investment and wage rates due to the forces of supply and demand for labor in competitive economies. The second is the increasing emphasis on cumulative knowledge, skills, and technologies in the production of resources. These two characteristics may together produce the historically novel conditions that (a) investments in offspring income have nondecreasing (i.e., constant or increasing) returns to scale at the population level; and (b) embodied capital of parents is positively associated with returns to investment in embodied capital of children with diminishing returns at the individual level set by the within-population distribution of costs of skill embodiment.

The apparently non-adaptive nature of modern fertility decisions (as measured by the number of descendants produced) rests on the evolved rule of thumb that fixed number of children not in terms of birth-spacing, but by the optimal allocation of parental investment. In the past, investment in growth and skill acquisition reached diminishing returns at a much lower level of investment. In the evolutionarily novel conditions of today, people in developed countries with skills-based, competitive labor markets make decisions to minimize their fertility to two or three children using the same psychological mechanisms that, in the past, produced much larger families. Now, people employ birth control and subvert the lactation-energy system that for millions of years used to translate parental investment into fertility.

We presented tests of a model of human fertility and the timing of reproduction in the life course using interviews with men living in Albuquerque, New Mexico, about their reproductive careers. The model assumes that men's decisions regarding fertility and investment in children are directly related to investments they received from their parents and to their investments in own education-related human capital. Specifically, it predicts that men who have higher levels of human capital will invest more in their children's human capital and exhibit lower fertility as a result. This prediction is derived from considering two principal trade-offs in modern societies with skills-based labor markets. The first trade-off is between investments in own human capital and the onset of reproduction. The second trade-off is between investments in children's human capital and total fertility. Alternative life histories result from a positive correlation between men's stock of human capital and rates of return from investments in own and in children's human capital. Male reproductive strategies, directed either toward more less-educated children or towards fewer more-educated children, impact on family formation strategies in terms of the timing of reproduction in the life course, number of mates, total fertility, likelihood of desertion, and the production of second families.

ACKNOWLEDGMENTS

Support for the research project, male fertility and parenting in New Mexico, began with two seed grants from the University of New Mexico Biomedical Research Grants, 1988 and 1989, and one from the University of New Mexico Research Allocations Committee, 1988. Further seed money as well as interim funding came from the William T. Grant Foundation (#89130589 and #91130501). The major support for the project came from the National Science Foundation 1990 to 1993 (#BNS-9011723 and #DBS-911552). Both National Science Foundation grants included Research Experience for Undergraduates supplements. Some of these analyses are based upon work supported under a National Science Foundation Graduate Research Fellowship granted to Kermyt G. Anderson.

The authors would like to thank Paul Amato, Alan Booth, Nan Crouter, John Gottman, Steven Mintz, Patricia Draper, William Marsiglio, and Catherine Surra for helpful comments on drafts of this paper as well as the many undergraduate and graduate students at the University of New Mexico who worked on the Albuquerque Men project in interviewing, coding, data entry, office management, and data management and analysis. We would also like to thank Ted Bergstrom, Erik Charnov, Phil Ganderton, Steven Gangestad, Kristen Hawkes, Kim Hill, Nick Blurton Jones, David Lam, and Robert Willis for stimulating discussions about the theory of fertility and Kishore Gawande for discussions on economic models.

REFERENCES

Barkow, J. (1989). *Darwin, sex, and status.* Toronto: Toronto University Press.
Becker, G. S. (1975). *Human capital* (2nd ed.). New York: Columbia University Press.

Becker, G. S. (1991). *A treatise on the family* (2nd ed.). Cambridge, MA: Harvard University Press.

Becker, G. S., & Barro, R. J. (1988). A reformulation of the economic theory of fertility. *Quarterly Journal of Economics, 103,* 1–25.

Becker, G. S., & Lewis, H. G. (1973). Interaction between quantity and quality of children. In T. W. Schultz (Ed.), *Economics of the family: Marriage, children, and human capital* (pp. 81–90). Chicago: University of Chicago Press.

Becker, G. S., Murphy, K. M., & Tamura, R. (1990). Human capital, fertility and economic growth. *Journal of Political Economy, 98,* s12–s37.

Becker, G. S., & Tomes, N. (1976). Child endowments and the quantity and quality of children. *Journal of Political Economy, 84,* s143–s163.

Becker, G. S., & Tomes, N. (1986). Human capital and the rise and fall of families. *Journal of Labor Economics, 4,* s1–s39.

Ben-Porath, Y. (1967). The production of human capital and the life cycle of earnings. *Journal of Political Economy, 75,* 352–365.

Betzig, L. L. (1986). *Despotism and differential reproduction: A Darwinian view of history.* Hawthorne, NY: Aldine.

Blake, J. (1989). *Family size and achievement.* Los Angeles, CA: University of California Press.

Blurton Jones, N. G. (1986). Bushman birth spacing: A test for optimal interbirth intervals. *Ethology and Sociobiology, 7,* 91–105.

Blurton Jones, N. G. (1987). Bushman birth spacing: A direct test of simple predictions. *Ethology and Sociobiology, 8,* 183–203.

Blurton Jones, N. G., Hawkes, K., & Draper, P. (1994a). Foraging returns of !Kung adults and children: Why didn't !Kung children forage? *Journal of Anthropological Research, 50*(3), 217–248.

Blurton Jones, N. G., Hawkes, K., & Draper, P. (1994b). Differences between Hadza and !Kung children's work: Affluence or practical reason? In E. S. Burch, Jr., & L. J. Ellanna (Eds.), *Key issues in hunter-gatherer research* (pp. 189–215). Oxford, England: Berg Publishers.

Blurton Jones, N. G., Hawkes, K., & O'Connell, J. F. (1989). Modeling and measuring the costs of children in two foraging societies. In V. Standen & R. Foley (Eds.), *Comparative socioecology: The behavioral ecology of humans and other mammals* (pp. 367–390). Oxford: Blackwell.

Blurton Jones, N. G., & Sibly, R. M. (1978). Testing adaptiveness of culturally determined behavior. Do bushman women maximize their reproductive success by spacing births widely and foraging seldom? In N. G. Blurton Jones & V. Reynolds (Eds.), *Human behavior and adaptation* (pp. 135–157). London: Taylor & Francis.

Bock, J. (1995). *The determinants of variation in children's activities in a southern African community.* Unpublished PhD dissertation, University of New Mexico.

Boone, J. (1986). Parental investment and elite family structure in preindustrial states: A case study of late medieval–early modern Portuguese genealogies. *American Anthropologist, 88,* 859–878.

Borgerhoff Mulder, M. (1987). On cultural and reproductive success: Kipsigis evidence. *American Anthropologist, 89,* 617–634.

Borgerhoff Mulder, M. (1988). Reproductive consequences of sex-biased inheritance for the Kipsigis. In V. Standen & R. Foley (Eds.), *Comparative socioecology of mammals and man* (pp. 405–427). London: Blackwell.

Borgerhoff Mulder, M. (1992). Reproductive decisions. In E. A. Smith & B. Winterhalder (Eds.), *Evolutionary ecology and human behavior* (pp. 339–374). Hawthorne, NY: Aldine de Gruyter.

Burck, C. G. (1976, May). A group profile of the Fortune 500 chief executives. *Fortune,* 173–177.

Chagnon, N. (1988). Life histories, blood revenge, and warfare in a tribal population. *Science, 239,* 985–992.

Charlesworth, B. (1980). *Evolution in age structured populations.* Cambridge: Cambridge University Press.

Charnov, E. L. (1993). *Life history invariants: Some explorations of symmetry in evolutionary ecology.* New York: Oxford University Press.

Cromer, A. (1993). *Uncommon sense: The heretical nature of science.* New York: Oxford.

Cronk, L. (1991a). Human behavioral ecology. *Annual Reviews in Anthropology, 20,* 25–53.

Cronk, L. (1991b). Wealth, status and reproductive success among the Mukogodo. *American Anthropologist, 93,* 345–360.

Denison, E. F. (1985). *Trends in American growth, 1929–1982.* Washington: Brookings Institute.

de Tray, D. N. (1973). Child quality and the demand for children. *Journal of Political Economy, 81,* S70–S95.

Downey, D. B. (1995). When bigger is not better: Family size, parental resources, and children's educational performance. *American Sociological Review, 60,* 746–761.

Draper, P., & Harpending, H. (1987). Parental investment and the child's environment. In J. Lancaster, J. Altmann, A. Rossi, & L. Sherrod (Eds.), *Parenting across the lifespan: Biosocial dimensions* (pp. 207–235). New York: Aldine de Gruyter.

Flinn, M. (1986). Correlates of reproductive success in a Caribbean village. *Ethology and Sociobiology, 9,* 1–29.

Hanson, L. A. (1982). The mammary gland as an immunological organ. *Immunology Today, 3,* 168–172.

Harpending, H. C., Draper, P., & Pennington, R. (1990). Cultural evolution, parental care, and mortality. In A. Swedlund & G. Armelegos (Eds.), *Health and disease in traditional societies* (pp. 241–255). South Hadley, MA: Bergin and Garvey.

Hart, B., & Risley, T. (1995). *Meaningful differences in the everyday experience of young American children.* Baltimore: Brookes.

Hawkes, K., O'Connell, J. F., & Blurton Jones, N. (1995). Hadza children's foraging: Juvenile dependency, social arrangements and mobility among hunter-gatherers. *Current Anthropology, 6*(4), 688–700.

Herrnstein, R. J., & Murray, C. (1994). *The bell curve: Intelligence and class structure in American life.* New York: Free Press.

Hill, K. (1993). Life history theory and evolutionary anthropology. *Evolutionary Anthropology, 2,* 78–88.

Hill, K., & Hurtado, A. M. (1996). *Ache life history: The ecology and demography of a foraging people.* Hawthorne, NY: Aldine de Gruyter Press.

Hoff-Ginsberg, E., & Tardif, T. (1995). Socioeconomic status and parenting. In M. Bornstein (Ed.), *The handbook of parenting* (Vol. 2, pp. 161–188). Hillsdale, NJ: Lawrence Erlbaum Associates.

Howie, P. W., Forsyth, J. S. Ogston, S. A., Clark, A., & du Florey, C. V. (1990). Protective effect of breast feeding against infection. *British Medical Journal, 300,* 11–16.

Hughes, A. (1986). Reproductive success and occupational class in eighteenth-century Lancashire, England. *Social Biology, 33,* 109–115.

Irons, W. (1979). Cultural and biological success. In N. Chagnon and W. Irons, (Eds.), *Evolutionary biology and human social behavior* (pp. 257–272). North Scituate, MA: Duxbury.

Irons, W. (1983). Human female reproductive strategies. In S. K. Wasser (Ed.), *Social behavior of female vertebrates* (pp. 169–213). New York: Academic Press.

Irons, W. (1990). Let's make our perspectives broader rather than narrower: A comment on Turke's "Which humans behave adaptively, and why does it matter?" and on the so-called DA-DP Debate. *Ethology and Sociobiology, 11,* 361–375.

Irons, W. (1993). Monogamy, contraception, and the cultural and reproductive success hypothesis. *Behavior and Brain Sciences, 16,* 295–296.

Irons, W. (1995). *Cultural and reproductive success in traditional societies.* Unpublished manuscript, Northwestern University.

Kaplan, H. (1996a). *The evolution of the human life course.* Unpublished manuscript, University of New Mexico.

Kaplan, H. (1996b). The competitive labor market theory of the demographic transition and the evolutionary economics of human fertility and parental investment. Unpublished manuscript, University of New Mexico.

Kaplan, H., & Hill, K. (1985). Hunting ability and reproductive success among male Ache foragers. *Current Anthropology, 26,* 131–133.

Kaplan, H., Lancaster, J. B., Bock, J., & Johnson, S. (1995). Does observed fertility maximize fitness among New Mexican men? A test of an optimality model and a new theory of parental investment in the embodied capital of offspring. *Human Nature, 6,* 325–360.

Kozlowski, J. (1992). Optimal allocation to growth and reproduction: Implications for age and size at maturity. *Trends Ecology and Evolution, 7,* 15–19.

Kozlowski, J., & Wiegert, R. G. (1986). Optimal allocation of energy to growth and reproduction. *Theoretical Population Biology, 29,* 16–37.

Kozlowski, J., & Wiegert, R. G. (1987). Optimal age and size at maturity in annuals and perennials with determinate growth. *Evolutionary Ecology, 1,* 231–244.

Lack, D. (1954). *The natural regulation of animal numbers.* Oxford: Oxford University Press.

Lack, D. (1968). *Ecological adaptations for breeding in birds.* London: Methuen & Co.

Lam, D. (1986). The dynamics of population growth, differential fertility, and inequality. *American Economic Review, 76,* 1103–1116.

Lancaster, J. B., & Kaplan, H. (1992). Human mating and family formation strategies: The effects of variability among males in quality and the allocation of male effort and parental investment. In A. Ehara, T. Kimura, O. Takenaka, & M. Iwamoto (Eds.), *Primatology today* (pp. 21–33). Amsterdam: Elsevier.

Lancaster, J. B., & Lancaster, C. S. (1987). The watershed: Change in parental-investment and family-formation strategies in the course of human evolution. In J. B. Lancaster, J. Altmann, A. S. Rossi, & L. R. Sherrod (Eds.), *Parenting across the life span: Biosocial dimensions* (pp. 187–205). Hawthorne, NY: de Gruyter.

Lee, P. C., Majluf, P., & Gordon, I. J. (1991). Growth, weaning and maternal investment from a comparative perspective. *Journal of Zoology, London, 225,* 99–114.

Lessells, C. M. (1991). The evolution of life histories. In J. R. Krebs & N. B. Davies (Eds.), *Behavioral ecology: An evolutionary approach* (3rd ed., pp. 32–68). Oxford: Blackwell Scientific.

Lesthaeghe, R., & Wilson, C. (1986). Modes of production, secularization, and the pace of fertility decline in western Europe, 1870–1930. In A. J. Coale & S. C. Watkins (Eds.), *The decline of fertility in Europe* (pp. 261–292). Princeton, NJ: Princeton University Press.

Lindert, P. H. (1986). Unequal English wealth since 1670. *Journal of Political Economy, 94,* 1127–1162.

Lloyd, D. C. (1987). Selection of offspring size at independence and other size-versus-number strategies. *American Naturalist, 129,* 800–817.

Low, B. (1990). Occupational status, landownership, and reproductive behavior in 19th-century Sweden: Tuna Parish. *American Anthropologist, 92,* 457–468.

McGinley, M. A., & Charnov, E. L. (1988). Multiple resources and the optimal balance between size and number of offspring. *Evolutionary Ecology, 2,* 77–84.

Mealey, L. (1985). The relationship between social status and biological success: A case study of the Mormon religious hierarchy. *Ethology and Sociobiology, 11,* 83–95.

Mincer, J. (1974). *Schooling, experience and earnings.* Chicago: National Bureau of Economic Research.

Newcomer, M. (1955). *The big business executive: The factors that made him. 1900–1950.* New York: Columbia University Press.

Oftedal, O. T. (184). Milk composition, milk yield and energy output at peak lactation: A comparative review. *Symposium Zoological Society of London, 5,* 33–85.

Pennington, R., & Harpending, H. (1988). Fitness and fertility among the Kalahari !Kung. *American Journal of Physical Anthropology, 77,* 303–319.

Perusse, D. (1993). Cultural and reproductive success in industrial societies: Testing the relationship at the proximate and ultimate levels (with comments). *Brain and Behavioral Sciences, 16,* 267–323.

Retherford, R. D. (1993). *Demographic transition and the evolution of intelligence: Theory and evidence.* Unpublished manuscript, Program on Population, East-West Center, Honolulu, Hawaii.

Roff, D. A. (1992). *The evolution of life histories: Theory and analysis.* New York: Chapman Hall.

Rogers, A. R. (1993). Why menopause? *Evolutionary Ecology, 7,* 406–420.

Rogers, A. R. (1994). Evolution of time preference by natural selection. *American Economic Review, 84,* 460–481.

Rogers, A. R., & Blurton Jones, N. G. (1992). *Allocation of parental care.* Unpublished manuscript, University of Utah, Salt Lake City.

Sheard, N. F., & Walker, W. A. (1988). The role of breast milk in the development of the gastrointestinal tract. *Nutrition Reviews, 46,* 1–8.

Simons, J. L. (1974). *The effects of income on fertility.* Chapel Hill, NC: Carolina Populations Center.

Smith, C. C., & Fretwell, S. D. (1974). The optimal balance between size and number of offspring. *American Naturalist, 108,* 499–506.

Stearns, S. C. (1992). *The evolution of life histories.* New York: Oxford University Press.

Stearns, S. C., & Koella, J. (1986). The evolution of phenotypic plasticity in life history traits: Predictions for norms of reaction for age- and size-at-maturity. *Evolution, 40,* 893–913.

Turke, P., & Betzig, L. (1985). Those who can do: Wealth, status and reproductive success on Ifaluk. *Ethology and Sociobiology, 6,* 79–87.

U.S. Bureau of the Census. (1985). *Current population reports, P-60,* No. 156, Table 35.

U.S. Department of Commerce. (1992). *U.S. census of population: General population characteristics: New Mexico.* Washington, DC: Bureau of Census.

U.S. Department of Transportation, Federal Highway Administration. (1993). *Highway statistics 1987.* TD2.22.991. Washington, DC: U.S. Government Printing Office.

Varian, H. R. (1992). *Microeconomic analysis* (3rd ed.). New York: Norton.

Vining, D. R., Jr. (1986). Social versus reproductive success: The central theoretical problem of human sociobiology. *The Behavioral and Brain Sciences, 9,* 167–216.

Vinovskis, M. A. (1994). Education and the economic transformation of nineteenth-century America. In M. W. Riley, R. L. Kahn, & A. Foner (Eds.), *Age and structural lag: Society's failure to provide meaningful opportunities in work, family, and leisure* (pp. 171–196). New York: Wiley.

Vitzthum, V. (1994). Comparative study of breastfeeding structure and its relation to human reproductive ecology. *Yearbook of Physical Anthropology, 37,* 307–349.

Voland, E. (1990). Differential reproductive success with the Krummerhorn population (Germany, 18th and 19th centuries). *Behavioral Ecology and Sociobiology, 26,* 65–72.

Weiss, Y., & Willis, R. (1985). Children as collective goods and divorce settlements. *Journal of Labor Economics, 3,* 268–292.

Whitehead, R. G., & Paul, A. (1981). Infant growth and human milk requirements: A first approach. *Lancet, 2,* 161–163.

Willis, R. J. (1973). A new approach to the economic theory of fertility behavior. *Journal of Political Economy, 81,* S14–S64.

Chapter 6

Why Should Fathers Father?

Patricia Draper
The Pennsylvania State University

The previous chapter, by Kaplan, Lancaster, and Anderson, does an excellent job of joining life-history theory from biology and theories of human capital from family economics. The relevance of both of these to issues of fertility is made compelling.

The findings about the ways in which components of men's human capital is translated into human capital of offspring are intriguing both for what the findings show about secular trends in fertility, consequences for child accomplishment, and for what they show about the importance of the child's mother in linking the father to the child. It is this issue, the mother as link to child and the nature of the father's relationships with the mother that I make the center of my remarks.

There are several things to keep in mind when we try to grasp the evolutionary big picture and to make sense of men in human families as we now find them in postindustrial western society. We humans of today carry with us the effects of selection in past environments. These effects are evident in our physical and behavioral makeup. Although we cannot know in detail the past physical and social environments in which our ancestors evolved, we can make various informed guesses, based on an understanding of how morphological, behavioral, and life-history features act together in other species. The ethnographic and historical literature provide data of another type, allowing us to see men playing various domestic and paternal roles. In these different settings, however, the concrete form of social institutions can vary so widely that a unitary picture of men

in families does not emerge. There are certain regularities of human experience that are worth reviewing for the purpose of thinking about men
in families in modern western society.

MORPHOLOGICAL AND LIFE-HISTORY TRACES
OF MALE PARENTAL INVESTMENT

I first review a few of the topics concerned with life-history theory, for they
are relevant to issues of human mating. Organisms must make decisions
about the allocation of energy to self (in the form of maintenance and
growth) versus commitment of energy to finding a mate and beginning
reproduction (Stearns, 1992). Similar trade-offs are faced with respect to
offspring—whether to have many offspring who necessarily are less inten-
sively nurtured or to have fewer offspring, each of whom receives propor-
tionately greater amounts of parental investment. Humans are like other
large mammals in showing life-history characteristics that favor long life
span, low fertility, slow maturation, long juvenile prereproductive period,
and large amounts of parental care (Hill, 1993). In some other ways,
humans are unlike other long-lived mammals. For example, humans attach
the male to the mother–offspring set; they retain multiple young at different stages of dependence under parental care, and they maintain lifelong
links between male and female parents and children.

In the evolutionary past in which our morphological and psychological
attributes were selected, we almost certainly lived in multifamily groups of
kin. Marriage, some form of sexual regulation between men and women,
is presumably some tens of thousands of years old. These multifamily
groups or bands lived by hunting and gathering at first, utilizing a sexual
division of labor that increased efficiency of food collection and provided
a system that was capable of relaxing pressure for productive work on older
people, immatures, and women who were pregnant or caring for newborns
(Lancaster & Lancaster, 1983; Lancaster & Lancaster, 1987). The provisioning of women and children is apparently an old human trait, one that
has, no doubt, made possible the evolution of some of the hallmarks of
our species, notably the neotonous state of new borns and their slow
progress to economic and social independence.

THE VIROCENTRIC CONTEXT OF MALE PARENTAL
INVESTMENT

The fathering behavior, however, took place in the context of an inclusive
social group. Looking at ethnographically described populations, either of
hunter-gatherers or low-energy food producers, we see that the importance
of the father was due to the fact that he not only provided resources

directly to his mate and children, but that he constituted a link for his conjugal family to his kin. Women, in our evolutionary past, who had an attached mate, benefited from his social networks and a wider system of reciprocity, presumably because her husband's kin recognized (consciously or otherwise) the inclusive fitness advantages of favoring kin. Paternal kin are especially important in the ethnographically described traditional societies, the majority of which practice patrilocality or virolocality, a custom that dictates that when women marry they leave their natal kin and go to live at the residence of the husband.

It is interesting that human groups are more likely to elect postmarital residence rules that favor keeping together men who are linked as brother–brother, father–son, than other sets of kin, such as, sister–sister or brother–sister or mother–son. The rule favoring coresidence of *agnates* (men linked to kinship groups through men but not through women) is not universally followed but is preponderant enough in samplings of world societies to have invited scholarly attention. The reasons behind this strategy are reasoned to lie in the dominance of men in the political sphere, in the superiority of men in roles of defensive or offensive force, and in the vulnerability of children that makes it too costly to involve children and their mothers in dangerous occupations or pursuits (Harris, 1993). The preponderance of kinship systems that reckon group membership through links through men, rather than through women, is thought to derive from many of the same principles that lead to coresidence of male kin (Fox, 1967; Keesing, 1975).

The significance of virolocality and other androcentric practices for our present purposes is to remind us that husbands and fathers in past times played different roles vis-à-vis wives and children than they do in westernized society, wherein married men live in urban areas and in nuclear families and, like their wives, are not enmeshed in local support networks of kin. At many times in our past history the significance of men as fathers may have been principally through their political roles in kin and extra kin settings. Today, when we think of men in families, we think of the personal and emotional ties men have to their single wives and children. In past social systems, the nuclear family was not necessarily an important unit with the separate and exclusive functions it carries today. Therefore, the impact of a man's ties to his wife and children were attenuated by the fact that the nuclear family did not have the fundamental significance it carries today.

THE MEANING OF MARRIAGE, DEEMPHASIS
OF THE SPOUSAL DYAD

Marriage meant for our ancestors, and still means for many people in the less economically developed areas of the world, an arrangement between the kin of the man and woman. The value of the marriage for cementing alliance and exchange between kin groups was typically much more important than the personal preference of mutual attraction between bride and groom. In the context of kin-based social institutions, the care of children was spread out among a variety of people, on the basis of their biological connection to the mother and the father.

THE BIOPOLITICAL ASYMMETRY OF GENDER

For most of human history, women have been protected by arrangements we now regard as archaic and repressive. However, women have also been held captive, not only socially but biologically. A consequence of the development of mammalian life-history strategy is to make females the reproductive monopolists. They gestate the conceptus and nurse the offspring, whereas the male role in reproduction is comparatively reduced. This is as true of human females as it is for females of nonhuman mammalian species. The variance in reproductive potential is very low in women, owing to their slow sexual maturation, singleton births, and limited reproductive life span. Furthermore, long gestation, long lactation, and intense involvement in child care for at least 3 or 4 years means that under past environments of adaptation, a woman's reproductive labor far outweighed that of men. In small-scale hunting and gathering societies, an orphaned child is at risk, particularly one who still nurses, or, if weaned, still requires carrying and close supervision. If the size of living groups is small, as is common among hunter-gatherers, an adequate surrogate caretaker cannot necessarily be provided from among other women who are nursing and carrying children of their own. Women, as mothers, in these circumstances are indispensable to their children. Women who lose children to death or who abandon children cannot recoup their losses by starting over with another mate because of their low reproductive capacity and their limited reproductive time span. A woman's past reproductive time cannot be recaptured, whereas a man can recapture lost offspring, at least in fitness terms, by starting over with another woman, necessarily a young one. For these reasons, it can be argued that women's reproductive behaviors and the strategizing that accompanies them have evolved under constraints in which children and mates, as individuals, were more valuable to women than children and mates were to men.

THE CONTROL OF FEMALE SEXUALITY

Different societies make attempts to guarantee to the father, and to the father's kin, certainty of the paternity of children born to the father's assigned mate or mates. This is achieved by controlling women's sexuality by such means as restricting their movements, providing for their supervision by interested parties, and by training women in sexual exclusiveness to the mate. Men are also regulated in how they can express sexual interest in women who are not their mates, although the "double standard," token punishment of male philandering versus comparatively severe punishment of female infidelity, is a cultural universal.

The emotionally laden content of female sexuality and cuckoldry is, of course, familiar to all and is the staple of ribaldry and tragedy around the world. That the subject should be so psychologically charged is testimony to the fact that male parental investment has been coaxed along at the level of species-typical behavior by the fact that men who provide care for their biological offspring leave more descendants than men who do not. The complicating factor in the reluctant parade of our kind toward a kind of fatherliness comparable to motherliness is that, given the biology of our reproduction, men cannot be sure their children are their own, unless other men are kept away. Yet, men cannot live alone with their mates, as the monogamous gibbons do, so a series of compromises are reached, none satisfactory, and all of them bearing hard on the control of women by men and by other women who are affected by any doubt men have of the paternity of their children.

In the great majority of ethnographically described societies, women are made tractable by being denied independent access to productive resources. Instead, women gain access to critical resources of land for gardening, water, domestic animals, and water or tools through men who possess ownership rights in these resources. Women have access to productive resources as daughters to fathers, sisters to brothers, wives to husbands, mothers to sons. The custom whereby property and use rights are assigned to men creates the perpetual jural minority of women, a widespread form of social inequity that persists to the present in many parts of the world.

There are societies in which the gender interests of women are not sacrificed in such a draconian manner to the gender interests of alliance groups of men. They are rather rare and share certain attributes. Some, but not all hunter-gatherer groups, have a fathering role for men that is not accompanied by the control of women by men. The !Kung San of Botswana, among whom I conducted research, were such an example (Draper, 1992). When the !Kung lived as hunter-gatherers, they occupied an arid environment of very scattered resources. This type of ecology did not support large settlements of people. The collecting work of women was as important and sometimes more important than the hunting work of men in producing a reliable source of calories (Lee, 1979). The total numbers of people available for mates was small, due to the small absolute size of the population and to the sizable distances between separate bands of !Kung. To raise a family required the close cooperation of a husband

and wife, together with regular coresidence and sharing with the kin of each. Under these particular circumstances, the reproductive interests of men and women were similar. About the best any man could do was to form a contractual relationship (of the sort suggested by Mintz, chap. 1, this volume) and hope that by joint work and the assistance of relatives, he and his wife could feed the small number of children born to the wife. Men played close, attentive, fathering roles and had companionate, egalitarian relations with their wives.

There are contrary examples of hunter-gatherers who do not exhibit gender egalitarianism (Hart & Pilling, 1960; Tonkinson, 1978). This is not a place for the listing of them, but it will suffice to say that sexually inegalitarian practices among hunter-gatherers are associated with environments that support larger congregations of people, in which the availability of foods is relatively rich and constant and also where the primary survivorship of the group is dependent on the skills and work of men. Arctic hunters are one example of these practices and the Tiwi of Northern Australia are another example of a southern latitude hunting and gathering society marked by extreme forms of patriarchal authority, gerontocracy, and polygyny.

THE MEANING OF POLYGYNY AND ITS EFFECTS
ON MALE PARENTAL INVESTMENT

Humans show a moderate degree of sexual dimorphism with men on the average having greater height, weight, bone mass, and heavier musculature. Sexual dimorphism indicates past intrasexual competition (Brace, 1973). The ethnographic literature and documents from ancient literate times makes it clear that polygyny was an available option in the majority of human societies, albeit one available to a minority of men, usually older ones who controlled greater resources (White & Burton, 1988). The point about polygyny as it relates to this chapter is that multiple mating, combined with male parental investment, must necessarily mean a dilution of the time men can spend with wives and children. The literature of sub-Saharan Africa is an excellent source to consult for understanding the dynamics of polygyny in this century (Oppong, 1987).

Men, particularly successful men who control resources, can have multiple mates. In the past (and some present societies in which polygyny is approved) some men who added additional wives to their households did not necessarily disadvantage their children, because an extended and enlarged group of kindred were available to absorb their care. Polygyny necessarily reduced the amount of contact between fathers and children, but the access of children to adults was not necessarily restricted in harmful ways. Today, in industrial society, we have a legal requirement of monogamy but, in reality, a form of de facto polygyny as a result of the dissolution of serial monogamous unions. Because of the legal requirement of monogamy, and because of our cultural value on monogamy and the ideal of companionate marriage, extramarital and subsequent-marital unions create disruptions of the pair bond and of the psychological and economic organization of households.

The temporally deep, evolutionary view and the temporally more shallow, but geographically diverse ethnographic view suggest that pair-bonding in various forms is a long-established pattern for humans in recent tens of thousands of years, if not longer. Changing our focus to the present case of western, post-industrial society requires some readjustments in our thinking if we are to continue to understand how a pattern of mating and parenting, evolved in a past context, can be expected to manifest itself in contemporary times.

The chapters in this volume demonstrate that the quality of fathering in modern, western society can be variable. There is a concern on the part of these authors to understand and to engineer away some of the bad variation when it takes the form of abandonment of family or exploitation and abuse of women and children. "Good" fathering, on the other hand, confers very impressive advantages to children who receive it. Lancaster, Kaplan, and Anderson show that fathers' achievements in human capital, when passed on to offspring, give the offspring measurable advantages that can be calculated concretely, in such ways as in children's lifetime earnings. Also important is the finding that increased time spent by fathers with children in their dependent years promotes the kinds of behaviors and skills that pay off in our society: Good social skills, peer relations, good grades, higher educational achievement, and more successful courtships and marriages.

A question naturally suggests itself: If what we are calling "good fathering" is so crucial now and if good fathering was also important in our evolutionary past, why is fathering so variable? Can we not expect that, over time, the same kind of selective pressures that have made women, on the average, reliable, lifelong advocates and actors on behalf of their children, would have made men tenacious, loyal, and dogged in the same way?

Why is there this variability? An evolutionary perspective suggests several lines of reasoning. In past environments of evolutionary adaptedness, the requirements of survival in certain environments may have been such that regular, stable inputs from investing fathers were not necessary and therefore the psychological properties of attention to, and interest in, children, which are routine in women, were not genetically encoded in men to the same degree. Another argument, is that given the different reproductive potential of the sexes, parental investment in men and women may never have been subject to the same selective pressures, regardless of the benignness or severity of the environment. There may have been few circumstances, over time, in which a mechanism for intense paternal solicitude can have evolved.

GENDER ASYMMETRY AND THE FATHERING ROLE

A point that is embedded in several of the chapters in this volume is that in many of the historically described situations in which men were central in families and their role was respected and economically valuable, the autonomy of women was severely restricted. What can we make of this association? Are male–female reproductive negotiations a zero sum game? Can we expect responsible fathering only in those societies or in those strata in society in which women are firmly under control and men act in concert with other men to guarantee themselves exclusive access to resources, holding property-less men at arms length and meanwhile monopolizing women of reproductive age who need the resources held by high-status men? A consequence of this arrangement is that large numbers of impoverished men are prevented from forming families due to their inability to gain resources (Dickeman, 1979). Is this the price of male parental investment?

The factors associated with important male familial roles in our own historical past, and in many ethnographically described nonwestern societies, form an interesting pattern. Some conditions favoring male parental roles are:

- No contraception.
- Difficulty of divorce.
- No abortion.
- Restriction of female sexuality.
- Restriction of female spatial mobility.
- Stigmatization of women who form informal unions.
- Stigmatization of children who lack legal fathers' guarantees to paternity certainty.
- Nonviability of mother–child households.
- No independent access of women to productive resources.
- Importance of male labor and male ownership of productive resources.
- Importance of family wage versus individual wage.
- Dependence of women on men and male affines for physical protection from rape and abduction.
- Jural minority of women.

- High cultural valuation of patriarchal principle, as father is seen as owner and symbol of the family.
- Misogyny, and so on.

Another list can be made of practices that go with the weakening of the central male role in the family. Some conditions apparently weakening the male role since the 1900s include:

- Rights to female sexuality no longer controlled by senior kin.
- Contraception is mainly under female control.
- Legalized abortion.
- Sexual revolution in which sex is not stigmatized.
- Nonmarital cohabitation is not stigmatized.
- Increased ease of divorce.
- Women have independent access to productive resources (e.g., entering into the labor market).
- Importance of the individual wage versus family wage.
- Economic viability of mother–child households.
- Political empowerment of women, votes for women, and legislation against gender discrimination.
- Women become the primary parent, gatekeeper through which fathers relate to children.
- Strong centralized government and police institutions that ensure public order, personal safety and private property, and so on.

What are we to make of contemporary life that, in the process of relieving women of severe and crippling restrictions, creates a situation in which it is less attractive to men to form families or to stay with the families they do form? In modern times we maintain that the biparental, fully fathered family is psychologically, economically, and socially superior, yet meanwhile we have removed many of the traditional prerequisites that went to men whose affluence enabled men to play a fathering role. Men who marry in our postmodern times have lost a number of advantages, which are now partially listed:

1. Men no longer get "free" personal and domestic services from women (who can now sell their own labor in the market).
2. Men cannot rely on support from largely female relatives and low-status males to help in the drudge work of domestic settings.
3. Given high demands of wage work facing both men and women, husbands surrender leisure time to spend in all-male "hangouts."

4. As women compete in the labor market, men lose the protected economic role that was previously guaranteed to them by virtue of their status as males and as members in alliance groups with other males.

5. Men surrender the conventional guarantees of paternity certainty because modern wives and mates are not only unsupervised by husbands or kin, but spending time in workplaces with men who are strangers.

6. Men in times past have been able to convert status won in competition with other men into the ability to attract mates and to father children. Once women have independent access to contraception, men do not have the power to father children by women, thereby solidifying the dependence of women on them.

7. Men as a group have no exclusive control over property and, therefore, women place less value on sexual partnerships with men.

8. The economic value of children has been lost. Having children now represents an economic drain.

CONCLUSION

There is every reason to assume that humans will continue to mate and bear children, however the institutional context within which mating and family formation occur has changed dramatically in recent decades. In former times in our own history, and at present in parts of the economically undeveloped world, men have received tangible rewards as a result of making formal marriages with women and fathering children. Their status is enhanced by assuming the role of head of household and the servile nature of women's status ensures them of an unpaid domestic labor force. Children's labor has economic value in agrarian and pre-industrial times. In societies with weak central governments, men can raise the status of their own kinship groups by increasing the number of children through births to multiple wives and by rising to political prominence as elders. Now the orthodox or classic returns to men for marrying, fathering, and supporting children have essentially disappeared. Children are costly to raise, local kinship groups are no longer useful in the political ambitions of men, and polygynous unions are increasingly outlawed.

Many questions can be raised about the future of men in families. In this postmodern era of information based economy, consumer services, and diminishing manufacturing jobs for skilled and unskilled workers, the research reported in this volume indicates that contributions by fathers incontrovertibly lead to enhanced performance and improved lives for children. Yet, as indicated earlier, the returns to men of investing time and energy in the support of children are not apparent to all. It may be that there is something to be gained by framing research questions around such questions as, "Why should fathers father?" and "How can the returns' on fathering be advocated or enhanced in order for men to perceive the advantage to increased frequency and quality of fathering?" Mothering, by and large, can be taken for granted, for reasons explored earlier, although here too, "good" mothering is not inevitable. Fathering is highly variable and problematic.

REFERENCES

Brace, C. L. (1973). Sexual dimorphism in human evolution. *Yearbook of Physical Anthropology, 16*, 31–49.

Dickeman, M. (1979). The ecology of mating systems in hypergynous dowry societies. *Social Science Information, 18*, 163–195.

Draper, P. (1992). Room to maneuver: !Kung women cope with men. In J. Campbell, D. Counts, & J. Brown, (Eds.), *Sanctions and sanctuary: Cultural perspectives on the beating of wives* (pp. 43–61). Boulder, CO: Westview Press.

Fox, R. (1967). *Kinship and marriage.* Middlesex, England: Penguin Books.

Harris, M. (1993). The evolution of human gender hierarchies: A trial formulation. In D. B. Miller (Ed.), *Sex and gender hierarchies* (pp. 57–79). Cambridge, England: Cambridge University Press.

Hart, C. W. M, & Pilling, A. R. (1960). *The Tiwi of northern Australia.* New York: Holt, Rinehart & Winston.

Hill, K. (1993). Life history theory and evolutionary anthropology. *Evolutionary Anthropology, 2*, 78–87.

Keesing, R. M. (1975). *Kin groups and social structure.* New York: Holt, Rinehart & Winston.

Lancaster, J. B., & Lancaster, C. S. (1983). Parental investment: The hominid adaptation. In D. J. Ortner (Ed.), *How humans adapt: A biocultural odyssey* (pp. 33–56). Washington, DC: Smithsonian Institution Press.

Lancaster, J. B., & Lancaster, C. S. (1987). The watershed: Change in parental investment and family formation strategies in the course of human evolution. In J. B. Lancaster, J. Altmann, A. S. Rossi, & L. Sherrod (Eds.), *Parenting across the lifespan* (pp. 187–205). New York: de Gruyter.

Lee, R. B. (1979). *The !Kung San: Men, women and work.* Cambridge, England: Cambridge University Press.

Oppong, C. (Ed.). (1987). *Sex roles, population and development and West Africa: Policy-related studies on work and demographic issues.* London: Heinemann.

Stearns, S. (1992). The evolution of life histories. New York: Oxford University Press.

Tonkinson, R. (1978). *The Marduddjara aborigines: Living the dream in Australia's desert.* New York: Holt, Rinehart & Winston.

White, M., & Burton, M. (1988). Causes of polygyny: Ecology, kinship and warfare. *American Anthropologist, 90*, 871–887.

Chapter 7

In Search of a Theory:
Men's Fertility and Parental
Investment in Modern Economies

William Marsiglio
University of Florida

As a sociologist with a social psychological background, no formal training in economics, and a penchant for microlevel theorizing, I find it challenging to comment on chapter 5 because its primary goal is to integrate threads from evolutionary biology and economic theories of life histories into a macrolevel theory of fertility and parental investment issues. This chapter underscored for me the diverse perspectives that can be brought to bear on fertility and family-related matters while also demonstrating the breadth of modern anthropology. Because the perspectives that inform this chapter are ones far removed from my own approach to conceptualizing paternity and male parenting, I do not critique certain features of the authors' highly detailed theoretical model, especially those related to economic principles. Ironically, the variables of most interest to me—sexual activity, contraception, gender, and identity—are largely absent from chapter 5. Moreover, because the amount of ground the authors covered in this chapter far exceeds what is typically attempted in one chapter, my comments will address only a limited number of issues.

I am intrigued by Kaplan, Lancaster, and Anderson's efforts to assemble an elaborate macrolevel explanation for why the fertility patterns of populations found in modern, industrialized societies do not jibe with evolutionary theory's predictions of how selectivity and notions of fitness shaped social patterns in hunting and gathering societies. I applaud Kaplan et al. for tackling this type of interdisciplinary project. The authors' theoretical work is thought provoking and, from what I can gather, unique. To their credit, the authors address a variety of theoretical issues and do a reasonable job of synthesizing these disparate ideas. Their discussion of the similarities between somatic effort in biological models and economists' views of investment in human capital is interesting. However, they can strengthen their work by demonstrating more clearly the relationship between their theoretical model and their empirical analyses—either those they have already conducted or others they may conduct in the future.

Kaplan et al.'s major thesis is that the mechanisms that evolved thousands of years ago to regulate fertility and parental investment levels have been greatly modified in modern economies in which skills-based competitive labor markets exist. The forces underlying modern economic systems have supposedly prompted individuals to develop reproductive adaptations that place greater weight on the quantity and quality of parental investment rather than the reproduction of large numbers of children. We are told that if we are to understand modern reproductive and paternal investment patterns, we must come to terms with the limitations of the crude selectivity and fitness thesis. This thesis must be augmented, then, with economic explanations for the transmission of embodied capital (e.g., strength, immune function, coordination, skill, and knowledge) from one generation to the next in modern economies where skills-based competitive labor markets produce novel conditions. Kaplan et al.'s argument seems consistent with contemporary sociobiological and behavioral-ecological theories, although it is unique due to its explicit reliance on economic principles. In this context, it is instructive to recall what Lamb, Pleck, Charnov, and Levine (1987) wrote 10 years ago:

> A key tenet of sociobiology or behavioral ecology is that individuals are designed to maximize their fitness *in the context of the options available to them* given the physical, economic, and social ecology. The goal is individual inclusive fitness, not propagation of the family, group, or species. Behavior is only optimal (in terms of fitness) in the context of a specific environment (broadly defined), and thus it is necessary to consider the constraints or facilitators of behavior represented by the social and physical environment. (p. 115)

Thus, if we accept the idea that individuals strive to "maximize their fitness" in response to their available options, as well as the constraints and enabling factors they encounter, it should come as no surprise that reproductive adaptations have emerged. The modern socioeconomic and cultural context is obviously quite different from what things were like when the mechanisms of selectively initially evolved. It seems logical then to hypothesize, as these authors do, that men with the most human capital will invest more in their children, but have fewer of them.

My biggest concern with this chapter is that gender issues do not assume a more central place in the theoretical framework that guides it. It appears to me that Kaplan et al.'s theoretical formulation treats reproduction and parenting as generic processes, rather than processes that are fundamentally shaped by gender issues in modern societies. Their approach is puzzling to me because they use data that is based exclusively on men's self-reports and this volume is devoted to studying men in families. I therefore wonder, in part because of my own theoretical biases, whether Kaplan et al. could enhance their current theoretical framework by dealing more explicitly with reproduction and parenting as gendered social processes. The basic macroeconomic principles they present using supply and demand curves are apparently silent on gender issues. All workers are conceptualized alike without considering how gender influences labor market activity on a structural or interpersonal level. Perhaps their economic theory is based implicitly on an understanding of men's labor market activity. If so, they should state this explicitly. Given similar types of circumstances, it may not really matter whether the workers the authors' theorize about are women or men. However, there are important gendered aspects to individuals' labor market activity. Would it not make sense then to take into account realities about segmented labor markets, corporate cultures, and income differentials when developing an integrated, economically informed theory about reproduction and parental investment?

It is common knowledge that men and women often think about and behave differently in the labor market and at home (Coltrane, 1996). Thus, the production of children the authors discuss often occurs within a negotiated, dyadic relationship that is likely to determine whether individuals are in the labor market, how they act if they are, and how they behave at home. These types of issues, some of which involve microlevel types of social processes, may not readily be compatible with the authors' type of theorizing and use of aggregate level data, but omitting them completely seems inappropriate if we are to understand such gendered phenomena as fertility and parental investment. Fertility and parental investment strategies are surely affected by men's and women's gendered attitudes about and activities in the home and workplace. In short, although Kaplan et al. mention in passing that cultural norms will probably play a role in shaping reproductive strategies, I suspect that their type of economic analysis would be enriched if it were more sensitive to the gendered nature of work in the modern economies to which they refer—as it is manifested inside and outside the home. My basic question, then, is: How might this theoretical framework be modified to explain more fully paternity rather than reproduction, and paternal investment rather than parental investment?

One possible way of developing this line of reasoning would be to consider how images of masculinities, fatherhood, and work have evolved over the years alongside the changing socioeconomic landscape Kaplan et al. describe. It would serve us well to recognize that the macrolevel fertility patterns they seem to attribute to the invisible hand and mechanisms guiding the economic system, actually find expression in the daily lives of individuals making decisions about sex, contraception, abortion, work, marriage, and family, all of which are shaped, to some extent, by men's and women's efforts to construct and manage their expression of gender in a particular sociohistorical context.

Having conveyed my general preference to see these authors incorporate a gender perspective into their theory, I now comment more specifically on several aspects of their chapter. The authors use a clever strategy to identify their sample through the Motor Vehicle Division (MVD) office in Albuquerque. To my knowledge, no other study has used this method to identify respondents, although this may change in the future. Researchers may want to take note, because this sampling technique could represent a relatively inexpensive alternative for identifying large numbers of male respondents of various ages. Those who use this strategy will need to be attentive, however, to possible biases associated with some men being more likely to conduct their business with the MVD through the mail—a pattern that may vary across states. Although this sampling strategy will not yield data as generalizable as those using national probability surveys, the comparisons the authors make with census data are encouraging. Furthermore, their methodology provided them with the opportunity to ask extensive and in-depth questions about a range of fertility-related issues.

One reason to temper our enthusiasm about the Albuquerque data is that these reports are based solely on men's cross-sectional retrospective accounts, and some of the measures are quite crude. Because demographers have voiced serious concerns about the reliability of men's fertility reports, I would encourage Kaplan et al. to at least speculate on the reliability of their respondents' reports and to consider how these potential biases may influence their conclusions. Mott (1983) analyzed data from the youth cohort of the National Longitudinal Survey of Labor Market Experience (NLSY) and demonstrated that young men in their teens and twenties were much less accurate than young women in reporting their fertility. Misreporting of one sort or the other was so pervasive that of the 728 male respondents who reported a live birth, 341 were found to have at least one discrepant record. Although many of these discrepant records dealt with children's birth dates, it was surprisingly common for children to "appear" and "disappear" from men's fertility histories during various waves of the NLSY panel survey. Interestingly, about 25% of fathers of children who were not living with them acknowledged their child for the first time in 1982, even though the child had been born prior to the 1981 survey. Overall, Mott found that men's reporting inconsistencies were not random; those men who were either never married, did not live with their child, or were African American were more likely than their counterparts to have inconsistencies in their birth histories. I also suspect that those men who are economically disadvantaged, have children from previous relationships, have been married more than once, and have had sex with many partners will be more likely to either intentionally or unintentionally misreport their fertility histories than their counterparts.

Overall gender differences in reporting are probably even more prominent when men are asked to recall fertility and parenting experiences that may have occurred decades ago. Unfortunately, few researchers have the luxury of having direct access to raw panel data that provides them the opportunity to do systematic data checks. Researchers using male fertility data from cross-sectional reports like the Albuquerque study must simply live with their original data. N᾽ data are perfect, of course, especially when it involves men reporting on their fertility, so we should not disregard the reports from this Albuquerque sample. In fact we should commend those who collected these unique data and encourage them to harvest this information as fully as possible.

The authors provide a wealth of information about men's fertility patterns, and, not withstanding the limitations of the parental investment measures, explore these issues as well. I briefly highlight several themes associated with these researchers' findings. One of the general themes that emerged from their data was that men's fertility patterns and investment tendencies were affected by their partners' characteristics. For example, men's rate of fertility was lowered if their partners already had had a child from a previous relationship, whereas men's fertility in previous relationships was not related to the probability of men begetting a child in a current relationship. Likewise, when indicators for women's and men's level of education were entered into statistical models, only women's education was related to the probability of men's procreation. These findings are consistent with common wisdom that understanding fathers' behavior often requires us to explore their relationships with their partners.

In addition to studying fertility patterns, Kaplan et al. examine what they admittedly view as crude measures of parental investment. One outcome they document is the probability of fathers no longer living with their children. Their discussion does not clarify how they define this concept and they do not take into account the ebbs and flows that often accompany men's coresident status involving their children (see Mott, 1990). Are we to assume that those men who cease to live with their children never co-reside with them again? What about those men who never wanted to, or were never given the opportunity to live with their child? Men who do not initially live with their children are becoming increasingly prevalent and should be included in analyses of contemporary coresidence patterns for fathers and their children. Significant issues are at stake here because it is debatable whether some children may experience more emotional trauma by developing strong attachments to fathers who ultimately leave them emotionally and physically than they would if they had never developed those attachments in the first place. Furthermore, we should not forget that there are a variety of complex links between marriage, partners' relationships, and the probability of nonresident fathers being involved with their children and paying child support (Arditti & Keith, 1993; Furstenberg & Cherlin, 1991; Nord & Zill, 1996; Seltzer, 1991; Veum, 1993).

The researchers' bivariate analysis also reveals a relationship between fathers' level of education and their likelihood of changing their coresident status with their children. In households with more educated fathers, fathers and their children are more likely to stay together. Conversely, those children born to fathers who have less embodied capital to transmit to them are more likely to have their coresidence pattern disrupted. The children of less educated fathers may, in one sense, have less to lose than their more advantaged peers in these situations, but their chances of having this marginal level of embodied capital replaced may be equally poor. Kaplan et al. apparently duplicate this finding in separate multivariate analyses not reported in this paper. Unfortunately, the researchers do not indicate what control variables were used. Age at first marriage is an important covariate that should be considered in this regard.

Kaplan et al. used a crude 2-item index to explore fathers' reported time investment in their children's lives. They found that having siblings close in age was associated with lower levels of fathers' time investment. This finding is consistent with my own research (Marsiglio, 1991) with fathers from the first wave of the National Survey of Families and Households (NSFH). Having other kids around presumably limits fathers' opportunities or need to spend time with their children, particularly because the major form of paternal involvement, defined in its narrow sense, involves play. The researchers might also want to consider using these data to examine how different sibling structures are related to fathers' time investment. Morgan and Harris' (1991) analysis of national data found that fathers spend more time with their daughters if they also have a son living at home.

Another noteworthy finding based on the Albuquerque sample is that fathers' report spending significantly less time with nonbiological children than their biological offspring. Again it would be useful to consider how this finding is affected by the genetic sibling structure. In other words, is fathers' involvement with their nonbiological children affected by whether their own children are living in the house as well? My research with the first wave of the NSFH found that fathers were more likely to play with their minor stepchildren when their own children lived at home.

The analysis that policymakers are likely to be most interested in involves fathers' reported financial contributions to their children. One appealing feature of this set of analyses is that the researchers estimate separate models for fathers' investment in their minor children as well as in their older children (18 to 23 years of age). In addition, a separate model is estimated for fathers' contributions to college expenses. The most important finding is that fathers report providing more financial support to the young children they live with who are their partner's biological children but not theirs, compared to the support they provide for their biological children living elsewhere. These results support Furstenberg and Cherlin's (1991) view of fatherhood as a package deal, that is, men's tendency to view their father roles as being connected to or contingent on their relationship with their children's mother. Meanwhile, fathers' contributions to their children when they are between the ages of 18 and 23 are influenced, not surprisingly, by whether they are genetically related to them. Fathers are more likely to provide financial support to their young adult genetic offspring. It would be useful if future analyses with these data controlled for the length of time fathers lived with their nonbiological children. I suspect that in those instances where fathers began to coreside with their children at a very young age that differences between genetic and nongenetic offspring would be attenuated. My own research with stepfathers indicates that those men who live with their child at an earlier age are more likely to adopt a fatherlike identity to them, which, I believe, would prompt them to feel a greater sense of obligation to help them out financially during their early adulthood years (Marsiglio, 1995). Although policymakers are most concerned about fathers' support of their nonresident biological children, the extent to which fathers contribute to their young adult children may influence their long-term well-being and the degree to which parents can transfer their embodied capital. Interestingly, fathers' financial contribution to their children that are 18 to 23 years of age was unaffected by the number of siblings. No explanation is offered for this counterintuitive finding.

In closing, I make two final points. First, my reading of chapter 5 left me with the impression that the authors' theorizing and analyses were being implicitly guided by a traditional image of rational, planned, marital childbearing. Even in their discussion section when the authors refer to the "earlier onset of reproduction among less educated men in recent cohorts" (p. 104) they speculated that this pattern may be due to recent welfare policies or educated men's increased postgraduate on-the-job training, but they do not mention that recent cohorts of men's fertility patterns are likely to be affected by the complex web of associations between human capital variables and patterns of sexual activity, contraceptive use, and abortion.

Second, I would like to draw attention to the significance of Kaplan et al.'s efforts to introduce themes associated with evolutionary biology when they theorize about men's fertility and parental investment patterns. Their work is consistent with the emerging trend that finds a growing and diverse body of social scientists devoting more attention to the role biological and evolutionary factors play in shaping social behaviors (Rossi, 1987). Although Kaplan et al. conclude that evolutionary processes in their crude form are of limited value in explaining fertility and parental investment patterns in modern economies, the underlying dynamics are thought to provide the foundation for how other key mechanisms or processes affect people's lives in modern societies. This resurgence in exploring sociobiological types of issues is slowly gaining credibility in the wake of a feminist revolution that has at times thwarted sober discussions about gender-related topics. I therefore anticipate that social scientists, including those who are interested in family life, will increasingly face pressures to expand their theoretical paradigms in the 21st century to include selective biological influences as explanatory and control variables.

REFERENCES

Arditti, J. A., & Keith, T. Z. (1993). Visitation frequency, child support payments, and the father–child relationship postdivorce. *Journal of Marriage and the Family, 55,* 699–712.

Coltrane, S. (1996). *Family man: Fatherhood, housework, and gender equity.* New York: Oxford.

Furstenberg, F. F., Jr., & Cherlin, A. J. (1991). *Divided families: What happens to children when parents part.* New York: Cambridge University Press.

Lamb, M. E., Pleck, J. H., Charnov, E. L., & Levine, J. A. (1987). A biosocial perspective on paternal behavior and involvement. In A. Lancaster & S. Rossi (Eds.), *Parenting across the life span* (pp. 111–142). New York: de Gruyter.

Marsiglio, W. (1991). Paternal engagement activities with minor children. *Journal of Marriage and the Family, 53,* 973–986.

Marsiglio, W. (1995). Stepfathers with minor children living at home: Parenting perceptions and relationship quality. In W. Marsiglio (Ed.), *Fatherhood: Contemporary theory, research, and social policy* (pp. 211–229). Thousand Oaks, CA: Sage.

Morgan, P., & Harris, K. M. (1991). Fathers, sons, and daughters: Differential paternal involvement in parenting. *Journal of Marriage and the Family, 49,* 531–544.

Mott, F. L. (1983). *Fertility-related data in the 1982 National Longitudinal Surveys of Work Experience of Youth: An evaluation of data quality and some preliminary analytical results.* Columbus: Ohio State University, Center for Human Resource Research.

Mott, F. L. (1990). When is a father really gone? Paternal–child conduct in father-absent homes. *Demography, 27,* 499–517.

Nord, C. W., & Zill, N. (1996). *Non-custodial parents' participation in their children's lives: Evidence from the Survey of Income and Program Participation (volumes I and II).* Report prepared for the Office of Human Services Policy, Office of the Assistant Secretary for Planning and Evaluation. U.S. Department of Health and Human Services. Rockville, MD: Westat Inc.

Rossi, A. S. (1987). Parenthood in transition: From lineage to child self-orientation. In J. B. Lancaster, J. Altmann, A. S. Rossi, & L. R. Sherrod (Eds.), *Parenting across the life span: Biosocial dimensions* (pp. 31–81). New York: de Gruyter.

Seltzer, J. A. (1991). Relationships between fathers and children who live apart: The father's role after separation. *Journal of Marriage and the Family, 53,* 79–101.

Veum, J. R. (1993). The relationship between child support and visitation: Evidence from longitudinal data. *Social Science Research, 22,* 229–244.

Chapter 8

Subjectivity and Practicality in Mating and Parenting Decisions

Catherine A. Surra
University of Texas at Austin

For researchers who study mate selection and the connections between the early history of heterosexual relationships and their long-term outcomes, Kaplan, Lancaster, and Anderson's chapter (this volume) holds special interest. The relevance of the chapter for mate selection lies in the linkages it makes between mating and parenting. Traditionally, no other theory of human mating or parenting explores these linkages. Developmental psychology, for example, focuses on how children are affected by the parental relationship and by their experiences in other contexts, such as schools and peer relationships. Social psychology explains mating in terms of the individual traits, behaviors, and interpersonal attitudes that shape attraction to particular partners and the development of closeness in relationships. Family sociologists who study mating are mostly concerned with the personal and social characteristics of mates and with mates' compatibility on these characteristics. In addition, family sociologists have concentrated on how the social structure limits the availability of mates with specific characteristics and how the presence or absence of people with specific characteristics affects marital pairings. If one were to read solely in the subject matter areas that traditionally have dealt with mating and parenting, the two behaviors would seem to be unrelated.

Kaplan et al. argue that in order to understand contemporary patterns of fertility and parental investments in children, we need to look at economic theories of resource allocation, as well as theories of the evolutionary origins of humans in hunting and gathering lifestyles. It is these theories that make the mating and parenting link.

THEORETICAL LINKAGES BETWEEN
REPRODUCTION AND MATE SELECTION

According to the theories of evolutionary biology that underlie the arguments by Kaplan et al. (chapter 5, this volume), individuals aim to maximize
their genetic fitness, or the contribution of their genes to subsequent
generations. In order to accomplish fitness, individuals must parent well;
to parent well, they need to fare well in the mating competition. In mating,
women and men have competing goals. Tension between the sexes in the
mating game comes, in part, from the costs associated with reproduction,
which differ greatly for the sexes (Buss, 1994; Trivers, 1972). Women's
investments of time, energy, and other resources in childbearing and
childrearing far exceed men's. Women, for example, spend much more
time than men just in the activities of gestation, childbirth, and lactation.
As a result, women's goals in mating differ from men's. Men are motivated
to reproduce, to ensure the propagation, survival, and growth of their
genes. Women will be better off if they mate with men who will provide
them and their offspring with a continuous, long-term source of aid and
resources. Women, therefore, must be more selective in the extent to
which they reproduce and in the mates with whom they reproduce. In
these ways, mating and parenting are inextricably linked in biological theory.

In addition, reproductive choices involve decisions about the allocation
of scarce resources. According to the biological theory utilized by Kaplan
et al., maximizing fitness involves trade-offs between current and future
reproduction and between the quantity and quality of offspring. These
trade-offs parallel problems of resource allocation found in economic theories of the family. The economic trade-offs are between present and future
consumption and between present and future income. Individuals must
decide how much to invest in the development of their own human capital
and in the human capital of their offspring. With respect to reproduction,
individuals must decide about how much to invest in offspring to maximize
fitness. Conflicts arise among the demands from these competing decisions.
Therein lie the key connections between biological and economic approaches to reproduction.

Kaplan and his co-authors maintain that individuals weigh the trade-offs,
and make decisions about reproduction and fertility by means of a complex
calculus. In writing about how people resolve the trade-offs, these authors
use the language of conscious decision making. Individuals are thought
to respond to environmental inputs and to make adjustments in their
behavior accordingly. Environmental inputs include such distal factors as
wage rates and the distribution of jobs in competitive markets, and more
proximate factors, such as the demands children make on parents. The

complex calculus involves psychological mechanisms by which individuals perceive the opportunities and constraints that exist in their environments, and act appropriately. Individuals are assisted with translating environmental inputs into useful knowledge by means of cultural norms. Norms function to transmit and reinforce a store of cultural knowledge to individuals. Cultural knowledge is especially useful when it provides individuals with information about how their present actions might relate to future outcomes (Kaplan et al., chapter 5, this volume), as in the case, for example, where members of the social network sanction the choice of endogamous mates to promote integration with the social group and long-term marital success (cf. Surra & Milardo, 1991).

According to Kaplan et al., psychological processes especially operate in determining the degree of parental investment in each child. Historically, at least, fertility was governed by physiological processes, such as age at weaning and energy flow to women. The authors argue that fertility is now lower than biological theories would predict because of a conflict between the fertility that our physiological responses and our psychological responses would permit. They imply that in modern societies "consciously desired fertility" is governed more by psychological than by physiological processes.

SUBJECTIVE EXPLANATIONS FOR CHOOSING A MATE

The questions I address in the next sections concern the linkages between mate selection and parenting that were proposed by Kaplan et al. Specifically, I examine the extent to which individuals perceive and act on reproductive considerations when they select mates, as Kaplan and his co-authors maintain that they do. One example of how economic and reproductive information might operate in mate selection is found in the way Kaplan et al. interpret their results showing that women's education, but not men's, predicts men's fertility. They suggest that some men may opt for a mate selection strategy in which they choose highly educated women as mates, which, in turn, allows for low fertility and high parental investment in their offspring. I examine more fully the extent to which individuals who are making mate selection decisions do evaluate the economic and reproductive potential of their mates and of their relationships. I present data that pertains to whether individuals consider relevant conditions in the environment and in their relationships. I also examine the extent to which individuals act on such information when it is available to them.

No one has systematically studied whether and how people actually consider reproductive potential when they select their mates. The closest research on this question is found in the work of Buss and others (see Buss, 1994, for a review), in which people's *preferences* for a mate have been examined in many different cultural contexts. These data show that preferences that are valued by men and women do correspond closely to what evolutionary theories would predict. There are two major problems with this research, however. First, it leaves completely unanswered the question of whether preferences for a mate are associated with mate selection behaviors. This question is important because the conditions that surround mate choices often limit people's ability to act only on their preferences. Second, we do not know whether preferences for a mate, as reported on questionnaires, enter into people's actual decision strategies in any way, as the theory and the interpretation of the data assume that they do.

My own research has examined people's subjective explanations for why they become more or less committed to marrying their partners over time, the objective influences that researchers believe are influential, and the long-term outcomes of subjective and objective influences on commitment. In the next section, I report on what the results of this research have to say about the role of reproductive considerations in mate selection.

A Method for Studying Subjective Explanations for Choosing a Mate

The method I use to study people's subjective explanations for changes in marital commitment was adapted from an interviewing procedure in which newlyweds were asked to recall how they became committed to wed over the course of their courtship (cf. Huston, Surra, Fitzgerald, & Cate, 1981). Newlyweds plotted from memory the history of their relationship on a graph that indicates how the chance of marriage to their partners changed over time. Chance of marriage, on the vertical axis, ranges from 0% to 100%, and is defined as respondents' estimates of the likelihood that they will eventually wed their partners, all things considered. The chance of marriage is a measure of marital commitment (cf. Surra & Hughes, 1997). Respondents are asked to take into account their own and their partners' thoughts about eventually marrying. They are asked to disregard how much they want to wed or are in love. If they are certain they will eventually wed, the chance is 100%. If they are certain they never will wed or if they have never thought about marriage, the chance is 0%. I used the graphing procedure to study two samples of newlyweds, who reconstructed the development of their commitment from memory (Surra, 1985, 1987; Surra, Arizzi, & Asmussen, 1988), and with two samples of premarital partners, who provided retrospective reconstructions of their relationships, as well as reports concurrent with the development of their relationships. The first sample of premarital partners consisted of 120 individuals (60 couples) who were mostly college students (e.g., Surra & Hughes, 1997; Surra & Longstreth, 1990). The second sample of premarital partners was 464 partners (232 couples) who were randomly selected from households in a large southwestern city (e.g., Jacquet & Surra, 1996). The qualitative data reported in this chapter are taken from the random sample of daters, except where indicated.

The graph is drawn by the interviewer sequentially, based on respondents' answers to a series of structured questions. First, the chance of marriage at the wedding date for newlyweds, or at the date of the interview for daters, is marked on the graph. Then the chance of marriage at the start of the relationship is marked. Respondents are then asked when they were first aware that the chance of marriage differed from its initial value, what the chance was at that time, and the shape of the line connecting the two points. Next they are asked, "Tell me in as specific terms as possible what happened from (date) to (date) that made the chance of marriage go (up/down) (___%)." Respondents provide an account of what happened, and then are asked, "Is there anything else that happened . . ." until they answer, "No." The series of questions is repeated for each time the respondent was aware that the chance of marriage had changed, until the graph reaches the endpoint. Each period of time the chance of marriage went up or down is called a *turning point.*

An advantage of this approach for studying the subjective considerations involved in mate selection is that it gets at the factors people think about, or at least say they think about, when making commitment decisions in a very open-ended way. It makes no a priori assumptions about what factors are influential, as questionnaires designed by researchers do. Respondents are not prompted to think about the influence of any specific factor, such as how their parents influenced their commitment or how much they thought about what a good spouse or parent their partners would be. The procedure simply asks people to report on their perceptions of what happened to prompt changes in commitment, thereby taking the emphasis off of strategic deliberation for people who do not engage in such thoughtful, conscientious approaches to commitment. In this way, the method gets at the phenomenology of marital commitment (Surra, Hughes, & Jacquet, in press), or the more proximate psychological mechanisms that affect marital decisions (cf. Kaplan et al., chapter 5, this volume).

Once gathered, the accounts of commitment are divided into separate reasons for commitment. Reasons are people's own explanations for acting as they do; as such, they are one influence on their behavior (Locke & Pennington, 1982). The reasons are classified into different categories according to their content. The categories were derived from a qualitative analysis of themes in accounts of commitment gathered from a sample of newlyweds (Surra, 1987). Although we are now coding reasons into one of 29 subcategories, the subcategories can be subsumed into four major categories. *Intrapersonal-normative reasons* are statements in which some characteristic of the self, the partner, or the relationship is evaluated against socialized beliefs about what relationships are like or what should occur. One male respondent from a sample of newlyweds said, for example, "She didn't trip over any 'no's' for what I wanted in a partner. I didn't want to marry a girl who feels that housework or cooking is degrading . . . or a girl who wouldn't compromise . . . or couldn't converse. I was very impressed." *Dyadic reasons* are references to interaction between partners (e.g., doing things together) and attributions about the nature of the partner or relationship (e.g., the partner's good or bad personality traits, how comfortable they are with one another, how enjoyable the relationship is). *Social network reasons* include interactions with and attributions about a variety of specific third parties, including parents, one's own and the partner's friends and relatives, co-workers, therapists, and alternative dating partners. Social network reasons include not only pressures from the network but also the partners' reactions to the network (e.g., getting along well with the other's friends). *Circumstantial reasons* are references to the role played by timing (e.g., holidays), elements of the situation (e.g., "There was just too much of a difference in geographical location"), and institutional or external events (e.g., the death of a family member; acceptance into college).

Subjective Explanations and the Reproductive Potential of Mates

Reasons that involve evaluations of the reproductive value of mates would fall into the category of intrapersonal-normative reasons. Intrapersonal-normative reasons have elements that are consistent with the ideas of Kaplan et al. regarding how individuals translate environmental inputs into useful information. In intrapersonal-normative reasons, characteristics or qualities of the partner are mentioned in combination with the belief that such qualities are necessary or desirable in an ideal mate or marriage. The evaluation of what is ideal or necessary is rooted in respondents' normative beliefs about the good and bad qualities of a marriageable partner or relationship. One women said, for example, "We worked very well together during that stressful time so I see that that's very positive in looking towards long term relationship like marriage [*sic*]." For this woman, the ability to work well together under stress was a good quality to have for a marriageable relationship. Intrapersonal-normative reasons are expressions of cultural norms that govern mate selection, and indicate the way in which such norms are internalized by individuals and become self-regulating

(Surra & Milardo, 1991). In other cases, norms are reinforced by means of direct sanctions by members of partners' local social network. Reasons for changes in commitment that involve such direct sanctions are coded into one of the subcategories that involve the social network.

Intrapersonal-normative reasons frequently involve considerations of the timing of marriage and parenthood in relation to partners' other activities. Partners' other activities may include travel, occupational development, and, as the data of Kaplan and his colleagues show, investments in education. The following quotation illustrates how one female is timing marriage against her education: "I . . . had considered that if I ever did get married I would like to wait until I got outa college." In other cases, intrapersonal-normative reasons involve economic considerations: A 10% increase in the chance of marriage was explained this way by a woman who recently had purchased a house: "We made a decision together . . . that I would get this house as property very amenable to renting 'cause it's very close to the university. . . . It's kinda been our investment. . . . For me at least [that] puts the relationship on a . . . much more stable ground in terms of it's probability of . . . a marital relationship."

Intrapersonal-normative reasons sometimes are direct evaluations of the partner's reproductive plans and potential. Partners sometimes weigh each other's plans regarding whether to have children and when to have them if they do want children. One man explained a 25% increase in the chance of marriage this way: "She doesn't want to have kids for another 8 or 9 [years]. . . . She and I both agree that [*sic*], I mean I'm only what 21, 22. And she's 23. And she doesn't want to get married for another 4 or 5 years and I don't either so . . . we have a lot of the same ideas." Another women said this about a 12% increase in the chance of marriage: "We're very . . . committed towards each other. . . . We're both very independent, both very, very career-minded. Neither one of us is very interested in children. . . . I think we will probably get married."

Partners typically get information about the reproductive and economic qualities of their mates from interactions with them, from interactions with third parties, and from other external events. In this case, a woman got parenting information from interaction with the social network: "My brother and his wife and, and their two children came. . . . He [her partner] got along very well with my nieces . . . and my nephews and although . . . I don't plan on having any children myself, they're very important to me, and I was a little worried because he doesn't necessarily like children very much. It was crucial that he . . . get along well with my nieces and nephews, and he did." She goes on to say that having the children, a 6-month-old and a 6-year-old, visit made her certain she did not want children, and strengthened the agreement between her and her partner that they strongly opposed having children.

The data on intrapersonal-normative reasons show that a minority of individuals pay attention to the reproductive value of their mates. In studies of newlyweds, such reasons are reported by about 39% of the sample (Surra et al., 1988). In the study of college-student daters, they were reported by about 33% of the sample. Compared with other categories of reasons, intrapersonal-normative reasons are infrequent; they constitute about 2% of the 1,763 reasons reported by newlyweds and about 2% of the 2,395 reasons reported by daters.

Just because such reasons are reported infrequently, relative to other reasons, does not mean they are unimportant, however. From a phenomenological perspective, even one intrapersonal-normative reason can exert a powerful influence on commitment, as in the case of this man from a sample of newlyweds, who explained an initial 75% increase in the chance of marriage this way: "I was 26. I figured I'd better get married pretty soon. . . . We were both livin' alone so I just decided [to wed]." Other support for the idea that intrapersonal-normative reasons may promote more rapid changes in commitment was found in a study of newlyweds. Newlyweds who reported a higher proportion of intrapersonal-normative reasons had courtships that accelerated rapidly to marriage, reached high levels of commitment earlier in relationships, and had fewer turning points in commitment (Surra, 1987; Surra et al., 1988). After 4 years of marriage, spouses had lower levels of marital satisfaction if, as newlyweds, they had reported that during courtship they frequently evaluated whether their partnership met their standards for a marriageable relationship. This finding may be a function of recurring doubts during courtship about whether the partner or the relationship was suitable for marriage (Surra et al., 1988).

An example of recurring doubts about the suitability of a mate is found in a woman with a master's degree who was cohabiting with her partner. She was supporting him financially, until her mother's medical crisis forced her to use up all of her savings. She said, "Looking at his potential as a mate . . . and as my mate, how well would he support himself and us . . . his potential was pretty low." Several months later he got a part-time job, but he did not make enough money to contribute his share of the rent. She then began to see other things that lowered his mate potential in her eyes, such as his silence during arguments. Again, she told him to pay rent or get out. Finally he got a better job, but by then she had doubts about whether he was mature enough to be a marriage partner. Eight months after her initial doubts, however, they attended a friend's wedding that was "very romantic." Now, she said, "Here's a guy whose finally getting his shit together. . . . And you've gotta have a vision of what you want for yourself. And it seemed like he had finally gotten a vision." She asked him to marry her, and they became engaged. Her doubts about his mate potential, however, continued for the next several months.

Some premarital partners do consciously weigh the economic, reproductive, and parenting potential of possible mates when they decide how committed they are to marrying. Such considerations are evidenced in intrapersonal-normative reasons for commitment. When characteristics of one partner do measure up to what the other finds desirable, when qualities of the relationship make it marriageable, or when partners agree on their beliefs about marriage, parenthood, education, and jobs, commitment increases. Conversely, when partners disagree or do not measure up, commitment declines. Recurring doubts about the suitability of a mate may portend difficulties with the long-term success of the relationship. Intrapersonal-normative reasons, however, are not the predomimant reasons why people become more or less committed to wed.

Subjective Explanations and Interpersonal and Social Considerations

Studies have shown that other processes are more common in the development of commitment to wed (cf. Surra et al., 1988; Surra & Hughes, 1997). Two processes by which commitment develops have been identified from a sample of dating partners (Surra & Hughes, 1997). The commitment processes were quantitatively derived from data on selected reasons for commitment and on the degree of instability of commitment evident in the graphs of changes in the chance of marriage. The processes are called *relationship-driven commitment* and *event-driven commitment*. For relationship-driven partners, commitment evolves with few reversals, and changes in commitment occur at a slow rate (10% per month, on average). The reasons for changes in commitment given by relationship-driven partners concern activities and time spent together and positive beliefs about their partner and their relationship. One male who had a relationship-driven commitment, for example, described the initial 10% increase in the chance of marriage over a 3-month period in this way: "We became closer. We started seeing each other, just the two of us. . . . I went away spring break and when I came back, we became closer. Then school and summer began so we spent a lot of time together and things just kept on getting closer." For the next 52% increase in the chance of marriage over 20 weeks, he referred again to spending time together, coded as behavioral interdependence, and positive beliefs about the partnership: "We spent more time with each other. . . . We were there for each other when problems came up." Relationship-driven men also referred more to the couple's joint network interaction and to positive beliefs involving the network. This same man, for instance, later said, "We went to her grandparents' condominium in Florida so her family invited me to go with them and stay down there." He also referred to their "families getting closer." On an objectively derived measure of compatibility between partners on their preferences for doing leisure activities, relationship-driven women were more compatible than were event-driven women. On standard questionnaire measures, relationship-driven partners reported less conflict, less ambivalence about getting seriously involved, more satisfaction at the start of the study, and greater increases in satisfaction over a 1-year period. The characteristics of relationship-driven commitments parallel the depiction of prototypical mate selection apparent in traditional theories. These partners seem to be compatibility testers, whose decisions about commitment to wed are rooted in information about how well they get along that is gathered from time spent together. Their explanations also focus on the social changes that are supposed to occur and do occur during premarriage; that is, the joining together of the partners' networks (Milardo, Johnson, & Huston, 1983) and positive reactions to the relationship on the part of the network (Surra & Milardo, 1991).

In contrast to relationship-driven commitments, event-driven commitments have relatively more downturns, and both positive and negative changes in commitment occur at a much faster rate (20% per month, on average). According to results from partners' accounts, the rockiness of their commitment stems from negative occurrences punctuated by positive ones. The accounts show a preponderance of references to conflict episodes, negative beliefs about the partner and the relationship, and negative beliefs involving the network. Explanations of network interaction focus on the partners' separate, rather than the joint network, suggesting that separate network interaction may prevail and may interfere with the development of a joint social group. Yet positive occurrences, usually involving episodes of disclosure between partners or interaction with the network, intervene to reverse sharp declines in commitment. A good example of these reversals is found in a woman who described an initial 10% increase in the chance of marriage in this way: "We had a long talk and we just sort of brought everything out that we were thinking out into the open and said it to each other," referring to how much they missed each other while apart and their thoughts of marrying one another. Beginning the eighth month of the relationship, however, their commitment took a downturn because "he didn't seem very sensitive to my needs at all. He just seemed very self-centered and noncaring." A drop in commitment from 45% to 10% over 1 month occurred because of a combination of negative beliefs about the relationship and separate network interaction: "I guess I started feeling really tied down. He started asking for things that he . . . could do for himself. I began to feel like his mother or something. . . . And my friends at the same time were asking me out . . . and I was never spending any time with the girls and I noticed myself losing some of my friends." Later, an upturn of 60% over a 2-week period was attributed to another disclosure incident: "We talked about getting married to each other. We just had a long talk and he said he thinks I'd be a good wife and a good mother and I said well, I think you'd be a good husband. . . . It just sounded really good." For this woman, the pattern of sharp positive changes in commitment alternating with negative changes was repeated during the second, nonretrospective phase of the study.

One good reason for the rockiness of event-driven commitments may be that event-driven women, at least, are less compatible with their partners on preferences for leisure activities, and event-driven men and women report more conflict over activities. On standard indicators, event-driven partners describe their relationships as more conflict-ridden, have more ambivalence about serious involvement, and are less satisfied. Despite the negativity of their relationships and of their own awareness of it, event-driven partners were no different from relationship-driven on several indicators of depth of involvement, including love; whether the relationship ends after 1 year; the length of their relationship; or whether they were casually involved, seriously involved, or engaged.

Whereas some individuals pay attention to the reproductive and economic potential of their partnerships, most individuals pay more attention to more immediate events, including their interactions with one another, interactions with third parties, to their reactions to interactions, and to their feelings and beliefs about their partnerships. Historical research, which has examined shifts in the bases of mate selection decisions from colonial America to the present, supports the idea that people have moved from practical to subjective considerations in mate selection (Gadlin, 1977; Rothman, 1984). To overstate the case: The search for a helpmate has shifted to the search for a playmate. The search for a helpmate was rooted in the industries of marital life and governed by the external constraints of a vigilant community and social circle (cf. Mintz, chapter 1, this volume). The search for a playmate is rooted in good feelings and intentions, and it requires that people introspect about and evaluate a subjective world of feelings and the interplay between two individuals.

Part of the reson why people seem to evaluate practical and economic considerations in a cursory manner may be that the concerns of childbearing have become less relevant to the concerns of mate selection. As the behavior of bearing children becomes less and less linked to the behavior of marriage (Saluter, 1994), the practical and economic considerations that seem central to the bearing and raising of children may become less important to mate selection. Because children are, in fact, born into many marital and non-marital unions, mating partners' relative lack of attention to the practical implications of their unions may be short-sighted.

The findings on the reasons why people become more or less committed to wed further suggest that individuals do not always act on the information they have in the ways that theories predict. Even when partners have data on the poor functioning of their relationships, even when they doubt the marriageability of their partners, and even when they feel bad about their relationships, some people will proceed with commitment, at least over the short-run. It is a myth that people who are dating do not see the bad points of their partners and their relationships. It is also a myth that relationship distress is something that erupts after marriage—after partners begin to recognize the negative qualities of their partnership (Surra, Batchelder, & Hughes, 1995). Instead, some relationships seem to progress toward marriage despite partners' awareness of the limitations of and problems with their partnership.

Why is this so? (cf. Surra & Hughes, 1997). One possibilty is individual differences in the ability to detect and to use information from interaction. The tendency to be deliberate, in general, or to be introspective about relationships, in particular, may prompt some people to pay closer attention than others to environmental inputs. Additionally, what appears to be clear-cut information to an outsider may be hard for an insider to interpret. Insiders do not have the benefit of seeing their relationship history plotted on a graph. In rocky relationships especially, people may respond to negative and positive occurrences as they happen, rather than to the developmental history of the relationship. Insiders' behavior may be constrained by influences that they deny or are unwilling to talk about. Premarital partners, for example, may become increasingly involved in unhappy relationships because they feel they are not marketable on the dating scene, are economically constrained, or are heavily invested in the relationship. These partners may be unaware of the full range of factors that influence their decisions to wed.

CONCLUSIONS

Kaplan et al. argue that, in modern societies, fertility and, by extension, mate selection decisions are governed by physiological mechanisms, by fitness maximizing motives, and by individuals' assessments of optimal levels of parental investment. Their model proposes that these decisions are well thought out and rooted in practical considerations. Is this an accurate assumption about the way people go about choosing mates and bearing children? Certainly, the findings just described suggest that the decisions are based less in practical and reproductive considerations than Kaplan et al. assume is the case. Although their data show a connection between, for example, education and parity, this does not necessarily mean that "men are consciously deciding to stop producing at lower parities so that they can invest both more time in their children and provide them with funding for education."

The model of fertility presented by Kaplan and colleagues leaves unexplained the possible interpersonal subjective and bases of men's fertility decisions. The data they themselves report indicate that overlooking the interpersonal in their theoretical model is problematic. Whenever characteristics of men's female partners are included in analyses, they predict men's fertility-related decisions as well as or better than the hypothesized predictors do. The most notable example is found in the prediction of the probability of a first birth for men. When women's education is entered into the model, the effect of men's education disappears. In other cases in which characteristics of mates are entered into the model, they are significant predictors of men's fertility behavior (e.g., women's education and the likelihood of dissolution). Likewise, characteristics of men's heterosexual relationships, such as number of prior relationships or length of relationship, or of the relationship context in which children were born, are significant predictors of their parental investments and of their children's outcomes.

The findings presented in this volume, including my own, those reported by Kaplan et al., and those reported by Amato (chapter 13, this volume), underscore the importance of the interpersonal and the subjective in mate selection and fertility decisions. Men's contributions to families can best be understood in the context of the contributions of other family members. Mate selection and fertility decisions, in particular, require theories and data that speak to the interpersonal, or how one partner affects the decision making of the other partner. In modern societies, understanding the role of the interpersonal, in turn, requires attention to the subjective bases of mate selection and fertility decisions.

ACKNOWLEDGMENTS

This research was supported by a grant (R01 MH47975) from the National Institute of Mental Health. I thank my colleagues in family economics, Vickie Hampton and Sue A. Greninger, for their assistance with the preparation of this chapter, and Karin Samii, Denise Bartell, and April Coover for their work on the qualitative analysis.

REFERENCES

Buss, D. M. (1994). *The evolution of desire: Strategies of human mating.* New York: Basic Books.
Gadlin, H. (1991). Private lives and public order: A critical view of the history of intimate relations in the United States. In G. Levinger & H. L. Raush (Eds.), *Close relationships: Perspectives on the meaning of intimacy* (pp. 33–72). Amherst: University of Massachusetts Press.
Huston, T. L., Surra, C. A., Fitzgerald, N. M., & Cate, R. M. (1981). From courtship to marriage: Mate selection as an interpersonal process. In S. Duck & R. Gilmour (Eds.), *Personal relationships 2: Developing personal relationships* (pp. 53–88). New York: Academic Press.
Jacquet, S., & Surra, C. A. (1996). *The association between parental divorce and the premarital relationships of young adults.* Unpublished manuscript, University of Texas, Austin.

Locke, D., & Pennington, D. (1982). Reasons and other causes: Their role in attribution processes. *Journal of Personality and Social Psychology, 42,* 212–223.

Milardo, R. M., Johnson, M. P., & Huston, T. L. (1983). Developing close relationships: Changing patterns of interaction between pair members and social networks. *Journal of Personality and Social Psychology, 44,* 964–976.

Rothman, E. K. (1984). *Hands and hearts: A history of courtship in America.* New York: Basic Books.

Saluter, A. F. (1994). *Marital status and living arrangements: March 1994* (Current Population Reports, Series P20, No. 484). Washington, DC: U.S. Government Printing Office.

Surra, C. A. (1985). Courtship types: Variations in interdependence between partners and social networks. *Journal of Personality and Social Psychology, 49,* 357–375.

Surra, C. A. (1987). Reasons for changes in commitment: Variations by courtship type. *Journal of Social and Personal Relationships, 4,* 17–33.

Surra, C. A., Arizzi, P., & Asmussen, L. (1988). The association between reasons for commitment and the development and outcome of marital relationships. *Journal of Social and Personal Relationships, 5,* 47–63.

Surra, C. A., Batchelder, M. L., & Hughes, D. K. (1995). Accounts and the demystification of courtship. In M. A. Fitzpatrick & A. L. Vangelisti (Eds.), *Explaining family interactions* (pp. 112–141). Thousand Oaks, CA: Sage.

Surra, C. A., & Hughes, D. K. (1997). Commitment processes in accounts of the development of premarital relationships. *Journal of Marriage and the Family, 59,* 1–17.

Surra, C. A., Hughes, D. K., & Jacquet, S. (in press). Commitment to marriage: A phenomenological approach. In W. H. Jones & J. Adams (Eds.), *The handbook of interpersonal commitment and relationship stability.* New York: Plenum.

Surra, C. A., & Longstreth, M. (1990). Similarity of outcomes, interdependence, and conflict in dating relationships. *Journal of Personality and Social Psychology, 59,* 501–516.

Surra, C. A., & Milardo, R. M. (1991). The social psychological context of developing relationships: Interactive and psychological networks. In W. H. Jones & D. Perlman (Eds.), *Advances in personal relationships* (Vol. 3, pp. 1–36). London: Jessica Kingsley.

Trivers, R. L., (1972). Parental investment and school selection. In B. Campbell (Ed.), *Sexual selection and the descent of man* (pp. 136–179). New York: de Gruyter.

Part III

MARITAL RELATIONS: WHAT DO MEN CONTRIBUTE?

Chapter 9

Toward a Process Model of
Men in Marriages and Families

John Mordechai Gottman
University of Washington

My social-psychophysiology laboratory is founded on a multimethod approach that collects simultaneous synchronized data on marital and family interaction as coded by observers, insider perceptions using video playback and interviews, and physiological data, as well as standard questionnaire and interview procedures, applied to representative samples. The research in my laboratory proceeds in distinct five stages. The first stage is the establishment of differential longitudinal trajectories with respect to the unfolding of central high-risk criteria, particularly divorce and the marital satisfaction of the remaining stable couples. The second stage is the identification of predictors of these differential trajectories. The third stage is the development of theory that organizes the predictors into a proposed coherent mechanism of change over time. For this stage, we have turned to various mathematical modeling approaches, particularly nonlinear dynamic modeling (Cook et al., 1995). The fourth stage is direct experimentation with highly specific, brief interventions to test this theory's ability to create proximal changes in marriages. The fifth stage includes clinical trials to create distal, lasting changes. We are currently in stages 4 and 5 of this work. The overarching goal is to build a process model of how marriages and families function and dysfunction. In this chapter, I describe the implications of our current work for the distinct process roles that men and women play in making marriages work.

A DEVELOPMENTAL PERSPECTIVE

The divide between the genders has its roots in infancy, in an overwhelming visual preference not, as one might expect, for female motherly forms, but in a preference for visual stimuli representing the same sex as the infant's. For example, in Bower's (1989) classic book, *The Rational Infant,* he noted that same-sex preference can be observed in infants less than 1 year of age in their preferences for visual stimulation. Female infants prefer viewing pictures even of female young preschool children, whereas male infants prefer viewing pictures of male children. The effect is so strong that in one of Bower's experiments he transformed films of a moving child to films of spots of light placed at each bodily joint of the moving child. The female infants even preferred watching the dots generated by pre-school female children, whereas the male infants preferred viewing the dots generated by male preschool children.

In the childhood relationships of very young children, by about 10 months of age some children begin preferring specific children as com-panions, and the roots of peer friendships then begin to emerge. In the preschool period, peer relations become extremely central to the lives of most children, and most children have a favorite playmate or best friend. About 65% of these best friendships are same-sex friendships, but 35% of them are opposite-sex friendships (Gottman & Parker, 1986). By about age 7, these opposite-sex friendships disappear dramatically in what looks developmentally like a step function, with a dramatic drop-off. The same effect can be observed not only in friendships, but also in casual interaction and play patterns. Eventually boys and girls form different worlds and stop playing with one another. They have little to do with one another until the onset of puberty, when there is a renewed interest in the opposite sex. Remarkably, the effect appears to be cross-culturally universal (see Mac-coby, 1990).

Many hypotheses have been suggested to explain the cross-culturally universal gender segregation effect that occurs in childhood at around age 7, such as sex differences in preference for rough and tumble play, but no one hypothesis has received universal acceptance among develop-mental psychologists. Recently, Maccoby (1990) suggested that the gender segregation effect may be related to the fact that in their social play, boys do not appear to accept influence from girls, whereas girls appear to accept influence from both boys and girls. She suggested that eventually girls move away from boys because of their inability to influence them. The evidence she amassed for her contention was impressive.

I wondered whether differences between men and women in adult cross-sex relationships are further compounded by the differential sociali-zation of young males and females that creates facially expressive women and inexpressive men, such as has been demonstrated in the work of Buck (1977). Buck asked mothers of preschool children aged 4 to 6 years old to guess which of a set of slides their child was viewing; mothers of 4-year-olds were equally adept at reading their sons or their daughters but, by age 6, they could read their daughters' faces far better than they could read their sons' faces. This finding appears to be related to the overwhelming concern that the Blocks reported in their longitudinal study that the parents of preschool children have in down regulating the emotional displays of their young boys before they start school, and developing in their boys the ability to control strong emotions.

Many writers pointed out that this differential socialization of emotion for the genders is quite dramatic and powerful. A few selected findings may be in order. We can, for example, study the play of children, and the repairs they make when the play falls apart. Young boys tend to play run-and-chase games with large groups over a wide geographical terrain. In the run-and-chase games, the object of the game is to keep the game going, and emotional events that occur are quickly handled with this objective in mind. If a child is upset or hurt, rapid negotiations occur to keep the game going. Often these repairs are made by changing the rules of the game to minimize the emotion. Girls, on the other hand, tend to play games in dyads close to the school building, and the object of the play appears to be more the relationship between the girls than the game they are playing. Their repairs involve discussing feelings and the events that generated them. Many of these same kind of gender differences can be observed in other contexts in children's emotional development, such as the best friend context that I have studied (Gottman & Parker, 1986).

These differences in the socialization of the genders obviously are not so monolithic, in the sense that huge individual differences exist, and these dual effects lead to a fascinating hypothesis that I discuss in this chapter. That hypothesis is that the differential socialization of emotion effects compound the gender segregation effect, so that, when the genders seek each other out in puberty, the difference that Maccoby noted in accepting and rejecting influence, particularly in the area of emotion, may become critical for the fate of cross-sex relationships. The hypothesis is that cross-sex relationships, particularly marriages, will work to the extent that men can accept influence from women.

As part of discussing this hypothesis we must lay to rest the false impression that has been created by recent misleading popularizations (such as Tannen's, 1990a, 1990b) of gender differences that suggests that women (in their use of language) are tentative in their attempts to be influential in cross-sex relationships. Nothing could be further from the truth. Although there is some evidence (e.g., the work of Aires, 1974, 1976, 1982; Aries, Gold, & Weigel, 1983) to suggest that women's use of language to try to influence people was tentative in the workplace, these trends have turned out to be largely secular, and more recent studies do not find these differences. They never existed in the family; women have never been tentative about how their families are to be run. In fact, it is a nearly universal finding among marital researchers that the wife generally has the responsibility for raising the issues and getting the couple to confront these issues. In most interaction sessions, the wife speaks first, presents the problem, and often the analysis of the problem and the tentative outlines for its solution.

Again, if we go back to the play of children, this is not surprising. I have observed the play of hundreds of young children and I have never once seen two young boys dress up and pretend to be grooms at a wedding. Pretending to be a bride is so common a game among girls that all dress-up areas of preschool classrooms I know of have mock bridal apparel. The differences do not end there. Much of the preferred play of young girls involves courtship, romance, and then playing house with babies. To put it simply, by the time girls start a family the whole subject is old hat, whereas for the male, the subject is generally quite new, and for most of his life he has avoided the whole topic. The new groom quickly finds, even in the courtship process, that he is dealing with an expert in terrain in which he is a rank amateur. This is true in all emotional and practical aspects of creating a home and a family. Clearly, the male who can allow himself to be socialized in this process is at a great advantage.

This differential concern with domestic themes in the play of young boys and its absence in the play of young boys can be dramatized by an example of a play session from a pair of 4-year-old cross-sex best friends I studied for a year, Eric and Naomi. They had been best friends from infancy, and they considered themselves engaged to be married. In one play session, Naomi wanted to use a new doll and pretend that the doll was their new baby and that they would then take the baby around to meet their friends. Eric went along with this game for about 10 minutes and then he suddenly said, "Naomi, this baby is *dead!* We have go to get it to the hospital right away and save its life." Naomi, going along with this wrinkle in the game, then rode in a very fast ambulance to the hospital (with Eric driving and Naomi urging him to please slow down), and then she assisted in the emergency surgery they both performed that eventually saved the dead baby's life. After this change in the play introduced by Eric, they continued the original theme of showing the baby off to their friends. At best, Eric put up with Naomi's domestic themes, and this is also typical of the gender divide from early childhood on. By the time the sexes come together in adolescence, girls and not boys have given an enormous amount of thought to the major issues of love, home, and family. They have also been socialized to be expert in emotion and emotional connection, which are the "stuff" of relationships. It makes sense that those men who can accept influence from women in these vital areas are probably going to have entirely different kinds of lives from those who reject this influence.

THE REJECTION OF INFLUENCE FROM WOMEN BY WIFE-BATTERING MEN

The dimension of rejecting influence from women became extremely salient in our observations of the marital interaction of violent couples in a longitudinal study that Neil Jacobson and I conducted. In this study there were three groups of couples, a group of extremely violent physically abusive couples, a control group of nonviolent but equally unhappily married couples, and a control a group of nonviolent and happily married couples.

It has been postulated that the battering of women is a natural extension of the patriarchy that largely defines our social structure (Dobash & Dobash, 1979). Evidence for this can be found in studies demonstrating wife abuse as being nearly 3 times more likely to happen in relationships where the husband dominates the decision-making process than when the wife dominates, and 8 times more likely than in egalitarian marriages (Murphy & Meyer, 1991; Straus, Gelles, & Steinmetz, 1980). There is also evidence showing that wives in higher status or income jobs than their husbands are more likely to be a victim of marital violence (Hotaling & Sugarman, 1986). Although patriarchy does not explain why some men batter and others do not, it has prompted the suggestion that men who do batter may do so in an attempt to obtain power in their relationships (Dutton, 1988). This implies that husband aggression should occur when the violent husband perceives a decrease in his marital power. Indeed, there is some evidence to support this contention. Babcock, Waltz, Jacobson, and Gottman (1993) found some evidence to support the hypothesis that batterers who had less power in their relationship were more physically abusive toward their wives. The struggle for influence may be a factor in distressed and violent marriages. The patriarchal nature of our social structure renders many women inherently less influential than their husbands. As such, another effect of this social structure could be that wives are more willing to accept influence from their husbands than their husbands are from them.

In a recent paper (Coan, Gottman, Jacobson, Babcock, & Rushe, in press), influence processes were examined because wife-battering men in their marital interactions reminded me of baseball players at automatic pitching machines, refusing to be influenced by anything their wives say, not only rejecting their wives complaints or any negative affect, but escalating it as well. In watching the marital interactions of violent men, I noticed a pattern we eventually decided to call the *bat-'em- back* hypothesis, because these men reminded me of baseball batters at automatic pitching machines in another way as well, in that they hit back every pitch thrown at them. The "pitches" usually appeared to be any low-level negative affect (or even reasonable neutral affect requests) from their wives (particularly complaints, whining, sadness, anger). Their "batting back" had an escalated "in your face" high intensity, characterized by our high intensity negative affect codes of contempt, belligerence, or defensiveness. It was striking how no violent man in our sample, in interaction with his wife, ever said anything like "Good point, I never thought of that," or "I'm beginning to see it your way," or "Maybe you are right here and I am wrong," or "I'm sorry." This pattern of rapid and sudden escalation of aggression is reminiscent of a pattern that G. R. Patterson (personal communication, 1995) described as characteristic of antisocial young men. We also were struck by the potential face-saving nature of this stance of attack and defensiveness.

To operationalize this pattern of rejecting influence, we turned to the most reliable empirical discriminator between happy and unhappy marriages, to what is called the *Negative Affect Reciprocity* model. This means that if one partner is affectively negative (sad, angry, etc.), the spouse is subsequently much more likely to be negative than he or she usually would be, using some way of comparing conditionals to unconditionals (base rates), such as a z-score or a covariance analysis. In this analysis, conditional frequencies are compared to unconditionals.

In this assessment we further refined the Negative Affect Reciprocity model by breaking it into two components. One is *reciprocation in kind* (e.g., anger is met with anger). The other is *escalation,* in which any lower intensity negativity like anger is met with either belligerence (which is provocative), contempt, or defensiveness. This escalation is designed to index the bat-'em-back hypothesis and to test the hypothesis that marriages will work to the extent that men accept influence from women.

We videotaped all couples for 15 minutes in our standard task of having the couple discuss 2 areas of continuing disagreement in their marriages, and attempting to resolve them. We used my observational coding system called the Specific Affect Coding System (SPAFF), which categorizes each second in terms of the dominant specific positive and negative emotion displayed. To assess this rejection of influence from the wife, in a sequential analysis of interaction patterns among the couples in this study, we examined the husband's consequent behavior of being either belligerent, contemptuous, or defensive, which we called *Rejects Influence.*

Even when the wife's antecedent emotion was neutral in affect during this problem-solving discussion, in an analysis of variance of the sequence wife neutral affect to husband rejects influence, the F-ratio was $F(3, 96) = 3.00$, with $p < .05$. Subsequent tests (Multiple Range Tests: least significant difference [LSD] test with significance level .05) revealed that violent men were significantly more likely than nonviolent men to reject influence (means, in seconds for these sequences: happy = 129.23, violent = 214.19, and distressed but nonviolent = 207.29). We found this same pattern when the wife's affect was mildly negative, with $F(3, 96) = 3.00$, $p < .05$. The means were 14.46 for the happy nonviolent group, 27.04 for the distressed nonviolent group, and 45.56 for the violent men. In an analysis of the equivalent sequence for the wives rejecting influence from the husband, as we expected, neither of these two sequences were significant.

So the summary of these analyses is that it is indeed the case that violent men are rejecting influence from their wives. A recent article by Nisbett (1993) suggested that the pattern of batting back using high-intensity negative affects may be related to an "honor code" these men may have about not accepting influence from a woman. We take only the following idea from Nisbett's research: For some men, there may be of a loss of face or dishonor in accepting influence from a woman. Nisbett's (1993) research was on a different matter. He attempted to explain the phenomenon of increased rates of violence (toward strangers, not to wives and children) throughout the southern region of the United States as compared to the north. In doing so, he proposed the existence of an "honor culture," derived form the Scotch–Irish sheepherding cultures who populated much of the southern region. As its name suggests, this culture is preoccupied with honor, to the extent that men feel more justified in resorting to violence in response to insult received by strangers than do people in the northern region. This construct might help us to explain the behavior and motivations of the batterer. Is it possible, for example, that batterers find the idea of accepting influence from their wives an affront to their honor, for which they feel justified in resorting to aggression and violence?

EXTENDING THESE RESULTS: EXAMINING INTERACTIVE PROCESSES IN A LONGITUDINAL STUDY OF DIVORCE PREDICTION AMONG NEWLYWEDS

Our next question was whether this notion of the husband rejecting influence from his wife was also predictive of marital dissolution among nonviolent couples. For an answer to this question, I turned to our longitudinal study of 130 newlyweds, a representative sample of newlyweds from the Seattle area. We ran these 130 couples over a 3 to 6 year period in cohorts of approximately 40 couples, and so our follow-up period has varied from 3 to 6 years. There were 18 divorces in that time. We then took 20 comparable couples very high in marital satisfaction, and 20 very low in marital satisfaction as comparison groups. Here we examined the same sequences in an attempt to predict both marital stability and marital happiness among intact couples.

In these analyses, four other models were of interest. One we called the *Negative Startup Model*, and our interest in it came from three sources: (a) our work showed that wives are consistently more likely than husbands to criticize (complain with added blaming), whereas husbands are consistently more likely than wives to withdraw emotionally as listeners from the interaction, a process we called *stonewalling*; (b) the work of Christensen and his associates, who identified a related marital interaction pattern they called the *demand–withdraw* pattern (Christensen & Heavey, 1990; Christensen & Shenk, 1991; Heavey, Layne, & Christensen, 1993), in which typically the wife demands that the couple solve the problem, whereas the husband typically withdraws; and, (c) the work of Patterson at the Oregon Social Learning Center in his writing about how coercive processes in families get started (Patterson, 1982). *Startup* is the escalation of conflict from neutral to negative affect. The startup model represents our best guess of what the wife's contribution may be toward the dissolution of marriages. It is potentially quite important. In one of our first analyses of marital interaction patterns predictive of dissolution, Gottman and Levenson (1992) found that graphs of the cumulative positive minus negative interaction over 15 minutes was highly predictive of the cascade toward divorce, with a lower ratio of positive to negative interaction of about 0.8 characteristic of dissolving marriages and a higher ratio of about 5.0 characteristic of stable marriages. I later examined these graphs, asking the question of how much of the interaction was necessary to make this prediction, the answer was about a minute of the startup is all that is necessary for 96% of the marriages in one longitudinal sample. Only 4% of the couples reversed an interaction that started off negative. Hence, the way the problem-solving conversation starts is likely to be critical, and this appears to be a role that women typically determine. These results are also consistent with our replicated findings about gender differences in the our observational divorce predictors termed the *four horsemen of the apocalypse* (e.g., Gottman, 1994) namely, that women are more likely than men to criticize (complain with blaming) whereas men are more likely than women to stonewall (withdraw emotionally as responsive listeners).

The second model is the *De-Escalation model* (Gottman, 1979), and it suggests that what is important in functional relationships is the de-escalation of conflict, which is moving from negative (either high or low intensity) to neutral affect. Gottman (1979) reported that men in happy marriages played a role of de-escalating negative affect, but only when it was low intensity. When it was high in intensity, men did not de-escalate in happy or unhappy marriages.

Another aspect of marital interaction that has received scant attention is the role of positive affect (such as humor, affection, and interest) in predicting the eventual fate of marriages. This is the *Positive Affect model,* namely that the amount of positive affect (humor, affection, interest) will predict divorce and marital happiness. Positive affect has been under-studied in marital interaction. An exception is Birchler, Weiss, and Vincent (1975), who used a self-report diary measure of "pleases" and "displeases," a precursor of the Spouse Observation Checklist, and a version of the Marital Interaction Coding System (MICS) to code either general conversation when they were supposedly setting up the equipment, and the Inventory of Marital Conflict discussion (IMC; Olson & Ryder, 1970). In the summary MICS code the positives were: agreement, approval, humor, assent, laugh, positive physical contact, and smile. Distressed couples produced an average of 1.49 positives per minute, whereas nondistressed couples produced an average of 1.93 positives per minute, a significant difference. In the home environment, distressed partners recorded significantly fewer pleasing and significantly greater displeasing events than was the case for nondistressed partners. The ratio of pleases to displeases also discriminated the groups (the ratio was 29.66 for nondistressed couples and 4.30 for distressed couples).

In our analyses we employed the SPAFF observational system that obtained considerably more detail and specificity than the MICS in the realm of emotion, for both positive and negative affect (Gottman, 1996). There are two forms of the Positive Affect model I was interested in. One simply suggests that positive affect will be randomly distributed throughout the conflict interaction, without any connection to other salient processes. This is a kind of noncontingent or *Good Will Positive Affect model.* Another model of positive affect suggests that positive affect is used in the service of the de-escalation of marital conflict, that is it is in the service of moving the overall affect from negative to a less negative (even a neutral affective) state. In this *Contingent Positive Affect model,* the underlying, or related purpose of the positive affect might involve physiological soothing of one's partner (Gottman, 1990).

An important aspect of positive affect concerns empathy, particularly as the recommended response to one's partner's negative affect. It is clearly the most influential process theory of what is functional in marriage, and here I call it the *Empathy model.* This model forms the basis of most complex multicomponent marital treatments (e.g., see Jacobson & Margolin, 1979). The hypothesis is that stable, happy marriages are characterized by empathetic exchanges during conflict resolution, and that ailing marriages are characterized by the absence of this empathy. That is, what is functional is for people to be able to be nondefensive and empathetic even when they feel they are being attacked by their spouse. In most marital therapies, this assumption is reflected in some form of the listener–speaker exchange.

I am sure that you are all familiar with this exercise. For example, let us say the wife starts as the speaker and the husband is the listener. She is asked to put her complaints as "I-statements." For example, she complains that she is hurt about the way he relates to their youngest child. She hates the way he ignores the boy and criticizes him. He then is asked to para-phrase both the content and feelings of his wife's message, and to check out his paraphrase. Then he is asked to empathetically validate her feelings. He is asked to suspend judgment, to respond nondefensively. This is what we recommend in our therapies about the expression of negative affect and the proper or functional response.

But where does this knowledge that the empathy pattern be basic to good marriage come from? In fact, it turns out that, historically, what we do is a version of what Carl Rogers said to do as a therapist. It's acceptance, nonjudgmental acceptance and empathy. That is where Guerney (1982) got his ideas many years ago when he suggested empathy training for couples. All the other marital therapies eventually followed his lead; in fact, they expanded this suggestion in creating Communication Skill Train-ing Components. What was the scientific justification for these communi-cation skills? How did these communication-oriented marital therapies know what to train? How did they decide that "I-statements" are better than "you-statements"? How was any of it decided? It may come as a surprise that, even in psychotherapy research, the original Truax three therapist process variables of accurate empathy, warmth, and genuineness were never shown to relate consistently to therapeutic outcome. In fact, a great deal of doubt was raised in studies by Bergin and Garfield in the late 1960s and early 1970s (e.g., Garfield & Bergin, 1971) about this hypothesis. Yet, for some reason, the Empathy model has become the basis of most marital therapies.

In the analyses we conducted, we sought to be able to make two types of predictions: (a) a marital stability prediction in which we combined the two stable groups (happy and unhappy) and attempted to predict divorce or stability from their Time-1 marital interaction (taken in the first 6 months of marriage), using various process models, and (b) a marital happiness prediction, in which, controlling for stability, we tried to predict a couple's Time-2 marital happiness or unhappiness (from their Time-1 marital interaction taken in the first 6 months of marriage) using various process models. For all sequences, when we examined a sequence that indexed a particular process model, if the results turned out to be statis-tically significant, we also conducted a covariance analysis, using the fre-quency of the consequent code as the covariate; this was a stringent ap-proach to the fundamental sequential connection question, "Was the consequent more predictable from the antecedent than its base rate of occurrence?" (Gottman & Roy, 1990). Without this test we cannot know if a high joint frequency of occurrence was not simply due to a high-base rate of the consequent, or if a low-joint frequency of occurrence is not simply due to a low-base rate of the consequent.

Finally, in our data analysis we constructed a path analytic model linking several salient theoretical process models, and attempted to fit the same model in our three criterion groups, and then to compare the same model across groups. Here is what we discovered.

Negative Affect

If we look at sequences that describe reciprocating negative affect in kind, that is, sequences where for example anger is met with anger and there is no escalation as in the bat-'em-back hypothesis, these sequences appear to be characteristic of all marriages. For the most part, they do not predict divorce or marital unhappiness. The only exception is that there is evidence that in the first few months of marriage, the wife in marriages that end up unstable are more likely to reciprocate low-intensity negative affect (not high-intensity) than is the case in marriages that are stable. None of these sequences were related to happiness among stable couples.

The sequences we hypothesized as indicating the refusal to accept one's partner's influence—the bat-'em-back hypothesis—revealed that only the husband's rejection of influence from the wife predicted divorce. (the covariance analyses yielded $F(1, 54) = 10.53$, $p = .002$, for husbands and $F(1, 54) = .98$, ns for wives). These sequences were nonsignificant for the happiness analyses.

The sequences indicating the Negative Startup Model are indexed by the couple moving from neutral to negative affect. The covariance analysis revealed that for the husband, $F(1, 54) = 1.03$, ns, whereas for the wife, $F(1, 54) = 10.81$, $p = .0001$. Hence, there was evidence only for wife negative startup predicting marital dissolution. These startup sequences were not predictive of happiness among intact couples.

Positive Affect Empathy Model

The usual way to operationalize the empathy sequences would be to look for sequences in which one partner expressed negative affect and the other partner validated this. We cast a wider net than the usual definition of empathy, examining all sequences in which one partner expressed low- or high-intensity negative affect and this was followed by either interest, affection, humor, or validation by the other partner. In the stability analyses, the F-ratios were .06, .24, .12, and .00, respectively, all of which were nonsignificant. These sequences occurred very infrequently for all couples, approximately 4 seconds out of 900, and they were predictive of neither stability or marital happiness among stable couples. Hence, to summarize, these empathic exchanges hardly ever occurred, and they predicted nothing.

Sheer Positive Affect

Next we examined pure positive affect. The amount of positive affect was significantly related to stability, with husband positive and wife positive, respective F-ratios 7.67, $p = .0076$, and 7.64, $p = .0077$ (stable husbands = 62.23 secs, unstable husbands = 31.76 secs, stable wives = 59.05, and unstable wives = 31.23 secs), with discriminant function $\chi^2(2) = 8.74$, $p = .0127$. It was also related to happiness, with F-ratios 5.27, $p = .0273$, and 8.25, $p = .0066$. The discriminant function was $\chi^2(2) = 8.14$, $p = .0171$. Hence, the amount of positive affect predicted both marital stability and happiness, and it was the only variable to do so. The positive-to-negative affect variable also performed well in these two regards.

What was very interesting was that the differences in the amount of positive affect among the three groups of couples (divorced, stable-unhappy, stable-happy) were about 30 to 40 seconds for all groups. What a short amount of time this seemed for it to be such a major predictor of marital outcomes. How were these 30 second employed by the couples? Were they used noncontingently, like a Good Will model would suggest? Or were they being used like a scalpel, in the service of some other social process important in the problem-solving interaction? For an answer to this question, we examined the relationship between de-escalation sequences and positive affect. We found that the de-escalation sequence, indexed by the couple moving from low-intensity negative to neutral affect, predicted marital stability only for the husband's de-escalation (in the covariance analyses, for the wife's de-escalation $F(1, 54) = 1.35$, ns, but for husband's de-escalation $F(1, 54) = 6.47$, $p = .014$). Hence, there was evidence of the importance only of the husband's de-escalation, and only of low intensity negative wife affect (which is a replication of results I reported in 1979). For the happiness analyses, the F-ratios were nonsignificant.

Parenthetically, it is interesting to speculate about a null effect in these analyses, namely, why is it that we do not find that husbands de-escalate their wives' *intense* negative affect? This null finding is completely in keeping with the phenomenon we consistently observed that husbands are more likely than wives to stonewall, or withdraw as listeners, not providing the usual listener back-channels, when the marital conflict becomes emotionally negatively intense. This tendency of men to withdraw emotionally when they are confronted with their wives' intense negative affect is potentially an important result from process marital research that probably relates to the greater tendency of men to withdraw from their children as well as their wives when the marriage is ailing. This effect is quite powerful. For example, developmental psychologists have discovered that by 7 to 9 months of age, young infants, when confronted with a potentially disturbing or frightening novel stimulus will look at their parent and read their parent's facial expression to determine whether to stop or to proceed with their explorations. This is called *social referencing*, and babies will do it with their fathers as well as with their mothers. However, there is even evidence that 1-year-old babies no longer socially reference their unhappily married fathers, whereas they do still socially reference their unhappily married mothers (Dickstein & Parke, 1988). This phenomenon probably indexes the father's withdrawal from both his wife and his baby in an ailing marriage. The roots of this male withdrawal from intense negative affect are not known, but Gottman (1994) reported that men are more likely to feel "emotionally flooded" (Ekman, 1984) by lower intensity negative marital events than are women. However, Levenson, Carstensen, and Gottman (1994) recently speculated that because other research on heartbeat awareness shows that men are more in tune with their bodies than women, men may be looking at their bodily reactions for affective cues about whether to engage or to withdraw, whereas women may look more to social cues for making this decision. Withdrawal may be men's way of taking care of themselves, a pattern that, unfortunately, has particularly negative consequences for their marriages and for their relationships with their children as well.

Path Analysis of the Contingent Positive Affect Model

Next, we conducted a path analysis to examine the relationship between de-escalation and positive affect. Recall that our analyses revealed that positive affect was the only variable that predicted marital stability and also was able to discriminate between stable happily married and stable unhappily married couples. To understand the role of positive affect, we constructed a path-analytic model between the following variables: positive affect, the sum of husband and wife bat-'em-back sequences, the sum of husband and wife de-escalation sequences, and the sum of husband and wife negative reciprocity sequences (combining low- and high-intensity negative affect reciprocity). The model we constructed, using the Bentler computer program EQS, was successful in fitting the covariance matrices of all three groups, stable and happily married. I then compared the models across groups, and the omnibus test showed that the path coefficients for the three groups were significantly different. Testing specific path coefficients with cumulative multivariate statistics, we found that: (a) Only in the stable, happy group was there a positive association between de-escalation and positive affect—in the other two groups, the path coefficient was negative; (b) the relationship between escalation or the bat-'em-back sequence and positive affect was more negative in the stable happy group than in the stable unhappy group and in the divorced group;

and, (c) the relationship between escalation and de-escalation was stronger in the stable, happy group than in the two other groups.

Hence, positive affect is not being employed by stable happy newlyweds in a noncontingent manner, but in the service of the de-escalation of conflict, and, I surmise, in the service of the kind of physiological soothing that facilitates effective and creative marital problem solving. These analyses are currently underway.

Summary

Except for the low-intensity reciprocation of wives in unstable marriages, surprisingly, negative affect reciprocity in kind appears to be characteristic of all marriages (the only other exception was reciprocated stonewalling, which was also characteristic only of unstable marriages). What did predict divorce was the wife's negative startup and then the husband's rejection of her influence, indexed by escalation of negative affect. This means that in unstable marriages, the wife starts the sequence, with low-intensity negative affect, probably adding criticism, and then the husband escalates it rather than de-escalates it, batting back any attempt she makes to influence him with her negative affect. In stable marriages, on the contrary, the wife expresses her complaints with a "softened startup" and then the husband both accepts influence and he also de-escalates whatever low-intensity negative affect the wife expresses. Note that this pattern is substantially different from the demand–withdraw pattern identified by Christensen and his associates. Here we are not flagging the critical husband patterns as withdrawal, but escalation. The combined picture we present is one of both husband escalation (refusal to accept influence), as well as husband withdrawal in the face of more intense wife negative affect. In the dissolving marriage, he first responds with rejection to her negative startups. Let her complain and criticize and he is instantly "in her face" and twice as negative. But, let her negative affect escalate, and he withdraws and becomes a stonewalling listener. Furthermore, the hypothesis we arrived at is that during conflict resolution, positive affect is used in the service of the de-escalation of conflict and perhaps its concomitant physiological soothing so that the marital interaction may proceed to creative and effective problem solving.

THE ETIOLOGY OF MARITAL DYSFUNCTION DURING CONFLICT RESOLUTION: TURNING TOWARD VERSUS TURNING AWAY IN EVERYDAY INTERACTIONS

Although these results and our previous results detail the specific marital processes predictive of the longitudinal course of marriages, they leave open the question of the etiology of these dysfunctional patterns. The overwhelming amount of research on marital processes has focused on the resolution of conflict. Recently we began investigating what we call couples' *repair attempts* at reversing a chain of negative affect during these conflict conversations. Repair attempts are potentially very important because they happen naturally even in the worst marriages at the rate of about 1 every 3 minutes, and they work to reverse negative patterns in marriages that are stable and happy.

However, we are led to the view that the context and form of the repair attempt are not predictive of its success, and that, in fact, there is nothing we can find in the conflict interaction itself that is predictive of the success of these repair attempts. For these reasons, we began working on a hypothesis that the etiology of dysfunctional marital interaction during conflict resolution lies in the way couples interact during more mundane, everyday nonconflict interaction contexts.

We first examined this a study in which the very first conversation couples had in our lab was a conversation about the events of their day after they had been apart for at least 8 hours. Of course, these conversations are significantly more neutral affectively than the conflict interactions. However, in examining the predictability of the ratio of positive to negative affect in the events of the day conversation of the same ratio in the conflict conversation, we found that in predicting the wife's ratio in the conflict conversation from the husband's and wife's ratios in the events of the day conversations, the multiple R was .71, $F(2, 62) = 31.99$, $p = .0000$. For the husband's conflict ratio, $R = .54$, $F(2, 62) = 12.46$, $p = .0000$. In other words, the simple ratio of positive to negative affect in mundane everyday conversations appears to set the stage for the same ratios in conflict conversations. We also know that these positive-to-negative ratios in the conflict context are good predictors of divorce or stability. For example, for serious considerations of marital dissolution in the next 4 years, the husband's ratio predicted this $F = 3.14$, $p < .05$, and the wife's $F = 6.75$, $p < .01$. Splitting on the husband's ratio during conflict, the positive to negative ratios were .97 for those considering dissolution and 1.75 for those not, and splitting on wives the same ratios were .42 and 1.56, respectively.

We videotaped 50 of our newlywed couples for 12 continuous hours in an apartment laboratory, and coded the 600 hours of interaction we obtained. Preliminary evidence suggests that codes we call *turning toward* versus *turning away*, by which mean contingent responsiveness to a partner's fairly neutral interest or excitement will also be strongly related to these positive-to-negative ratios and to the success of repair attempts made during conflict resolution.

This balance of turning toward versus turning away in everyday, mundane, and possibly fairly "mindless" interaction moments may be critical for building a theory of an emotional bank account of the etiology of dysfunctional or functional marital interaction patterns during conflict resolution. Our theory is that the balance of turning toward versus turning away will determine either positive or negative sentiment override (Weiss, 1980). *Positive and Negative Sentiment Overrides* are concepts proposed by Weiss in 1980. Weiss suggested that reactions during marital interaction may be determined by a global dimension of affection or disaffection rather than by the immediately preceding valence of the stimulus. To evaluate the existence of these overriding sentiments, one must look for discrepancies between insider and outsider in characteristic evaluations of particular messages. In Positive Sentiment Override (PSO) a spouse tends to perceive even affectively negative messages as neutral or positive. In Negative Sentiment Override (NSO), a spouse tends to perceive even affectively neutral messages as negative. Notarius et al. (1989) evaluated the validity of this hypothesis in a remarkably creative study in which they employed a sequential stream of behavior and cognitions to operationalize a number of hypotheses linking behavior and cognition. They found that distressed wives were more negative, were more likely to evaluate their partner's neutral and negative messages as negative (suggesting the operation of a negative sentiment override), and given a negative evaluation of their partner's antecedent message, were more likely to offer a negative reply than were all other spouses. It is important to note that this finding is quite specific. It is a very important precise finding because it is opposite to the general gender difference finding in negative attributions, in which men are more likely than women to rehearse distress-maintaining attributions when the marriage is distressed (Holtzworth-Munroe & Jacobson, 1985).

To summarize, I think that PSO determines the success of repair attempts during conflict resolution. And what determines PSO? I propose that the couples ratio of positive to negative affect in nonconflict interaction determines it. I call this the *Emotional Bank Account* model of marriage, and it means that PSO is determined by how much "emotional money in the bank" the couple has. Our data supports this theory.

THE HUSBAND'S LOVE MAP AND FONDNESS AND ADMIRATION SYSTEM

One of the objectives of our newlywed study was to search for buffers against the precipitous decline in the wife's marital satisfaction that seems to accompany about 75% of all newlyweds as they make the transition to parenthood (e.g., see Cowan & Cowan, 1992). Our study is only one of two studies (Markman's is the other; see Markman, Renick, Floyd, & Stanley, 1988; Markman, Floyd, Stanley, & Storaasli, 1988) that studied the couple in the early stages of marriage; other studies have begun in the second trimester of pregnancy. We analyzed our oral history interview data taken in the first few months of marriage, and found that four variables provided the major buffers. Couples who did not decline in marital satisfaction following the birth of their first child had four characteristics that emerged from our coding of this interview. It is interesting that 3 of the 4 buffer variables turned out to be from the husband. They are the husband's spontaneous expressions of fondness and admiration of his wife (r = .43, $p < .01$), the husband's "we-ness" ($r = .33$, $p < .05$) (by which we mean a philosophy of companionate solidarity that is indexed by the tendency to use inclusive words like "we" and "us" in describing a period in the relationship or one's own views), and the amount of what we call *cognitive room* for the relationship both husbands and wives have allocated (husband's, $r = .46$, $p < .001$, and wife's, $r = .46$, $p < .001$), by which we mean the details of the relationship's history, as well as the details of their partner's everyday world. We call this latter dimension a *Love Map*, because it appears to represent an active guide each spouse creates and maintains about the partner and the marriage. Thus, we have found that the same variables that predict marital stability or divorce continue to predict the longitudinal course of the remaining intact marriages who go on to become parents and act as a buffer against the decline in marital satisfaction after the arrival of the first child.

Some Implications of Focusing on Nonconflict Interaction

Marital therapy is known to universally have a huge relapse problem; in general, only about 20% to 30% of couples who make initial gains in marital satisfaction have maintained these gains after 2 years (e.g., see Jacobson & Addis, 1993). One possible explanation for the relapse problem is that the setting conditions for dysfunctional problem solving lie in the couple's nonconflict, everyday interactions. I have suggested this in the Emotional Bank Account model. Another potential advantage of focusing on nonconflict interaction is that one reason that many couples may engage in so much conflict is that they do not seem to know how to make a satisfying emotional connection in other, potentially more pleasurable contexts. In my interviews of our violent couples, I was struck by the intense loneliness of both people in the violent marriage, and by how little they appear to share everyday events that most couples thrive on, such as weekend outings, marital dates, groups activities like church events, sports, and so on. Even their TV viewing seems to be isolated or without much interaction. Coming together in emotionally low-cost activities might be one way of restoring whatever processes have failed in the distressed marriage. One example of where this appears to be most promising is in ritualizing a stress-reduction daily conversation. In this conversation, the husband's empathy would seem to have its proper place. The wife complains about something or someone other than the husband, and the husband empathizes. This type of "we against others" gossip and emotional support seems to be quite common in the events of the day conversations of our subjects, and it tends to be physiologically soothing. We think that training empathy in the context of conflict resolution, in which the spouse is the target, may be effective for a small proportion of couples, but it is tantamount to emotional gymnastics for the rest. It may be the major source of relapse in marital therapy, in which the therapy is trying to build in and sustain an unnatural (but potentially effective) process that can only be sustained by the continual presence of a trained therapist.

THE IMPORTANCE OF THE SYMBOLIC VALUE INHERENT IN IRRECONCILABLE CONFLICTS, AND OF MEN ACCEPTING INFLUENCE

In recent pilot work designed to obtain proximal changes in marital interaction, we discovered an underlying dynamic that explains what happens in marriages locked in irreconcilable conflicts. We developed an interview about these conflicts called the dreams-within-conflict interview. This interview explores the symbolic meanings, metaphors, narratives, and hidden dreams within each entrenched position. By the time we saw couples who have these conflicts, they had often gone through a five-stage processes of entrenchment of their positions. These five stages are: (a) the dreams are in opposition, (b) entrenchment of positions, (c) fears of accepting influence, (d) vilification of one's partner, and finally, (e) emotional disengagement. Our proximal intervention has two components. The first attempts to reveal the dreams, narratives, stories, and metaphors inherent within each position, as well as each partner's fears of the other's position. For many couples, a lot has to happen to make the marriage safe enough for these dreams and fears to emerge. The second component of the intervention attempts to change influence patterns so that each dream can be supported within the marriage. The major challenge is usually to get the husband to accept influence from his wife, and, for some husbands, we employed individual response training tapes as well so that this process will be more face-saving for the husband. We called this the *yield to win* intervention, patterned after the art of Aikido. The goal is to change the marriage into one that supports each person's dreams, hopes, and aspirations, and calms fears.

The next part of our picture about the husband's role in marriage and family dynamics emerged from our research on the links between the marriage, parenting, and child outcomes, and I move to a consideration of fathering.

THE UNIQUE ROLE OF FATHERS IN FAMILIES

The importance of fathers has been pointed out for some time by several writers, most notably Parke (1981, 1996), Lamb (1981, 1986, 1987), and Levant (1988). In general, mothers tend to be more verbal and directing, whereas fathers are more physical and arousing (see Parke, 1981, for a review). In the emotion area, mothers also appear to exert their influence via direct instruction, whereas fathers appear to have their effects primarily through play. There is substantial research evidence that parenting practices also differ based on a child's gender (e.g., MacDonald & Parke, 1984), and that this distinction begins at an early age, continuing in varying forms throughout childhood. In the emotion arena, Fivush (1991) found mothers making gender distinctions in the emotion arena: When they talked to their 3-year-old sons and daughters about anger and sadness, they talked more to their daughters about sadness, and more to their sons about anger. Furthermore, a number of studies found that it is fathers more than mothers who treat their children differently based on their gender, particularly in the areas of discipline and physical involvement (Fisher & Fagot, 1993; Maccoby & Martin, 1983; Mulhern & Passman, 1981; Starrels, 1994). Kerig, Cowan, and Cowan (1993) also found that it was fathers, not mothers, who distinguished between sons and daughters in a laboratory teaching task, particularly when faced with marital conflict and disagreement regarding parenting style. Distressed fathers of daughters were more authoritarian (more cold, angry, and disengaged) than distressed fathers of sons, and these differences were exacerbated by the level of marital conflict. However, mothers did not show these differences. Kerig, Cowan, and Cowan (1993) found that maritally dissatisfied parents of girls were more negative than dissatisfied parents of boys, and dissatisfied fathers were more critical than dissatisfied mothers; the most negative parent was the father of a daughter. The mothers tended to be critical of daughters only when they asserted themselves (see also Pratt, Kerig, Cowan, & Cowan, 1992).

Probably the most important recent set of discoveries about fathers concerns their special and unique role in intense positive affective play with their children. The work of Parke, MacDonald, and their associates revealed that fathers' physical play with their young children is the vehicle capable of teaching the children a great deal about affect regulation, and that this learning has implications for the children's relationships with their peers. For example, MacDonald (1987) compared the dyadic interactions of parents and their sons classified as popular or rejected by peer sociometric ratings. Popular boys and their parents (popular dyads) were able to maintain longer bouts of physical play and showed more positive affect than rejected boys and their parents (rejected dyads). Physical play is an especially useful setting for looking at regulation processes because of the potential for overstimulation and the need for mutual regulation. Children typically express their displeasure when their optimal level for stimulation is exceeded. MacDonald found that the frequency of overstimulation was much higher in the rejected dyads than the popular dyads, especially for boys and their fathers. Parents of rejected children were less able to keep the stimulation within the child's optimal level. Children in these dyads were more likely to try to avoid and to make negative responses to stimulation (for other evidence of linkages between the family system and the child peer system see Bhavnagri and Parke, 1991; Booth, Rose-Krasnor, & Rubin, 1991; Cassidy, Parke, Butkovsky, & Braungart, 1992; Cohn, Patterson, & Christopoulos, 1991; Gottman & Katz, 1989; Ladd & Hart, 1992; MacDonald & Parke, 1984; Pettit, Harrist, & Bates, 1991; Putallaz, Costanzo, & Smith, 1991).

RESEARCH ON HOW MARRIAGES RELATE
TO PARENTING AND CHILD OUTCOMES

In a second line of longitudinal studies we have conducted since 1985, we investigated the relationships between marital interaction, parenting, and child outcomes. In this research, we searched for the effects of children on marriage, the effects of the marriage on children, and for ways that parents can buffer their children when they are in an ailing marriage. We first discovered that contemptuous and belligerent (hostile) marital interaction, which predicts divorce, also predicts the development of externalizing behavior problems in children (e.g., aggression), whereas a demand–withdraw marital interaction pattern predicts the development of internalizing problems in children (e.g., depression and anxiety). We discovered that the development of externalizing problems involves the spillover of marital conflict, affecting the father's parenting and the child's regulatory physiology through the father. However, the development of internalizing problems involves the spillover of marital conflict, affecting the mother's parenting and the child's regulatory physiology through the mother. These latter two results are a replication and extension of the Cowans' findings.

The major organizing construct in our research has been our construct of meta-emotion. *Metacommunication* is communication about communication. *Metacognition* is cognition about thinking. *Meta-emotion* is emotion and thoughts about emotion. It includes such things as people's emotions, metaphors, narratives, and philosophies about anger and sadness, both in themselves and in their children.

We conducted a meta-emotion interview with parents and we noticed that there as those parents who are aware of the emotions in their lives, particularly the negative emotions, who can talk about them in a differentiated manner, are aware of these emotions in their children, and assist their children with their emotions of anger, sadness, acting like an "emotion coach." Briefly, our major results confirm and extend the writing of one of our most intuitive and insightful clinicians, Ginott (1994), who began writing in the 1960s and wrote three seminal books before his untimely death by cancer. There is a parental meta-emotion philosophy we call *emotion coaching*, in which parents notice low-intensity emotions in their children, see this as an opportunity for intimacy or teaching, are accepting of these emotions or wishes in their children, and then do limit setting, problem solving, and value transmission with their children. The opposite, a *dismissing* meta-emotion philosophy was one in which parents felt that the child's sadness or anger were potentially harmful to the child, that it was the parents' job to change these toxic negative emotions as quickly as possible, that children needed to realize that these negative emotions would not last and were not very important, and that it was the parent's job to convey to the children a sense that they could "ride out" these negative emotions without damage.

We found that emotion-dismissing families can be sensitive to their children's feelings and want to be helpful, but their approach to sadness is to ignore or deny it as much as possible. Often they perceive a child's strong emotion as a demand that they fix everything and make it better. They hope that the dismissing strategy will make the emotion go away quickly. They often convey a sense that the child's emotion is something they may be forced to deal with, but it is not interesting or worthy of attention in itself. They may describe sadness as something to get over, ride out, but look beyond and not dwell on. They often use distractions when their child is sad to move the child along, and even use comfort, but within specified time limits, as if they are impatient with the emotion itself. They prefer a happy child, and find these negative states in their child quite painful. They don't present an insightful description of their child's emotional experience. They typically do not problem solve, they do not see the emotion as beneficial, or as any kind of opportunity, either for intimacy or for teaching. Many dismissing families may see their child's anger as enough cause for punishment or a "time out."

We found significant differences between mothers and fathers on emotion coaching. Fathers coached significantly less than mothers, particularly when their children were sad. In the following excerpt a father responds to his daughter's sadness by emphasizing the importance of her not remaining sad. The father focuses on a myriad of distractions. At the same time he dismisses his child's sadness, he also conveys affection in the concern he shows that his child not be unhappy.

I: How do you react when she is sad?

F: I pamper her.

I: What do you do?

F: I just hold her, carry her around. I ask her if she needs anything. Ah, if she needs mostly if she needs anything, or I just talk to her.

I: What do you talk about?

F: Hmmm? "What do you want?" Well, back to needs again, uhhh, "You want to watch television?" "Can we get you a movie or anything like that?" "You want to go upstairs?" "You want to go outside?" Just, I don't know. Just work with her and see what she answers back with cause then you find out. *You have to respond to her needs. . . .* But, ah, she's usually never sad. [italics added]

To summarize, emotion dismissing parents tend to hear primarily the *demand aspect* of the child's sadness, a demand that they make the world perfect for the child and fix everything so the child will not have to be sad. They tend to view the negative affect in their child as toxic, so they want to change their child's negative affect to positive, through tickling, distraction, or minimizing. They want to teach their children that they can endure the negative state and put it behind them.

Consider how an emotion coaching father advised his child about how to deal with being sad about peer rejection:

F: . . . so, Joshua's sad. I try really hard to understand why it's that way. Why are you feeling sad? And, umm, him being just a little boy, I think you can't expect too much of him. But *I try to find out why he's feeling that way.* Some kid might have hit him or someone might have made fun of him or something. But my feelings towards him are my goodness, my heart just goes out to him. I try to stop everything else at that moment and really empathize with him and try to support him and help him feel better. [italics added]

This is part of a coaching problem-solving process. It contrasts very well with the following example from a dismissing parent:

F: Yeah, [I tell him] not to really worry about it. If he comes in and says one of his friends took his toys, I'll just say, Well don't worry about it, he'll bring it back, you know. Or, you know, *he says, "he hit me." Don't worry about it, he probably didn't mean it, it was probably an accident. Just to take it lightly, don't dwell on it,* but I don't sit there and say, you shouldn't be upset. That's fine, he can be upset all he wants, but just *teach him to roll with the punches and get on with his life.* [italics added]

There were five components of emotion coaching:

1. Is aware of low intensity child emotions.
2. Sees the child's emotion as an opportunity for intimacy or teaching.
3. Helps the child verbally label the emotions while the child is having the emotions.
4. Empathizes with or validates the child's emotions. (e.g., using affection, soothing).
5. Helps the child problem solve (sets limits, discusses goals, strategies, and values).

The Relationship Between Our Meta-Emotion Variables and the Parents' Marriage

We found that the meta-emotion variables are related to how the parents resolve their marital conflict. Some selected results are: Fathers who are aware of their own sadness were more affectionate in the marital conflict interaction, and their wives were significantly less contemptuous and belligerent; fathers who accept their own sadness were less likely to stonewall; fathers who coach their children's sadness were less disgusted, less defensive, and more affectionate, their wives were also less defensive and more affectionate; and fathers who coach their children's anger were more affectionate and their wives are less contemptuous, less belligerent, less defensive, and more affectionate. Furthermore, the meta-emotion variables are related to marital satisfaction and marital stability. Awareness of one's own and one's children's emotions and emotion coaching were uniformly related to higher marital satisfaction at Time-1 and at Time-2, fewer serious considerations of separation and divorce, less actual separation, and, if separation did occur, to shorter separations, and less likelihood of divorce. Hence an emotion-coaching meta-emotion structure was related to greater marital stability and to greater marital satisfaction. This is particularly true of the father's meta-emotions about anger and the mother's meta-emotions about sadness.

Furthermore, we found that the meta-emotion variables are related to the physical health of the parents; in particular, the father's health was related to his awareness of his own sadness, and the mother's physical health was related to her awareness of her sadness, her coaching of her child's sadness, her husband's awareness of his anger, and to her awareness of her own anger. To control for reporting biases (men tend to underreport illness), we also used the Krokoff (1985) health index, which asks each spouse to report on their partner's health. Once again, the meta-emotion variables were predictive of reports of greater physical health.

We also found that the meta-emotion variables were related to the parents' philosophy of marriage as measured by our oral history interview. The results show that the meta-emotion variables are not isolated and limited to only the parent–child family subsystem, but are also related to the couple's philosophy of marriage. For example, in marriages in which the father was aware of his sadness, during the oral history interview, the father was more likely to spontaneously express fondness for his wife, to talk about the importance of we-ness or a companionate philosophy of marriage, and the couple was more likely to say that it is important to discuss emotional issues, to believe that marital conflict is worth the struggle, and to feel less chaotic and out of control of their lives. The father's awareness of his anger was related to his expressions of fondness for his wife, his expressions of we-ness and his wife's expressions of we-ness in the interview. The father's awareness of his child's anger was related to greater fondness expressed by the father toward his wife, greater we-ness expressed by the father and mother and less of a conflict-avoiding philosophy of marriage expressed by the father. The father's coaching of his child's anger was also related to his expressions of fondness toward his wife, his and his wife's expressions of we-ness, the couple being more likely to say that it is important to discuss emotional issues, to believe that marital conflict is worth the struggle, and to feel less chaotic and out of control of their lives. There was a similar pattern for mothers.

We also found that *meta-emotion discrepancy* between parents was predictive of divorce. We computed two variables to index this discrepancy, the squares of the differences between spouses in coaching anger (a variable we called x), and coaching sadness (a variable we called y), respectively. These two variables alone were able to predict divorce or marital stability in a discriminant function analysis with 80% accuracy (Wilks' λ for $x = 4.85$, $p < .05$, Wilks' λ for $y = 5.25$, $p < .05$). The F-ratio for the multiple regression for divorce was $F(2, 47) = 4.16$, $p < .05$, $R = .39$.

The implications of a meta-emotion discrepancy on coaching *sadness* was that to the extent that there is a discrepancy, the father was less likely to coach the child's sadness ($r = -.31$, $p < .05$) and the child's anger ($r = -.46$, $p < .001$); the equivalent correlations for the mother's coaching of sadness and anger were not significant ($r = .13$ and $-.08$, respectively). The implications of a meta-emotion discrepancy on coaching *anger* was that to the extent that there is a discrepancy, the father was less likely to coach the child's sadness ($r = -.57$, $p < .001$) and the child's anger ($r = -.59$, $p < .001$); the equivalent correlations for the mother's coaching of sadness and anger were not significant ($r = -.21$ and $-.10$, respectively).

Is it possible that the meta-emotion variables tap a fundamental quality about emotional connection in the marriage as well as in the parent–child system? Could it be the case that many fundamental incompatibilities in marriage come from having divergent views about emotion, that is, disparate meta-emotion structures? We think that this is a real possibility, and wish to elevate these findings into a hypothesis about marital stability: Spouses who have different meta-emotion structures will have unstable marriages and their interaction will be characterized by disappointment, negativity, criticism, contempt, defensiveness, and by eventual emotional withdrawal. We suggest that this meta-emotion compatibility is another fundamental dynamic that operates to either to make marriages work or not work.

Meta-Emotion and Parenting

Emotion coaching was embedded in a network of parenting variables. That is to say, the variables we derived from the meta-emotion interview had validity in a laboratory teaching task. In particular, emotion coaching was positively correlated with what we call *Scaffolding/praising* parenting, and negatively correlated with what we call *Derogatory parenting*. Scaffolding/Praising parenting is a pattern of teaching a child by providing only minimal information so that the child can get started on the learning task, waiting for the child to do something right, praising the child, and then offering more information about the task. Derogatory parenting involves an opposite pattern of teaching, in which a lot of information is presented at high density in an excited, impatient manner, the parent waits for the child to do something wrong, and then uses criticism, mockery, and intrusiveness to correct the child. Intrusiveness involves taking over for the child and it communicates a sense that the child must be incompetent.

These different types of parenting interactions are likely to be quite powerful for the child, particularly with fathers. In an edited book titled *Sons Writing About Their Fathers,* (Keyes, 1992), most of the contributors did not feel they knew their fathers very well, rarely expressed love toward them, and rarely received affection or understanding from them. Cristopher Hallowell wrote that when he was 6 or 7 years old, his father tried to teach him to build a wooden box, saying "If you can't build a box square, you can't build anything." When he built his first box, it was far from perfect. It wobbled and rolled, but, nonetheless, he was proud of his work. But his father, on examining his work, scowled and told him he didn't get it square and that he would never be a good builder. He wrote, "each time I lifted the top . . . never far away was a picture of my father's disapproving look" (Keyes, 1992, p. 17). Our data suggest that major effects exist in determining the social, affective, and cognitive development of children by whether fathers are emotion coaches for their children, and whether their style of parenting involves Scaffolding/praising or Derogatory parenting. The father's parenting is determined by his meta-emotion structure. We also discovered that the father's parenting and his interaction with his wife are completely parallel.

Summary of Our Results on Emotion Coaching

Our results in predicting the longitudinal course of children's emotional, social, and cognitive development were quite consistent. The children of emotion-coaching parents are better off as they develop. They are better able to regulate their own emotions, to not be disorganized by their negative feelings. They are better able to focus their attention (measured by Stroop performance scores). They have less negative interactions with their friends and other children at school. They whine less. They are seen more positively by their teachers. They are not as likely to develop behavior problems. They are more resistant to infectious illness. We predicted this relationship because part of our theorizing involves the child's regulatory physiology, and this involves the measurement of vagal tone. The vagus nerve is the tenth cranial nerve; it is the major parasympathetic nerve; it also innervates the thymus gland and the thymus makes T-cells. We discovered that children who have emotion coaching parents are on entirely different developmental trajectories than children who have emotion dismissing parents. At age 8, they have higher reading and mathematics scores in school, even controlling for their initial (age 5) intelligence.[1] This means that if two children have the same IQ, the one with emotion coaching parents will achieve more than the one with dismissing parents. This effect is mediated by regulatory physiology and the child's increased ability to focus attention.

The theoretical model we developed to account for these outcomes suggests that these effects are mediated through the development of the child's regulatory physiology. Our evidence suggests that the child's ability to self-soothe when upset physiologically by a negative event at age 5 is strongly predictive of the child's ability to down regulate negative emotions at age 8. Interestingly, the children of emotion-coached parents had a significantly higher increase in heart rate in response to parental criticism as well as a faster recovery. This is also interesting because usually a higher response is accompanied in the physiological literature with slower recov-

---

[1]To test this hypothesis, we performed a regression analysis forcing in the three IQ scales (WPPSII Block Design, Picture Completion, and Information Scaled Scores) before entering the mother's awareness of her own sadness in predicting the child's math scores, and in a second analysis before entering the father's coaching of the child's anger. The F-ratios for change were computed, as well as the partial correlations. For the prediction of the child's mathematics scores from the mother's awareness of her own sadness, the F-ratio for change was $F(4, 48) = 6.12$, $p < .05$ (partial correlation = 0.34). For the prediction of the child's reading-comprehension scores from the father's coaching of the child's anger, the F-ratio for change was $F(4, 44) = 9.41$, $p < .01$ (partial correlation = 0.37). For the prediction of the child's total score from both the mother's awareness of her own sadness and the father's coaching of the child's anger, the two variables were summed for the analysis; the F-ratio for change was $F(4, 45) = 4.13$, $p < .05$ (partial correlation = 0.29).

ery, not a faster recovery. The autonomic systems of these children are both responsive and labile as well as resilient. To summarize, we found that part of the effect of emotion coaching is mediated through physiological processes. The children of emotion-coaching parents have lower resting heart rates than the children of emotion-dismissing parents, and when they experience emotion their hearts recover more quickly. They are better able to soothe their bodies when they are upset. They carry around fewer stress-related hormones (adrenaline and cortisol) in their bodies.

We discovered that fathers are very important in the development of these regulatory processes in their children. Fathers can either do a great deal of harm to their children's emotional development (if they are derogatory) or a great deal of good (if they use Scaffolding/praising and are emotion coaching). Contrary to current thinking reflected in such popular books as *Fatherless America* (Blankenhorn, 1995; Popenoe, 1996), it's not just the father's presence that matters but how he is present that matters. A father who is emotionally engaged with his children also tends to be emotionally engaged with his wife.

One of our recent results assessed the extent to which the parenting variables can buffer children from the harmful effects of dysfunctional marital conflict and the harmful effects of marital dissolution itself. The harmful effects of both hostile marital conflict and of marital dissolution were quite dramatic in our data. We were quite amazed to find that children were totally buffered from the each negative effect of dysfunctional marital conflict and from marital dissolution for every outcome but the child's negative affectivity. Children are not buffered by these four buffering variables from feeling sad and anxious.

I have a theory about what mediates these effects. I think that when parents emotion coach their children's negative emotions while the children are having these emotions, the brain of the child experiences the emotion differently. I think that the emotional experience becomes a left-frontal or bilateral process rather than a right-frontal process. Usually negative emotions that are related to our withdrawal from the world like disgust, sadness, and fear are processed in the right frontal lobe. Emotions that are related to our engagement with the world, like amusement, interest, curiosity, joy, and (interestingly) anger, are processed in the left frontal lobe. The left hemisphere of the brain also contains major centers for language processing that could be engaged when parents help children verbally label their emotion. We think that when a withdrawal emotion is ordinarily just experienced, the processing that occurs on the right frontal lobe leads to physiological arousal (the heart beats faster and the blood flows faster after a ventricular contraction) because the right frontal lobe has direct connections with the limbic system and the brain stem, and from there to autonomic centers. When a parent helps a child with a withdrawal emotion the way emotion-coaching parents do, the left frontal lobe increases its activation and the nature of the emotional experience changes. The child experiences a greater sense of emotional control, approach, and well-being even while having the withdrawal emotion. This leads to the child being able to self-soothe the physiological arousal that usually accompanies this negative withdrawal emotion. The child becomes better at calming down and focusing attention, and subsequently continuing to engage with the world. We are currently planning studies to test these ideas.

THE FATHER'S "KID LOVE MAP"

In our intervention program for parents we have extended to idea of the marital Love Map to the *Kid Love Map*. The idea came from a case we saw for the Connie Chung television show a few years ago. The father was a physician who was the head of an intensive care unit for sick infants. He was extremely dedicated to his important work. He slept in the hospital an average of 20 nights a month. The marriage was in serious trouble and the couple was in marital therapy. This father was so disengaged from his family that when the film crew asked him what the name of the family dog they had had for two years was, he said he didn't know. He also didn't know where the back door to the couple's home was, and he did not know the names of his children's friends. This husband and father had become emotionally disengaged from his family. The therapy consisted of understanding how that had happened and changing it. The therapy (after 2 years of follow-up) was highly successful. Since then, we discovered that almost all mothers and some fathers actively create a "map" of their children's worlds, their daily activities, the flow of events in school, the names and characters of their friends, their preferences and so on. We find that creating this Kid Love Map is the beginning of more meaningful interactions with one's child.

WHY WOULD THE FATHER'S VARIABLES
BE SO IMPORTANT IN THESE DATA?

It is important to speculate about why the husband's and the father's data would be so important in creating models of both marital and child outcomes. One possibility of why the fathers' data is more important than the mothers' data in accounting for variation in child process and outcome variables is that there is less variability in the behaviors of mothers than the behavior of fathers. Indeed, we found that the variance of fathers' affective behaviors (Scaffolding/praising vs. Derogatory/critical) during our laboratory teaching task was 3 times that of mothers. If mothers tend to be more uniformly positive in this task, but fathers are more variable, then we can expect the behavior of fathers to be more powerful in our models. The situation was reversed in a recent study of family processes conducted in Greece. Roe (1980) conducted a study of the effects of spanking on empathy in 10-year-old Greek island children. In these islands, the fathers tend to be away most of the time, and their relationships with their children tends to be cold and punitive. However, there was great variability in the mother–child relationships. This is the reverse of the situation in our data. She found that spanking and fear of their fathers was characteristic of their low-empathic children (assessed by the Feshbach and Roe Situational Test). However, some of those subjects whose fathers were away most of the year scored high on empathy, even though spanking was common for mothers as well as fathers. The results are explained by the very positive relationship some of these children have with their mothers and the distant, ambivalent relationship they typically have with their fathers. The suggestion is that spanking within the context of a warm relationship with the mother was not deleterious.

Even if this type of explanation is sensible, we need to inquire about why there would be so much variability in the behavior of the men in our studies. The answer lies in studying the massive sociological changes that various forces in our current culture are bringing to bear on men. Within this context we can interpret one of our results as saying that those men who can accept influence from their wives and who are more emotionally engaged with their wives and with their children are way ahead of the game in the area of meaningful, satisfying, and lasting family relationships. But what are these forces that are polarizing the men in our samples?

The Changing American Family

The structure of the family in the United States has changed dramatically over the last 30 years. The Census Bureau noted that the traditional nuclear family defines only about half of families today (56% of White children live in a nuclear family, 26% of African American children, and 38% of Hispanic children). However, when the definition of nuclear family is expanded to include two-parent families (blended and adoptive families), 71% of children live in two-parent families. In 1960, the figure was 88% of children living in two-parent families. Among African Americans, 42% of children live in two-parent families today.

Part of these changes are due to the rising incidence of pregnancies outside of marriage. In 1950, only 4% of all births was to unmarried women. In 1980 the figure was 18.4% , in 1986, the figure was 23%, and in 1991, the figure was 29.5% (National Center for Health Statistics, 1993). The statistics for White American mothers were 11% in 1980 and 21.8% in 1991. In comparison, African American mothers had 55.2% of their babies out of marriage in 1980, and 67.9% in 1991. In 1991, Hispanic mothers had 39% of their babies outside of marriage.

Although most of these women eventually marry, in 1989, 28% of all households were headed by women, up from 21% in 1970. Among African Americans, the figure today is 40%, and for Hispanic families the figure today is 23% (Chadwick & Heson, 1992). About 50% of children who live in mother-only households are poor, whereas about 24% of children who live in father-only households are poor (U.S. Bureau of the Census, 1994). This is true despite the fact that 70% of these single-parent households have the parent working.

These demographic changes are a combination of rising divorce rates (two thirds of recent marriages are likely to experience a disruption; Martin & Bumpass, 1989), and the rising incidence of teenage pregnancy and an increase of births by unmarried women at every socioeconomic level.

The family has also changed dramatically as a function of the increasing proportion of women who work. In 1960, 36% of women worked, whereas the comparable figure in 1988 was 56%. If we consider women with young children, in 1950 12% of mothers worked, whereas today the figure is 57% (Chadwick & Heson, 1992). Many writers have commented on the fact that despite the high increase of two-earner households, the average family income has not increased very much since 1975 (Information Please Almanac [IPA], 1992).

The world today is a more dangerous place to raise children than it was 30 years ago. Today, every 21 minutes there is a murder in the United States and 1 violent crime every 17 seconds. Today, 1 of every 5 high school children carries a gun (*New York Times*, January 9, 1995). The number of arrests of males under 18 for all reasons increased from 1,260,123 in 1989 to 1,355,638 in 1990; the equivalent figures for females under age 18 were 351,541 in 1989 and 398,904 in 1990. There is a high incidence of violent crimes against teenagers, and this figure has been increasing over time (IPA, 1992, p. 824). Gang violence has become a national problem, with gang members armed with automatic assault weapons (IPA, 1992, p. 830), with its concomitant urban gang warfare, drive-by shootings, turf bullets, and killing of informers. In 1989, it was estimated that there were 1,500 youth gangs nationwide, with more than 120,500 members. The drug problem has become quite serious. The proportion of newborns exposed to drugs is between 11% and 18% in several surveys of hospitals conducted in 1988, and the proportion is increasing; the incidence and prevalence of drug abuse is also increasing (Information Please Almanac, 1992, p. 444). Children are under increased risk from drugs: In 1990, high school students spent 651 million dollars on all narcotics. In 1990, students in grades 6 through 12 consumed an estimated 6,173 pounds of cocaine and 74,956 pounds of marijuana.

The Changing American Father

There is converging evidence that the workplace does not support fathers in dual-career marriages spending time after work hours with the family. A recent *New York Times* article (October 12, 1994) summarized a number of these studies. Men in families whose wives stay home to take care of children earn 25% more than men whose wives work, and they are likely to get more promotions as well. One study, conducted by Stroh (Stroh, Brett, & Reilly, 1992) on 348 male managers at 20 Fortune 500 companies found that traditional fathers had 20% higher raises than the men with working wives. Reitman's (Schneer & Reitman, 1993) study of 231 men who received MBA degrees in the late 1970s, found, that men whose wives were at home with the children earned 25% more than men whose wives held jobs. Reitman's study found that men in more traditional marriages earned $24,140 more per year than men whose wives worked; salaries were for 1993, adjusted for number of hours worked, number of years experience, field of employment, and career interruptions. The adjusted salary increases of traditional men from 1987 to 1993 was 64%, compared to 45% for men whose wives worked. Traditional men worked an average of 53.7 hours per week, compared to 51.9 for men whose wives worked (difference was not significant). One suggestion made in the article by Reitman was that bosses, who tend to be older and are more likely to be in more traditional marriages, and are more likely to give raises and promotions to men who are more similar to themselves. It is also possible that men whose wives work are less aggressive in their motivation because they know they have another income coming in; however, there was no evidence to support this hypothesis in any study. Rather, it is more likely that men who do things like playing golf on Sundays with the boss or with clients, or who go out for a drink with the boss after work instead of going home are rewarded with promotions and higher raises (Brett, Stroh, & Reilly, 1993; Schneer & Reitman, 1993). These differences in salary are quite striking, particularly if one thinks of them in the context of the fact that in the United States, college graduates earn an average of only $12,000 more per year than high school graduates.

Where Have All the Fathers Gone?

It is a startling fact that after divorce, a very small proportion of fathers see their children more than once a year (Doherty, 1995). A number of studies suggest that the quantity and quality of fathering (but not mothering) is mediated through the quality of the marriage. This means that when the marriage is ailing, fathers tend to withdraw from their children as well as their wives, although this is not true for women. Many writers and legislators (including the President of the United States) have suggested that there is a national crisis in child support payments after divorce.

It was not always considered tolerable that fathers would vanish after divorce. In fact, until the evolution of the Tender Years Doctrine, the father traditionally got custody of the children after a divorce, and were considered morally responsible for their upbringing and education. Tibbits-Kleber, Howell, and Kleber (1987) wrote:

> In Roman society continuing through the Middle Ages, children were regarded as the father's property. . . . However, as a result of the influences of the Industrial Revolution, in addition to the importance and emphasis placed upon childhood, awards began to favor the mother. . . . The 1889 court opinion. . . . [led to the] "tender years doctrine," which was a presumption, not a law, [that] basically stated that "nature had given women a unique attachment to children and that the baby would thus receive better care from its mother." (p. 28)

The "tender years" were considered to be birth to age 7. The Tender Years Doctrine was gradually replaced by the guiding principle that custody awards are to be made with the "best interests of the child" in mind.

Iron John and the Fathers of the Past

The Hite report (Hite, 1987) asked men whether they had a close relationship with their fathers. The study, although not a representative sample, startlingly revealed that over 90% of men claimed that their relationships with their fathers were not close. This kind of result has been echoed in the cry of anguish in what Levant (1992) called the "Mythopoetic Men's Movement," represented, in part, by the writings of the poet Robert Bly (1990). The phrase "father hunger," initially introduced by Herzog and used by many of the writers of this movement, undeniably represents an echo of the great pain caused by the emotional absence of fathers in the United States in the past. Levant (1992) wrote:

> It is important to acknowledge Bly's and his associates' contributions, in tilling the barren soil of men's groups for many years, in successfully engaging large numbers of men in a process of reexamining masculinity, and in Bly's modeling (through openness about his own work on his relationship with his alcoholic father) the grieving process that many men need to go through in order to come to terms with their relationships with their own fathers. (p. 382)

Later in his paper, Levant described typical processes he observed in his groups with fathers in his Fatherhood Project. He wrote:

> One man would start to speak, bottom lip quivering, struggling to maintain control: "You know, the reason why I am here is so that my little son Jimmy will not grow up to feel as bad about me as I feel about my own dad." This would open the flood gates, and the men would pour out their stories and their grief about their own fathers: Never knowing their fathers; nor how their fathers felt as men; nor if their fathers ever really approved of them. This acutely painful feeling of father loss is very widespread and requires grief work to resolve. Bly's most significant accomplishment may have been to facilitate this process of grieving on a large scale. (1992, p. 39)

However, Levant critiqued the Mythopoetic Men's Movement. He described a weekend retreat he attended in 1991 led by Bly. In this weekend Bly (1992) urged men to "reject the path of the 'soft male,' which he views as feminist-inspired" (p. 383). Indeed, Bly wrote about marriage as follows:

> A contemporary man often assumes that a woman knows more about a relationship than he does, allows a woman's moods to run the house, assumes that when she attacks him, she is doing it "for his own good." Many marriages are lost that way. (p. 64)

Bly thus confounds emotional communication with dominance or power struggles, suggesting that confrontations in marriage be viewed as attacks and that men guard against letting a woman's moods run the house. Levant (1992) suggested that this movement is "not helpful, and potentially destructive" (p. 383). One reason Levant offered this appraisal is that "the essentialist thrust, which requires separation from women, is exactly the opposite of what is required. Men today . . . need a closer connection with women, not a more attenuated one" (p. 384).

The Issue Is Not Just Whether Fathers Are There but How They Are There

In the longitudinal study we are conducting with Jacobson on marital violence, a mother reported a story to us about her husband. One evening the father and his 5-year-old son were roughhousing in the living room when the boy accidentally got his lip hurt and began to cry. The father took the crying child into the kitchen and took out a meat cleaver and said to the boy, "If you don't stop crying, I'm going to cut your lips off!" The child stopped crying. This child was so terrified of his father that whenever the father asked the boy to do anything the boy did it immediately. Such behavior is, of course, quite unusual in 5-year-olds, and it speaks to the great fear that this child had of his father.

As we have noted in this book, fathers, even when they are present can either do a great deal of harm to their children or a great deal of good. Even fathers who are not as abusive to their children as the father we just described can hurt their children's development with Derogatory parenting. They can also do a great deal of good. Our point is simple: It is not enough for fathers to be in their children's lives. They need to be there as emotionally engaged and sensitive fathers. Our results are quite consistent with the writings of Parke (1981, 1996).

Sons Writing About Their Fathers

I referred to the edited book by Keyes (1992) on sons writing about their fathers. The book provides many poignant examples of father hunger. Most of the contributors did not feel they knew their fathers very well, rarely expressed love toward them, and rarely received affection or understanding from them. Son after son in this collection of essays said they never really felt close to their father, that they felt uncomfortable with their fathers, that they hated their fathers, that there was a strong sense of competition between them, and that they saw their fathers as terrifying, angry, authoritarian people. Moments of closeness were often mysterious and mixed, often obtained during a hunting expedition, or a sporting event. Sons seemed to yearn for their fathers to express pride and respect toward them as well as love and acceptance.

The so-called emotionally absent father has apparently been absent for his daughters as well as his sons (see Sharpe, 1994). The evidence seems fairly clear that for a large proportion of children today, their fathers have been distant emotionally, disrespectful, and derogatory, and often they have also been unkind and unaffectionate. Sometimes this has been a result of their attempts to toughen up and masculinize their boys and their discomfort with their girls.

However, Levant's (1988) review about education for fatherhood showed that the fathers of today are undergoing great changes. Levant's optimistic review cited support for a model of a reciprocal relationship between husband's participation in housework and wives' work over time. In the 1960s time-budget studies showed that men's participation in housework was much less than their wives (1 to 1.6 hours per day, compared to 7.6 to 8 hours per day for wives). In this era, husbands increased their participation in housework only slightly if their wives worked (Robinson, 1977; see Hawkins, Marshall, & Meiners, 1995). However, by the mid-1970s, husbands' and wives' participation in housework showed evidence of having changed: Husbands were spending 3.3 hours per day if their wives did not work and 3.9 hours per day if their wives did work, whereas working wives spent 4 hours per day and nonworking wives spent 6.8 hours per day on housework. Furthermore, and probably more important, the evidence suggests an increasing general trend in husbands' psychological involvement with their own families, placing the importance of their families toward their psychological well-being above that of work. Levant (1988) wrote "This trend (that men experience their family role as more psychologically significant than their work role) is so far-reaching that its ramifying effects have yet to be fully appraised" (p. 254). These changes may be occurring more in the area of child care than in the area of housework (N. Crouter, personal communication, 1996).

No doubt all these changes occurring simultaneously is part of the cause of the great variability of fathering in our data. This variability includes strong trends away from fathers being involved with their children's emotions. As the religious right gains strength in the United States, there is also a movement of some fathers toward authoritarian parenting in childrearing patterns of discipline. In the United States, the religious right has reacted to the child advocacy movement as if it were a movement of the government designed to take away what they claim are the rights of parents to use corporal punishment with their children, and especially to not have corporal punishment of children be viewed as child abuse. Thus, they are advocating corporal punishment of children as part of what they see as strengthening the family. An example is Christian ministry advocate Dennis Rainey, part of the *Family Life Today* series of books and other media presentations, who will do a week in his radio show on the positive aspects of spanking (B. Coffin, personal communication, 1995). This point of view is well-expressed in a recent manual from this school about spanking, which instructs parents in how to spank their children (see also Dobson, 1997). As part of this series of books there is a book by Chase (1982) titled, *Discipline Them, Love Them.* In the book "Method 2" is spanking, which is justified by biblical quotations that sparing the rod spoils the child. The book then goes on to suggest 5 "principles" and 7 steps about spanking, such as "Do not spank in anger" (p. 27). Chase (1982) then wrote:

A parent's conversation during these seven steps might sound like this: (Place the child on your lap). "Timmy, what did mommy say about throwing your ball in the house?" . . . "Yes, that's right, no ball playing in the house. But what did you do?" . . . "Yes, you disobeyed the rule. What happens when you disobey Mommy or Daddy?" . . . "That's right, we give you a spanking. We love you, Timmy, and want to help you learn how to obey and do what's right. A spanking now will help you to remember to do the right thing next time." (Lay the child over lap, and give a few brief, but painful swats on the buttocks *until Timmy stops his angry cry and cries softly.* Return child to your lap and hold him close. Be quiet a moment to allow for crying) . . . "Timmy,

are you sorry you disobeyed Mommy and threw the ball in the house?"
. . . "Good, I'm glad, and I forgive you. Now sweep up the broken glass
from the picture that fell down when the ball hit it. I'll hold the dustpan."
(p. 28, italics added)

This book appears to be part of parenting advice suggestive of the 18th-
century idea that the child's will must be broken as part of discipline. The
expected changes in the child's crying is quite reminiscent of this philosophy. It is not unlike the comments of a father in our study, who said:

F: . . . you teach people to do right or wrong at least as they perceive
      it. And you teach them to react as they feel they should and not
      be ashamed for it. . . . And if they do something wrong to take the
      consequences for it. Dawn picks her nose, I've told her many, many
      months ago, that every time I see her finger in her nose, that I'm
      going to slap her hand.

I: Um-hmm.

F: Slap the back of her hand. And I used to grab her hand and hold
      it and slap it, you know, and sometimes pretty hard even. Now I
      said, Dawn, "What did you just do?" She says, "Put my finger in my
      nose." (He imitates a scared child's voice.) And I said, "What do
      we do then?" She says, "Slap my hand." And I said, "Why don't you
      put it out there then," and she holds it out and I slap her hand.

Another force pushing men toward more authoritarian family patterns
is the "Promise Keepers" movement. This is a fundamentalist Christian
movement of many hundreds of thousands of men. It was organized by
former University of Colorado football coach Bill McCartney. A recent
article on the movement by Waggenheim (1995) quoted from a manual
that these men are issued in "instructing husbands how to reclaim their
manhood." The manual read:

The first thing to do is to sit down with your wife and say something like
this: "Honey, I've made a terrible mistake. I've given you my role. I gave up
leading this family and I forced you to take my place. Now I must reclaim
that role." Don't misunderstand what I'm saying here. I'm not suggesting
that you *ask* for your role back. I'm urging you to *take it back*. If you simply
ask for it, your wife is likely to say, "Look, for the last ten years, I've had to
raise the kids, look after the house, and pay the bills. I've had to get a job
and still keep up my duties in the home. I've had to do my job *and* yours.
You think I'm just going to turn everything back over to you?" Your wife's
concerns may be justified. Unfortunately, however, there can be no compromise here. If you're going to lead, you must lead. Listen. Be sensitive.
Treat the lady gently and lovingly. But *lead*. (Waggenhein, 1995, p. 80)

The forces pushing fathers toward authoritarian parenting are not limited to the religious right. For example, as Levant noted, the Men's Movement has not advocated that men become more emotionally sensitive to their children. In fact the Men's Movement has suggested that men avoid becoming *feminized,* by which they mean emotionally more expressive and responsive. This is related to a macho reaction we see in our sample against what is perceived as women's approach to emotion. For example, consider the following excerpt from a meta-emotion interview from the father we just quoted as having said "every time I see her finger in her nose, that I'm going to slap her hand."

F: You'll find that I'm very cold in this whole thing, in this whole survey, you'll find that I don't react the way most people, especially my wife.

I: Hmm.

F: My wife is exceptionally emotional.

I: Hmm.

F: That's one of our real problems too. Of course you didn't ask any questions about that, but she is highly emotional and I'm very unemotional.

I: So you have different styles.

F: I cry at my grandmother's and grandfather's funerals and every once in a while a movie. (Laughs.)

I: Um-hmm.

F: But she cries over everything. You know, she can sit and watch a movie and blubber through the whole thing.

I: Um-hmm.

F: You know, she sees a dead animal beside the road, she's an animal lover, she wants cats, I'd just as soon shoot them, but, you know, that type of thing, she gets real, real affectionate over that. That goes back to our daughter too. You know the two of us have a harshness and a leniency.

I: Right.

Misogyny plays a role in some of these forces that are attempting to influence men. To the extent that the advice of the mythopoetic movement leads to dismissing children's emotions and more derogatory parenting, it is potentially harmful to children. These attitudes may be malleable. Our data suggest that fathers having some education at the college level was significantly (but not strongly) related to the likelihood of his awareness of low intensity sadness and anger in his children and to his being an emotion coach ($r = .32$, $p < .01$, and $r = .24$, $p < .05$, respectively).

On the other hand, in addition to Levant's reviews, Schwartz's (1994) book, *Peer Marriage,* has suggested that the opposite phenomenon is at work. Some men are moving toward a far less authoritarian and more emotionally involved stance toward their children. Many men are establishing equalitarian relationships with their wives in which they play an equal and active role in household work and child care. Schwartz suggested that these men pay a price for having this kind of marriage; their careers are not as well-developed as the careers of traditional men. She also suggested that their sex lives may not be as satisfying as those of traditional men. However, she also suggested that there are great rewards that come from emotional connection with spouse and children for these men who have peer marriages.

No doubt some of these factors are responsible for the great variability in fathering (compared to mothering) in our data. In our analyses of variance the test for inhomogeneity of variance in parenting across parents was always statistically significant. In our data, for derogation alone, fathers had three times the variance of mothers. The Greek Island Study of Roe (1980) suggests an analogous picture, but one in which the greater variability was in mothering, and mothers accounted for great variance in child outcome (a measure of child empathy). In the Greek Islands, the fathers are described uniformly as harsh, cold, and distant. Mothers, on the other hand, are described as quite variable, with some mothers compensating for the father's distance by having a close relationship with their children. In this case we might expect that mothers have the potential to account for more of the variance in child outcome than fathers. Perhaps a similar process is occurring in the United States today, with the largest variance in fathers rather than mothers.

Indeed, when we examine the effects of mothers in modern Toronto when an extremely wide range of families is considered, the effects of variations in mothering is quite large. Pepler (1995) recently reported the results of a study of mothers who were either homeless, were recruited from battered women's shelters, or came from intact two-parent families. A significant proportion of the variance in the development of psychopathology in children was accounted for by variation in mothering (see also Pepler, King, & Byrd, 1995).

Thus, converging lines of evidence suggest that fathers in the United States and Canada may be undergoing increasing polarization over time. The forces that mediate this change involve the increased stresses on families, the loss of a clear breadwinner role as a greater percentage of women pursue not just work but meaningful careers, the increased pressure on fathers from the workplace to avoid family life and become workaholic, and the increased pressure fathers feel from within due to their own disappointments with their fathers and their own father hunger, and the increased value that today's fathers are placing on family life compared to work.

The changes in fathering occurring today have led some writers such as Levant (1992) to propose a new ethic for fathers, one that is both masculine and emotionally connected. Levant called for a program that increases men's abilities to be empathic and emotionally expressive, increasing men's abilities to experience a wide range of emotions (Levant called this dealing with men's relative "alexithymia," and says that for many men at first their main emotions are "stress" and "anger," but that after the group experience they report more of the "vulnerable" emotions of sadness and fear; Levant, personal communication, 1994), and men's greater expression of anger, rage and violence. These skills form the basis for Levant's program for creating involved and emotional fathers instead of distant and detached fathers (Levant & Kelly, 1989). Levant (1992) wrote:

> To help men overcome alexithymia, we first worked with them to develop a vocabulary for emotions, particularly the vulnerable ones, such as hurt, sadness, disappointment, rejection, abandonment, and fear, as well as the tender ones, such as warmth, affection, closeness, and appreciation. We then asked the men to keep an Emotional Response Log, noting when they experienced a feeling that they could identify, or a buzz that they became aware of, and what circumstances led up to that feeling or buzz. The logs were then discussed in the group, with emphasis on learning how to apply verbal labels to emotional states. *We also taught men to tune into their feelings through watching and discussing immediate play-backs of role-plays designed to engender feelings. By pointing out the nonverbal cues and asking such questions as "What were your feelings, Don, when you grimaced in that last segment?", fathers learned how to access the ongoing flow of emotions within. The video play-back was so effective at times that we came to refer to it as the "mirror to a man's soul."* (p. 389, italics added)

However, despite our conclusions about fathering becoming polarized today, the overwhelming trend is still for fathers to spend relatively little time with their children compared to mothers. A recent study (Rustia & Abbott, 1993) concluded that the "culture of fatherhood has changed more rapidly that the conduct of fatherhood," meaning that fathers' role performance lagged behind their rhetoric.

CONCLUSIONS

In the past we have tended to minimize the contribution of men to the well-being of marriages and families. It is quite clear from these studies that men play a vital role (but not all of the role) in the stability and eventual happiness success of marriages and families, as well as in their children's physical, emotional, social, and cognitive development. It is clear to us that we are in the middle of an historic worldwide transition in the economic, political, and psychological empowerment of women, one that is long overdue, and one that is still struggling with misogyny. Increasingly, women will not continue to put up with the particular circle of hell that a demeaning marriage has always entailed for them. As part of these changes, in many western industrialized societies men have lost the sole breadwinner role, and men today are at a loss as to what is expected of them in families. There are no manuals, and there is no formal training in schools. In Sweden the government has been encouraging fathers to take paid leaves after the birth of a child, and instruction on how to play with your baby is now a part of birth preparation training for both fathers and mothers (Hedenbro, personal communication, 1996). But in the United States, the concern voiced by both political parties in presidential elections is pure rhetoric. Coontz's (1992) book, *The Way We Never Were*, demonstrates convincingly that this rhetoric is reminiscent of the Gilded Age of the past century, in which the false myths of a "strong family that stood on its own feet" were extolled politically, backed only by a moralistic approach against the problems of the poor, and a policy that militated against social action that would provide real governmental support to families.

There is no question that our research suggests that those husbands who have a fondness and admiration system for their wives, who actively build a cognitive map of their wife's world and of the relationship, who turn toward their wives on an everyday basis, and who can accept influence from their wives, are clearly way ahead of the game, as long as they are wedded to women who soften their startup of the conflict and do not reciprocate low-intensity negative affect. Our longitudinal research with newlyweds suggests that these men also tend to sail through the transition to parenthood, an that they also become emotionally involved fathers. Not only are their marriages more stable and more satisfying, but their children are on an entirely different developmental trajectory, one that affects their cognitive, affective, social, and physical development. We do not know very much about these men, except to say that, as far as we can tell at the moment they do not seem different from all the other men we also study. We do not yet know how to change the men who are not like them, but that is clearly the next step for both intervention design and for the construction of theory.

REFERENCES

Aries, E. (1974). Interaction patterns and themes of male, female, and mixed groups. *Dissertation Abstracts International, 35*(6-B), 3084.

Aries, E. (1976). Interaction patterns and themes of male, female, and mixed groups. *Small Group Behavior, 7*, 7–18.

Aries, E. J. (1982). Verbal and nonverbal behavior in single-sex and mixed-sex groups: Are traditional sex-roles changing? *Psychological Reports, 51,* 127–134.

Aries, E. J., Gold, C., & Weigel, R. H. (1983). Dispositional and situational influences on dominance behavior in small groups. *Journal of Personality and Social Psychology, 44,* 779–786.

Babcock, J. C., Waltz, J., Jacobson, N. S., & Gottman, J. M. (1993). Power and violence: The relationship between communication patterns, power discrepancies and domestic violence. *Journal of Consulting and Clinical Psychology, 61*(1), 40–50.

Bhavnagri, N. P., & Parke, R. D. (1991). Parents as direct facilitators of children's peer relationships: Effects of age of child and sex of parent. *Journal of Social and Personal Relationships, 8*(3), 423–440.

Birchler, G., Weiss, R., & Vincent, J. (1975). Multimethod analysis of social reinforcement exchange between maritally distressed and nondistressed spouse and stranger dyads. *Journal of Personality and Social Psychology, 31,* 349–360.

Blankenhorn, D. (1995). *Fatherless America: Confronting our most urgent social problems.* New York: Basic Books.

Bly, R. (1990). *Iron John: A book about men.* Reading, MA: Addison-Wesley.

Bly, R. (1992). The hunger for the king in a time with no father. In C. Scull (Ed.), *Fathers, sons, and daughters* (pp. 60–71). New York: Putnam.

Booth, C. L., Rose-Krasnor, L., & Rubin, K. H. (1991). Relating preschoolers' social competence and their mothers' parenting behaviors to early attachment security and high-risk status. *Journal of Social and Personal Relationships, 8*(3), 363–382.

Bower, T. G. R. (1989). *The rational infant.* New York: Freeman.

Brett, J. M., Stroh, L. K., & Reilly, A. H. (1993). Pulling up roots in the 1990s: Who's willing to relocate? *Journal of Organizational Behavior, 14,* 49–60.

Buck, R. (1977). Nonverbal communication of affect in preschool children. *Journal of Personality and Social Psychology, 35,* 225–236.

Cassidy, J., Parke, R. D., Butkovsky, L., & Braungart, J. M. (1992). Family–peer connections: The role of emotional expressiveness within the family and children's understanding of emotion. *Child Development, 63*(3), 603–618.

Chadwick, B. A., & Heson, T. (1992). *Statistical handbook on the American family.* New York: Oryx.

Chase, B. N. (1982). *Discipline them, love them.* Elgin, IL: David Cook Publishing Co.

Christensen, A., & Heavey, C. L., (1990). Gender and social structure in the demand/withdraw pattern, *Journal of Personality and Social Psychology, 59*(1), 73–81.

Christensen, A., & Shenk, J. L. (1991). Communication, conflict, and psychological distance in distressed, clinic, and divorcing couples. *Journal of Consulting and Clinical Psychology, 59*(3), 458–463.

Coan, J., Gottman, J., Jacobson, N. S., Babcock, J., & Rushe, R. (in press). Men rejecting influence from women in violent marriages. *Violence and Victims.*

Cohn, D. A., Patterson, C. J., & Christopoulos, C. (1991). The family and children's peer relationships. *Journal of Social and Personal Relationships, 8*(3), 315–346.

Cook, J., Tyson, R., White, J., Rushe, R., Gottman, J., & Murray, J. (1995). Mathematics of marital conflict: Qualitative dynamic modeling of marital interaction. *Journal of Family Psychology, 9,* 110–130.

Coontz, S. (1992). *The way we never were.* New York: Basic Books.

Cowan, P. A., & Cowan, C. P. (1992) Becoming a family: Research and intervention. In I. Sigel & A. Brody (Eds.), Family research. Hillsdale, NJ: Lawrence Erlbaum Associates.

Dickstein, S., & Parke, R. D. (1988). Social referencing in infancy: A glance at fathers and marriage. *Child Development, 59,* 506–511.

Dobash, R. E., & Dobash, R. P. (1979). *Violence against wives: A case against the patriarch.* New York: Free Press.

Dobson, J. (1997). *The new dare to discipline.* Wheaton, IL: Tyndale House.

Doherty, W. J. (1995). The vanishing American father. In W. J. O'Neill, Jr. (Ed.), *Family: The first imperative.* Cleveland, OH: The William J. & Dorothy K. O'Neill Foundation.

Dutton, D. G. (1988). *The domestic assault of women: Psychological and criminal justice perspectives.* Boston: Allyn & Bacon.

Ekman, P. (1984). Expression and the nature of emotion. In K. R. Scherer & P. Ekman (Eds.), *Approaches to emotion.* Hillsdale, NJ: Lawrence Erlbaum Associates.

Fisher, P. A., & Fagot, B. I. (1993). Negative discipline in families: A multidimensional risk model. *Journal of Family Psychology, 7*(2), 250–254.

Fivush, R. (1991). Gender and emotion in mother–child conversations about the past. *Journal of Narrative & Life History, 1*(4), 325–341.

Garfield, S. L., & Bergin, A. E. (1971). Therapeutic conditions and outcome. *Journal of Abnormal Psychology, 77,* 108–114.

Ginott, H. (1994). *Between parent and child.* New York: Avon. (Original work published 1965)

Gottman, J. M. (1979). *Marital interaction: Experimental investigations.* New York: Academic Press.

Gottman, J. M. (1994). *What predicts divorce?* Hillsdale, NJ: Lawrence Erlbaum Associates.

Gottman, J. M. (1990). How marriages change. In G. R. Patterson (Ed.), *New directions in family research: Depression and aggression.* Hillsdale, NJ: Lawrence Erlbaum Associates.

Gottman, J. M. (Ed.). (1996). *What predicts divorce?: The measures.* Hillsdale, NJ: Lawrence Erlbaum Associates.

Gottman, J. M., & Katz, L. F. (1989). The effects of marital discord on young children's peer interaction and health. *Developmental Psychology, 25,* 373–381.

Gottman, J. M., & Levenson, R. W. (1992). Marital processes predictive of later dissolution: Behavior, physiology and health. *Journal of Personality and Social Psychology, 63,* 221–233.

Gottman, J. M., & Parker, J. (Eds.). (1986). *Conversations of friends.* New York: Cambridge University Press.

Gottman, J. M., & Roy, A. K. (1990). *Sequential analysis: A guide for behavioral researchers.* New York: Cambridge University Press.

Guerney, B., Jr. (1982). *Relationship enhancement.* San Francisco: Jossey-Bass.

Hallowell, C. (1992). Daddy. In R. Keyes (Ed.), *Sons on fathers* (p. 17). New York: Harper-Collins.

Hawkins, A. J., Marshall, C. M., & Meiners, K. M. (1995). Exploring wives' sense of fairness about family work: An initial test of the distributive justice framework. *Journal of Family Issues, 16,* 693–721.

Heavey, C. L., Layne, C., & Christensen, A. (1993). Gender and conflict structure in marital interaction: A replication and extension. *Journal of Consulting and Clinical Psychology, 61910,* 16–27.

Hite, S. (1987). *The Hite Report: Women and love—a cultural revolution in progress.* New York: Knopf.

Holtzworth-Munroe, A., & Jacobson, N. S. (1985). Causal attributions of married couples: When do they search for causes? What do they conclude when they do? *Journal of Personality and Social Psychology, 48,* 1398–1412.

Hotaling, G. T., & Sugarman, D. B. (1986). An analysis of risk markers in husband to wife violence: The current state of knowledge. *Violence and Victims 1*(2), 101–124.

Information Please Almanac. (1992). New York: McGraw Hill.

Jacobson, N. S., & Addis, M. E. (1993). Research on couples and couple therapy: What do we know? Where are we going? *Journal of Consulting and Clinical Psychology, 61,* 85–93.

Jacobson, N. S., & Margolin, G. (1979). *Marital therapy.* New York: Brunner-Mazel.

Kerig, P. K., Cowan, P. A., & Cowan, C. P. (1993). Marital quality and gender differences in parent–child interaction. *Developmental Psychology, 29*(6), 931–939.

Keyes, R. (1992). *Sons on fathers.* New York: HarperCollins.

Krokoff, L. J. (1985). The anatomy of negative affect in working-class marriages. *Dissertation Abstracts International, 45*(7-A), 2041.

Ladd, G. W., & Hart, C. H. (1992). Creating informal play opportunities: Are parents' and preschoolers' initiations related to children's competence with peers? *Developmental Psychology, 28*(6), 1179–1187.

Lamb, M. E. (Ed.). (1981). *The role of the father in child development.* New York: Wiley.

Lamb, M. E. (Ed.). (1986). *The father's role: Applied perspectives.* New York: Wiley.

Lamb, M. E. (Ed.). (1987). *The father's role: Cross-cultural perspectives.* Hillsdale, NJ: Lawrence Erlbaum Associates.

Levant, R. F. (1988). Education for fatherhood. In P. Bronstein & C. Cowan (Eds.), *Fatherhood today: Men's changing role in the family* (pp. 253–275). New York: Wiley.

Levant, R. F. (1992). Toward the reconstruction of masculinity. *Journal of Family Psychology, 5,* 379–402.

Levant, R. F., & Kelly, J. (1989). *Between father and child.* New York: Penguin.

Levenson, R. W., Carstensen, L. L., & Gottman, J. M. (1994). Influence of age and gender on affect, physiology, and their interrelations: A study of long-term marriages. *Journal of Personality and Social Psychology, 67*(1), 56–68.

Maccoby, E. E. (1990). Gender and relationships: A developmental account. *American Psychologist, 45*(4), 513–520.

Maccoby, E. E., & Martin, J. A. (1983). Socialization in the context of the family: Parent–child interaction. In E. M. Hetherington (Ed.), *Handbook of child psychology* (Vol. 4, pp. 1–102). New York: Wiley.

MacDonald, K. (1987). Parent–child physical play with rejected, neglected, and popular boys. *Developmental Psychology, 23*(5), 705–711.

MacDonald, K., & Parke, R. D. (1984). Bridging the gap: Parent–child play interaction and peer interactive competence. *Child Development, 55,* 1265–1277.

Markman, H. J., Floyd, F. J., Stanley, S. M., & Storaasli, R. D. (1988). Prevention of marital distress: A longitudinal investigation. *Journal of Consulting and Clinical Psychology, 56,* 210–217.

Markman, H. J., Renick, M. J., Floyd, F. J., & Stanley, S. M. (1993). Preventing marital distress through communication and conflict management training: A 4- and 5-year follow-up. *Journal of Consulting and Clinical Psychology, 61,* 70–77.

Martin, T. C., & Bumpass, L. (1989). Recent trends in marital disruption. *Demography, 26,* 37–51.

Mulhern, R. K., & Passman, R. H. (1981). Parental discipline as affected by the sex of the parent, the sex of the child, and the child's apparent responsiveness to discipline. *Developmental Psychology, 17*(5), 604–613.

Murphy, C. M., & Meyer, S. L. (1991). Gender, power and violence in marriage. *The Behavior Therapist, 14*(4), 95–100.

National Center for Health Statistics (1992). Advance report of final statistics, *Monthly vital statistics report, 42, No. 3* [Suppl.]. Hyattsville, MD: Public Health Service.

New York Times. (1995, Janurary 9).

New York Times. (1994, October 12).

Nisbett, R. E. (1993). Violence and U.S. regional culture. *American Psychologist, 48*(4), 441–449.

Notarius, C. I., Benson, P. R., & Sloane, D. (1989). Exploring the interface between perception and behavior: An analysis of marital interaction in distressed and nondistressed couples. *Behavioral Assessment, 11,* 39–64.

Olson, D. H., & Ryder, R. G. (1970). Inventory of marital conflicts (IMC): An experimental interaction procedure. *Journal of Marriage and the Family, 32,* 443–448.

Parke, R. D. (1981). *Fathers.* Cambridge, MA: Harvard University Press.

Parke, R. D. (1996). *Fatherhood.* Cambridge, MA: Harvard University Press.

Patterson, G. R. (1982). *Coercive family process.* Eugene, OR: Castalia Press.

Pepler, D. (1995). *Varieties of mothering.* Presentation at the Society for Research in Child Development Meeting, Indianapolis, IN, April 1995.

Pepler, D., King, G., Craig, W., & Byrd, B. (1995). The development and evaluation of a multisystem social skills group training program for aggressive children. *Child & Youth Care Forum, 24,* 297–313.

Pettit, G. S., Harrist, A. W., & Bates, J. E. (1991). Family interaction, social cognition and children's subsequent relations with peers at kindergarten. *Journal of Social and Personal Relationships, 8,* 383–402.

Popenoe, D. (1996). *Life without father: Compelling new evidence that fatherhood and marriage are indispensable for the good of children and society.* New York: Free Press.

Pratt, M. W., Kerig, P. K., Cowan, P. A., & Cowan, C. P. (1992). Family worlds: Couple satisfaction, parenting style, and mothers' and fathers' speech to young children. *Merrill-Palmer Quarterly. 38*(2), 245–262.

Putallaz, M., Costanzo, P. R., & Smith, R. B. (1991). Maternal recollections of childhood peer relationships: Implications for their children's social competence. *Journal of Social and Personal Relationships, 8*(3), 403–422.

Roe, K. V. (1980). Toward a contingency hypothesis of empathy development. *Journal of Personality and Social Psychology, 39*(5), 991–994.

Robinson, B. (1977). Sex-typed attitudes, sex-typed contingency behaviors and personality characteristics of male caregivers. *Dissertation Abstracts International, 37,* 5003.

Rustia, J. G., & Abbott, D. (1993). Father involvement in infant care: Two longitudinal studies. *International Journal of Nursing Studies, 30,* 467–476.

Schneer, J. A., & Reitman, F. (1993). Effects of alternate family structures on managerial career paths. *Academy of Management Journal, 36,* 830–843.

Schwartz, P. (1994). *Peer marriage.* New York: Free Press.

Sharpe, S. (1994). *Fathers and daughters.* New York: Routledge.

Starrels, M. E. (1994). Gender differences in parent–child relations. *Journal of Family Issues, 15*(1), 148–165.

Straus, M. A., Gelles, R. J., & Steinmetz, S. J. (1980). *Behind closed doors: Violence in the American family.* Garden City, NY: Anchor Books.

Stroh, L. K., Brett, J. M., & Reilly, A. H. (1992). All the right stuff: A comparison of female and male managers' career progression. *Journal of Applied Psychology, 77,* 251–260.

Tannen, D. (1990a). Gender differences in typical coherence: Creating involvement in best friends' talk. *Discourse Processes, 13,* 73–90.

Tannen, D. (1990b). *You just don't understand: Women and men in conversation.* New York: William Morrow & Co.

Tibbits-Kleber, A. L., Howell, R. J., & Kleber, D. J. (1987). Joint custody: A comprehensive review. *Bulletin of the American Academy of Psychiatry and the Law, 15,* 27–43.

U.S. Bureau of the Census. (1994). Live births, deaths, marriages, and divorce: 1950 to 1992. *Statistical Abstract of the United States: 1994* (114th ed.). Washington, DC.

Waggenheim, J. (1995). Among the promise keepers. *New Age Journal, March/April, 1995,* 78–130.

Weiss, R. L. (1980). Strategic behavioral marital therapy: Toward a model for assessment and intervention. In J. P. Vincent (Ed.), *Advance in family intervention, assessment and theory* (Vol. 1, pp. 229–271). Greenwich, CT: JAI Press.

Chapter 10

Gender, Power, and Emotional Expression: Social and Historical Contexts for a Process Model of Men in Marriages and Families

Scott Coltrane
University of California, Riverside

In the last several decades, social science research has brought us closer to understanding the internal dynamics and social significance of marriages and families. As this volume demonstrates, however, much of this research has focused on women and children, with the role of men in families relegated to the background. Because fathers' actions were assumed to be relatively unimportant to child development, men were left out of many psychological studies of parenting practices before the 1970s (Parke, 1981, 1996). Similarly, because men's proper family role was assumed to be that of economic provider, many sociological studies of household functioning did not collect information from husbands, even when the research focus was supposedly on family power (Bernard, 1981; Blood & Wolfe, 1960). More recent family studies have more often included men, although few have measured precisely what men actually do, and even fewer have been methodologically or theoretically sophisticated enough to determine why men act the way they do or what potential influence their actions have on wives, children, or the larger society.

The research of Gottman and his colleagues at the University of Washington provides a major corrective to the previous lack of detailed empirical data on the behavior of men in marriages and its association with marital stability and child development. The psychologists conducting this multi-faceted research program deserve praise for generating detailed substantive findings and for developing and testing theories about men in families. As a sociologist, I am not qualified to comment on the clinical and physiological aspects of their work. Nevertheless, I can evaluate the sociological implications of their work, and place some of their psychological findings in broader social context.

Cross-disciplinary dialogues are often limited by conflicting paradigmatic assumptions, and tend to focus on what might have been done differently. In the comments that follow, I adopt such an outsider's perspective—puzzling over methodological choices, challenging analytical inferences, questioning the significance of findings, and comparing study results to others from historical, sociological, and cultural studies. I appreciate the precision of Gottman's data and the elegance of the study design. I offer these comments as a way to better understand and evaluate the results.

Gottman's research relies on multiple methods of data collection (i.e., observations, self-reports, videotaping, interviews, questionnaires, etc.); multiple types of data (i.e., quantitative and qualitative; structured and unstructured; behavioral and attitudinal; physiological [cardiovascular, respiratory, & skin conductance], psychological, demographic, and social, etc.); multiple sources of data (i.e., self-report, observer evaluations, video coders, teacher ratings, parent/spouse ratings, achievement tests, polygraphs and electrocardiograms, etc.); multiple sites and time periods (i.e., both cross-sectional and longitudinal designs, with data collected in the home and at the laboratory); and multiple comparison groups (i.e., sample subjects grouped according to couple's domestic violence or marital satisfaction). The basic procedure in most of these studies has been to bring subjects into a research laboratory and have husbands and wives discuss and attempt to solve continuing disagreements in their marriage. These conflict interactions are videotaped and coded by student assistants, down to the level of small differences in verbal and nonverbal expression. Several years later, subjects are recontacted and additional information is collected. Massive amounts of data are generated using instruments with proven psychometric reliability.

Quantitative data on husband–wife interaction sequences is then correlated with various other demographic, psychological, health, and physiological data, and used to predict later outcomes such as divorce. More recently, the research also includes parent–child interaction codes and parenting philosophy variables that are correlated with child outcomes as measured by teacher evaluations, achievement tests, and parental reports. Typically, subject couples are divided into subgroups ($n = 15$–60) on the basis of responses to marital adjustment questionnaires or violence self-reports, and comparisons are then made between the interaction patterns of stable and unstable couples, or more recently, between domestically violent, distressed but nonviolent, and happy and nonviolent groups (e.g., Babcock, Waltz, Jacobson, & Gottman, 1993; Cordova, Jacobson, Gottman, Rushe, & Cox, 1993; Gottman, 1993; Jacobson, Gottman, Waltz, Rushe,

Babcock, & Holtzworth-Munroe, 1994). Using structural equation modeling and sequential analysis, Gottman and his colleagues have been able to isolate many different associations between laboratory interaction patterns and outcome variables, and to compare these associations across subject groupings.

As noted in Gottman's chapter for this volume, major findings relating to marriage include that divorce is associated with Negative Affect Reciprocity in laboratory interactions: The wife complains or criticizes; the husband responds with belligerence, contempt, or defensiveness; the wife gets more angry or cries; and the husband withdraws. Husbands who have been physically violent toward their wives are found to be more likely than others to rapidly and suddenly escalate negative emotions, a pattern labeled *rejects wife's influence.* In contrast, stable and happy couples are less defensive and more empathetic: "the wife expresses her complaints with a 'softened startup' and then the husband both accepts influence and he also de-escalates whatever low-intensity negative affect the wife expresses" (p. 162). Concerning parenting, Gottman finds that fathers' interactions with their wives and children are parallel: Husbands in stable, happy marriages are more aware of their own emotions (especially sadness), are empathetic with their children as well as wives, and tend to accept children's expression of anger and sadness more than other fathers. The emotional coaching that these fathers provide for their children parallels their scaffolding/praising, and correlates with enhanced cognitive, emotional, and social development in the children.

Gottman suggests that these findings reflect effective meta-emotional philosophies and marital interaction styles that create strong marriages and well-adjusted children. In this chapter, he also speculates about the links between gender socialization, emotional self-regulation, physiological functioning, marital happiness, effective parenting, and desirable child outcomes. One of his most important findings is that what husbands and fathers do in, and for, families is more important than their presence. He and his colleagues are now working toward developing specific interventions and eventually running clinical trials that will test some of their hypotheses about how to improve marital and family processes.

I find Gottman's ambitious and productive research program to be very helpful in describing how men interact with their wives and children, and in formulating questions about the impact of various behavioral and emotional patterns. His careful and creative multimethod, multitopic approach allows us to move beyond abstract theories and superficial self-reports of how men act in families. Nevertheless, we should be aware of some of the limitations of these data and guard against making unfounded inferences or unwarranted generalizations. In addition, there are some important theoretical and political issues that Gottman's research does not address.

In the comments that follow, I address these issues by focusing on the importance of gender and power to the perception and regulation of emotional experience. I suggest that we can better understand men's interactions within marriages and families by analyzing the political, cultural, and historical contexts in which they occur.

METHODOLOGICAL ISSUES

Inferences from multimethod, multitopic research of this type are limited by characteristics of the sample, the subgroup divisions and comparisons being made, the laboratory procedures used, the measurement strategies employed, the selection of variables for final multivariate equations, and many other research design issues. For example, in similar research attempting to assess the impact of family processes on children's development under conditions of economic distress during the midwest farm crisis of the 1980s, it was found that individual perceptions of economic pressure were much better predictors of marital and parental dysfunction and deleterious child outcomes than objective measures of economic hardship at the household level (Conger & Elder, 1994). This finding does not mean that income loss plays no causal role in the dysfunctional interactions of distressed families, nor that we should try to help impoverished couples by convincing them they are not so poorly off. How people interpret and react to income or asset loss is clearly important to family functioning, but our theoretical models and intervention strategies ought to focus on the fundamental causal problem—in this case, widespread and unprecedented farm foreclosures. Like Gottman's studies, the midwest farm family studies gathered a wealth of observational and self-report data on marital interactions and parenting practices, and associated it with various child outcomes using state-of-the art structural equation modeling. It is important to note, however, that neither the perception of economic pressure nor the negative affect exchanged in distressed families fundamentally caused the negative child outcomes that ensued. The real culprit was national and global economic structuring leading to a massive number of foreclosures against family farms.

In general, Gottman, like Conger and Elder (1994) exercises caution in making causal attributions based on the complex data discussed in his chapter. For example, he finds that positive affect and de-escalation in the lab conflict sessions are associated with positive marital outcomes, but he acknowledges that these behaviors do not exist in isolation. Instead, he postulates that dysfunctional conflict resolution techniques observed in the lab probably have roots in the ways that couples relate in everyday nonconflict situations, and recommends ritualizing stress-reduction daily conversations rather than just training for empathy in conflict situations. In other cases, causal attributions, although qualified, are made with less caution: "what is functional is for people to be able to be nondefensive and empathetic even when they feel they are being attacked by their spouse" (p. 157); "the way the problem-solving conversation starts is likely to be critical, and this appears to be a role that women typically determine"; and "the Startup model represents our best guess of what the wife's contribution may be toward the dissolution of marriages" (p. 56).

Even though a large amount of observational data has been collected from different time points, structural equation models cannot tell us what causes what in real life. To say that an observed interaction sequence, or a self-report measure, predicts divorce or marital stability only means that the two variables are associated, not that one causes the other. Thus, the finding that "an emotion-coaching meta-emotion structure was related to greater marital stability and to greater marital satisfaction" (p. 171) implies only that they co-vary, not that if one were to coach people to focus on emotions in this way that it would lead to better marital relations. Gottman claims that "the father's parenting is *determined* by his meta-emotion structure" (p. 173, italics added), but I would just as readily interpret the self-reported emotional philosophy as an account that the father constructs in response to his own parenting practices, to his wife's views, and other social situational factors. As noted in the following section, I presume that many supposedly independent variables in these studies (such as meta-emotion philosophy and marital interaction patterns), along with many dependent variables (such as marital satisfaction, marital stability, and child well-being), are similarly strongly shaped by more structural factors such as social class.

Gottman's use of divorce or "divorce consideration" as criterion variables in his longitudinal research is a major improvement over earlier cross-sectional marital adjustment studies that merely correlated self-report variables. Nevertheless, conceptual problems may be introduced by selecting comparison groups based on marital adjustment or marital satisfaction. Instruments like the Locke-Wallace Marital Adjustment Test and the Dyadic Adjustment Scale, used extensively by Gottman, have been criticized for being conceptually "fuzzy" and biased toward reports of socially desirable attitudes and practices (Edmonds, 1967; Trost, 1985). Do lower scores on these scales indicate "bad" marriages, unhappy marriages, divorce proneness, few shared activities, frequent disagreements, argumentativeness, inexpressiveness, independence, unconventionality, low commitment to the idea of marriage, or simply embeddedness in class-linked gender segregated social networks? Dividing sample groups on the basis of extremely high or low marital adjustment scores (omitting couples in the middle) and documenting differences in how groups talk about recurring conflicts may not tell us much about what makes marriages work in everyday life. Fortunately, the interventions, experiments, and clinical trials planned by Gottman and his colleagues should be able to address this issue.

SOCIAL CLASS BIAS AND ETHNIC DIVERSITY

Like most laboratory research, the studies reported by Gottman suffer from potential biases introduced through the use of small, relatively homogeneous samples. Details on the income, race, ethnicity, occupation, education, living conditions, and related characteristics of couples studied by Gottman are not provided in this short chapter. Nevertheless, most of the studies referenced in the chapter used newspaper advertisements to recruit subjects from university towns, a strategy promoting volunteer bias that often results in samples with disproportionate numbers of White middle-class couples. For example, a recent paper reporting on negative reciprocity in marital interaction (Cordova et al., 1993) used three comparison groups: "domestically violent" couples ($n = 29$), with a mean annual income of $29,880 (husband = $20,376, wife = $9,504); "distressed nonviolent" couples ($n = 15$), with a mean annual income of $35,232 (husband = $25,848, wife = $9,384); and "happily married" couples ($n = 13$), with a mean annual income of $61,104 (husband = $43,308, wife = $17,796). Note that mean incomes for all groups are relatively high, that the husband's mean income in each group is more than double the wife's, and that both husbands and wives in the "happy" group earn approximately twice as much as those in the other two groups. Other differences between groups included older age and more education for the "happy" group.

Valuable information about marital processes can be obtained using these volunteer samples and comparing subgroups, but serious questions arise when one attempts to apply the results to other groups. Without random selection of subjects, the use of inferential statistics is unwarranted, and findings cannot be generalized to the larger population. Even when volunteer subjects are initially screened and selected on the basis of self reports for certain behaviors (such as domestic violence), they are rarely representative of the entire population of people with that specific behavior. Without precisely documenting the characteristics of sample couples and controlling for ethnicity and socioeconomic status at each stage of the analytical process, it is impossible to determine whether these results might apply to other groups.

The sorts of interaction processes identified by Gottman as being associated with stable, happy marriages and successful children are those valued among college-educated professional couples. Working-class social networks are traditionally segregated by gender and spouses have not typically conceived of each other as best friends or emotional confidants—a pattern more common among upper middle-class Americans (Rubin, 1976, 1994). Similarly, emotion coaching and Scaffolding/Praising are styles of child-rearing admired by many White middle-class mothers and some fathers, but they may not be functional or desirable for all U.S. families. Authoritative parenting (Baumrind, 1971) is usually contrasted with authoritarian or permissive parenting styles, which are assumed to be less effective in producing successful, self-actualizing children. But authoritative parenting practices are only functional within certain social contexts, and it is unlikely that they apply equally well to all social classes, races, and ethnicities (Chao, 1994; Taylor, 1994).

Positive parenting that includes Scaffolding/Praising and emotion coaching is advocated by many child development professionals and is promoted by many popular advice manuals, but it is definitely linked to social-class position. As Melvin Kohn and his colleagues demonstrated, parenting practices and ideal images of children are associated with one's role in the overall economy. Distinctive parenting styles are associated with different class cultures and serve to prepare children to occupy specific positions in a highly stratified labor market (Kohn, 1977). In modern industrial societies, an emphasis on individualism, emotional display, and creative self-expression is characteristic of parenting that implicitly trains children to be managers and professionals. An emphasis on obedience, conformity, and self-regulation is associated with training children to be order-takers in working-class and lower-level white-collar jobs.

HISTORICAL VARIABILITY

An emphasis on emotional self-fulfillment in marriage and for one's children is not only related to social class, but is also a product of modern historical developments. In previous eras, in different regions, and among different groups of people, conceptions of children and their needs were often very different from what they are today. Because of relatively harsh living conditions, and also because the sentimental individualism of the modern era had not yet blossomed, emotional involvement with children was considerably more limited (Ariès, 1964; Shorter, 1975; Synnott, 1983). Prevailing images of children often lacked our modern emphasis on the innocence and purity of children. Religious teachings, particularly those of the American Puritans and Methodists, stressed the corrupt nature and evil dispositions of children, and fathers were admonished to demand strict obedience and use swift physical punishment to cleanse children of their sinful ways (Muir & Brett, 1980).

As productive work gradually became separated from the home in the modern era (a slow and uneven process—see Mintz, chap. 1, this volume), the image of children shifted dramatically, especially among the more privileged classes. No longer sinful creatures valued for their work efforts, children came to be seen as "precious little angels" (Synnott, 1983, p. 79). Relying on insurance company records and court cases, the historical sociologist Viviana Zelizer (1985) showed how the economically useful child of previous times was transformed into an "economically worthless, but emotionally priceless child" (p. 3) as we moved into the 20th century. Traditional forms of child labor came to be seen as harmful and inappropriate for those of tender years (although working-class children, Black children, and immigrant children, like their mothers, still had to work to survive). The middle-class family came to be idealized as the only place where innocent and pure children could and should be protected. No longer considered evil creatures whose will had to be broken by their fathers, children had become precious creatures who needed nurturing and support from their mothers (Coltrane, 1996).

Among subgroups of the U.S. population, emotionally indulgent childhood ideals often remained severely out of touch with everyday reality. For example, scholars debate how much White middle-class family norms and childrearing ideals actually affected the lives of African Americans over the past 200 years (Burgess, 1995; McDaniel, 1990). Images of children among the rich White southern gentry in the 19th century were certainly much different than those held by the slaves who were forced to work on their plantations (Griswold, 1993; McDaniel, 1994). And turn-of-the-century immigrant children in New York were not granted the opportunities to seem as innocent as their wealthier contemporaries (Coltrane, 1997). In addition, important historical events, like war or economic depression, changed the way that people conceived of children and their inherent needs, encouraging us to view them as potential soldiers or supplemental breadwinners (see, e.g., Elder, 1974; Elder, Modell, & Parke, 1993; Hareven, 1982). These historical examples, like the ones presented in Mintz's chapter, show that there has been considerable variability in American men's involvement in families, at least since the 19th century. In addition, they suggest that the modern emphasis on emotional coaching and authoritative parenting is class-, culture-, and time-bound. Because Gottman's findings about meta-emotion philosophies are limited to a specific group, time, and place, we should resist the temptation to universalize them.

GENDER AND POWER

I was troubled by Gottman's use of terms like *accepts influence* to describe battered wives' reactions to hostile husbands, or *rejects influence* to describe husbands' continued belligerence and escalation of conflict. To his credit,

Gottman attempted to place domestic violence in a social context, described husbands' antagonistic interaction style as "in your face," and included brief reference to patriarchy and misogyny. Nevertheless, with such heavy emphasis on the marital interaction sequences associated with negative outcomes, I worry that readers might erroneously blame battered women for the putative role they play in provoking violence. Research consistently shows that there are virtually no actions that women can take to avoid provoking their habitually violent husbands (Gelles & Straus, 1988).

Gottman suggests that violent husbands who are powerless are most likely to batter their wives, and that women play an important role in initiating negative interactions by beginning the laboratory sessions with criticisms. As other researchers using detailed microcoding have suggested, it is more likely that wives use more negative affect than husbands during marital interaction because of their subordinate position (Krokoff, 1987; Margolin & Wampold, 1981; Stets & Burke, 1996). It is probably inappropriate to refer to men who aggressively harass and intimidate their wives as *powerless,* regardless of their lack of verbal acuity. Focusing on the men's standpoint—the lived reality of their lives—will typically produce a picture of men's felt powerlessness. We must be careful to acknowledge that these same men exercise considerable power, particularly over their wives, but also over other women and over some men. This contradictory co-existence of felt powerlessness and actual (if latent) power is quite common for men. Other family violence research suggests that men's subjective sense of powerlessness—of lost or slipping privilege—is often a precursor to wife-beating or sexual abuse (Coltrane, 1997; Lisak, 1991). This does not mean, however, that these men are less powerful than their wives. If they didn't possess some measure of social, cultural, and interactional power, they would not be able to get away with repeatedly beating them.

We can better understand Gottman's findings about violent husbands if we appreciate the historical and institutional contexts of marriage, and the unequal gender relations that it has promoted. Our social customs and legal institutions have treated the marriage relationship as a kind of property relationship, with the wife losing rights to act on her own behalf when she got married. Until relatively recently, the courts upheld husbands' rights of "domestic chastisement" and men were rarely punished for hitting, or even raping, their wives. In some states today, it is still a legal impossibility for a wife to bring legal charges against her husband for raping her, and in a few states, women still lose other legal rights on marrying (Coltrane, 1997). Thus, we can see that institutionalization of the romantic ideal of marriage as an equal emotional partnership between spouses is a relatively recent development, even though the companionate ideal has deep historical roots. The main point is that men continue to enjoy more benefits and privileges from marriage than do women (Collins & Coltrane, 1995;

Thompson & Walker, 1989). In my own work, I have begun to move toward an understanding of gender and emotional expression in marital relationships based on concepts like entitlement, obligation, and gratitude (Coltrane, 1996; Pyke & Coltrane, 1996).

Entitlement, Obligation, and Gratitude in Marriage

All marriages have implicit emotional rules that shape the exchange of displeasure, tolerance, or appreciation between husbands and wives (Erickson, 1993; Ferree, 1990). Hochschild and Machung (1989) called this the *marital economy of gratitude* (p. 18) suggesting that husbands' and wives' gendered self-images contribute to viewing some actions in their marriage as gifts and others as burdens. Marital economies of gratitude include implicit rules about who should be entitled to certain services, who is obligated to perform which tasks, and who should express gratitude when waited on or helped. Such things are continually and subtly negotiated in all couples, but the spouse with more power typically dictates the terms of these negotiations and the spouse with less power typically spends more time aligning emotions with expectations. As many researchers and theorists have noted, the exercise of power through emotional economies is rarely direct or explicit, but it is nevertheless a latent and integral component of all marriages (e.g., Blumberg & Coleman, 1989; Komter, 1989; Pyke, 1994; Thompson & Walker, 1989).

As Gottman's paper begins to suggest, marital power dynamics both shape and reflect how men and women express themselves emotionally. Research confirms that most American women value close emotional relationships more than men and therefore choose to spend more of their time and effort getting romances started and keeping them going, and are also more likely to terminate them when their emotional needs are not met (Cancian, 1987; Chodorow, 1978; Rubin, 1983; Thompson, 1993; Wood, 1994). Not only have women generally worked to get men to notice them, but they have also taken the lead in talking about relationships, taught men how to talk about their feelings, and have sometimes given in to men's sexual advances out of a sense of obligation. These actions relate to the larger gender balance of power in the society and show that women have traditionally been more dependent on marriage than men (Cancian, 1987; Sattel, 1992). This dependence has encouraged women to emphasize relationships, pay more attention to men's feelings than men pay to women's, and be less impulsive than men about falling in love or wanting to get married. To most people, these gender differences in approach to heterosexual emotional relationships appear to be natural and unchanging, but in fact, they are socially constructed.

THE SOCIAL CONSTRUCTION OF GENDER
IN MARRIAGES AND FAMILIES

Sociologists Candace West and Donald Zimmerman (1987) suggested that to be considered competent members of a society, we are all required to "do" gender. We accomplish this by acting in a manly or womanly fashion, or at least close enough to it to be considered a man or woman, boy or girl. According to West and Zimmerman, doing gender is not a choice: We cannot avoid being labeled, or labeling others, as fitting (or not fitting) socially accepted gender categories, even if we recognize that these categories are inappropriate or changing (see also Cahill, 1983; Kessler & McKenna, 1985). The "doing gender" concept alerts us to the idea that gender is not a single fixed "thing." In fact, there are now, and have always been, multiple forms of masculinity and multiple forms of femininity (Connell, 1987, 1995; Lorber, 1994).

Global differences in behavior and disposition between men and women are learned through repeated interaction with other people who share similar views about gender. Much of this learning takes place when we socialize children as discussed later. The gender differences that develop seem so entrenched that they are taken for granted, but they are not instincts, and they are subject to modification after people become adults. Even in the area of emotional support and caregiving, where women do more of it than men, gender differences tend to be significantly reduced or disappear when researchers control for the structural conditions under which people live (Umberson, Chen, House, Hopkins, & Slaten, 1996). For instance, when women's jobs are similar to men's, the amount and type of care they provide family members, extended kin, and friends becomes more similar (Gerstel & Gallagher, 1994). Also, when women and men experience similar conditions of support and caring, they have similar psychological reactions, including levels of depression and alcohol use (Umberson et al., 1996). In other words, similar family conditions and expectations elicit similar psychological reactions from individuals, regardless of gender. In spite of the fact that most people believe that things like maternal instinct, feminine intuition, and male aggressiveness, are built into us by nature, these characteristics are primarily attributed to individuals based on the social roles they play.

The obvious biological differences between males and females—like women's ability to bear children and nurse infants—do play into the social roles that women and men play, but in a less decisive way than most people think. As Howard and Hollander (1997) suggested, "the pervasive cultural belief in the significance of biology may be as important a determinant of behavior as biology itself" (p. 156). In other words, our belief about natural

gender differences is at least as important as any actual underlying physiological differences between the sexes. Even if there are underlying biological differences that promote certain traits or behaviors (and this is a
hotly debated topic among social scientists), for the traits and behaviors
to survive, they must also be supported by the culture and continually
reproduced through the rituals of daily interaction (Kessler & McKenna,
1985; Lorber, 1994; West & Zimmerman, 1987).

When social scientists have conducted careful experimental studies on
the workings of gender in social interaction—like asking a mixed-sex group
to complete a complex task—they find that men and women respond in
remarkably similar fashion to similar social circumstances (Bem, 1993;
Howard & Hollander, 1997; Ridgeway, 1991; Spence, Deaux, & Helmreich,
1985). Given the same sorts of resources, pressures, demands, and concerns, men and women act similarly. The catch is that women and men
rarely face the same resources, pressures, demands and concerns, especially
if they get married and have children together (Lorber, 1994).

An appreciation for how gender is constructed in and through family
obligations might help us better understand the significance of the marital
interaction patterns observed by Gottman (especially when the recurring
problems that couples discuss in the lab concern housework, childrearing,
or money). The gender-linked meanings associated with housework and
paid work influence how couples divide labor, with women routinely assuming responsibility for most of the mundane repetitive household tasks
like cooking and cleaning, and husbands usually seeing themselves as the
main breadwinner (Coltrane, 1996; Hood, 1983; Perry-Jenkins & Crouter,
1990; Thompson & Walker, 1989). Because the economy of gratitude differs
among couples, however, different patterns of negotiation emerge, resulting in various allocations of labor and different levels of marital satisfaction
(Perry-Jenkins & Folk, 1994). In some two-earner couples, for example,
wives' careers and earnings are valued and their husbands respond by
doing more of the housework. In other marriages, however, wives' careers
and earnings are viewed as a threat to the manhood of their husbands
(Pyke, 1996) or devalued in such a manner that the breadwinner role and
its entitlements are not conferred to wives (Bielby & Bielby, 1992; Hood,
1983). Even within the same marriage, husbands and wives can assign
different symbolic meanings to various tasks, leading to protracted conflicts
or continued negotiation about who should do what and who owes what
to whom (Pyke & Coltrane, 1996; McHale & Crouter, 1992).

I am suggesting that what couples argue about in the laboratory interaction sessions might be worthy of further exploration. Because money,
children, and housework are typical sources of conflict in married couples
(Blood & Wolfe, 1960; Coltrane, 1996; Scanzoni & Scanzoni, 1988), it is
important to look at how assumptions about gender and underlying power

imbalances affect negotiations over who does which tasks and who spends how much money on which items. If there is built-up resentment over an unfair division of labor or wasteful spending, and a long history of failed negotiations to change the situation, then we would expect more negative emotions to surface in the start-up phase of the laboratory interaction. Knowing what the argument is about, and what its history is, might enable us to make better guesses about how to stop the negative escalation sequence that Gottman and his colleagues have isolated. Without understanding something about underlying gender and power issues, however, it is difficult to say whether specific individual actions are appropriate, or whether an emotionally charged interaction sequence is functional or dysfunctional for the marriage.

SOCIALIZING CHILDREN INTO GENDER INEQUALITY

Gottman's chapter begins with a discussion of how gender differences between boys and girls are cross-culturally universal, with girls accepting the influence of both girls and boys, but boys rejecting the influence of girls. This is an interesting observation that fits nicely with his laboratory findings of differences between men's and women's styles of marital interaction. I think this topic is worthy of further study, but I would suggest that the social and structural conditions surrounding child socialization are probably more constitutive of these gender differences than Gottman implies.

The most important insight from research on gender socialization is that because boys and girls are treated differently and put into different learning environments, they develop different needs, wants, desires, skills, and temperaments; in short, they become different kinds of people—men and women—who hardly question why they are different or how they ended up that way. Although the specific social and psychological processes through which gender socialization occurs are the subject of much debate, the basic underlying model is that of the self-fulfilling prophecy (Bem, 1993; Merton, 1948; Rosenthal & Jacobson, 1968). Because people think boys and girls are supposed to be different, they treat them differently and give them different opportunities for development. This differential treatment promotes certain behaviors and self-images that recreate preconceived cultural stereotypes about gender. The process repeats itself over and over in a kind of unending spiral across the generations, so that even though gender stereotypes are being constantly recreated and modified, they seem natural and impervious to change.

It is not just that boys and girls are naturally and fundamentally different in some unchanging way. Rather, in order to be considered competent members of society, they must learn how to fit in as appropriately gendered individuals. Because gender tends to be very important to the adults in our society, children are called on to conform to the gender standards currently in force. In order for children to develop an identity, they must also develop a gender identity, and they must work to make their actions and thoughts conform to what the people around them expect. Children literally claim a gender identity as they interact with adults and other children (Cahill, 1986; Thorne, 1993). Thus children, as well as adults, are required to "do gender" in an ongoing way (West & Zimmerman, 1987; West & Fenstermaker, 1993).

In findings similar to those reported by Gottman, psychologist Sandra Bem (1993) reported that boys are more rigidly socialized to gender norms and allowed less cross-over behavior than girls: She found that it was easier for girls to be tomboys than for boys to be "sissies." In her study of children's play on elementary school playgrounds, sociologist Barrie Thorne (1993) elaborated these findings when she discovered that high-status girls were most able to cross gender boundaries and play in boys' games, but boys who tried this were usually ridiculed. Contrary to Gottman's suggestion of cross-cultural universality, Thorne found that there was considerable cross-over between girl's culture and boy's culture. Supporting Gottman's assertion, on the other hand, she found that girls were much more likely to try to get into boys' games than the reverse. According to Thorne, playground rituals like "cooties" and chase-games represent "borderwork" that reinforce gender differences and erect boundaries between boys and girls.

On the playground and at home, both girls and boys learn that they should conform to gender-appropriate behaviors, but studies find that boys are encouraged to conform to masculine ideals more than girls are encouraged to conform to feminine ideals. In addition, boys tend to receive more rewards for gender conformity than girls (Wood, 1994). In part, this is because boys tend to get more attention than girls. Children, as well as adults, generate more restrictive gender rules for young boys than for young girls (Bem, 1993). Another consistent finding across studies is that fathers enforce gender stereotypes more than mothers, especially in sons. This is generally true across types of activities, including toy preferences, play styles, chores, discipline, interaction, and personality assessments (Caldera, Huston, & O'Brien, 1989; Fagot & Leinbach, 1993; Lytton & Romney, 1991). If men became more involved in raising children, but continued to enforce gender stereotypes like these studies suggest, then active fathering could have gender-polarizing effects in the next generation. Alternately, if men began to behave more like conventional mothers, their propensity to sex-type children would decrease (Coltrane, 1996). By bringing gender and power back into the child-socialization picture, as well as into the marital-interaction picture, we should be able to better interpret Gottman's emerging findings about meta-emotion philosophies, emotional coaching, and men's influence on child development.

PREDICTING THE FUTURE

Turning to sociological changes in men's family roles in the last part of the chapter, Gottman offers some tentative predictions about the future. He suggests that enormous variability in men's family roles is a recent development, whereas others have drawn on historical sources to show that a tremendous range of variation has existed in American men's family roles for at least 150 years (Griswold, 1993; Mintz, chap. 1, this volume). Again, Gottman's review of contemporary trends would benefit from the recognition of cross-class and cross-ethnic diversity, attention to the ways that power helps construct masculinity, and acknowledgment of the property relations embedded in the institution of marriage. Nevertheless, I appreciated Gottman's acknowledgment of "increasing polarization" among North American fathers, reminiscent of sociologist Frank Furstenberg's (1988) discussion of the increase in both "good dads" and "bad dads" (pp. 193–218).

The demographic trends Gottman summarizes need to be extended. The decrease in number and percent of conventional nuclear family households has increased even further (DeVita, 1996). Rates of teenage birth and nonmarital birth have actually leveled off and are now falling (National Center for Health Statistics, 1995, 1996). The trend toward greater labor force participation for women has continued unabated. The gap between rich and poor in America continues to widen, and more children than ever before are living in poverty (DeVita, 1996; Weinberg, 1996). The figures on the number of high school students carrying guns, in contrast, and assumptions about continued increases in violent crime appear to be overstated.

What is most compelling about the conclusion to Gottman's chapter is the contribution it can make to political debates about the importance of fathers. His findings counter recent rhetoric from neoconservatives like David Blankenhorn (1995) and David Popenoe (1996), who claim that father absence and single motherhood are the root cause of contemporary society's evils. Echoing Parke (1981, 1996), Gottman stresses that what really matters is what fathers do in and for families, not just whether they are married to the mother or living in the same household with their children. Gottman advocates turning more men into husbands who are empathetic toward their wives. Similarly, he advocates turning fathers into emotionally attuned parents who can meet their children's needs. According to the process model he proposes, this would lead to satisfying stable marriages and positive developmental outcomes for the children. I concur that these are worthy goals.

I worry, however, that a focus on minute marital interaction patterns will not get us there. In my view, we need to focus on the social conditions that allow a shrinking White middle class to become emotionally sensitive spouses and parents whereas people of color and single mothers suffer economic hardship. I worry that if we ignore class, race, and gender biases we will not be able to get the majority of couples to "de-escalate negative affect." I worry that we might blame women for being too critical when they are trying to salvage a marriage, or that we will encourage battered women to assume responsibility for placating abusive husbands. And finally, I worry that if we value the presence of fathers over their actions, we will go back to patriarchal laws that treat women and children as the property of the "master of the house." In spite of my worries, I thank John Gottman for raising important questions about how we can help men become better partners and parents.

REFERENCES

Ariès, P. (1964). *Centuries of childhood: A social history of family life* (R. Baldick, Trans.). New York: Random House.

Babcock, J. C., Waltz, J., Jacobson, N. E., & Gottman, J. (1993). Power and violence—The relation between communication patterns, power discrepancies, and domestic violence. *Journal of Consulting and Clinical Psychology, 61,* 40–50.

Baumrind, D. (1971). Current patterns of parental authority. *Developmental Psychology Monographs, 4,* 1, part 2.

Bem, S. L. (1993). *The lenses of gender.* New Haven, CT: Yale University Press.

Bernard, J. (1981). The good provider role: It's rise and fall. *American Psychologist, 36,* 1–12.

Bielby, W., & Bielby, D. D. (1992). I will follow him: Family ties, gender role beliefs, and reluctance to relocate for a better job. *American Journal of Sociology, 97,* 1241–1267.

Blankenhorn, D. (1995). *Fatherless America: Confronting our most urgent social problem.* New York: Basic Books.

Blood, R. O., Jr., & Wolfe, D. M. (1960). *Husbands and wives.* New York: Free Press.

Blumberg, R. L., & Coleman, M. T. (1989). A theoretical look at the gender balance of power in the American couple. *Journal of Family Issues, 10,* 225–250.

Burgess, N. J. (1995). Female-headed households in sociohistorical context. In B. J. Dikerson (Ed.), *African American single mothers* (pp. 21–36). Thousand Oaks, CA: Sage.

Cahill, S. E. (1986). Childhood socialization as a recruitment process: Some lessons from the study of gender development. *Sociological Studies of Child Development, 1,* 163–186.

Caldera, Y. M., Huston, A. C., & O'Brien, M. (1989). Social interactions and play patterns of parents and toddlers with feminine, masculine, and neutral toys. *Child Development, 60,* 70–76.

Cancian, F. (1987). *Love in America.* New York: Cambridge University Press.

Chao, R. K. (1994). Beyond parental control and authoritarian parenting style. *Child Development, 65,* 1111–1119.

Chodorow, N. (1978). *The reproduction of mothering: Psychoanalysis and the sociology of gender.* Berkeley, CA: University of California Press.

Coltrane, S. (1996). *Family man: Fatherhood, housework, and gender equity.* New York: Oxford University Press.

Coltrane, S. (1997). *Gender and families.* Thousand Oaks, CA: Pine Forge Press.

Collins, R. & Coltrane, S. (1995). *Sociology of marriage and the family: Gender, love, and property.* Chicago: Nelson Hall.

Conger, R. D., & Elder, G. H., Jr. (Eds.). (1994). *Families in troubled times: Adapting to change in rural America.* New York: de Gruyter.

Connell, R. W. (1987). *Gender and power: Society, the person and sexual politics.* Stanford, CA: Stanford University Press.

Connell, R. W. (1995). *Masculinities.* Berkeley, CA: University of California Press.

Cordova, J. V., Jacobson, N. S., Gottman, J. M., Rushe, R. & Cox, G. (1993). Negative reciprocity and communication in couples with a violent husband. *Journal of Abnormal Psychology, 102,* 559–564.

DeVita, C. (1996). The United States at mid-decade. *Population Bulletin, 50,* 4. Washington, DC: Population Reference Bureau.

Edmonds, V. H. (1967). Marriage, conventionalization: Definition and measurement. *Journal of Marriage and the Family, 29,* 681–688.

Elder, G. H. (1974). *Children of the Great Depression.* Chicago: University of Chicago Press.

Elder, G. H., Modell, J., & Parke, R. D. (1993). *Children in time and place: Developmental and historical insights.* New York: Cambridge University Press.

Erickson, R. J., (1993). Reconceptualizing family work: The effect of emotion work on perceptions of marital quality. *Journal of Marriage and the Family, 55,* 888–900.

Fagot, B. I. & Leinbach, M. D. (1993). Gender-role development in young children: From discrimination to labeling. *Developmental Review, 13,* 205–224.

Ferree, M. M. (1990). Beyond separate spheres: Feminism and family research. *Journal of Marriage and the Family, 52,* 866–884.

Furstenberg, F. F., (1988). Good dads—bad dads: Two faces of fatherhood. In A. Cherlin (Ed.), *The changing American family and public policy* (pp. 193–218). Washington, DC: Urban Institute.

Gelles, R. J., & Straus, M. A. (1988). *Intimate violence.* New York: Touchstone.

Gerstel, N. & Gallagher, S. (1994). Caring for kith and kin—gender, employment, and the privatization of care. *Social Problems, 41,* 519–39.

Gottman, J. M. (1993). The roles of conflict engagement, escalation, and avoidance in marital interaction: A longitudinal view of five types of couples. *Journal of Consulting and Clinical Psychology, 61,* 6–15.

Gottman, J. M. (1994). *What predicts divorce?* Hillsdale, NJ: Lawrence Erlbaum Associates.

Gottman, J. M., Katz, L. F., & Hooven, C. (1996). Parental meta-emotion philosophy and the emotional life of families: Theoretical models and preliminary data. *Journal of Family Psychology, 10,* 243–268.

Griswold, R. (1993). *Fatherhood in America: A history.* New York: Basic Books.

Hareven, T. K. (1982). *Family time and industrial time: The relationship between the family and work in a New England industrial town.* Cambridge, UK: Cambridge University Press.

Hochschild, A, & Machung, A. (1989). *The second shift: Working parents and the revolution at home.* New York: Viking.

Hood, J. A. (1983). *Becoming a two-job family.* New York: Praeger.

Howard, J. & Hollander, J. (1997). *Gendered situations, gendered selves: A gender lens on social psychology.* Thousand Oaks, CA: Sage.

Jacobson, N. S., Gottman, J. M., Waltz, J., Rushe, R., Babcock, J., & Holtzworth-Munroe, A. (1994). Affect, verbal content, and psychophysiology in the arguments of couples with a violent husband. *Journal of Consulting and Clinical Psychology, 62,* 982–988.

Kessler, S. J., & McKenna, W. (1985). *Gender: An ethnomethodological approach* (2nd ed.). Chicago: University of Chicago Press.

Kohn, M. L. (1977). *Class and conformity.* Chicago: University of Chicago Press.

Komter, A. (1989). Hidden power in marriage. *Gender & Society, 3,* 187–216.

Krokoff, L. J. (1987). The correlates of negative affect in marriage. *Journal of Family Issues, 8,* 111–135.

Lisak, D. (1991). Sexual aggression, masculinity, and fathers. *Signs, 16,* 238–262.

Lorber, J. (1994). *Paradoxes of gender.* New Haven, CT: Yale University Press.

Lytton, H. & Romney, D. M. (1991). Parents' differential socialization of boys and girls: A Meta-analysis. *Psychological Bulletin, 109*(2), 267–296.

McDaniel, A. (1990). The power of culture: A review of the idea of Africa's influence on family structure in antebellum America. *Journal of Family History, 15,* 225–238.

McDaniel, A. (1994). Historical racial differences in living arrangements of children. *Journal of Family History, 19,* 57–77.

McHale, S. M., & Crouter, A. C. (1992). You can't always get what you want: Incongruence between sex-role attitudes and family work roles and its implications for marriage. *Journal of Marriage and the Family, 54,* 538–547.

Margolin, G. & Wampold, B. E. (1981). Sequential analysis of conflict and accord in distressed and nondistressed marital partners. *Journal of Consulting and Clinical Psychology, 49,* 554–567.

Merton, R. K. (1948). The self-fulfilling prophecy. *Antioch Review, 8,* 193–210.

National Center for Health Statistics. (1995). Births to unmarried mothers: United States, 1980–92 (Ventura, S. J.). *Vital Health Statistics, 21*(53). Washington, DC: U.S. Department of Health and Human Services.

National Center for Health Statistics. (1996). *Monthly Vital Statistics Report, 45,* 3, supp. 2. Washington, DC: U.S. Department of Health and Human Services.

Muir, F., & Brett, S. (1980). *On Children.* London: Heinemann.

Parke, R. D. (1981). *Fathers.* Cambridge, MA: Harvard University Press.

Parke, R. D. (1996). *Fatherhood.* Cambridge, MA: Harvard University Press.

Perry-Jenkins, M., & Crouter, A. C. (1990). Men's provider-role attitudes: Implications for household work and marital satisfaction. *Journal of Family Issues, 11,* 136–156.

Perry-Jenkins, M. & Folk, K. (1994). Class, couples, and conflict: Effects of the division of labor on assessments of marriage in dual-earner families. *Journal of Marriage and the Family, 56,* 165–180.

Popenoe, D. (1996). *Life without father: Compelling new evidence that fatherhood and marriage are indispensable for the good of children and society.* New York: Martin Kessler/Free Press.

Pyke, K. (1994). Women's employment as a gift or burden? Marital power across marriage, divorce, and remarriage. *Gender & Society, 8,* 73–91.

Pyke, K. (1996). Class-based masculinities: The interdependence of gender, class, and interpersonal power. *Gender & Society, 10,* 527–549.

Pyke, K. & Coltrane, S. (1996). Entitlement, obligation, and gratitude in family work. *Journal of Family Issues, 17,* 60–82.

Ridgeway, C. (Ed.). (1991). *Gender, interaction, and inequality.* New York: Springer-Verlag.

Rosenthal, R., & Jacobson, L. (1968). *Pygmalion in the classroom: Teacher expectations and pupil's intellectual development.* New York: Holt.

Rubin, L. (1976). *Worlds of Pain: Life in the working class family.* New York: Basic Books.

Rubin, L. (1983). *Intimate strangers.* New York: Harper & Row.

Rubin, L. (1994). *Families on the fault line: America's working class speaks about the family, economy, and ethnicity.* New York: Harper Collins.

Sattel, J. W. (1992). The inexpressive male. In M. S. Kimmel, & M. A. Messner (Eds.), *Men's Lives* (pp. 350–370). New York: Macmillan.

Scanzoni, L. D., & Scanzoni, J. (1988). *Men, women, and change.* New York: McGraw-Hill.

Spence, J. T., Deaux, K., & Helmreich, R. L. (1985). Sex roles in contemporary American society. In G. Lindzey & E. Aronson (Eds.), *Handbook of Social Psychology* (pp. 149–178). New York: Random House.

Stets, J. E. & Burke, P. J. (1996). Gender, control, and interaction. *Social Psychological Quarterly, 59,* 193–220.

Shorter, E. (1975). *The making of the modern family.* New York: Basic Books.

Synnott, A. (1983). Little angels, little devils: A sociology of children. *Canadian Review of Sociology and Anthropology 20,* 79–95.

Taylor, R. L. (Ed.). (1994). *Minority families in the United States: A multicultural perspective.* Englewood Cliffs, NJ: Prentice Hall.

Thompson, L. (1993). Conceptualizing gender in marriage: The case of marital care. *Journal of Marriage and the Family, 5,* 557–569.

Thompson, L., & Walker, A. J. (1989). Gender in families: Women and men in marriage, work, and parenthood. *Journal of Marriage and the Family, 51,* 845–871.

Thorne, B. (1993). *Gender Play: Girls and Boys in School.* New Brunswick, NJ: Rutgers University Press.

Trost, J. E. (1985). Abandon adjustment. *Journal of Marriage and the Family, 47,* 1072–1073.

Umberson, D., Chen, M. D., House, J. S., Hopkins, K., & Slaten, E. (1996). The effects of social relationships on psychological well-being: Are men and women really so different? *American Sociological Review 61,* 837–857.

Weinberg, D. H. (1996). A brief look at postwar U.S. income inequality. *Current Population Reports, Household Economic Studies,* P60–191. Washington DC: U.S. Bureau of the Census.

West, C., & Fenstermaker, S. (1993). Power and the accomplishment of gender: An ethnomethodolgical perspective. In P. England (Ed.), *Theory on Gender/Feminism on Theory* (pp. 151–174). New York: de Gruyter.

West, C., & Zimmerman, D. (1987). Doing gender. *Gender & Society, 1,* 125–151.

Wood, J. T. (1994). *Gendered lives: Communication, gender, and culture.* Belmont, CA: Wadsworth.

Zelizer, V. (1985). *Pricing the priceless child: The changing social value of children.* New York: Basic Books.

Chapter 11

The Importance of Variation Among Men and the Benefits of Feminism for Families

Julia McQuillan
Myra Marx Ferree
University of Connecticut

Gottman (chap. 9, this volume) offers several provocative ideas in his very wide-ranging chapter. In addressing these ideas, we are not interested in criticizing any of his detailed evidence or arguments as such, but instead will attempt to extend a few of them. The goal is to highlight the differences in our approach to the issues he raised and bring evidence of our own to bear on some of his assertions. This chapter is limited to three such interesting points of convergence and divergence, described briefly first, and then examined in more detail.

First, Gottman makes a strong case for the importance of the husband's ability to accept influence from his wife as a predictor of marital violence, overall marital satisfaction, and the likelihood of divorce. He therefore describes the socialization processes of boys and girls, emphasizing how childhood play and friendship patterns differentially prepare men and women for the demands of marriage. But such an explanation, based on generic differences between the categories "women" and "men," tends to obscure important differences among men and among women. These differences are in fact crucial to Gottman's basic project of explaining why some marriages work and others do not, and how men and women can learn to make their marriages work better. If marital conflict all boils down to gender differences in playground behavior, his project would be doomed. But, as his data suggests, a key issue is variation among men.

The second point concerns the significance of gender stereotypes, both in regulating and legitimating certain behaviors, and in understanding the significance of nonstereotypical behavior. Gottman often explains men's counterproductive marriage behaviors in terms of stereotypical patterns, such as an inability to recognize and manage emotion. We focus instead on the cross-stereotypical and counterstereotypical behaviors in which some men already engage that seem to relate to more satisfying and enduring relations. We distinguish *cross-stereotypical activity*—engaging in behavior characteristically expected of and ascribed to the other sex—from *counterstereotypical* activity, that is, engaging in behavior not conventionally expected of men. We make this distinction because it is important to challenge the cultural assumption that everything that is not masculine must be feminine and vice versa. This helps open up space for marital behavior that is not strongly gender-typed, and we argue that such behavior helps both husbands and wives relate to each other and to their children more productively.

Third, we extend the discussion of the politics of marriage. We applaud Gottman for naming, critiquing, and challenging the forces urging a return to authoritarian fatherhood (i.e., the dangers of the Promise Keepers, the followers of Robert Bly, and other men's movements that are specifically part of the backlash against feminism). But we urge an extension of this effort to include the positive effects of feminism for families that is implicit in his chapter. His data supports the conclusion that feminism is good for families, and we offer additional, more explicit arguments in support of this contention.

EMPHASIZING VARIABILITY AMONG HUSBANDS

We agree with the contention that some men may have particular difficulty accepting influence from their wives, and that such an inability to accept influence may be central to marital dissatisfaction and the likelihood of divorce. Gottman grounds his argument in developmental sex differences research, but we find it provocative not as identifying a general difference between women and men as generic classes of people, but as a difference *among* men. Not all of the men respond to mildly negative comments from their wives with "contempt, belligerence, or defensiveness" (p. 154), which is how Gottman defines rejecting influence. And yet we know that some men do respond in these ways.

Kurz's (1995) study of women in divorce provides a qualitative sense of what this type of relationship is like; she quoted one woman as saying, "My ex-husband didn't have an emotional vocabulary. Everything was fine or he was very, very angry. He used his anger to control. It scared me" (p. 50). Or, as another said, "I was afraid of saying what I really thought . . . I walked on eggshells about that" (p. 51). This is a real pattern and a gendered one, one that frightens women, makes marriages unhappy and needs desperately to change.

But the unanswered question that Gottman's research raises is what differences exist in male identity or experience that lead some men more than others to be able to accept influence from their wives? To say that batterers do not accept influence from their wives, but instead respond to any level of negative affect with increased negativity (the "bat 'em back" hypothesis, chap. 9, this volume), certainly describes the problem with greater precision than before, but we are left wondering which men can and cannot say "you're right" to their wives and wondering how likely each of these types might be.

Using a different methodological approach, we did a preliminary analysis of variations among husbands in their ability to accept influence from their wives. Using survey research, we gain in generalizability, but lose some of the advantages of direct observation and process measures available in laboratory studies such as Gottman's. We compiled a random sample of 382 Connecticut dual-earner couples (described in Ferree, 1991). We chose two questions that most closely match Gottman's idea of the husband's ability to accept influence, using wives' reports. Wives were asked: (a) When you feel unhappy about something your husband is doing or not doing, whatever it might be, is it very easy, easy, difficult, or very difficult to raise this issue with him? and (b) When you do tell him your opinion on this, does he listen and usually change his behavior, listen but only sometimes try to change, listen but usually do nothing, or refuse to even really listen to you?

Husbands whose wives find it very easy to raise issues or who change at their wives request are considered willing to accept influence. Almost one third of the wives (31%) report that it is very easy to raise issues with their husbands, and one fifth (20%) report that their husbands listen and change when she raises a concern about his behavior (see Tables 11.1a, 11.1b, 11.1c). This suggests that not all husbands, as Gottman himself found, are unwilling to accept their wife's influence. Although this measure does not actually observe processes and has all of the biases of self-reports at one point in time, it has the strength of coming from a larger sample.

Our data is consistent with Gottman's in that we also found higher levels of marital satisfaction among couples with husbands who accept influence from their wives. In our data, the third of all wives who say it is very easy to raise issues with their husbands are happier than other wives (80% are very happy compared to 52% of the non-acceptors) and their husbands also report greater satisfaction (75% are very happy compared to 53% of the non-acceptors). Also, when wives say that husbands are willing to change something that is bothering her when she asks him to, both they themselves and their husbands separately say they are significantly more satisfied with the marriage.

TABLE 11.1a
Husband and Wife Marital Satisfaction (Separately) by
the Wife's Report of Husband's Willingness to Accept Influence
(Measured by How Easy It Is for Her to Raise Issues)*

	How Easy Is It to Raise Issues?		
	Very Easy	Less Than Very Easy	Total N (Percent of Total)
Wife's marital satisfaction:			
Percent extremely satisfied	80%	***52%	229
Husband's marital satisfaction:			
Percent extremely satisfied	75%	**53%	226
Total Percent	31%	69%	100%
(N)	(118)	(260)	(378)

*Only the extremely satisfied are shown—those less than extremely satisfied can be calculated from the total sample N.
**p = .0001.
***p = .00001.

TABLE 11.1b
Husband and Wife Marital Satisfaction (Separately) by the
Wife's Report of Husband's Willingness to Accept Influence
(Measured as Willingness to Change When the Wife Asks)

	How Often Does He Change?		
	Usually	Sometimes to Never	Total N
Wife's marital satisfaction:			
Percent extremely satisfied	82%	***55%	228
Husband's marital satisfaction:			
Percent extremely satisfied	77%	**55%	225
Total Percent	20%	80%	100%
(N)	(74)	(304)	(378)

**p = .0001
***p = .00001

It is important to look at the likelihood of men's accepting or rejecting influence from their wives not as a general characteristic of men's personality, but as an approach to marriage that accentuates the gendered inequalities that are often structured into it. What are some of these structured inequalities in marriages? Husbands tend to be older, more educated, wealthier, have higher prestige jobs, and have more authority at work.

TABLE 11.1c
Marital Satisfaction (Husbands and Wives Separately) for Wives Who
Feel Understood by Their Husbands Compared to Those Who Do
Not Feel Very Understood by Their Husbands (Empathy)

	Wife Feels Very Well Known by Her Husband	Wife Feels Fairly-to-Not Very Well Known by Her Husband	Total N
Percent of wives extremely satisfied	85%	***38%	230
Percent of husbands extremely satisfied	74%	***47%	228
Total Percent and N	48% (182)	52% (200)	100% (382)

***$p = .00001$.

It is possible that some of these structural characteristics distinguish between husbands that accept influence and husbands that do not.[1] In our data, the only pattern we found is that husbands who are younger (under 36 years old) are more willing to accept influence from their wives: 38% of wives with younger husbands report it is very easy to raise issues compared to 25% of wives of older husbands (chi-square = 7.096, $p = .007$), and 25% of wives with younger husbands report that their husbands change when asked to compared to 14% of wives with older husbands (chi-square = 8.133, $p = .004$).

Gottman also introduced the concept of a Love Map as an important feature of successful marriages. We did not have variables that can directly measure the quality of each spouse's Love Map, but we did have the wife's subjective sense of how well her husband knows and understands her. Wives were asked "How well do you think your husband understands you— your feelings, your likes and dislikes, and any problems you may have? Is it very well, fairly well, not very well, or not well at all?" Almost half (48%) of wives reported feeling very well known by their spouses, suggesting at least some husbands are successful at overcoming any weakness they may have from differential socialization. Similar to Gottman, we found that in marriages in which the wife feels understood by her husband, a much greater percent of both husbands and wives have higher satisfaction. Thus,

---

[1]The pattern might be more complex than this statement implies. Hochschild (1989) described a couple in which the husband allows his wife to work at a job that she earns more money than he does only if she maintains her domestic duties at the same level she did when not employed. In this couple doing gender, and the power relations of gender, are carefully maintained, but not immediately apparent, given the information that she earns more than her husband.

we emphasize the need to look to factors that will foster empathy and responsiveness in men, and recognize that there is already a base of variation on which to build.

SEPARATING CROSS-STEREOTYPICAL FROM COUNTERSTEREOTYPICAL BEHAVIOR

How can husbands be encouraged to relate to women and children in ways that are more productive of happy and stable marriages and better functioning children? Here we focus on the uses of stereotypes to interpret behavior, both on the part of couples themselves and by the researchers studying them. As Thorne (1993) pointed out in her study of children's interactions, observers tend to focus on the behaviors that are most readily interpretable in gender stereotypical terms, leaving the many exceptions aside. Gottman, too, is often quick to interpret actions in gendered terms. For example, he sees the significant positive effect of husbands' de-escalation of wives' low-level, in contrast to high-level, negative affect on marital stability as reflecting men's generic tendency to be emotionally swamped and so to adopt withdrawal and stonewalling tactics. This conforms to culturally available ideas about how men behave, but it does not attempt to explain why this difference is surrounded by other less stereotypical nonsignificant effects. For example, men's de-escalation of low-level affect has no effect on marital happiness and women's de-escalation of both low- and high-level negative affect has no effect on either marital stability or happiness.

To see husbands and wives as not always the same and to adopt explanations that truly take gender into account are important steps forward from non-gender-specific analyses (Ferree, 1990; Thompson & Walker, 1989). But, in taking gender into account in the models we develop, we need to be particularly careful that we not notice and interpret only the most stereotypically gendered behaviors. The existing base of variation among men—as among women—is an important aspect of this reality.

When Gottman's data show that his models successfully differentiate happy from unhappy marriages or stable ones from unstable ones, he is often finding that men do engage in significant numbers in nonstereotypical behaviors. As he recognizes, the statistical reality is that we can only find significant differences when there is variation involved, and in many ways the statistical importance of men's behavior reflects the greater variability in men's relations to their families than in women's styles of involvement. In other words, it is important to recognize that not all men withdraw in low-level negative affect sequences; some men in some circumstances are engaging in counterstereotypical behavior. Gottman's and our data shows that it is good for their marriages that they do.

We also would further distinguish between the two concepts mentioned previously: counterstereotypical and cross-stereotypical. *Counterstereotypical* describes behavior by one gender that does not conform to the prevailing stereotype of that gender, such as men not stonewalling or withdrawing from their families or husbands not rejecting influence from their wives. *Cross-stereotypical* describes behavior that conforms to social expectations of the other sex, such as men being nurturant to children or actively coaching their children to express emotions. If one immediately assumes that men who are not conforming to a certain stereotype of masculinity must therefore be fitting an apparently equal and opposite stereotype of femininity, we narrow the range of permissible behavior for men and women alike. One goal is to consider how certain types of counterstereotypical and cross-stereotypical behaviors are good for both men and women, and might be detached from their exclusive association with masculinity or femininity.

For example, with regard to cross-stereotypical behavior, note the critical role that Gottman finds in husbands' ordinary interactions with their wives. Those husbands who spontaneously express fondness and admiration, use inclusive "we" language, and know more and think more about the relationship are likely to maintain happier marriages after children are born. It is wives who are stereotypically supposed to expend such effort on the relationship, yet it is husbands' cross-stereotypical interaction patterns that make a difference. Of course, these gender-specific effects may be found because there is little or no variation among wives. All wives are expected to fit a supportive pattern, and most actually manage to do so.

But explaining the cross-stereotypical behavior of men and encouraging change for social justice remains the crucial problem (Connell, 1995). Thorne's (1993) studies of children suggested that it is much more threatening to a boy to be a sissy than for a girl to be a tomboy, because anything associated with girls has lower status. Recognizing the value and significance of skills and knowledge that have been associated with girls and women is important, but unless, and until, girls and women have the same status as boys and men, it may be more useful to redefine these as nongender-specific behaviors than to encourage men to adopt a more feminine style.

The importance of counterstereotypical behavior also emerges in Gottman's discussion of childrearing and meta-emotion. In his research, meta-emotion, that is, emotions and thoughts about emotion, relates to the role of parents as emotion coaches for their kids, teaching children how to manage rather than dismiss their feelings. Here Gottman argues both that mothers emotion coach more than fathers, and some families, as a whole, emotion coach more than others. Again, to say that women do something more than men is not to say that men do not do it. Indeed,

Gottman's paper provides a wonderfully sensitive case of a father emotion coaching his son on how to deal with sadness. He finds some intriguing relationships between men who emotion coach their children's sadness also being more affectionate and less defensive to their wives. Bem's (1983) work on gender schema suggested that men who feel less restricted in how they express masculinity are also happier with themselves and less anxious more generally. Rather than being concerned about identifying a uniquely male contribution to families and children, as Gottman sometimes seems to be, we suggest that it better reflects the reality of good fathers and husbands to appreciate how they avoid limiting themselves to just what is typically or stereotypically masculine.

We examined the relationship between cross-stereotypical behavior and counterstereotypical behavior to both how well the wife feels her husband understands her (his empathy) and the wife's marital satisfaction. The husband's counterstereotypical behavior, measured as accepting influence, is significantly associated with knowing his wife better ($B = .53$, $p = .0001$), but husband's cross-stereotypical housework participation (engaging in tasks usually done by wives, i.e., preparing meals, doing laundry, and household cleaning) is not a significant predictor of knowing his wife, but is in the expected direction ($B = .08$, $p = .24$). Both the wife feeling understood ($B = .50$, $p = .0001$) and the husband's acceptance of influence ($B = .30$, $p = .0001$) are significant predictors of wives' marital satisfaction, but husband's cross-stereotypical participation in female-stereotyped chores is not ($B = .07$, $p = .24$) (see Table 11.2a).

In order to test some of Gottman's ideas about the importance of husbands' and wives' approaches to emotions, we looked at the congruence of husbands and wives responses to how much housework their spouse does. They were each asked: "When you think about the amount of housework your wife/husband does, do you usually, sometimes, or never feel: disappointed, pleased, guilty, embarrassed, angry, proud?" Given that nearly all wives do a disproportionate share of housework, we assume some level of grievance, whether expressed as such (anger or disappointment) or not. Husbands who feel guilty or embarrassed sense their wives' emotions and respond empathetically (even if not by actually doing more housework). Our focus is on the quality of the husband's response to his wife's anger, disappointment, or lack of either within the couple as a unit. Couples were grouped into three categories:

1. Emotionally aware husbands—those who feel guilt or embarrassment when their wives feel anger and/or disappointment (222 or 58% of the sample).
2. Very emotionally aware husbands—those who feel guilt and/or embarrassment even though their wives say they are not feeling angry or disappointed (65, or 17% of the sample).

TABLE 11.2a

Regressions of How Well the Wife Feels Her Husband
Knows Her and the Wife's Marital Satisfaction on
Cross- and Counterstereotypical Behavior

	Wife's Report of How Well She Feels Her Husband Understands Her	Wife's Marital Satisfaction (WMSAT)[4]
	B	B
HCOUNTER[1]	.53***	.30***
HCROSS[2]	.08	.07
WKNOWN[3]	—	.50***
Constant	2.94***	1.55***
R-square	.13***	.34***

[1]HCOUNTER = a dummy variable indicating that the husband engages in counterstereotypical behavior, that is, he accepts influence from his wife.

[2]HCROSS = a dummy variable indicating that the husband engages in cross-stereotypical behavior, measured as being responsible for any of 3 predominantly female-typed tasks (preparing meals, laundry, or housecleaning).

[3]WKNOWN = How well do you think your husband understands you—your feelings, your likes and dislikes, and any problems you may have? Is it (a) not at all, (b) not very well, (c) fairly well, (d) very well? (These are the reverse of what is reported in the text to make for easier interpretation in the analysis.)

[4]WMSAT = All in all, how satisfied would you say you are with your marriage: (a) Not too satisfied, (b) somewhat satisfied, (c) satisfied, or (d) extremely satisfied? (These are reversed from the actual text for ease of interpreting the regression analysis.)

3. Emotionally unaware husbands—those that do not feel guilt nor embarrassment, even though their wives feel angry or disappointed (95, or 25% of the sample).

These measures tap husbands' overall emotional responsiveness to their wives in the context of their amount of housework. Emotionally aware husbands have wives who feel better understood and both they and their wives have higher marital satisfaction than husbands who are less emotionally aware (see Table 11.2b).

In sum, it is not helpful to think about men generically, as not aware of their emotions or not able to express emotion. Both Gottman's and our data suggest that marriages appear to be both happier and more stable when both spouses are similar in their approach to emotions in ways that are counterstereotypical for men. Greater awareness and emotional responsiveness on the part of men—even when not accompanied by more substantive shifts in responsibility for cross-stereotypical chores—seems to create better relationships for both spouses. Moreover, it also seems to support counterstereotypical, but positive fathering. When parents differ,

TABLE 11.2b
Husband and Wife Marital Satisfaction (Separately) by the
Quality of the Husband's Response to the Wife's Feelings
About the Amount of Housework He Does

| | How Emotionally Aware Is the Husband? | | | |
	Very Aware	Aware	Unaware	Total N (Percent of Total)
Wife's marital satisfaction:				
Percent extremely satisfied	80%	60%	48%	230
How well does the wife feel her husband knows and understands her? Percent very well	63%	50%	33%	182
Total Percent	17%	58%	25%	100%
(N)	(65)	(222)	(95)	382

*For the marital satisfaction question, the Pearson χ^2 = 16.18, 2 d.f., p = .00031.
*For the how well understood question, the Pearson χ^2 = 15.112, 2 d.f., p = .00052.
[1]The "emotionally aware" categories were created from responses to a question about how each spouse feels about the amount of housework the other spouse does. Husbands who feel embarrassed or guilty even though the wife does *not* feel angry or disappointed are "very aware," husbands who feel embarrassed or guilty when the wife is angry or disappointed are "aware," and husbands who do not feel guilty or embarrassed even though their wife feels angry or disappointed are "unaware."

it is likely to reflect fathers being less engaged in coaching than other fathers, rather than these mothers being either more or less coaching than other mothers. Again, the basic picture tends to be one of variation (not all husband and fathers dismiss emotions) and one where such counter-stereotypical behavior by men makes for happier marriages. Putting the focus of attention on these cases, rather than treating them as less important exceptions to the rule, opens up the question of the social conditions and practices that encourage men to adopt cross- and counterstereotypical, and often highly productive, practices in their families.

FEMINISM IS GOOD FOR FAMILIES

We agree with Gottman that the issue for children is not whether fathers are present, but how men are present in children's lives. As Heiss's (1996) analysis also suggested, for both White and African American families, it is not if fathers are present, but how they are involved in their child's life that matters. Heiss compared mother-only and two-parent families, and found that parental involvement (frequency of parent–child conversation, extent to which the parent knows the doings and whereabouts of the respondent, and the mother's hopes for the child's future) was more important than family structure (father present or not) in predicting school performance.

Although the statistics that Gottman cites to describe the social conditions of men and women are open to many different interpretations, we particularly want to stress the political and policy issues in the data he reviews. For example, we are struck by how male managers who are married to women with full-time jobs earn less even though they do not work fewer hours. Gottman attributes this difference to men with more family demands being less available for work-centered male bonding activities like golf on weekends. This is part of the complaint that working mothers have always brought against the system: Advancement is predicated on a gender-based division of labor in which men are freed for work-based activities by wives' domestic labor, and why employed mothers say they "need a wife." To some extent, at least in the middle and upper classes, this need is met by hiring help and buying more expensive, prepared foods. However, that solution implies that the work at home, emotional as well as physical, that is conventionally the responsibility of mothers and wives, will not get done. A political solution that forces women back into the home to provide this labor is neither feasible nor desirable.

Gottman's work suggests that happier marriages, as well as children who thrive, are the product of both men and women who invest a lot in knowing their partners and children (what he calls having a more elaborate Love Map), and who are aware of, and responsive to, emotions. Because this is counterstereotypical involvement on the part of husbands and fathers, it also appears to have a more significant effect on outcomes. We would stress that this is not because women's involvement as wives and mothers does not matter, but because it is still the less variable background condition for most marriages and childrearing situations (Gottman's data on the inhomogeneity of variance supports this claim). Although Gottman is right to note the social forces pushing men toward more authoritarian marriage and parenting styles, this political trend seems more than ever to be counterproductive.

What people seem to need to manage happy and stable marriages is, instead, men whose masculinity is more counterstereotypical: a style of manliness that is not afraid to accept influence from women, to recognize and express emotion, and to give cognitive room to the marriage relation as such. Gottman is not shy about naming the religious right and various associated men's movements as influential forces pushing men toward authoritarian and stereotypical forms of masculinity and attempting to renew patriarchal family relations. We suggest he might go further and be equally explicit about naming feminism as a key force encouraging changes that are better for families, helping men and women to seek ways of bringing men back into families in non-authoritarian ways, both at the individual level by validating the expression of counterstereotypical behaviors, and at the societal level by urging legal and social changes such as the Family Leave Act and flex-time.

Feminism has made strides in increasing the social legitimacy of competitiveness and aggression in women, as the boom in women's sports has helped us all to see. The steps toward increasing the legitimacy of men accepting influence—or even leadership—from women, and expressing empathy and showing emotional responsiveness to their wives, and even coaching emotion in their children, are perhaps smaller and more tentative. Nonetheless, the greater variability shown in men's participation as fathers and husbands today helps to explain their statistical significance and should make clear to us that such changes are no less socially important. Although we appreciate Gottman's concern with improving marriages one at a time, as sociologists, we are more concerned with examining the social conditions that allow men to improve their performance as husbands and fathers generally or that put economic barriers in their way; these conditions include government policy. Title IX (equal funding of sports for women in federally funded schools) made a giant step forward for women in sports; perhaps it is time to consider social policies that will make similar steps for men in families easier.

This is not to suggest that only self-identified feminist men will make good fathers and husbands. Coltrane (1996) described a husband and wife who arranged their work schedules to allow genuine co-parenting of their two children. Neither considers him or herself feminist, nor are they choosing their arrangement for stated ideology or gender politics. Instead, they explain their arrangement as fitting their desire to best take care of their children and their marriage—an unconventional way to reach conventional goals. Although explicitly not feminist, the husband in this couple would be considered open to his wife's influence and sensitive to his own, his wife's, and his children's emotions. Yet we would argue that the social conditions that make their arrangement even conceivable are in a large part due to feminist changes. The value a husband places on his wife's advanced degree and her career, and the validity of his claims as a primary parent at school and in their social lives, are both shaped and reinforced through social change that would be inconceivable without more than 20 years of feminist pressure.

In this sense, we see feminist claims for change in government, in corporations, and in men's and women's expectations of themselves and each other as the real force advancing family values in U.S. society today. Although those who advocate a resurgence of authoritarian relations may be able to make it too hard for many women to leave dangerous and destructive marriages, Gottman's data suggests that this will not make the marriages any happier or better environments for raising children. Instead of seeing feminism as a threat to families and marriages, as some on the right would portray it, we take Gottman's data as one more basis for arguing that feminist directions in changing social conditions for men and women are among the most promising recipes for happy and stable marriages with thriving children.

ACKNOWLEDGMENT

This research is supported in part by grant SES 88–11944 from the National Science Foundation.

REFERENCES

Bem, S. L. (1983). Gender schema theory and its implications for child development: Raising gender aschematic children in a gender schematic society. *Signs: Journal of Women in Culture and Society, 8,* 598–616.

Coltrane, S. (1996). *Family man: Fatherhood, housework, and gender equity.* New York: Oxford University Press.

Connell, R. W. (1995). *Masculinities.* Berkeley, CA: University of California Press.

Ferree, M. M. (1990). Beyond separate spheres: Feminism and family research. *Journal of Marriage and the Family, 52*(4), 866–884.

Ferree, M. M. (1991). The gender division of labor in two-earner marriages: Dimensions of variability and change. *Journal of Family Issues, 12*(2), 158–180.

Heiss, J. (1996). Effects of African American family structure on school attitudes and performance. *Social Problems, 43*(3), 246–267.

Hochschild, A. (with Machung, A.). (1989). *The second shift.* New York: Viking.

Kurz, D. (1995). *For richer, for poorer: Mothers confront divorce.* New York: Routledge.

Thompson, L., & Walker, A. (1989). Gender in families: Women and men in marriage, work and parenthood. *Journal of Marriage and the Family, 51,* 845–871.

Thorne, B. (1993). *Gender play: Girls and boys in school.* New Brunswick, NJ: Rutgers University Press.

Chapter 12

Marriage in Men's Lives

Steven L. Nock
University of Virginia

Professor Gottman has provided a detailed analysis of the micro-environment of marriages. His research has demonstrated the impressive consequence of commonplace tactics and introduced terms that are now conventional topics in research: the cascade toward divorce, stonewalling, flooding, and the Horsemen of the Apocalypse. His prediction studies of divorce and his research on violence have directed our attention to the importance of some well-known psychological processes such as empathy, but also to some new ways of thinking, such as focusing on meta-emotions. His detailed method of sequential coding and his integration of psychophysiological perspectives (even using such approaches as catastrophe theory) make his work arguably the most detailed microanalysis of marriage and divorce available.

A sociological perspective on marriage also addresses such topics. However, it rarely gets to the immediate lives of the partners in such detail. Therefore, in my comments, I take several of Gottman's central observations and move away from the moments of interaction and consider the social and institutional contexts in which they occur. I focus on how marriage matters for men by looking at what married men are expected to be—at the roles that our society presumes and encourages men to assume. This perspective views the intimate life of any married individual as also being influenced by social structure (i.e., laws, religion, custom, convention) that is a basic sociological perspective.

In particular, I take my lead from the following observations in Gottman's chapter:

1. Marriages will work to the extent that men can accept influence from their wives.
2. Some husbands find accepting such influence to be an affront to their honor.
3. Some fundamental incompatibilities in marriage arise from divergent views about emotion.
4. Some fathers may focus on work and achievement more than on their own children.

There is a sociological theme related to gender that unites these seemingly disparate points, at least with respect to married men. That theme focuses on marriage as a social institution and venue for the expression and development of adult masculinity. My work on this subject examines marriage as a socially patterned framework for men's expression of masculinity.

MARRIAGE AND MASCULINITY

For the past several years, I have been studying how and why marriage changes men. Many researchers have found that men benefit in tangible ways from their marriages, and many have suggested that "his" marriage is better than "hers." My work focuses on "his" marriage and asks why men benefit from matrimony. I begin with the observation that marriage is not some point on a continuum of relationship possibilities. That is, marriage is not quantitatively different from other types of relationships. It is fundamentally different in a qualitative way. This is because marriage is a social structure, or social institution, governed and surrounded by countless soft boundaries that originate in law, religion, economy, education, and public opinion.

The difference between a long-term cohabiting relationship and a marriage is not one of degree. It is a substantive difference because of the way these two relationships are defined by others. Cohabiting couples may enjoy virtually every other thing that married couples enjoy except one: The unmarried couple is exempt from the vast set of laws, assumptions, expectations, and norms that govern marriage. The normative assumptions and legal expectations surrounding marriage are unlike those in any other type of relationship. A sociologist will consider such social structures in an attempt to understand the cause of behavior. This does not deny the importance of any of the things Gottman has discussed. Rather, it offers a perspective on how social forces are involved in them.

A married man can say to his wife: "I am your husband. You are my wife. I am expected to do certain things for you, and you likewise. We have pledged our faithfulness. We have sworn to forego others. We have a binding commitment to our children. We have a responsibility to our relatives and they have a binding responsibility to us." These are not simply sentiments. They are *legally* enforceable. Others will expect these things and will act accordingly. And when this man says to someone "I would like you to meet my wife" that simple declaration says a great deal. No other type of relationship shares this essential feature.

Marriage thus contains elements that originate outside the married couple. This institutional aspect of marriage is part of the relationship of any two married people. Marriage is a form of capital. It is a template. And this aspect of marriage, the normative rules surrounding it, helps us understand how and why men benefit from it.

After reviewing domestic-relations law, religious doctrine, the Bible, Supreme Court decisions, and public opinion, I formulated an elementary definition of marriage as it is expressed in our social structure—although not necessarily in the lives of every married couple. This I refer to as a *normative definition* of marriage. Understand that this is not necessarily a descriptive statement about modern marriages (although it actually comes quite close). Rather, it is a cultural definition, a statement of how U.S. society defines the institution of marriage.

MARRIAGE AS A DISPLAY OF GENDER

Marriage is the elemental environment in which gender is produced. This means that gender exists as it is displayed. As Fenstermaker (cited in Berk, 1985) noted, the household is the gender factory. The dimensions of normative marriage (e.g., heterosexuality, maturity, etc.) are powerful symbols that husbands use in the ongoing everyday display of gender.

A long line of sociological writing has focused on how gender is produced in everyday encounters. Goffman, for example, showed that gender is one ingredient in what other people see as our essential nature—that is, gender is something that endures and persists. People know one another as males or females, even when they know very little else. The gender stereotypes that inform our sense of masculinity or femininity are embedded in all social institutions—the law, the economy, religion, and so on. This gives gender a coercive quality. People who deviate in obvious ways from the ordinary are treated differently. The effeminate male, the masculine woman, or the androgynous person whose gender cannot be discerned pay various prices for their departures from convention.

The universal cultural imperative heard in the order to "be a man" implies that it does not go without saying, and that manliness is less natural than one might think (Badinter, 1992). But almost all societies provide a mechanism by which this can be done. And they provide a method by which males may sustain their claims to masculinity.

So, how do males become "men" in U.S. society? What are the rituals and public rites that announce and sustain this status? In my forthcoming book *Marriage in Men's Lives* (Nock, 1998), I show that traditional normative marriage is the American way of making men.

Throughout the world, anthropologists have found that three social roles define masculinity. These are universal, so far as we know. In all known societies, adult men should be fathers to their wives' children, providers for their families, and protectors of wives and children. This trinity of social roles defines masculinity in an inherently sociological way. It focuses on those things that men are expected to be. So closely connected are the ideas of masculinity and marriage that in many cultures, males who do not pass the rites of manhood are denied the rights of marriage.

COMPONENTS OF NORMATIVE MARRIAGE

A model of normative marriage includes the following six components, all but one of which are operationalized in my research:

1. The decision to marry is an individual choice, based on love. There is a marriage market.
2. Maturity is a presumed requirement for marriage.
3. Marriage is a heterosexual relationship.
4. Marriage ordinarily involves childbearing.
5. Husbands are the heads of, and the principal earners in a marriage.
6. Sexual fidelity and monogamy are requirements for marriage.

Whether an individual couple conforms to all of these dimensions is not particularly important, and some clearly do not (empirically, of course, most do). Instead, these expectations are a form of social control. Because it is institutionalized, normative marriage establishes boundaries for behavior and aspirations. It is a force greater than the married couple because it represents the collective sentiments of others. And it is in these rules that we may find a partial explanation for why men benefit from marriage.

Psychological and epidemiological studies have repeatedly documented the better physical and mental health of married than single men. There are even benefits for wives (Crum, Helzer, & Anthony, 1993; Hu & Goldman, 1990; Reissman & Gerstel, 1985). But the quality of the marriage appears to be critical for women. Women appear to benefit from a good marriage. They do not appear to benefit from a bad marriage. However, this is decidedly not true for men. Overall, for the types of outcomes considered by most researchers, the quality of the marriage is largely irrelevant for husbands. For men, differences in psychological and physical health are associated with marital status; for women, they are associated with marital quality (Gove, Hughes, & Style, 1983; Hughes & Gove, 1981).

One very obvious explanation for such findings, of course, is that marriage is selective. Not all who wish to marry actually do so. It is possible that the least healthy men are unattractive marriage partners. There are mundane and prosaic aspects of marriage that might make it appear that married men are healthier—lack of time to visit the doctor, for example.

Alternatively, marriage may actually cause the differences that have been found in comparisons between married and unmarried men. Marriage involves a different lifestyle than bachelorhood. Wives are important sources of help and assistance to their husbands. Men may be encouraged by wives to visit their doctors and attend to their health, and the greater social involvement of married people may minimize some types of mental health problems by providing networks of support (see, e.g., Waite, 1995).

CHALLENGES TO NORMATIVE MARRIAGE

In my search for clues about how marriage affects men, I found that considering challenges to traditional marriage was quite helpful in identifying significant dimensions of marriage that matter, at least to large numbers of people. There is a general theme to challenges to traditional marriage in law, religion, and public opinion.

For most of the century, adult men's lives were defined by marriage. As mature adults, men were also "good providers." The mature man was a stable husband and father. To be anything else traditionally implied that a man was somehow less than a man. The adult male who could not, or worse, would not provide for his wife and family was not only a failure, he was not really a man.

We are now seeing a questioning and rejection of certain elements of traditional marriage. More than anything else, the gendered nature of marriage is being questioned.

Whereas other dimensions of traditional marriage have undergone change (e.g., the idea that sex or childbearing occurs only in marriage), the most direct challenge to the basic institution of marriage has been the assumption that the husband is the head of the household.

We may read such trends as calling into question the idea that to be an adult male means to be a husband who provides for a wife and family.

But despite widespread commentary and critiques, has the association between marriage and masculinity been broken? Is the definition of masculinity no longer connected to men's roles as husbands and fathers? Can males be "men" without marrying? I propose that they cannot.

HOW MARRIAGE AFFECTS MEN

So, finally we may ask, how would we expect marriage to change a man? What are the dependent variables? In light of the points I raised, we can make simple predictions about what happens when a man marries or when his marriage becomes more or less traditional (i.e., consistent with the normative model).

1. *Adult achievement.* Providing for a family is a central part of normative marriage and masculinity. Married men, and men in more normative marriages will achieve more than others.

2. *Social participation.* High levels of engagement and involvement in public, as opposed to private affairs is part of the masculine image. More particularly, the model of masculinity that I use predicts that marriage will foster greater involvement in organizations where participation is governed by clearly defined rules and standards wherein the man is an occupant of a clearly defined role. A husband is more likely to join a church or other formal organization than a health club because the former are defined by rules of membership.

3. *Philanthropy.* Giving is a direct extension of the marital roles of provider and protector. My model of gender predicts that marriage will foster a particular type of giving and helping. Married men's gifts and assistance are likely to be patterned by role expectations. A married man is less likely to help out a friend and more likely to help his church or close relatives. His philanthropy will be patterned by rules of membership.

For example, consider the very simple comparison of men before and after marriage on three measures of adult achievement (data are from the National Longitudinal Survey of Youth, 1979–1993 panels and results are based on pooled cross-section time series techniques with fixed-effects). The bars in Figs. 12.1, 12.2, and 12.3 show the change in the outcome that followed a change in marital status. All such changes are in addition to those normally associated with aging. In other words, any effect plotted in these figures is in addition to changes that were occurring independently of a change in marital status. For all three outcomes considered, marriage is associated with gains in achievement.

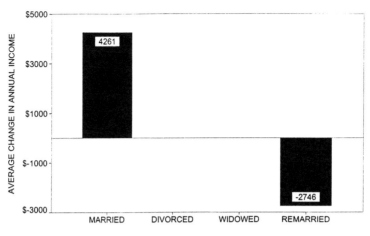

FIG. 12.1. Average change in annual income as a result of changes in marital status. Data from the "National Longitudinal Survey of Youth" (1979–1993).

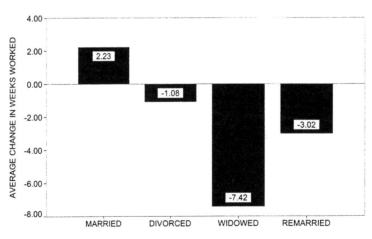

FIG. 12.2. Average change in weeks worked as a result of changes in marital status. Data from the "National Longitudinal Survey of Youth" (1979–1993).

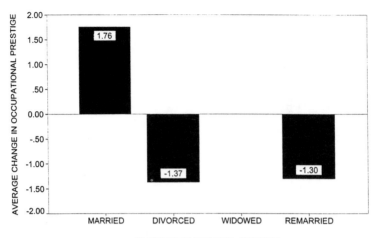

FIG. 12.3. Average change in occupational prestige as a result of changes in marital status. Data from the "National Longitudinal Survey of Youth" (1979–1993).

More compelling is how variations in normative marriage are associated with changes in such outcomes. I study this by operationalizing the dimensions of normative marriage (i.e., the independent variables) as follows (there is no way to operationalize the assumption of heterosexuality in marriage because it is a constant):

1. Free choice is measured as the age-specific sex ratio of unmarried persons. The higher this value, the less valuable a man is on the marriage market, and the more valuable is his current marriage.
2. Maturity is measured as economic independence. I simply compute what proportion of the total family income is generated by the couple through wages and investments.
3. Parenthood is measured by counting the number of biological children who reside in the household.
4. Husband as head is measured with a conventional strategy that shows the proportionate dependence of one spouse on the other's income. A +1 means the husband earns all income and −1 means the wife earns all income.
5. Fidelity and monogamy are measured by determining the number of years a man has been married to this particular woman.

In Figs. 12.4, 12.5, and 12.6, the effects of each dimension of normative marriage are plotted by comparing the minimum and maximum effect. At the left of each figure the changes in outcomes associated with the minimum change in each dimension are plotted. At the right, the changes in outcomes associated with the maximum change in each dimension are plotted. Each line is drawn to reflect the consequence of a change in one dimension of marriage from the minimum to the maximum level. As these figures show, changes from less to more traditional (i.e., normative) marriages are associated with increases in adult achievement.

Similar results were found for the other two areas in which men are predicted to change as a result of their marriages. So what are we to conclude?

CONCLUSION

To return to the four points raised by Gottman. The ability or willingness of men to accept influence from their wives, or men's sense of a "code of honor" could be translated as what it means to be (or appears to be) masculine. These ideas do not originate solely within the marriage; rather, they are part of a cultural model of both masculinity and marriage. With

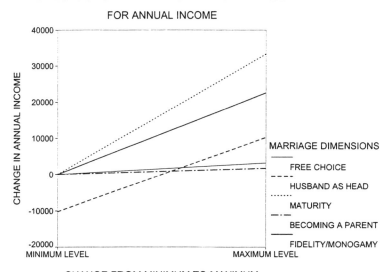

FIG. 12.4. Effects of changes in marriage dimensions for annual income.

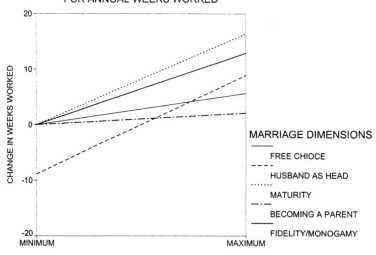

EFFECTS OF CHANGES IN NORMATIVE MARRIAGE
FOR ANNUAL WEEKS WORKED

MARRIAGE DIMENSIONS

——— FREE CHIOCE

- - - - HUSBAND AS HEAD

······· MATURITY

—·— BECOMING A PARENT

——— FIDELITY/MONOGAMY

CHANGE FROM MINIMUM TO MAXIMUM

Data from the National Longitudinal Survey of Youth: 1979-1993

FIG. 12.5. Effects of changes in marriage dimensions for annual weeks worked.

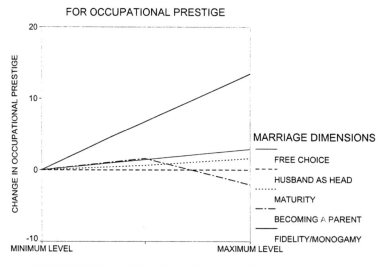

EFFECTS OF CHANGES IN NORMATIVE MARRIAGE
FOR OCCUPATIONAL PRESTIGE

MARRIAGE DIMENSIONS

——— FREE CHIOCE

- - - - HUSBAND AS HEAD

······· MATURITY

—·— BECOMING A PARENT

——— FIDELITY/MONOGAMY

CHANGE FROM MINIMUM TO MAXIMUM LEVEL

Data from the National Longitudinal Survey of Youth: 1979-1993

FIG. 12.6. Effects of changes in marriage dimensions for occupational prestige.

236

respect to the divergent meta-emotions, the idea that men and women may have different views on emotion is also something we find clues about in cultural definitions of marriage and masculinity. The way emotion is expressed can be seen as a form of gender display. Likewise, men's over-involvement in work might be understood as a response to what men internalize about the provider/protector role. It is not surprising that Gottman describes the emergence of social movements stressing how important it is for men to maintain their masculinity within the framework of modern marriages.

My point is a very simple one. In attempting to understand the process of marriages and the dynamics involved, we may benefit by examining the details of intimate interaction as well as the sociocultural context of gender in marriage. As husbands, men's behaviors must be understood in the context of our cultural definition of masculinity.

REFERENCES

Badinter, E. (1992). *XY: On masculine identity* (L. Davis, Trans.). New York: Columbia University Press.

Berk, S. F. (1985). *The gender factory.* New York: Plenum Press.

Crum, R. M., Helzer, J. E., & Anthony, J. C. (1993). Level of education and alcohol abuse and dependence in adulthood: A further inquiry. *American Journal of Public Health, 83,* 830–837.

Gove, W. R., Hughes, M., & Style, C. B. (1983). Does marriage have positive effects on the psychological well being of the individual? *Journal of Health and Social Behavior, 24,* 122–131.

Hu, Y., & Goldman, N. (1990). Mortality differentials by marital status: An international comparison. *Demography, 27*(2), 233–250.

Hughes, M., & Gove, W. R. (1981). Living alone, social integration, and mental health. *American Journal of Sociology, 87,* 48–74.

National longitudinal survey of youth. (1995). (Machine-readable data file). Center for Human Resource Research: The Ohio State University, Columbus, OH.

Nock, S. L. (1998). *Marriage in men's lives.* New York: Oxford University Press. Manuscript submitted for publication.

Reissman, C. K., & Gerstel, N. (1985). Marital dissolution and health: Do males or females have greater risk? *Social Science and Medicine, 20*(6), 627–635.

Waite, L. J. (1995). Does marriage matter? *Demography, 32,* 483–507.

Part IV

FATHERS: WHEN DO THEY MAKE A DIFFERENCE?

Chapter 13

More Than Money?
Men's Contributions to
Their Children's Lives

Paul R. Amato
University of Nebraska–Lincoln

A couple of generations ago, American men understood what it meant to
be fathers. The consensus of the 1950s, as codified in the structural func-
tionalism of Parsons and Bales (1955), held that men were the instrumental
leaders of their families. Fathers were responsible for the family's social
status, provided economic support, dispensed discipline, and served as role
models of employment and achievement. Mothers, as the socioemotional
leaders of the family, were responsible for domestic chores, child care,
and meeting the emotional needs of family members. Of course, there
were marked individual differences—as well as racial, ethnic, class, and
geographical variations—in how men and women enacted their parental
roles. Nevertheless, the instrumental father depicted by Parsons and Bales
was the cultural ideal, and one that described the behavior of many men.

During the last 40 years, the cultural consensus about fatherhood has
disintegrated. The economic recessions of the 1970s and 1980s increased
male unemployment and eroded men's wages, making it more difficult
for fathers to fulfill the breadwinner role. Partly in response to men's
declining economic opportunities, mothers moved into the paid labor
force in large numbers (Hernandez, 1993). An increase in women's educational attainment, a decline in family size, and the spread of an ideology
of gender equality facilitated this movement. Dual-earner families came to
replace good-provider families, and the specialized division of labor between men and women began to blur.

As women became more like fathers, so men were expected to become
more like mothers. The belief that parents should share child care shifted

241

from a minority opinion in the 1960s to a majority opinion in the 1980s (Thornton, 1989). People believe that fathers should be involved with children because it relieves the burden experienced by employed mothers. But many people also assume that children benefit when fathers provide child care, are highly involved in children's lives, and are affectionate and emotionally expressive. After all, if maternal love and attention are good for children, then two nurturant parents should be better than one.

Children might benefit from a less specialized, more androgynous nuclear family—one in which fathers and mothers share breadwinning and caregiving roles equally. But the "degendering" of family roles has not gone smoothly. Although men have increased their participation in child care over the last 30 years, the amount of change has been small (Coltrane, 1995; Pleck, 1997). Indeed, many men are reluctant to take on extra child care duties, preferring instead to let their employed wives do a "second shift" (Hochschild, 1989). And although some wives accept this state of affairs with equanimity, other wives experience the household division of labor as a major source of marital tension (Pina & Bengtson, 1993; Yogev & Brett, 1985).

Changes in family structure have exacerbated this problem. The rise in single-mother households (due to increases in divorce and nonmarital birth) has reduced the amount of time that men spend living with children over the life course (Eggebeen & Uhlenberg, 1985). Furthermore, many nonresident fathers see their children infrequently and pay no child support or less than they should (Furstenberg & Nord, 1985; Seltzer & Bianchi, 1988). Increasingly, American children are being raised with little or no assistance from fathers. These changes in behavior and family structure have led to a contradictory situation: At a time when some men are becoming more involved with children, men (as a group) are spending less time with children than ever before (Furstenberg, 1988).

We generally ask questions about fundamental social arrangements during times of rapid social change. It is not surprising, therefore, that the dramatic shifts that have occurred in family life during the last 40 years have led many people to raise questions about the significance of fathers. If most fathers can no longer exclusively claim the breadwinner role, and if most fathers are unwilling or unable to share the role of caregiver, then what exactly are fathers good for? The answer to this question is not only of theoretical interest, but also has practical consequences for the formation of family policy—and for the lives of individual fathers and children.

In this chapter, I assess the importance of fathers in children's lives. My task has three components. First, I present a conceptual analysis of the potential contributions that fathers, as well as mothers, make to their children's development, attainment, and well-being. Second, I review recent studies to assess the degree of empirical support for the existence of father effects. Several authors have provided excellent reviews of this literature (Biller, 1993; Lamb, 1981, 1987; Popenoe, 1996; Radin & Russell, 1983; Snarey, 1993). However, most prior reviews focus on paternal involvement in childrearing and do not consider other dimensions of potential influence, such as fathers' human capital and income. Furthermore, previous reviews tend to focus on two-parent families and do not consider the impact of nonresident fathers. I attempt to go beyond previous reviews by considering multiple dimensions of paternal influence and by including studies of nonresident as well as resident fathers. Third, I supplement the literature review with a new analysis based on a unique 12-year longitudinal study of parents and young adult offspring.

THEORY

As children develop, they actively use whatever resources are present in their social and physical environments. Fathers and mothers are usually (but not always) the central members of children's social networks. Consequently, children's development is bound up with the quantity and quality of resources that parents provide. Following Coleman (1988, 1990), I divide parental resources into human capital, financial capital, and social capital. Children are also affected by the genetic resources provided by parents, as reflected in physical appearance, health status, the heritable component of cognitive ability, and temperament. Biological influence, however, is beyond the scope of the present review.

Human Capital

Human capital refers to parents' possession of skills, knowledge, and traits that facilitate achievement in U.S. society (Becker, 1991). Broadly construed, human capital includes verbal and numeric ability, occupational skills, effective work habits, and knowledge of correct forms of speech and dress. A key indicator of parents' human capital is years of education. Fathers and mothers with a high level of human capital are able to foster their children's cognitive skills and socioeconomic attainment by providing stimulating home environments, encouraging high occupational aspirations, and modeling everyday behaviors (such as regular participation in the labor force) that children learn through observation.

Financial Capital

Financial capital refers to income, or goods or experiences purchased with income, that parents provide to their children. Examples of these resources include wholesome food, adequate shelter in safe neighborhoods, access to high-quality schools, commodities that facilitate children's academic success (books, computers, travel, and private lessons), and support for college attendance.

Social Capital

Social capital, as defined by Coleman (1988, 1990) is a resource that adheres in the relationships between people. In the present context, social capital refers to family and community relations that benefit children's cognitive and social development. In this chapter, I focus on two aspects of social capital: the co-parental relationship and the parent–child relationship.

The Co-parental Relationship. The co-parental relationship represents a resource for children that is inherently dyadic. In this context, Coleman (1990) discussed the importance of *closure,* that is, a strong link between two (or more) adults who each have a relationship with the child. Although single parents can provide individual resources to children, it takes two interacting parents (married or otherwise) to provide dyadic resources.

One benefit of a positive co-parental relationship for children is the modeling of dyadic skills. These skills include providing emotional support, showing respect, communicating openly, and resolving disputes through negotiation and compromise. Children who learn these skills through observation of parental models are likely to experience positive relationships with peers, and later, with intimate partners.

In addition, parents with a cooperative relationship are able to present a united authority structure. When parents agree on the rules for children and support one another's decisions, children learn that parental authority is not arbitrary. Parental agreement also means that children are not subjected to inconsistent discipline following misbehavior. Social closure between parents helps children to learn and internalize social norms and moral values. Also, a respect for hierarchical authority, first learned in the family, makes it easier for young people to adjust to social institutions that are hierarchically organized, such as schools and the workplace (Nock, 1988).

Finally, the nature of the relationship between parents can affect children through its impact on parent–child relationships. For example, wives with hostile and abusive husbands are likely to feel distracted, emotionally drained, and irritable. As a result, they may be unresponsive or short-tempered when dealing with their children. In contrast, wives with supportive and helpful husbands are likely to have positive feelings that allow for more effective parenting. Similarly, support from mothers is likely to improve the quality of fathers' parenting.

The Parent–Child Relationship. In terms of children's development, the amount of time that parents and children spend together is not as important as the nature of the interaction that occurs between them. In particular, parental support and control are dimensions of parental behavior that represent key resources for children (Baumrind, 1968; Maccoby & Martin, 1983; Rollins & Thomas, 1979). Support is reflected in behaviors such as affection, responsiveness, encouragement, instruction, and everyday assistance. These behaviors facilitate children's positive development by conveying a basic sense of trust and security, reinforcing children's self-conceptions of worth and competence, and promoting the learning of practical skills.

Control is reflected in rule formulation, discipline, monitoring, and supervision. Through these processes, children learn that their attempts to affect the environment must operate within a set of socially constructed boundaries. In addition, by explaining the reasons behind rules (induction), parents help children to internalize rules and engage in self-regulation. Parental control is harmful, however, if it is enforced with coercive punishment, such as hitting. Furthermore, as children grow into adolescence, it is necessary for parents to relax their degree of regulation. If parents are too restrictive, adolescents do not have opportunities to develop new forms of competence, profit from their mistakes, and learn to accept responsibility for their own decisions. Excessive control may also generate feelings of resentment toward parents, thus eroding parent–child affection. Nevertheless, parental monitoring is still necessary to ensure that adolescents do well in school and do not drift into delinquent or antisocial activities.

Summary of the Conceptual Model

The conceptual model assumes that children's development is related to the quality of human, financial, and social capital that parents provide. This perspective assumes that fathers as well as mothers are capable of providing all three of these resources. Of course, in the United States, fathers and mothers have tended to provide different types of resources to children, with fathers providing social status and income, and mothers providing child care and emotional support. Most observers believe that cultural and historical factors have shaped gender differences in parenting, although others argue that fathers and mothers are biologically predisposed to specialize in certain tasks (Becker, 1991; Popenoe, 1996; Rossi, 1984). But in spite of cultural, historical, or biological pushes in either direction, the fact remains that any type of resource, in principle, can be provided by either fathers or mothers.

Nevertheless, not all fathers provide the resources just described. Some fathers are poorly educated, experience chronic unemployment, and earn little money; some fathers engage in chronic warfare against their wives; and some fathers are uninterested or abusive toward their children. Rather than serving as resources, these fathers may increase the level of stress in children's lives. Therefore, one must consider not only the extent to which fathers are involved with children, but also the extent to which they provide useful resources. In other words, if fathers are important, then they have the potential for harm as well as good.

The conceptual model that guides my analysis appears in Fig. 13.1. Note the causal ordering among the four types of paternal resources. In the model, paternal human capital (as reflected in education) is positively related to paternal financial capital (as reflected in earnings). This assumption is based on the well-replicated finding that education is a fundamental predictor of income (U.S. Bureau of the Census, 1992b). Both education and income, in turn, exert a positive influence on children's social capital, as reflected in the quality of the coparental relationship (Conger et al., 1990; Elder, 1974; Lewis & Spanier, 1979; Voydanoff, 1991) and the father–child relationship (Conger et al., 1992, 1993; Elder, Nguyen, & Caspi, 1985; McLoyd, 1989; McLoyd & Wilson, 1991; Sampson & Laub, 1994; Simons, Beaman, Conger, & Chao, 1993). Finally, the quality of the coparental relationship is positively related to the quality of the parent–child relationship (Belsky, 1984; Davies & Cummings, 1994; Grych & Fincham, 1990), especially for fathers (Belsky, Youngblade, Rovine, & Volling, 1991; Booth & Amato, 1994; Cummings & O'Reilly, 1997; Peterson & Zill, 1986). Previous research, therefore, amply documents all of the proposed linkages between categories of paternal resources.

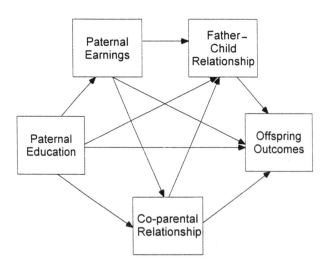

FIG. 13.1. Conceptual model of father influence.

HYPOTHESES

In the remainder of this chapter, I consider four hypotheses:

Hypothesis 1: Fathers' education is positively associated with children's well-being.

Hypothesis 2: Fathers' income is positively associated with children's well-being.

Hypothesis 3: The quality of the co-parental relationship (as reflected in the extent to which fathers model constructive dyadic skills, cooperate with mothers in childrearing, and are emotionally supportive of mothers) is positively associated with children's well-being.

Hypothesis 4: The quality of the father–child relationship (as reflected in the level of support and effective control exercised by fathers) is positively associated with children's well-being.

To assess the degree of support for these hypotheses, I carried out a review of relevant empirical studies. Given the large number of studies involved, I limited my search to articles, chapters, and books published since 1980, along with a few recent conference papers. In addition, I restricted my search to studies that examined child (and adolescent) outcomes in four broad categories: (a) cognitive ability and academic achievement, (b) conduct problems, (c) psychological adjustment and self-esteem, and (d) social competence and peer relations. I also included studies of young adult offspring if they utilized comparable (but age appropriate) outcomes, such as educational attainment, delinquency or criminal behavior, depression, and the size of social support networks (I discuss studies of young adults separately, however).

In evaluating the evidence, I pay particular attention to studies that control for maternal resources in estimating the effects of paternal resources. This is because paternal and maternal characteristics, such as education and childrearing behaviors, are likely to be positively correlated. To determine if fathers make unique contributions to children's welfare, therefore, it is necessary to incorporate maternal and paternal variables in statistical models.

After assessing each hypothesis in general, I consider the extent to which support for each varies with (a) children's gender, (b) children's race, and (c) family structure. In relation to the last point, any assessment of the importance of fathers must take into account the fact that more than half of all children in the United States today spend part (or all) of their childhoods living apart from their fathers.

Finally, to supplement previous literature, I carried out a new analysis using 12-year longitudinal data on parents and young adult offspring.

LITERATURE REVIEW

Fathers' Human Capital

The first hypothesis states that paternal education is associated with positive outcomes among children. Much of the research relevant to this hypothesis has focused on socioeconomic outcomes among offspring in late adolescence or young adulthood. Of 13 studies examining the association between fathers' and offspring's education, only one shows no statistical significance (Conklin & Daily, 1981). Another shows positive estimated effects for fathers' education but not for mothers' (Wilson, Peterson, & Wilson, 1993). However, the most common result is for fathers' and mothers' educations to predict offspring's education, even with both variables in the equation simultaneously (Alwin & Thornton, 1984; Behrman & Taubman, 1985; Cohen, 1987; Haveman, Wolf, & Spaulding, 1991; Hill & Duncan, 1987; Jencks, Crouse, & Mueser, 1983; Kalmijn, 1994; Krein, 1986; Mare, 1981; Rumberger, 1983; Teachman, 1987). Fathers' education is also positively associated with the occupational status and earnings of offspring, even with mothers' education controlled (Jencks et al., 1983; Kerkhoff, Campbell, & Trott, 1982; Kiker & Condon, 1981; Sewell, Hauser, & Wolf, 1980).

Paternal education is also positively associated with young children's grade point averages (Alwin & Thornton, 1984; DiMaggio, 1982), cognitive and achievement test scores (Alwin & Thornton, 1984; Amato, 1987; Blau & Grossberg, 1992; Mercy & Steelman, 1982; Parcel & Menaghan, 1994; Steelman & Doby, 1983), and school attendance (Browne & Rife, 1991). Although most studies have examined school-related outcomes, others show that paternal education is related positively to children's self-esteem, life skills, social competence, and cooperativeness (Amato, 1987; Roberts, 1987). A few studies fail to yield significant results (Smith, 1989; Wright, Peterson, & Barnes, 1990). Nevertheless, the great majority of studies suggest beneficial effects of having well-educated fathers. Most (but not all) of these studies control for maternal education. Furthermore, many of these studies show that fathers' education is positively associated with children's outcomes independently of family income, indicating that some of the effect of fathers' education is direct and not mediated by earnings.

Is father's education more important for sons than daughters? Some studies show that paternal education predicts outcomes for sons but not daughters (Rumberger, 1983), but other studies show the reverse pattern (Cohen, 1987). And several studies that search for differences between sons and daughters fail to find them (Hill & Duncan, 1987; Kalmijn, 1994; Teachman, 1987). Overall, the literature suggests that daughters as well as sons benefit from having well-educated fathers.

Do the effects of paternal education hold across racial and ethnic groups? Several studies show positive links between paternal education and offspring's cognitive skills (Steelman & Doby, 1983) and high school completion (Rumberger, 1983) among Blacks as well as Whites. Similarly, paternal education predicts test scores equally well among Whites and Asian Americans (Chen & Stevenson, 1995). Although the number of studies is small, they suggest that the impact of paternal education is similar across racial and ethnic groups.

Nonresident Fathers. The studies reviewed above deal mostly with fathers in two-parent households. Does the education of nonresident fathers yield similar results? Coleman (1988) noted that parents' human capital is largely irrelevant to children if parents are not involved actively in children's lives. Based on this assumption, one would expect the effects of paternal human capital to be stronger when children experience separations from fathers at older ages, as this allows more time for paternal influence to occur. For children who are young at the time of parental separation, fathers' human capital may be influential only under conditions of close and regular contact. However, divorces tend to occur when children are relatively young, and many fathers do not maintain frequent contact. These considerations suggest that the influence of paternal human capital may be weaker for nonresident than for resident fathers.

Two studies of children in single-mother households are consistent with this reasoning. Knox and Bane (1994) and Murnane, Maynard, and Ohls (1981) found that maternal education, but not paternal education, is associated with children's educational attainment and test scores, respectively. Nevertheless, additional studies that present relevant data are needed before one can reach any meaningful conclusion.

Fathers' Financial Capital

The second hypothesis states that fathers' financial capital is positively related to children's well-being. Many studies have examined the effects of family income on children; most of these have focused on poverty, rather than affluence. Nevertheless, these studies have documented the harmful toll that economic hardship takes on children. Poverty is associated with poor nutrition and health problems (Klerman, 1991), low school grades, an elevated risk of dropping out of school (Levin, 1986), and a higher incidence of emotional and behavioral problems, such as depression, low self-esteem, conduct disorders, and conflict with peers (McLoyd, 1989; McLoyd & Wilson, 1991).

In spite of this consistency, surprisingly few studies have attempted to disentangle the effects of paternal and maternal income. However, because women earn less money than men and are less likely to be in full-time employment, wives contribute only about one third of the income in dual-earner households, with husbands contributing the other two thirds (U.S. Bureau of the Census, 1992b). Consequently, the effects of family income on children are due mainly to fathers' income. In other words, most children are poor either because their fathers earn little money or because their fathers are absent and pay little or no child support. In this sense, most of the effects of poverty are effects of fathers' (low) income. Research by McLanahan and Sandefur (1995), which showed that income differences between single-mother and two-parent households account for about one half of the gap in children's socioeconomic outcomes, was consistent with this interpretation.

Nevertheless, to test the second hypothesis adequately, it is necessary to estimate the effects of paternal and maternal income separately. It is also necessary, in testing this hypothesis, to control for paternal education in order to avoid spurious associations. Two studies that carried out appropriate tests showed that fathers' earnings are positively associated with the education attainment (Hill & Duncan, 1987) and earned income (Behrman & Taubman, 1985) of adult sons and daughters. Other studies yield less clear results. For example, Blau and Grossberg (1992) found that fathers' income is positively associated with children's cognitive test scores at the bivariate level, but not when mothers' income is controlled. Rumberger (1983) found that fathers' earnings are negatively associated with dropping out of high school among White females, but not among White males. Furthermore, this study found no significant associations for Black or Hispanic students of either gender. Overall, the evidence suggests that fathers' earnings are positively associated with some offspring outcomes, but the number of studies is disappointingly small.

Nonresident Fathers. Does paternal income matter for children living in single-mother households? Under these circumstances, it is not the total income of nonresident fathers, but the amount that is transferred to children, that one would expect to affect children's well-being. Therefore, the most relevant studies to answer this question are those that estimate the impact of fathers' payment of child support.

Ideally, studies should control for maternal income in assessing the importance of paternal child support. Because marriages tend to be homogamous in terms of education, maternal income may be positively associated with paternal income, and paternal income is a good predictor of fathers' payment of child support (Braver, Fitzpatrick, & Bay, 1991; Seltzer, 1991). Consequently, any observed "effects" of paternal child support may really be due to maternal income. Paying child support is also positively correlated with fathers' contact with children (Furstenberg, Morgan, & Allison, 1987; Seltzer, Schaeffer, & Charng, 1989), fathers feeling that they have control over their children's upbringing (Braver, Wolchik,

Sandler, Sheets, Fogas, & Curtis, 1993; Teachman, 1991), and the quality of relations between parents (Teachman, 1991). And because contact with children creates opportunities for conflict between parents (Amato & Rezac, 1991), paying child support can also increase interparental discord. Because maternal income, paternal contact, and interparental conflict all might affect children's well-being, it is desirable to control for these variables in assessing the role of child support.

Several studies, using an impressive variety of large data sets, have revealed positive associations between the amount of child support paid by nonresident fathers and measures of children's well-being. Furstenberg, Morgan, and Allison (1987), using the National Survey of Children, found that fathers' child support payments are negatively related to mothers' and teachers' reports of behavior problems. McLanahan, Seltzer, Hanson, and Thomson (1994), using the National Survey of Families and Households, found that fathers' payment of child support is positively associated with mothers' reports of children's school grades and negatively associated with mothers' reports of school behavior problems. King (1994), using the National Longitudinal Survey of Youth, found that payment of child support is positively associated with children's reading and math scores. Finally, Knox and Bane (1994), using the Panel Study of Income Dynamics, and Graham, Beller, and Hernandez (1994), using the Current Population Survey, found that fathers' payment of child support is positively associated with children's years of attained education. In general, these associations do not vary with the sex or race of children (Furstenberg, Morgan, & Allison, 1987; King, 1994). Furthermore, several of these studies controlled for the confounding variables just discussed (maternal income, paternal contact, and interparental conflict), thus increasing our confidence in the findings.

However, not all studies are in agreement. Three studies based on the NLSY fail to find consistent positive effects of child support. Baydar and Brooks-Gunn (1994) found that fathers' payment of child support is positively but not significantly associated with daughters' reading scores. Similarly, Heard (1995) found no link between payment of child support and children's self-esteem, behavior problems, school problems, or delinquency. And Argys, Peters, Smith, and Brooks-Gunn (1995) found that payment of child support is not only positively associated with math and reading scores among African Americans, but also with higher behavior problems. Finally, Simons, Whitbeck, Beaman, and Conger (1994), using a sample of children in Iowa, found that fathers' child support payments are negatively related to sons' (but not daughters') externalizing behavior at the bivariate level, but not when controlling for the quality of fathers' parenting and the extent of interparental conflict.

In summary, although contradictory studies exist, the balance of evidence suggests that fathers' payment of child support benefits children.

Presumably, these benefits occur for the same reason that fathers' income benefits children in two-parent households. That is, regular child support payments improve children's health and nutrition, increase the amount of stimulation in the home environment, and improve children's access to educational resources. Alternatively, the payment of child support may benefit children indirectly by lowering the level of stress experienced by mothers—an explanation as yet untested. Furthermore, although existing studies suggest links between child support and school behavior and achievement, links with other child outcomes, such as psychological adjustment, self-esteem, and peer relations, are less clear.

The Father's Role in the Co-parental Relationship

The third hypothesis states that fathers can have a positive impact on children through the co-parental relationship, that is, by providing positive models of dyadic behavior, backing up mothers' authority, and giving emotional support to mothers. Although relatively few studies have examined the co-parental relationship itself, a large number have examined marital conflict, which is a reasonable proxy. In support of the hypothesis, reviews of the literature consistently conclude that marital discord is negatively associated with children's academic success, conduct, emotional adjustment, self-esteem, and social competence (Cummings & O'Reilly, 1997; Davies & Cummings, 1994; Emery, 1988; Grych & Fincham, 1990). Although some of the effects of marital discord appear to be mediated through parent–child relationships (with distressed parents being relatively unsupportive and punitive), other effects appear to be direct.

Although most of these studies use global measures of marital quality, a few attempt to separate the father's contributions to marital discord from the mother's. For example, Conger and Elder (1994) found that when fathers show little warmth toward mothers, mothers are more hostile toward fathers and engage in harsher and less consistent discipline toward their children. Similarly, Boyum and Parke (1995) found that when fathers display a good deal of positive affect toward mothers, children tend to be popular with peers. Other studies suggest that the extent to which fathers undermine or support mothers in the parenting role is critical. For example, Kandel (1990) found that mothers' ratings of disagreements with fathers over childrearing are associated with poor child adjustment. Similarly, Brody et al. (1994) found that mothers' reports of co-caregiver support from their husbands (e.g., talking over the child's behavior) and co-caregiver conflict (e.g., disagreements over how to raise the child) are associated with children's self-control and academic competence in the expected direction. Overall, these studies support the hypothesis that fathers affect children's well-being to the extent that they strengthen or weaken the co-parental alliance.

In general, studies show that interparental discord increases the risk of problems for sons as well as daughters. And although relatively few studies have focused on non-Whites, similar processes appear to occur among African American families (Brody et al., 1994). Overall, the benefits of a positive co-parental relationship appear to be shared among diverse groups of children.

Nonresident Fathers. What about the relationship between never-married or divorced parents? All things being equal, it is easier for married parents than for unmarried parents living in separate households to maintain a positive co-parental relationship. Indeed, even among relatively involved fathers, most engage in "parallel parenting" rather than co-parenting following divorce (Furstenberg & Nord, 1985; Maccoby & Mnookin, 1992).

Nevertheless, studies consistently show that the level of conflict and cooperation between parents is one of the best predictors of children's postdivorce adjustment (see Amato, 1993, for a review). For example, Buchanan, Maccoby, and Dornbusch (1991) found that the stress of feeling caught between hostile parents after divorce predicts poor outcomes for adolescents. Similarly, Healy, Malley, and Stewart (1990) found that children exhibit more behavior problems if parents engage in legal conflict following marital dissolution. Guidubaldi et al. (1986) noted that mothers' satisfaction with the postdivorce relationship with fathers is associated with a variety of independently assessed positive outcomes among sons and daughters. And Heath and MacKinnon (1988) showed that parental cooperation is positively associated with social competence among children living in single-mother households. Overall, these studies suggest that fathers, as part of a parental partnership, have the potential to benefit children in single-mother households, much as they benefit children in two-parent households.

The Father–Child Relationship

The fourth hypothesis states that the quality of the father–child relationship is positively related to children's well-being. My literature review uncovered 59 studies published since 1980 that examined associations between paternal behavior and child or adolescent outcomes in two-parent families. Although this is undoubtedly only a sample of the total population of studies published, there is no reason to suspect that it does not reflect larger trends in the literature. Most of these studies examined paternal support (or a similar construct), although a number also examined aspects of paternal control, such as monitoring, induction, or punishment. Of these studies, 50 (85%) found significant associations between father support (or noncoercive control) and measures of children's well-being in the predicted direction. This pattern would appear to support the hypothesis that paternal support and noncoercive control are beneficial to children. However, several qualifications to this conclusion are necessary.

Of the 59 studies, 20 examined associations between paternal and child variables using a single source of data and without controlling for maternal variables; of these, 18 yielded significant results in the hypothesized direction. For example, Barnes (1984) found that adolescents' ratings of paternal nurturance are negatively related to self-reports of deviance, including drug use, truancy, and stealing. However, because adolescents provided information on both the independent and dependent variables, shared method variance may be responsible for this finding.

Another 21 studies used multiple sources but did not control for maternal characteristics. These studies employed two strategies. The first was to use one source of data for the independent variable and a second source for the dependent variable. For example, Forehand and Nousiainen (1993) found that children's ratings of paternal acceptance predict teachers' ratings of social competence and conduct. The second strategy was to collect reports from multiple sources and use structural equation methods to form latent variables from the shared variance. For example, Conger et al. (1992, 1993) used reports from parents, children, and observers to create latent variable reflecting paternal nurturance and child adjustment and found these to be positively correlated. All 21 studies that used multiple sources (but no controls for maternal variables) yielded significant findings. These studies increase our confidence that father and child variables are correlated in the real world—not just in people's minds. However, these studies do not tell us if fathers' contributions have an impact above and beyond that of mothers. To address this issue, it is necessary to turn to studies that controlled for maternal characteristics.

Nine studies estimated father effects while controlling for maternal characteristics but relied on a single source of data; of these, six yielded significant results. For example, Astone and McLanahan (1991) found that fathers' monitoring of school progress is positively associated with high school students' grades, attendance, attitudes toward school, and graduation, even with mothers' monitoring in the equation. Similarly, Coombs and Landsverk (1988) found that, controlling for feelings of closeness to mothers, feelings of closeness to fathers are associated with less substance use among adolescents. However, although these six studies suggest a unique role for fathers, they may be affected by same-source bias, as noted earlier.

Another nine studies controlled for maternal characteristics and relied on independent sources; of these, five yielded significant results. For example, Amato (1989) found that children's reports of paternal and maternal support are independently associated with parents' reports of children's social competence and self-control. Similarly, Forehand, Long,

Brody, and Fauber (1986) found that with the quality of the mother–child relationship controlled, the father–child relationship (as reported by parents and adolescents) predicts offspring's grade point average (as reported by teachers). The other studies that found significant effects include Browne and Rife (1991), Galambos and Silbereisen (1987), and Patterson and Dishion (1988).

A few quick calculations reveal that studies that control for maternal characteristics yield weaker evidence of father effects than do other studies. Of the 41 studies that did not control for maternal characteristics, 95% yielded significant results. But of the 18 studies that controlled for maternal characteristics, only 61% yielded significant results. Although the majority of studies in the latter group still suggest evidence of father effects, more studies that use independent sources and control for maternal characteristics are sorely needed.

Associations between the quality of the father–child relationship and children's well-being appear to generalize across a variety of subgroups of children. Although some studies suggest stronger effects for sons than daughters (Mosley & Thomson, 1995), most studies show effects for children of both genders (Barber, Chadwick, & Oerter, 1992; Crouter, McHale, & Bartko, 1993; Hundelby & Mercer, 1987). Few studies have examined different racial and ethnic groups. However, Mosley and Thomson (1995) found that the estimated effects of father involvement are similar for Black and White children. Similarly, Coombs and Landsverk (1988) found that closeness to fathers is related to less substance use among both White American and Hispanic youth. Furthermore, the finding of a link between paternal behavior and children's outcomes has been reported in a variety of countries, including Australia (Amato, 1989), Germany (Barber, Chadwick, & Oerter, 1992), Canada (Hagan, MacMillan, & Wheaton, 1996) and Israel (Radin & Sagi, 1982).

Studies of Adult Offspring. A number of studies have also estimated father effects using samples of adult offspring. Several of these studies show that adults who have positive relationships with fathers tend to have higher levels of achievement or psychological well-being, even with the mother–child relationship controlled (Amato, 1994; Barber & Thomas, 1986; Barnett, Marshall, & Pleck, 1992; Harris, Furstenberg, & Marmer, 1996). All of these studies, however, relied on same-source data. Furthermore, not all studies are in agreement on this point. Umberson (1992) and Barnett, Kibria, Baruch, and Pleck (1991) found significant associations between the quality of father–child relationships and young adults' subjective well-being at the bivariate level, but not when the quality of the mother–child relationship is controlled. Longitudinal studies based on independent sources provide additional evidence of father effects. Father support during childhood and adolescence is associated with upward mobility (Snarey, 1993), being happily married and having strong support networks (Franz, McClelland, & Weinberger, 1991), and being empathic (Koestner, Franz, & Weinberger, 1990), although only the last studies controlled for mother support. Overall, the weight of the evidence supports the notion that the quality of the early father–child relationship continues to be a salient correlate of well-being into adulthood, although reliance on same-source data limits the certainty of this conclusion.

Nonresident Fathers. Divorce is often followed by a decline in the quality and quantity of contact between fathers and children. Nevertheless, some nonresident fathers manage to see their children frequently and maintain positive relationships. If the father–child relationship is an important resource for children, then a weakening of this relationship following divorce should disadvantage children.

I was able to locate 36 studies published since 1980 that examined children's relationships with nonresident fathers and children's well-being. Although most studies assessed the frequency of contact, others attempted to assess the quality of the father–child relationship. In general, these studies do not provide support for the hypothesis that maintaining ties with nonresident fathers benefits children. Of the 36 studies, 16 found that contact (or some other dimension of the father–child relationship) is positively associated with children's well-being, whereas 20 did not. Indeed, several studies found that contact with fathers is negatively related to children's well-being. These results appear to clash with the results of studies of two-parent households, which generally suggest positive father effects.

There are several explanations for the preponderance of null results. First, children may disengage psychologically from nonresident fathers, with the paternal relationship becoming less salient over time. However, this interpretation is inconsistent with qualitative studies showing that children maintain strong emotional attachments to fathers for years following divorce, even when little contact occurs (Wallerstein & Blakeslee, 1989). For example, when asked to draw their families, young children from divorced families typically include nonresident fathers in their pictures (Spigelman, Spigelman, & Englesson, 1992).

Another explanation is that father contact provides opportunities for parents to quarrel. Although contact with fathers may be beneficial, conflict between parents may cancel out, or even reverse, any potential good. Support for this interpretation comes from a study by Amato and Rezac (1994), which found that contact with nonresident fathers following divorce appears to lower sons' behavior problems when conflict between parents is low, but appears to increase sons' behavior when conflict between parents is high. Two other studies have obtained similar results (Hetherington, Cox, & Cox, 1982; Healy, Malley, & Stewart, 1990).

Another likely explanation for the less-than-overwhelming evidence of father effects focuses on the nature of the father–child relationship. Contact between nonresident fathers and children tends to be recreational (for example, going out to eat and to see movies), rather than instrumental. Compared with fathers in two-parent households, nonresident fathers provide less help with homework, are less likely to set and enforce rules, and provide less monitoring and supervision of their children (Amato, 1987; Furstenberg & Nord, 1985). If noncustodial fathers no longer play the role of parent, then mere contact, or even sharing good times together, may not contribute in a positive way to children's development.

Consistent with this interpretation, studies with null results tend to examine the frequency of visitation only, whereas those with significant results tend to measure meaningful aspects of the parent role. For example, Barber (1994) found that adolescents who frequently obtain advice from noncustodial fathers (about educational plans, employment goals, and personal problems) are less likely than other adolescents to experience symptoms of depression. Similarly, Simons et al. (1994) found that the quality of noncustodial fathers' parenting (as reflected in emotional support, giving reasons for decisions, providing consistent discipline, and praising children's accomplishment) is negatively related to externalizing problems among adolescent sons and daughters. Indeed, in both studies, the quality of the father–child relationship largely accounted for the significant bivariate differences between adolescents in divorced and two-parent households.

These studies suggest that nonresident fathers play an important role in their children's lives to the extent that they are able to provide appropriate support, guidance, and monitoring—especially if this occurs within the context of cooperation between parents. This interpretation is consistent with a study by Young, Miller, Norton, and Hill (1995) who found, in two-parent households, that children's reports of fathers' intrinsic support (as reflected in encouragement, trust, and talking over problems) are positively correlated with children's life satisfaction. In contrast, children's reports of fathers' extrinsic support (as reflected in going out to dinner, buying things, and seeing movies together) are not related to children's life satisfaction. Seen from this perspective, the results for nonresident fathers are consistent with those for fathers in two-parent households. Unfortunately, extrinsic parenting within the context of minimal interparental cooperation is the pattern typically observed among nonresident fathers.

Summary

In general, research tends to support the four hypotheses just outlined. The first hypothesis, dealing with the importance of fathers' human capital, is strongly supported in studies of two-parent households, although existing literature is insufficient to allow conclusions about nonresident fathers. The second hypothesis, dealing with the importance of fathers' financial capital, receives support from studies of two-parent households, although the number of studies that distinguish between fathers' and mothers' earnings is small. Fathers' financial contributions in the form of child support also appear to benefit children in single-mother households. Taken together, these studies suggest that fathers continue to be important for the same reasons that they have been important traditionally, that is, by serving as models of achievement, sources of knowledge about the workplace, and providers of financial support.

Studies also support the third and fourth hypotheses, based on fathers' social capital. Many studies of two-parent households suggest that fathers benefit children to the extent that they promote a positive marital relationship, and more specifically, a positive co-parental relationship. Furthermore, a cooperative co-parental relationship (although difficult to attain) appears to improve the well-being of children living in single-mother households. In relation to the fourth hypothesis, studies of two-parent households suggest that paternal support and effective control are good for children. This appears to be true even when we take into account the level of support and control exercised by mothers, although the number of studies providing strong evidence is disappointingly small. Evidence for the importance of the father–child relationship is weaker for nonresident fathers than for resident fathers. Taken together, however, the evidence regarding social capital suggests that fathers contribute more than money to their children's lives, although more research is necessary to reach a firm conclusion.

DATA ANALYSIS

To supplement the literature review, I present new data from the study entitled Marital Instability Over the Life Course (Booth, Amato, Johnson, & Edwards, 1993). The great majority of studies just reviewed examined only one type of paternal resource. And few of these studies considered mothers' characteristics along with those of fathers. In contrast, the present analysis involves a simultaneous test of all categories of paternal resources: human capital (as reflected in fathers' education), financial capital (as reflected in fathers' earnings), and social capital (as reflected in the quality of the marital and the father–child relationship). The present analysis also includes comparable variables for fathers and mothers. In addition, the present analysis supplements previous work by focusing on an understudied age group: offspring in young adulthood.

This project began in 1980 as a longitudinal study of approximately 2,000 married individuals. In 1992, we interviewed 471 young adult offspring of the original respondents. The analysis in this chapter is limited to 384 offspring who lived with both biological parents in 1980 and were between the ages of 7 and 19 in that year. In 1992, offspring ranged in age from 19 to 31, with a median age of 23. The sample was almost equally split between sons and daughters. However, because only 7% of the offspring were non-White, and because only 10% experienced parental divorce, it was not possible to examine variations by race or family structure. For more details on this study, see Amato, Loomis, and Booth (1995), or Booth and Amato (1994).

Dependent Variables

I used six outcomes to assess multiple domains of offspring's well-being in 1992. These outcomes were roughly similar to those employed in studies of younger children and adolescents. Offspring were the source of information for all outcomes.

Many studies of children have focused on peer relations. Correspondingly, I created two latent variables that reflected the size of offspring's social support networks. Two items dealt with ties to kin: "How many of your relatives do you feel emotionally close to?" and "How many of your relatives do you feel you could talk with about problems in your family?" Offspring were instructed not to count parents or relatives living in the same household in answering these questions. Similarly, two items dealt with close friends: "How many people do you consider to be very close friends?" and "How many of your friends do you feel you could talk with about problems in your family?" Respondents were instructed not to count relatives in answering these latter two questions.

Other studies of children have focused on psychological adjustment. In the present study, I used three latent variables to capture aspects of psychological well-being in early adulthood. To measure life satisfaction, respondents rated the extent to which they were satisfied with seven aspects of their lives: neighborhood, job or career, house or apartment, friends, hobbies or leisure activities, families, and financial situation. Psychological distress was based on eight items from the Langner (1962) scale of psychiatric symptoms. Respondents reported the frequency during the last year of experiencing somatic symptoms (such as headaches) as well as periods of negative affect (such as feeling isolated and alone). Finally, six items from Rosenberg's (1965) scale assessed self-esteem.

I subjected these measures to a confirmatory factor analysis. To accomplish this (along with the other analyses reported in the following section), I used the AMOS (Analysis of Moment Structures) program with maximum likelihood estimation. This analysis involved the two items reflecting ties to kin, the two items reflecting ties to friends, and split-halves (odd vs.

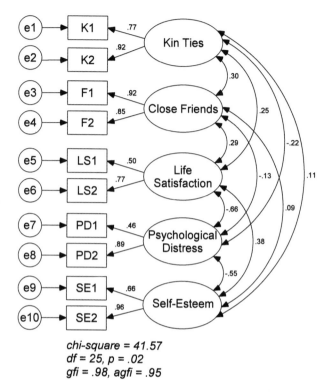

chi-square = 41.57
df = 25, p = .02
gfi = .98, agfi = .95

FIG. 13.2. Measurement model for offspring outcomes.

even items) of the life satisfaction, psychological distress, and self-esteem scales. The measurement model appears in Fig. 13.2. Although the chi-square value for the hypothesized model was significant, the goodness of fit indices revealed a close fit to the data. Note that some of the latent variables had moderate to high correlations. For example, psychological distress correlated at −.66 with life satisfaction and at −.55 with self-esteem. However, decreasing the number of latent variables resulted in significantly poorer fitting models ($p < .001$). Consequently, I retained the five variable model for all analyses.

I also included offspring's years of education as a sixth measure of well-being. Fourteen percent of young adults were still attending school in 1992. However, eliminating these individuals did not change the results, so I included them in all analyses. Previous research strongly suggests that educational attainment is a cause of other positive outcomes, such as strong support networks, a sense of well-being, high self-esteem, and good mental health (Kessler, 1982; Ross & Wu, 1995). For this reason, I assume that education is not only a positive outcome in its own right, but also has consequences for the other outcomes just described.

Effects of Fathers' Human and Financial Capital

The first causal model estimated the effects of parents' human and financial capital on offspring's outcomes in 1992. It included paternal education, maternal education, paternal earnings, and maternal earnings, all measured in 1980. Parents were the source of information for these variables. The model included mothers who were not in the paid labor force during the previous year (38%), and hence, had no income. In the model, the education of each parent is assumed to be a cause of that parents' income. I also assumed that fathers' income influences mothers' income. If fathers earn relatively little money, then mothers may find it necessary to increase their hours of employment to raise total family income. In contrast, if fathers earn high earnings, then mothers are free to relax their hours of employment (if they wish) and spend more time in other pursuits. Of course, many mothers are in the labor force because they want to be—not because their families need the money. For this reason, I also experimented with other causal assumptions.

The results of this analysis appear in Fig. 13.3. Although the latent variable model is fully recursive, only significant paths ($p < .05$) are shown in the figure. Because the analysis involves tests of directional hypotheses, one-tailed tests are used to determine statistical significance.

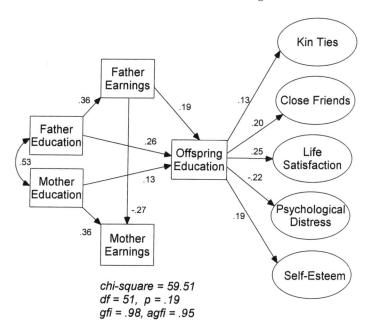

chi-square = 59.51
df = 51, p = .19
gfi = .98, agfi = .95

FIG. 13.3. Causal model based on fathers' and mothers' human and financial capital.

The estimates shown in Fig. 13.3 suggest that fathers' education and earnings directly increased children's education but had no direct effects on the other outcomes. However, children's education increased kin ties, close friends, life satisfaction, and self-esteem, and lowered psychological distress. Consequently, fathers' education and earnings appear to have indirect effects on these social and psychological outcomes. The model also indicates that fathers' education had an indirect effect on offspring's education via fathers' earnings. Multiplying the paths reveals that the indirect effect of fathers' human capital through earnings $(.36 \times .19 = .07)$ was considerably weaker than the direct effect of fathers' human capital $(.26)$.

Note that mothers' education also increased children's education in the model. However, mothers' earnings were not significantly associated with children's education. Although not shown, the beta was only $-.01$. The absence of an effect for maternal income may reflect the fact that women earn considerably less than men. Although many parents may use mothers' earnings to meet daily expenses, they may use fathers' earnings to pay for big-budget items, such as children's educational expenses. This finding is not an artifact of the proposed causal path between fathers' and mothers' earnings in the model. If that path is omitted (or reversed), then mothers' income still fails to predict children's education (or any other outcome). Additional analyses indicate that the estimated effects of paternal education and income did not vary with children's gender. (Readers should note, however, that the estimated effects of maternal education were stronger for daughters than for sons—but this is another story.)

How large are these estimated effects? One way of answering this question is to refer to the unstandardized partial coefficients (not shown). These indicate that every year of paternal education, net of income, increased children's education by about one fifth of a year. This effect size is comparable to results reported in other studies of educational transmission across generations (Alwin & Thornton, 1984; Hill & Duncan, 1987; Jencks, Crouse, & Mueser, 1983; Teachman, 1987). In relation to the effects of offsprings' education, each year of education increased the number of close kin by .18 and the number of close friends by .27. Furthermore, each year of offsprings' education increased life satisfaction by .12 of a standard deviation, decreased psychological distress by .10 of a standard deviation, and increased self-esteem by .09 of a standard deviation. In other words, offspring with 16 years of education, compared with those who had 12 years, had about one more close relative, about one more close friend, and scored between one half and one third of a standard deviation higher on measures of psychological well-being. These effects, although not overwhelming, are large enough to be nontrivial.

Effects of Fathers' Social Capital

Fathers provide social resources to their children, as just noted, to the extent that they maintain a unified authority structure with mothers, model positive dyadic behaviors, and provide emotional support to mothers. The present data set does not contain direct measures of the co-parental relationship. However, it contains measures of the extent to which parents experience the marital relationship as problematic, lack commitment to the marriage, and engage in chronic, unresolved conflict. Given that it is extremely difficult to maintain a positive co-parental relationship under these conditions, the present measures serve as close proxies for the quality of co-parenting.

I used five scales from the 1980 parent interview. Parents responded to a list of 14 potential marital problems by indicating if they or their partner had the problem. These problems included getting angry easily, feeling jealous, not talking enough, not being at home enough, and having sex with someone else. I used the sum of *fathers' marital problems* and *mothers' marital problems* as separate indicators. Similarly, parents reported whether they or their spouse (a) had ever thought that their marriage was in trouble, (b) were thinking about getting a divorce, (c) had discussed the possibility of a divorce with friends or family, and (d) had raised the possibility of getting a divorce with the other spouse. By adding positive responses to these items, I constructed measures of *fathers' marital instability* and *mothers' marital instability*. Finally, I drew on a four-item *marital conflict* scale. These items referred to parents' reports of disagreements in general, conflict over the household division of labor, the frequency of serious quarrels, and whether physical violence had occurred in the relationship.

The measurement model for these variables appears in Fig. 13.4. Each of the five observed indicators had a moderately high loading on the latent variable, *marital discord*. I allowed the error terms for the two marital problems indicators and the two divorce proneness indicators to be correlated because they were based on parallel sets of items. The model fit the data well, as reflected in a nonsignificant probability value and high scores on the goodness of fit indices.

To measure the quality of parent–child relationships, I relied on scales of father and mother support. In 1992, offspring responded to a series of 5 retrospective questions about their relationships with their parents when they were teenagers. These questions dealt with receiving help with homework, receiving help with personal problems, having talks, showing affection, and feeling close. Separate scales were created for fathers and mothers.

The measurement model for *father support* and *mother support* appears in Fig. 13.5, where each scale is shown in split half form (even vs. odd items).

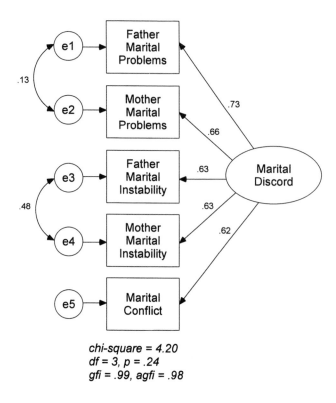

chi-square = 4.20
df = 3, p = .24
gfi = .99, agfi = .98

FIG. 13.4. Measurement model for marital discord.

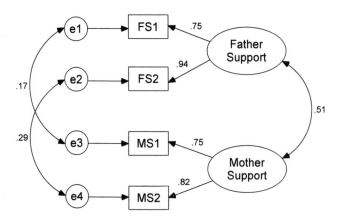

FIG. 13.5. Measurement model for father and mother support.

The loadings of each indicator on the latent variables were respectably high. To improve the fit of the model, I allowed the error terms for each half scale to correlate across parents, as these halves were based on parallel items. To save a degree of freedom, it was necessary to constrain the two covariances to be equal. Because there were no excess degrees of freedom, the model fit the data perfectly. Note that the correlation between father support and mother support was positive and moderately high. This indicates that offspring who recalled their fathers positively also tended to recall their mothers positively, and vice versa. However, combining the two into a single latent variable resulted in a significantly worse fitting model ($p < .001$). Consequently, the best interpretation would appear to be that young adults have separate recollections of fathers and mothers (rather than a generalized recollection of parents), but that these separate recollections are moderately correlated. (For this reason, I allowed the error terms for these two variables to be correlated in the causal model to be described.)

The results of the structural equation analysis based on social capital appear in Fig. 13.6 (as before, only significant paths are shown). This model fit the data well, as reflected in a nonsignificant probability value and high scores on the goodness of fit indices. The inclusion of marital discord, father support, and mother support did not change the earlier

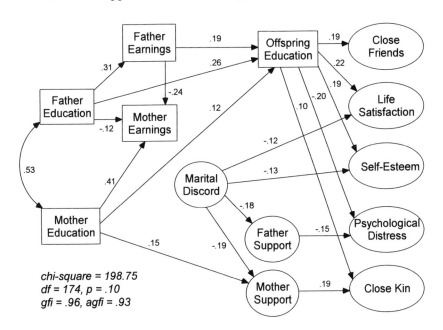

FIG. 13.6. Causal model based on fathers' and mothers' human, financial, and social capital.

results for fathers' education or income. As before, paternal education and income predicted children's educational attainment, and children's educational attainment, in turn, predicted forms of social and psychological well-being.

In relation to social capital, the model suggests that a high level of paternal support lowered children's psychological distress, whereas a high level of maternal support increased the number of close kin. The latter finding may be related to the fact that mothers tend to play the kin-keeper role in families. The model also suggests that marital discord had a direct negative effect on offspring's life satisfaction and self-esteem. In addition, marital discord appeared to lower paternal and maternal support; this implies that marital discord indirectly increased children's psychological distress and weakened their kin ties through its disruption of parent–child relationships. Supplementary analyses indicated that the estimated effects of marital discord, father support, and mother support did not vary with children's gender.

How large are these effects? Examination of the unstandardized partial coefficients (not shown) reveals that a person with the highest observed paternal support score has a predicted level of psychological distress that is .57 of a standard deviation lower than a person with the lowest observed paternal support score (net of the other variables in the model). Effect sizes for marital discord, life satisfaction, and self-esteem are comparable in magnitude. Once again, although these estimated effects cannot be described as strong, they are large enough to be nontrivial.

Interestingly, the model suggests that parental human and financial capital were not related to parental social capital, with one exception. Maternal education increased maternal support, but there was no corresponding association for fathers. These findings suggest that parents' human, financial, and social capital have largely independent consequences for children's long-term well-being.

Discussion of Findings

Overall, the results of my analysis suggest that fathers influence their children's well-being through a combination of human, financial, and social capital—findings that are congruent with the trends in the literature noted earlier. Fathers' and mothers' educations have independent estimated effects on children's educations. In addition, fathers' income appears to have long-term consequences for offspring that are independent of mothers' income. The model suggests that a high level of paternal education and income benefit offspring primarily through improving children's educational attainment; children's education, in turn, has positive implications for a variety of other outcomes. The results also indicate that an uncooperative, conflict-ridden relationship between fathers and mothers is detrimental to multiple aspects of offspring's well-being. Consistent with other studies, some (but not all) of the estimated effects of interparental discord are mediated through disruptions in parent–child relationships. Finally, paternal support seems to have modest beneficial consequences for offspring, as reflected in lowered psychological distress. These estimated effects are modest in magnitude, but this may be due to the fact that most independent variables were based on parents' reports in 1980, and the outcomes were based on offspring's reports in 1992. (The measures of parental support, which were obtained retrospectively from offspring, are the exception.)

The present study also demonstrates the necessity of controlling for mothers' characteristics when estimating father effects. If maternal support is omitted from the model, then paternal support is significantly associated with four of the six outcomes (not shown). But as the model in Fig. 13.6 indicates, this declines to one significant association with maternal support in the model. The same thing is true for maternal support if paternal support is omitted from the model. This suggests, on the one hand, that paternal support is largely redundant once we have information on maternal support. But on the other hand, the model does not suggest many unique effects of maternal support either. Due to the positive correlation between paternal and maternal support, neither variable appears to be doing much in the model, even though both are related to most of the outcomes when examined separately.

To gain an overall picture of the relative importance of fathers and mothers, I carried out a series of stepwise multiple regression analyses in which each offspring outcome was predicted by all of the paternal variables (fathers' education, income, marital problems, divorce proneness, and support), followed by all of the corresponding maternal variables. I then reversed the procedure. This made it possible to partition the explained variance into three components: variance uniquely accounted for by fathers, variance uniquely accounted for by mothers, and variance accounted for jointly by fathers and mothers. (I omitted one variable, marital conflict, because it could not be partitioned between mothers and fathers.)

These results appear in Fig. 13.7. Although some of the total R^2 values are not large, they are all statistically significant. The figure reveals that fathers account for more of the variance in offspring's education, psychological distress, and self-esteem than do mothers. In contrast, mothers account for a larger share of the variance in kin ties and close friends than do fathers. Finally, fathers and mothers account for roughly equal amounts of the variance in life satisfaction. Note, however, that the joint component tends to be as large as (or larger than) either of the individual components. This indicates that it is difficult to disentangle empirically the separate

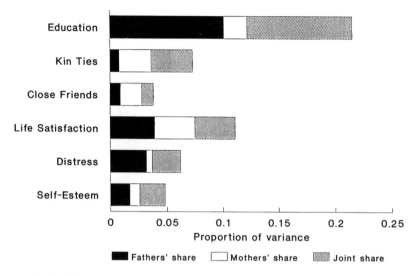

FIG. 13.7. Percentage of variance in offspring outcomes accounted for uniquely and jointly by fathers and mothers.

effects of fathers and mothers because their characteristics tend to be positively correlated. Taking into account the shared variance, these results suggest that fathers are about as important as mothers in predicting children's long-term outcomes.

UNANSWERED QUESTIONS

Previous studies, as well as the data analysis presented in this chapter, suggest that fathers influence their children's lives in multiple ways. However, several ambiguities in the research literature limit our ability to reach straightforward conclusions about fathers.

What Do Nonresident Fathers Contribute?

The most convincing case for the importance of fathers is based on evidence from two-parent families. But the evidence regarding nonresident fathers is less clear. It is tempting to conclude that the absence of significant associations between frequency of contact and children's outcomes means that nonresident fathers play only a minor role in their children's lives. Yet, this conclusion clashes with the findings that (a) nonresident fathers' payment of children support facilitates children's educational achievement, (b) interparental cooperation following divorce is a good predictor of children's divorce adjustment, and (c) nonresident fathers' investment in the parental role (through providing support and effective control) is positively related to children's well-being. Although many gaps in our knowledge exist, current data suggest that nonresident fathers have the potential to contribute to their children's development in a manner comparable to that of resident fathers, that is, by providing financial resources, by cooperating with and supporting mothers, and by enacting intrinsic (rather than extrinsic) aspects of the parent role. The appropriate question for future research, therefore, is not whether nonresident fathers are important, but why so many nonresident fathers fail to provide these resources to their children, thus wasting their potential.

What Are the Contingencies?

Rather than trying to determine whether fathers are important in an absolute sense, it may make more sense to inquire about the conditions under which fathers are more or less useful to their children. Although relatively few studies have addressed this issue, several provide useful clues. For example, paternal support may be especially useful when families are subjected to disruptive life events. Under these circumstances, positive father involvement may buffer potentially vulnerable children from stress. Existing studies provide some support for this idea. For example, Hagan, MacMillan, and Wheaton (1996) found that frequent moving lowers children's attainment, presumably because it disrupts their school routines and neighborhood networks, but the effects of moving are ameliorated when fathers are highly involved with their children. Similarly, Mosley and Thomson (1995) found that time spent with fathers is positively related to daughters' school performance in poor families, but not in nonpoor families. In addition, Simons, Lorenz, Wu, and Conger (1993) found that economic stress lowers the quality of mothers' parenting, but only if they receive little emotional support from their husbands. These studies all suggest that fathers are especially useful to children when families are experiencing difficult times.

In addition, fathers may be particularly important when children have problematic relationships with mothers. When mothers are ill, depressed, hostile, or have substance abuse problems, involved and competent fathers may help to compensate for deficits experienced by children. Similarly, fathers may be especially important to offspring whose mothers are deceased. Consistent with this idea, Barnett et al. (1991) found that adult daughters' psychological well-being is related more strongly to their relationships with fathers when their mothers are deceased than when their mothers are alive. Similarly, Amato (1994) and Barnett et al. (1991) found that the father–child relationship is more important for single than for married offspring. Both findings suggest that fathers are especially salient when close relationships with other significant others are lacking. In general, inquiring about the contingencies under which fathers are more or less important would move our understanding beyond simple "main effects" models of paternal influence.

How Important Is Social Capital Beyond the Family?

Previous research is limited in its consideration of social capital. Although many studies have dealt with the marital relationship and children's relationships with parents, researchers have given comparatively little attention to the links between parents and other community groups and institutions—an important component of Coleman's (1988, 1990) concept of social capital (see Furstenberg & Hughes, 1995, for an exception). For example, parents provide social capital when they maintain contact with extended family, enroll their children in organized sports, are involved with their children's schools, or help their adolescent or young adult offspring find employment. The extent to which fathers provide these resources, and their consequences for children, is not well-understood.

Father Effects or Child Effects?

Another limitation of previous research is that it rarely considers the extent to which observed associations between father and child variables might be due to the effects of children on fathers (Ambert, 1992; Belsky, 1991). Studies of paternal human capital and financial capital are exempt from this criticism, as children's educational achievement is unlikely to influence fathers' education or income. However, studies that estimate the effects of paternal support and control on children are vulnerable to this problem. It is quite likely, for example, that well-behaved children increase positive paternal involvement, whereas poorly behaved children increase paternal rejection and harshness. One way that future studies can address this limitation is to use structural equation methods with longitudinal data to model reciprocal influences over time between fathers and children—a strategy that I did not observe in any of the studies reviewed for this chapter. A second possibility is to use experimental methods to vary paternal behavior and observe the consequences for children. This strategy has been used to demonstrate mother effects. For example, Parpal and Maccoby (1985) varied maternal behavior experimentally and found that children were subsequently more compliant when mothers behaved in a responsive manner than in a nonresponsive manner. Similar experiments could be designed to demonstrate father effects.

Are Father Effects Genetic?

Researchers rarely consider the possibility that genetic factors might account for observed associations between paternal variables and child outcomes (Belsky, 1991). For example, an inherited component of intelligence could account for the link between fathers' and offspring's educational attainment. Similarly, an inherited antisocial trait could account for the observed association between fathers' harsh discipline and children's behavior problems. Nevertheless, it is unlikely that genetic factors can account completely for father effects. For example, Patterson and Dishion (1988) found that fathers' harsh and explosive parenting predicted children's antisocial behavior, even when controlling for fathers' antisocial personality. This study (and others like it) suggest that parental personality traits are transmitted to children at least partly through childrearing practices, and not entirely through genetic inheritance. Nevertheless, additional studies that distinguish genetic from other types of contributions from fathers would help to clarify this issue.

How Important Are Stepfathers?

Another limitation of this literature is the lack of attention to stepfathers. Due to a high rate of divorce and remarriage, an increasing number of children in the United States are living in stepfather families. Currently, of all children living in two-parent households, 15% live with a stepfather (U.S. Bureau of the Census, 1992a). Biological fathers who live with their children tend to invest more resources in their children than stepfathers invest in their stepchildren. But it is also true that many men invest more resources in their stepchildren (with whom they share a household) than in their biological children (who live elsewhere) (Furstenberg, 1988). Some studies have compared the well-being of children living with stepfathers and continuously married parents. Few, however, have considered how the human, financial, and social capital of stepfathers affects children's lives. Given the large number of children living in stepfamilies, this is a curious omission.

What Has Changed?

Two generations ago, Parsons and Bales (1955) argued that fathers primarily contribute to their children's lives in instrumental ways, that is, by providing social status, generating income, and serving as models of employment and achievement. Current research suggests that fathers continue to be important for their contributions of human and financial capital. Current research also suggests, however, that children benefit when fathers are involved in socioemotional aspects of family life. And yet, there is little reason to believe that this was not always so. In the 1950s, as in the 1990s, children benefited when their fathers cooperated with and supported their mothers, provided assistance and emotional support, and set consistent rules and monitored their behavior. Indeed, fathers in the past may have provided a wider range of resources to children than we give them credit for.

If this is true, then the current trend for fathers to be less involved in their children's lives (due to shifts in family structure) represents a net decline in the level of resources available to children. Compared with resident fathers, nonresident fathers share less of their human capital with children, invest less money in their children, find it more difficult to form cooperative alliances with their children's mothers, and spend less time enacting the parent role. Of course, some children (and mothers) are better off having little contact with fathers, especially when nonresident fathers are abusive, antisocial, or have substance use problems. Nevertheless, the majority of noncustodial fathers have the potential to be a positive force in their children's lives. Consequently, a policy challenge is to find incentives to make a larger number of nonresident fathers behave more like the "good dads" in two-parent households.

ACKNOWLEDGMENTS

I thank Alan Booth, David Johnson, Stacy Rogers, and Lynn White for helpful comments on an earlier draft of this paper, and I thank Julie Harms-Cannon for assistance with library research. This research was supported by Grant 5 R01 AG04146 from the National Institute on Aging and Grant 1-HD28263 from the National Institute of Child Health and Human Development.

REFERENCES

Alwin, D. F., & Thornton, A. (1984). Family origins and the schooling process: Early versus late influence of parental characteristics. *American Sociological Review, 49,* 784–802.

Amato, P. R. (1987). *Children in Australian families: The growth of competence.* Sydney, Australia: Prentice Hall of Australia.

Amato, P. R. (1989). Family processes and the competence of primary school children and adolescents. *Journal of Youth and Adolescence, 18,* 39–53.

Amato, P. R. (1993). Children's adjustment to divorce: Theories, hypotheses, and empirical support. *Journal of Marriage and the Family, 55,* 23–38.

Amato, P. R. (1994). Father–child relations, mother–child relations, and offspring psychological well-being in early adulthood. *Journal of Marriage and the Family, 56,* 1031–1042.

Amato, P. R., Loomis, L. S., & Booth, A. (1995). Parental divorce, marital conflict, and offspring well-being in early adulthood. *Social Forces, 73,* 895–916.

Amato, P. R., & Rezac, S. (1994). Contact with nonresidential parents, interparental conflict, and children's behavior. *Journal of Family Issues, 15,* 191–207.

Ambert, A. (1992). *The effect of children on parents.* New York: Haworth Press.

Astone, N. M., & McLanahan, S. S. (1991). Family structure, parental practices, and high school completion. *American Sociological Review, 56,* 309–320.

Argys, L. M., Peters, H. E., Smith, J. R., & Brooks-Gunn, J. (1995, May). *The impact of child support dollars on child well-being.* Paper presented at the Annual Meeting of the Population Association of America, New Orleans.

Barber, B. K., Chadwick, B. A., & Oerter, R. (1992). Parental behaviors and adolescent self-esteem in the United States and Germany. *Journal of Marriage and the Family, 54,* 128–141.

Barber, B. K., & Thomas, D. L. (1986). Dimensions of fathers' and mothers' supportive behavior: The case for physical affection. *Journal of Marriage and the Family, 48,* 783–794.

Barber, B. L. (1994). Support and advice from married and divorced fathers: Linkages to adolescent adjustment. *Family Relations, 43,* 433–438.

Barnes, G. M. (1984). Adolescent alcohol abuse and other problem behaviors: Their relationships and common parental influences. *Journal of Youth and Adolescence, 13,* 329–348.

Barnett, R. C., Kibria, N., Baruch, G. K., & Pleck, J. H. (1991). Adult daughter–parent relationships and their associations with daughters' subjective well-being and psychological distress. *Journal of Marriage and the Family, 53,* 29–42.

Barnett, R. C., Marshall, L. N., & Pleck, J. H. (1992). Adult son–parent relationships and their associations with son's psychological distress. *Journal of Family Issues, 13,* 505–525.

Baumrind, D. (1968). Authoritarian versus authoritative parental control. *Adolescence, 3,* 255–272.

Baydar, N., & Brooks-Gunn, J. (1994). The dynamics of child support and its consequences for children. In I. Garfinkel, S. S. McLanahan, & P. K. Robins (Eds.), *Child support and child well-being* (pp. 257–284). Washington, DC: The Urban Institute.

Becker, G. S. (1991). *A treatise on the family* (rev. ed.). Cambridge, MA: Harvard University Press.

Behrman, J., & Taubman, P. (1985). Intergenerational earnings mobility in the United States: Some estimates and a test of Becker's intergenerational endowment model. *Review of Economics and Statistics, 67,* 144–151.

Belsky, J. (1984). The determinants of parenting: A process model. *Child Development, 55,* 83–96.

Belsky, J. (1991). Parental and nonparental child care and children's socioemotional development: A decade in review. In A. Booth (Ed.), *Contemporary families: Looking forward, looking back* (pp. 122–140). Minneapolis, MN: National Council on Family Relations.

Belsky, J., Youngblade, L., Rovine, M., & Volling, B. (1991). Patterns of marital change and parent–child interaction. *Journal of Marriage and the Family, 53,* 487–498.

Biller, H. B. (1993). *Fathers and families: Paternal factors in child development.* Westport, CO: Auburn House.

Blau, F. D., & Grossberg, A. J. (1992). Maternal labor supply and children's cognitive development. *Review of Economic and Statistics, 74,* 474–481.

Booth, A., Amato, P. R., Johnson, D. R., & Edwards, J. N. (1993). *Marital instability over the life course: Methodology report for fourth wave.* Unpublished manuscript, Department of Sociology, University of Nebraska–Lincoln.

Booth, A., & Amato, P. R. (1994). Parental marital quality, divorce, and relations with offspring in young adulthood. *Journal of Marriage and the Family, 56,* 21–34.

Boyum, L. A., & Parke, R. D. (1995). The role of family emotional expressiveness in the development of children's social competence. *Journal of Marriage and the Family, 57,* 593–608.

Braver, S. L., Fitzpatrick, P. J., & Bay, R. C. (1991). Noncustodial parents' report of child support payments. *Family Relations, 40,* 180–185.

Braver, S. L., Wolchik, S. A., Sandler, I. N., Sheets, V. L., Fogas, B., & Curtis, B. Y. (1993). A longitudinal study of noncustodial parents: Parents without children. *Journal of Family Psychology, 7,* 9–23.

Brody, G., Stoneman, Z., Flor, D., McCrary, C., Hastings, L., & Conyers, O. (1994). Financial resources, parental psychological functioning, parent co-caregiving, and early adolescent competence in rural two-parent African-American families. *Child Development, 65,* 590–605.

Browne, C. S., & Rife, J. C. (1991). Social, personality, and gender differences in at-risk and not-at-risk sixth grade students. *Journal of Early Adolescence, 11,* 482–495.

Buchanan, C. M., Maccoby, E. E., & Dornbusch, S. M. (1991). Caught between parents: Adolescents' experience in divorced homes. *Child Development, 62,* 1008–1029.

Chen, C., & Stevenson, H. W. (1995). Motivation and mathematics achievement: A comparative study of Asian-Americans, Caucasian-Americans, and East Asian high school students. *Child Development, 66,* 1215–1234.

Cohen, J. (1987). Parents as educational models and definers. *Journal of Marriage and the Family, 49,* 339–351.

Coleman, J. (1988). Social capital in the creation of human capital. *American Journal of Sociology, 94,* 95–120.

Coleman, J. (1990). *Foundations of social theory.* Cambridge, MA: Harvard University Press.

Coltrane, S. (1995). The future of fatherhood. In W. Marsiglio (Ed.), *Fatherhood: Contemporary theory, research, and social policy* (pp. 255–274).Thousand Oaks, CA: Sage.

Conger, R. D., & Elder, G. H., Jr. (1994). *Families in troubled times.* New York: de Gruyter.

Conger, R. D., Conger, K. J., Elder, G. H. Jr., Lorenz, F. O., Simons, R. L., & Whitbeck, L. B. (1992). A family process model of economic hardship and adjustment of early adolescent boys. *Child Development, 63,* 526–541.

Conger, R. D., Conger, K. J., Elder, G. H. Jr., Lorenz, F. O., Simons, R. L., & Whitbeck, L. B. (1993). Family economic stress and adjustment of early adolescent girls. *Developmental Psychology, 29,* 206–219.

Conger, R. D., Elder, G. H. Jr., Lorenz, F. O., Conger, K. J., Simons, R. L., Whitbeck, L. B., Huck, S, & Melby, J. N. (1990). Linking economic hardship to marital quality and instability. *Journal of Marriage and the Family, 52,* 643–656.

Conklin, M. E., & Daily, A. R. (1981). Does consistency of parental educational encouragement matter for secondary school students? *Sociology of Education, 45,* 254–262.

Coombs, R. H., & Landsverk, J. (1988). Parenting styles and substance use during childhood and adolescence. *Journal of Marriage and the Family, 50,* 473–482.

Crouter, A. C., McHale, S. M., & Bartko, W. T. (1993). Gender as an organizing feature in parent–child relationships. *Journal of Social Issues, 49,* 161–174.

Cummings, E. M., & O'Reilly, A. W. (1997). Fathers in family context: Effects of marital quality on child adjustment. In M. E. Lamb (Ed.), *The role of the father in child development* (3rd ed.). New York: Wiley.

Davies, P. T., & Cummings, E. M. (1994). Marital conflict and child adjustment: An emotional security hypothesis. *Psychological Bulletin, 116,* 387–411.

DiMaggio, P. (1982). Cultural capital and school success: The impact of status culture participation on the grades of U.S. high school students. *American Sociological Review, 47,* 189–201.

Elder, G. H., Jr. (1974). *Children of the Great Depression.* Chicago: University of Chicago Press.

Elder, G. H., Jr., Nguyen T. V., & Caspi, A. (1985). Linking family hardship to children's lives. *Child Development, 56,* 361–375.

Eggebeen, D. J., & Uhlenberg, P. (1985). Changes in the organization of men's lives. *Family Relations, 34,* 251–257.

Emery, R. (1988). *Marriage, divorce, and children's adjustment.* Newbury Park, CA: Sage.

McLoyd, V. C., & Wilson, L. (1991). The strain of living poor: Parenting, social support, and child mental health. In A. C. Huston (Ed.), *Children in poverty: Child development and public policy* (pp. 105–135). Cambridge, MA: Cambridge University Press.

Mercy, J. A., & Steelman, L. C. (1982). Familial influence on the intellectual attainment of children. *American Sociological Review, 47*, 532–542.

Mosley, J. & Thomson, E. (1995). Fathering behavior and child outcomes: The role of race and poverty. In W. Marsiglio (Ed.), *Fatherhood: Contemporary theory, research, and social policy* (pp. 148–165). Thousand Oaks, CA: Sage.

Murnane, R. J., Maynard, R. A., & Ohls, J. C. (1981). Home resources and children's achievement. *Review of economics and statistics, 63*, 369–377.

Nock, S. L. (1988). The family and hierarchy. *Journal of Marriage and the Family, 50*, 957–966.

Parcel, T. L., & Menaghan, E. G. (1994). *Parents' jobs and children's lives.* New York: de Gruyter.

Parpal, M., & Maccoby, E. E. (1985). Maternal responsiveness and subsequent child compliance. *Child Development, 56*, 1326–1334.

Parsons, T., & Bales, R. F. (1955). *Family socialization and interaction process.* Glencoe, IL: Free Press.

Patterson, G. R., & Dishion, T. J. (1988). Multilevel family process models: Traits, interactions, and relationships. In R. A. Hinde & J. Stevenson-Hinde (Eds.), *Relationships within families: Mutual influences* (pp. 283–310). Oxford: Clarendon Press.

Peterson, J. L., & Zill, N. (1986). Marital disruption, parent–child relationships, and behavior problems in children. *Journal of Marriage and the Family, 49*, 295–307.

Pina, D., & Bengtson, V. L. (1993). The division of household labor and wives' happiness: Ideology, employment, and perceptions of support. *Journal of Marriage and the Family, 55*, 901–912.

Pleck, J. H. (1997). Paternal involvement: Levels, sources, and consequences. In M. E. Lamb (Ed.), *The role of the father in child development* (Third edition). New York: Wiley.

Popenoe, D. (1996). *Life without father.* New York: The Free Press.

Radin, N. & Russell, G. (1983). Increased father participation and child development outcomes. In M. Lamb & A. Sagi (Eds.), *Fatherhood and Social Policy* (pp. 191–218). Hillsdale, NJ: Lawrence Erlbaum Associates.

Radin, N., & Sagi, A. (1982). Childrearing fathers in intact families, II: Israel and the USA. *Merrill-Palmer Quarterly, 28*, 111–136.

Roberts, W. L. (1987). Two-career families: Demographic variables, parenting, and competence in young children. *Canadian Journal of Behavioural Science, 19*, 347–356.

Rollins, B. C., & Thomas, D. L. (1979). Parental support, power, and control techniques in the socialization of children. In W. R. Burr, R. Hill, F. I. Nye, & I. Reiss (Eds.), *Contemporary theories about the family. Vol. 1. Research-based theories* (pp. 317–364). Glencoe, IL: The Free Press.

Rosenberg, M. (1965). *Society and adolescent self-image.* Princeton, NJ: Princeton University Press.

Ross, C. E., & Wu, C. (1995). The links between education and health. *American Sociological Review, 60*, 719–745.

Rossi, A. S. (1984). Gender and parenthood. *American Sociological Review, 49*, 1–19.

Rumberger, R. W. (1983). Dropping out of high school: The influence of race, sex, and family background. *American Educational Research Journal, 20*, 199–220.

Sampson, R. J., & Laub, J. H. (1994). Urban poverty and the family context of delinquency: A new look at structure and process in a classic study. *Child Development, 65*, 523–540.

Seltzer, J. A. (1991). Legal custody arrangements and children's economic welfare. *American Journal of Sociology, 96*, 895–929.

Seltzer, J. A., & Bianchi, S. M. (1988). Children's contact with absent parents. *Journal of Marriage and the Family, 50*, 663–677.

Seltzer, J. A., Schaeffer, N. C., & Charng, H. (1989). Family ties after divorce: The relationship between visiting and paying child support. *Journal of Marriage and the Family, 51,* 1013–1019.

Sewell, W. H., Hauser, R. M., & Wolf, W. C. (1980). Sex, schooling, and occupational status. *American Journal of Sociology, 86,* 551–583.

Simons, R. L., Beaman, J., Conger, R. D., & Chao, W. (1993). Child experience, conceptions of parenting, and attitudes of spouse as determinants of parental behavior. *Journal of Marriage and the Family, 55,* 91–106.

Simons, R. L., Lorenz, F. O., Wu, C., & Conger, R. D. (1993). Social network and marital support as mediators and moderators of the impact of stress and depression on parental behavior. *Developmental Psychology, 29,* 368–381.

Simons, R. L., Whitbeck, L. B., Beaman, J., & Conger, R. D. (1994). The impact of mothers' parenting, involvement by nonresidential fathers, and parental conflict on the adjustment of adolescent children. *Journal of Marriage and the Family, 56,* 356–374.

Smith, T. E. (1989). Mother–father differences in parental influences on school grades and educational goals. *Sociological Inquiry, 59,* 88–98.

Snarey, J. (1993). *How fathers care for the next generation.* Cambridge, MA: Harvard University Press.

Spigelman, G., Spigelman, A., & Englesson, I. L. (1992). Analysis of family drawings: A comparison between children from divorced and non-divorced families. *Journal of Divorce and Remarriage, 18,* 31–54.

Steelman, L. C., & Doby, J. T. (1983). Family size and birth order as factors on the IQ performance of Black and White children. *Sociology of Education, 56,* 101–109.

Teachman, J. D. (1987). Family background, educational resources, and educational attainment. *American Sociological Review, 52,* 548–557.

Teachman, J. D. (1991). Contributions to children by divorced fathers. *Social Problems, 38,* 358–371.

Thornton, A. (1989). Changing attitudes toward family issues in the United States. *Journal of Marriage and the Family, 51,* 873–894.

Umberson, D. (1992). Relationships between adult children and their parents: Psychological consequences for both generations. *Journal of Marriage and the Family, 54,* 664–674.

U.S. Bureau of the Census. (1992a). *Households, families, and children: A 30-year perspective.* Washington, DC: U.S. Government Printing Office.

U.S. Bureau of the Census. (1992b). *Statistical abstract of the United States. 1992* (112th ed.). Washington, DC: U.S. Government Printing Office.

Voydanoff, P. (1991). Economic distress and family relations: A review of the eighties. In A. Booth (Ed.), *Contemporary Families: Looking Forward, Looking Back* (pp. 429–445). Minneapolis, MN: National Council on Family Relations.

Wallerstein, J. S. & Blakeslee, S. (1989). *Second chances: Men, women, and children after divorce.* New York: Ticknor & Fields.

Wilson, S. M., Peterson, G. W., & Wilson, P. (1993). The process of educational and occupational attainment of adolescent females from low-income rural families. *Journal of Marriage and the Family, 55,* 158–175.

Wright, D. W., Peterson, L. R., & Barnes, H. L. (1990). The relation of parental employment and contextual variables with sexual permissiveness and gender role attitudes of rural early adolescents. *Journal of Early Adolescence, 10,* 382–398.

Yogev, S., & Brett, J. (1985). Perceptions of the division of housework and childcare and marital satisfaction. *Journal of Marriage and the Family, 47,* 609–618.

Young, M. H., Miller, B. C., Norton, M. C., & Hill, E. J. (1995). The effect of parental supportive behaviors on life satisfaction of adolescent offspring. *Journal of Marriage and the Family, 57,* 813–822.

Chapter 14

Paternal Influence and Children's Well-Being: Limits of, and New Directions for, Understanding

Jay Belsky
The Pennsylvania State University

Paul Amato has done an impressive job of succinctly summarizing much of the recent evidence that purportedly highlights effects of fathering on the development and functioning of children and young adults, both in maritally intact and father-absent homes. To supplement this, he has presented thoughtful analyses, based on his survey of the literature of retrospective data on fathering gathered on a large sample of young adults whose parents have been studied for quite some time. Especially useful in Amato's analysis of his own data and that of others is his adoption of Coleman's (1988, 1990) conceptualization of parental resources. By distinguishing educational, economic and more psychological assets that parents can contribute to their progeny, Amato successfully integrates work done in separate disciplines that all too often remains unrelated.

In the course of his survey of the apparent effects of fathers' human, economic, and social capital on their children's well-being, Amato frequently highlights several limitations of much of the available research that tempers any conclusions that can be drawn from this ever-growing body of evidence. Repeatedly he notes, for example, that many studies included measures of fathering and child functioning based on single sources of information, such as a parent's or child's report. Results of such inquiries can clearly inflate estimates of fathering effects, if only because they may reflect more the results of shared method variance than actual paternal influence. It would seem useful, then, in any further attempt to composite results across studies to actually organize the database in terms of measurement independence. Simply put, to what extent do investigations that rely on single sources of information on fathers and children generate results suggestive of father effects quite at odds, at least in terms of effects sizes, with what derives from investigations in which there is not such shared method variance?

As another example of a repeatedly acknowledged methodological issue, Amato points out that many presumed assessments of paternal influence fail to take into consideration the effects of mothers. In consequence, influence that might be shared by mothers and fathers is attributed exclusively to fathers, and this may again inflate estimates of parental influence that is uniquely paternal. Once more we can wonder, then, how the results of the studies surveyed look when one distinguishes investigations that discount maternal effects before estimating father effects from those that do not (and probably cannot). More than anything else, Amato's insightful consideration of this issue of unique and shared influences of mothers and fathers reminds us that when it comes to thinking about paternal contributions to child development, there is need to conceptualize the father in family terms. Although the same is true for mothers, it remains the case that most efforts to study maternal influences rarely consider the possibility that effects of parenting attributed to mothers may be as much that of fathers. One can only hope that the point Amato makes with regard to fathering is heard by all those investigators who exclusively study mothers and mothering.

Although the issues of shared method variance and of unique fathering effects, like some others, are raised repeatedly throughout Amato's survey of research findings to highlight the limits of the available database, there are other important methodological—and derivative conceptual—issues that do not receive any real attention until the very end of his chapter. These, it seems to me, are even more central for accurately appraising the limits of our current understanding of father effects than several of those which receive so much more attention throughout Amato's review of recent research on father influence. Thus, it is around two of these issues that Amato indisputably acknowledges, but does not dwell on to any great extent, that I organize this commentary. They concern the temporal nature of the database—that is, whether study findings derive from cross-sectional or longitudinal designs—and the related issue of child effects. I discuss these interrelated issues before sharing some data on effects of fathering and mothering that derive from an investigation of families rearing toddlers carried out in collaboration with Keith Crnic (Belsky, Woodworth, & Crnic, 1996a, 1996b). My purpose in presenting these data is to underscore points Amato makes and points to be made in my analysis of methodological issues that might have merited more—or at least earlier—attention in Amato's analysis, as well as to raise one important issue that was not considered at all by Amato. I am referring here to the prospect that not all children are equally affected by fathering (or, more generally, by parenting), and thus the need to consider the role of child characteristics (other than gender) as moderating the effect of fathers and especially fathering on child development.

LONGITUDINAL DESIGNS AND CHILD EFFECTS

When research pertaining to effects of fathers and fathering on the development of children and young adults is surveyed and summarized without extensive and continued consideration of the longitudinal or cross-sectional nature of research designs, it is difficult to evaluate what findings and, thus, what percent of the database is likely to highlight actual father effects. Results of cross-sectional studies, as Amato acknowledges in the final section of his chapter, are open to alternative explanation. To cite the very good illustration Amato uses himself when briefly mentioning this critical issue, a contemporaneous association between paternal nurturance or rejection and problematic child behavior may reflect as much the effect of a troublesome child on a father as it does a father on his child. It would seem imperative, then, in considering the evidence that putatively chronicles effects of fathers and especially of fathering to systematically distinguish between cross-sectional and longitudinal studies. However much a study may be compromised when it comes to drawing inferences about parental influence by the fact that its design cannot discount behavior-genetic influences, it would seem even more limited if there is no temporal ordering of the measures of fathering and of child functioning.

A longitudinal design does not ameliorate all inferential problems, however, even those not related to genetic influences. This can be seen most clearly in studies that endeavor to evaluate father effects relatively late in development, for example, during the period of adolescence. Much of the recent research cited by Amato has as its focus parental and child behavior in the second decade of life. Even if assessments of fathering are obtained in such work weeks, months, or even a few years before child outcomes are measured, there are still problems with drawing causal inferences if child functioning has not also been measured at the time when fathering was first assessed. Unless such earlier child behavior can be discounted, it remains eminently possible that apparent effects of fathering at one point in time on child development at some later point are actually part of a more bidirectional process in which the putative father effects are sequelae of child effects. Consider in this regard Barber's (1994) finding that adolescents who frequently obtained advice from their noncustodial dads were less likely to be depressed than were other adolescents, or Simons, Whitbeck, Beaman, and Conger's (1994) result indicating that the quality of a noncustodial father's parenting was negatively related to his offspring's externalizing problem behavior. Quite conceivably, both findings could reflect child effects masquerading as father effects. After all, it seems rather possible that a child prone to depression might be less likely to evoke advice from her father or that a child's problem behavior might be more likely to evoke negative fathering. Not only, then, does it seem necessary to distinguish results putatively documenting father effects that derive from cross-sectional and longitudinal studies, but it would appear to be just as important to distinguish investigations that have controlled for possible child effects from those that have not.

In conclusion, the main point to be made is not that the research surveyed by Amato is without value. As both a reviewer of research and a researcher, I am quite aware that it is far easier to sit on the sidelines and be a design critic than it is to implement and bring to fruition the kind of work reviewed in the preceding chapter. But given the tendency of both psychologists and sociologists to interpret associations between a parent attribute or behavior and a child outcome as evidence of parental influence, and the structural weaknesses of many research designs, it would seem useful to distinguish investigations that afford stronger inference of father effects from those that afford weaker inferences. One might anticipate that the magnitude of putative father effects would decline as designs became more inferentially powerful. Thus, the strongest effects would emerge from cross-sectional designs, with weaker associations between measures of parent and child in longitudinal designs that do not discount plausible child effects, and still weaker effects in longitudinal designs that do discount such child effects. Ultimately, the weakest effects might be those emanating from such longitudinal studies that incorporate behavior-genetic designs (i.e., twin and adoption studies), although these would likely be the ones whose findings one might have the most confidence in. Unless, and until, some effort is made to array the database in this manner, it will be difficult to even guess at how much the apparent effects of fathering surveyed by Amato may be inflated due to limitations in research designs.

FATHERING, MOTHERING, CO-PARENTING AND THE DEVELOPMENT OF TODDLERS

In an effort both to apply the prescriptions just advanced and follow the strategy that Amato used to examine unique and shared effects of mothering and fathering and of the effects of marital processes using his own data, I present results of analyses geared toward examining the effects of mothering, fathering and co-parenting on two aspects of toddler functioning, externalizing problem behavior and inhibition. My specific purpose in presenting the data that I do is to highlight (a) the differential effects of mothering, fathering and co-parenting on these two aspects of children's functioning at 3 years of age and (b) to raise the possibility that our field may be both under- and overestimating effects of parenting by carrying out analyses that implicitly presume that all children are equally affected by the same family experiences. To be noted at the outset is that the approach adopted to addressing both of these issues is to rely on longitudinal data, and take into consideration potential child effects. Like so much other family-based research, the work to be presented is limited by its inability to take into consideration behavior-genetic influences.

METHODS

The participants in our study of families rearing toddlers are 123 working- and middle-class, maritally intact, White families from small-town and semi-rural central Pennsylvania who are rearing firstborn sons. The sample focuses exclusively on sons because of our interest in the origins of externalizing problem behavior and the fact that males are far more likely than females to evince such problems in the post-toddler years. Needless to say, such a restricted sample clearly limits the generalizability of the results to be presented.

The design of our research included an extensive parental report and lab-based assessment of infant temperament/emotionality at 1 year of age, repeated observations of family interaction during the second and third year of the child's life, and outcome evaluations of child externalizing behavior problems and of inhibition at age 3. Ultimately, we seek to illuminate potential influences of mothering, fathering, and co-parenting on these developmental outcomes over and above any effects of early temperament/emotionality.

Early Emotionality Assessments

In order to observe the separable constructs of infant positive and negative emotionality, mothers and fathers completed parent-report measures of temperament when infants were 10 months of age. Then when children were 12 and 13 months of age, they were videotaped in a series of laboratory procedures designed to evoke positive and negative emotional responses. By means of LISREL, we succeeded in creating two, relatively independent latent constructs reflective of positive and negative emotionality. Importantly, these constructs, which were used to create composite variables for purpose of the analyses presented in this chapter, proved replicable with the first and second halves of our sample, showed good discriminant validity across a 6-month period, and were comprised principally of observed behavior rather than of parental reports. (See Belsky, Hsieh, & Crnic, 1996, for a full report on the measurement of infant emotionality.) Thus, unlike most assessments of temperament, particularly those used in studies of problem behavior, we are not dependent exclusively or even principally on the kind of parent-report measures that have been shown to bear little relation to more objectively made assessments (Seifer, Sameroff, Barrett, & Kratchuk, 1994). This is a most critical point in light of the fact that at least one of our dependent constructs, that of externalizing problem behavior, is based on parental reports. In consequence, shared method variance will not be a limiting factor in our analyses.

Mothering, Fathering, and Co-parenting Assessments

In order to assess family interaction processes, eight home visits were carried out across the second and third year of the child's life, with pairs of visits scheduled 1 week apart at 6 month intervals (i.e., 15, 21, 27, and 33 months). These visits each afforded an hour of naturalistic observation, typically in the late afternoon and early evening around dinnertime, during which parents were instructed to go about their everyday routine and disregard the presence of the home observer as much as possible. The observer's job was to not disrupt family routines while taking detailed notes about parental efforts to control the child and spousal actions, in which one parent supported or undermined the implicit or explicit goals of the other parent. Every 15 minutes, the observer took a 5-minute break to review and elaborate on the notes taken during the preceding observation period and complete a set of ratings of family members. The notes were then elaborated on at the end of the home visit when the observer dictated a detailed narrative record, relying on the notes and audiotapes of family conversation during the home visit, which was subsequently typed for coding.

For purposes of this report, we rely on two different sets of home-visit data, averaged across all home visits during the second and third year of life. First, we have ratings of parenting that, when summed across the four 15-minute observation epochs at each visit and averaged across the 2 days at each age of measurement, yielded two separate—and identical—factors when subject to factor analysis at 15, 21, 27 and 33 months. One factor, labeled *Positive Parenting*, was comprised of individual ratings of sensitivity, positive affect, cognitive stimulation and detachment (reflected); the other, labeled *Negative Parenting*, was comprised of individual ratings of negative affect and intrusiveness. For purpose of the analyses presented in this report, these two factor-based composites were further composited by subtracting Negative Parenting from Positive Parenting, separately for each parent, at each age of measurement, before averaging the resulting grand composites over time.

Two measures of co-parenting were composited, each of which was based on codings of the narrative records of family interaction rather than on the ratings made during the home visits themselves (see Gable, Belsky, & Crnic, 1995, for details). *Supportive Co-parenting* reflects the number of times that one parent supported the goal of the other parent, either (a) by simultaneously directing the child to do essentially the same thing that the other parent was directing the child to do (e.g., "stop jumping on the couch"); (b) by reiterating what the first parent directed the child to do after the first parent had directed the child to do something (e.g., "you heard your mother, get down from the couch"); or (c) by elaborating on the first parent's directive in a manner consistent with it (e.g., "come here and I will read you a book"). *Unsupportive Co-parenting* reflects the number of times that one parent was observed to undermine the agenda of the other parent. Such negative co-parenting could take a variety of forms, including presenting a contrasting emotional response to the child (e.g., mother is irritated by the child's couch jumping and father laughs at child), giving competing directives to the child (e.g., "get off the couch" vs. "how high can you jump"), or openly disagreeing with the other parent in front of the child (e.g., "why can't he jump on the couch; he won't get hurt"). For purposes of this report, a grand co-parenting measure was created by subtracting the unsupportive score from the supportive score at each age of measurement and then averaging across the four ages of assessment.

Externalizing Problem Behavior and Inhibition Assessments

In terms of child outcomes, externalizing problem behavior was measured by averaging the mother-report and father-report scores on this dimension of problem behavior derived from the Child Behavior Checklist (Achenbach, Edelbrock, & Howell, 1987) administered when children were 36 months of age. Our measure of inhibition was based on ratings of children's reticence to engage in 21 different activities or interactions with experimenters across two visits to our laboratory when children were 36 and 37 months of age. Low ratings reflected no reticence and high ratings reflected a great deal of reticence, as when a child was unwilling to put on a special vest on entering the lab, proved unresponsive to a puppet's request that he pick up a toy that had fallen off a puppet stage, or was hesitant to respond to the examiner's questions during the administration of portions of an intelligence test (for full details, see Park, Belsky, Putnam, & Crnic, 1997). To be noted is that the composite inhibition score that was based on the average of all ratings was independent of the composite externalizing problem behavior score $(r = .14, p > .05)$.

EFFECTS OF MOTHERING, FATHERING,
AND CO-PARENTING

In order to assess the effects of mothering, fathering, and co-parenting on externalizing problems and inhibition, hierarchical regression analyses were used. The regression equation consisted of three blocks of variables. First entered were the predictors of early positive emotionality, negative emotionality, and their interaction, in order to control for the effects of early temperament and thus discount rival interpretations of family influences emphasizing child effects. The second block of predictors consisted of the grand composite measures of positive-minus-negative mothering and positive-minus-negative fathering and the interaction of these two parenting terms. Inclusion of the latter term enabled us to test the hypothesis raised by Amato that the influence of one parent may be moderated by that of the other parent. Finally, a third block of variables was entered, which included the grand unsupportive-minus-supportive index of co-parenting, as well as two interaction terms reflecting the interaction of this co-parenting measure with each of the composite measures of mothering and fathering. Inclusion of these interaction terms enabled us to determine whether an effect of co-parenting was contingent on patterns of mothering and fathering.

Most interestingly, the results of these analyses were quite different for the two dependent constructs under consideration. First, early emotionality accounted for an insignificant 4% of the variance in externalizing problems, providing no evidence that parent-reported behavior problems at 3 years of age were a function of (objectively measured) early temperament. In the case of inhibition, however, early temperament accounted for a significant 8% of the variance ($p < .05$), and it was the interaction of positive and negative emotionality that was principally responsible for this effect (beta = $-.18$, $p < .05$). Further consideration of this interaction revealed that the children most inhibited at 3 years of age were those who, as infants, evinced high levels of negativity and low levels of positivity (see Park et al., 1997).

Once the contribution of early emotionality was controlled (to discount child effects), the block of parenting variables accounted for a significant and additional 7% of the variance in the case of externalizing problems ($p < .05$) and 10% of the variance in the case of inhibition ($p < .01$). Perhaps more noteworthy, however, was the apparent differential impact of mothering and fathering on these two child outcomes. Whereas the standardized regression coefficient in the case of externalizing problems was significant for mothering ($-.26$, $p < .05$), indicating that more positive and less negative mothering predicted fewer externalizing problems, the comparable beta weight was insignificant in the case of fathers ($-.12$, $p > .05$). In contrast, it was fathering that predicted inhibition (beta = .28, $p < .01$) rather than mothering ($-.02$, $p > .05$) once early emotionality was controlled. These results, consistent with those of Arcus, Gardner, and Anderson (1992), although perhaps surprising to some, indicate that the more positive and less negative fathers were to their toddlers, the more inhibited they became relative to what would have been predicted on the basis of their early temperaments. Conversely, the less positive and more negative the fathers were, the less inhibited and more uninhibited children became (for extended discussion of these results, see Park et al., 1997). In sum, then, whereas mothers seemed to determine, in part, how problematic their 3-year-old's behavior was, it was fathering that appeared to affect how inhibited (or uninhibited) their offspring became. To be noted is that in the case of neither inhibition nor externalizing problems did any evidence emerge to indicate that the contribution of one parent was moderated by that of the other parent.

Once both early temperament and parenting were taken into account, the effect of co-parenting was tested. Only in the case of externalizing behavior did this block of variables contribute significantly to the prediction of child functioning, adding a significant and additional 7% of the variance to the explanation of this child outcome ($p < .05$). Somewhat counterintuitively, however, the standardized regression coefficient indicated that with all other variables in the model controlled, that more supportive and less unsupportive co-parenting was predictive of more externalizing problems (.28, $p < .01$). Clearly these results are difficult to reconcile with many others in the literature linking marital difficulties with problem behavior. At the current time, we simply do not have a clear understanding of this result.

In sum, although the two prediction models accounted for essentially the same amount of variance in the two outcomes under investigation (R^2: .18 and .19 for externalizing and inhibition, respectively), and were both statistically significant at the .01 level, the pattern of prediction was decidedly different. Indeed, when the two regression equations were compared by χ^2 difference test, they were found to be reliably different ($p < .01$), clearly suggesting that processes of influence in the case of inhibition are quite different than in the case of externalizing problems. More specifically, it appears that whereas mothering and co-parenting are important to understanding the development of externalizing problem behavior, it is infant emotionality and fathering that principally explain inhibition at 3 years of age. The differential effect of mothering and fathering is especially apparent in the top of Fig. 14.1, which depicts the unique and shared effect of the two parenting predictors in a manner consistent with that used by Amato.

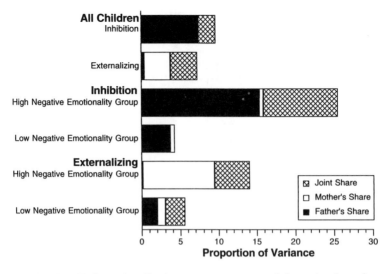

FIG. 14.1. Variance in offspring outcomes accounted for uniquely and jointly by mothers and fathers.

THE MODERATING EFFECT OF EARLY NEGATIVE EMOTIONALITY

Virtually all the research surveyed by Amato, like much of that pertaining to family influences on child development (including the work just reported), presumes that all children are affected by family experiences in the same general manner. After all, most research linking family processes and child functioning fails to take child characteristics into account except, perhaps, in the case of child gender, as when differential effects for boys and girls are considered. Needless to say, this gender-oriented approach was not possible in the analyses just presented, as the sample consists exclusively of boys.

There would seem to be both theoretical and empirical reasons to question the logic of carrying out assessments of family effects without regard to characteristics of the child. First, and from the theoretical side, there is the organismic-specificity hypothesis advanced by Wachs and Gandour (1983), which stipulates that not all children are affected in the same way by even the very same experiences. An angry complaint by a father may register quite differently when experienced by two different children. Similarly, praise for a job well-done may carry more meaning for one child than for another. Drawing on evolutionary logic, I recently advanced some biological reasons why it should be the case that different children are differentially affected by the same experience (Belsky, 1997). Here I briefly outline my reasoning once more.

Because the future is always uncertain, no biological organism, humans included, can be certain what its progeny will encounter as they develop. Thus, neither humans nor any other living organism can be sure what heritable features of its progeny will enable it to survive, grow, and, ultimately, successfully reproduce. In light of this uncertainty, evolution has crafted a reproductive system in the case of sexually producing species that mixes maternal and paternal genes and, thereby, creates diverse offspring. Such diversity is advantageous to the parents because it hedges their reproductive bets. Whereas one progeny might be well-suited to flourish in one ecological niche, another might be better suited to flourish in a different niche. By diversifying the genetic character of offspring, sexual reproduction increases the range of uncertain future environments in which some progeny might prove to be reproductively successful.

Following this same logic highlighting the benefit of diversity in the face of an uncertain future, it seems reasonable that parents might further hedge their bets and increase the collective reproductive return on their offspring by varying the degree to which offspring are susceptible to environmental influence. That is, the probability that some of a parent's progeny would thrive and thus reach reproductive age capable of conceiving, bearing, and rearing young who could themselves be reproductively successful would seem to be increased if the parent produced offspring that varied in terms of whether their behavioral tendencies were *fixed* or *plastic*. Those with fixed attributes (or particular fixed attributes) would be prepared to fit and thus flourish in fewer niches, but should have a very high rate of success when the niche for which they were prepared was encountered. It would also make sense, however, in terms of hedging bets against the uncertainty of futures that progeny would face, to bear offspring who are plastic, learn well and who are thus more susceptible than the fixed type to environmental, including family, influence. Such individuals might never fit any ecological niche as well as a fixed type, but such an individual would likely have a wider range of niches into which he or she could succeed and could be prepared, through rearing experiences, to fit.

One might imagine, given this conceptualization, progeny with genotypically fixed phenotypes who are likely to thrive especially in hostile and dangerous environments, others who are similarly genotypically fixed to flourish in ecologies based on cooperation and trust, and still others with genotypically plastic phenotypes capable of learning from experience so as to fit either of these environments to greater or lesser extent depending on their learning experiences and socialization histories. In a more refined form, one might think in terms of genotypically plastic individuals whose range of variation is broad or constrained. Thus, one such person might be capable of learning not to be hostile and aggressive, but be especially quick at acquiring such an interpersonal orientation given the right learning conditions (e.g., hostile rearing). Another person might be capable of learning not to be so cooperative and trusting, but be especially adept at acquiring such an interpersonal orientation given the right rearing conditions (e.g., nurturant rearing). And still another genotypically plastic individual might be especially proficient at acquiring either orientation should that orientation be promoted in his or her rearing milieu. In other words, one need not think in terms of a single fixed type and a single plastic type, but in more-and-less plastic and fixed types, with varying reaction ranges. Moreover, one can think about fixedness and plasticity in general or specific to a certain behavioral tendency. The basic point, though, is that we may have been making a basic mistake in assuming that nature has designed humans so that they are all equally capable of developing in any and all directions as a function of their rearing environment.

It is not unreasonable to ask at this point is whether there is any evidence that might be consistent with such theorizing—in fact there is. Most notable, perhaps, are Suomi's (1995) studies of selectively bred "laid back" and "uptight" rhesus monkeys who differ dramatically in the extent to which they are shy, inhibited, and fearful. What is most interesting is that it is the uptight monkeys who seem most responsive to rearing condition, becoming leaders when reared by highly skilled foster mothers, but into incompetent playmates and sexual partners when reared by highly unskilled mothers. Interestingly, the laid back monkeys show not nearly this range of reaction to dramatically different rearing conditions as do the more emotionally negative uptight monkeys.

What about humans? Not inconsistent with Suomi's (1995) findings are those of Kochanska (1993) who examined the influence of mothering on the development of conscience and self-control. As in Suomi's research on monkeys, it is the more negatively emotional infants who are most susceptible to parental influence. According to Kochanska (1993), such infants are more likely to be affected by the quality of care they receive when it comes to developing a conscience and developing self-control because they are more anxious than other infants and so are more emotionally motivated to follow parental directives. Children less anxious and fearful may simply find parental directives and threats of punishment less motivating and are thus less affected by the same socializing behavior that appears to affect more anxious and negative infants so much more.

Deater-Deckard and Dodge (1997) also reported results consistent with these others, this time in response to my evolutionary theorizing about, differential susceptibility to environmental influence (Belsky, 1997). More specifically, it was elementary school children whose mothers (retrospectively) described their children's temperaments as more resistant to intrusion and persistent in pursuing forbidden objects at 6 months of age whose externalizing problems were most strongly linked to harsh maternal discipline. Once again, then, we find that infant temperament appears to moderate the effect of parenting on socioemotional development, this time in the mid-childhood years.

In light of these results and the aforementioned theorizing, we reexamined effects of parenting and co-parenting on the problem behavior and inhibition of our toddlers after dividing our sample at the median on our nonretrospective and behaviorally based index of negative emotionality. This enabled us to determine whether parenting effects in particular were stronger in the case of toddlers who scored high in negativity as infants. Results consistent with those just summarized were most clearly evident in the case of our prediction of inhibition: parenting and co-parenting accounted for a significant 25% of the variance in inhibition among children who scored high in negativity as infants, but an insignificant 10% of the variance in the case of children who scored low in negativity. The two equations, moreover, were significantly different from each other ($p < .05$). The unique and shared variance in inhibition explained by mothering and fathering (but not co-parenting) in the two emotionality groups is displayed in Fig. 14.1.

With respect to externalizing behavior, a significant 16% of the variance was explained by parenting and co-parenting in the case of the high-negativity group ($p < .05$), with the corresponding figure in the case of the low-negativity group being 14% ($p < .05$). Despite this similarity in total variance explained in the two emotionality groups, the equations for each group were marginally different from each other ($p < .10$). This was due to the fact that the predictive power of parenting and co-parenting in the two equations—and thus in the two emotionality groups—was decidedly different. Consistent with the studies just summarized, parenting explained a significant 14% of the variance in externalizing problems in the case of the high-negativity group ($p < .05$), but only an insignificant 5% of the variance in the low-negativity group. Figure 14.1 also depicts unique and shared variance attributable to mothering and fathering (but not co-parenting) in the prediction of externalizing problems in the two emotionality groups.

In the case of co-parenting, the predictive power for the two groups was opposite of what was found with respect to parenting: An insignificant 2% of the variance was explained by co-parenting (once parenting was accounted for) in the high-negativity group, but a significant 9% of the variance was explained by this predictor in the low-negativity group ($p < .05$). Exactly why this unanticipated differential prediction of parenting and co-parenting should emerge across emotionality groups remains unclear. Unfortunately, because we are aware of no studies of marital effects that take into consideration characteristics of children (other than gender), there are no results to compare our co-parenting findings to. Thus, at the present time we must be cautious about breathing too much meaning into them. This would seem to be less the case with respect to the parenting effects just chronicled because they are clearly consistent with the afore-mentioned work of Suomi (1995), Kochanska (1993), and Deater-Deckard and Dodge (1997).

CONCLUSIONS

Four basic "take home" messages emerge from this commentary on Amato's chapter. First, not all research findings are equal in terms of the confidence that one can place in them. Effects attributable to fathers and fathering de-rived from cross-sectional studies are less convincing than those from longitudinal studies, but it is longitudinal inquiries that make some effort to control for child effects or take into account in some manner the develop-mental history of the father–child relationship that yield more convincing evidence of father effects. Even such research, however, is subject to infer-ential problems because of its inability to discount alternative behavior-ge-netic explanations. This analysis suggests that it might be useful to review data on fathering with integrity of research design as a basic organizing principle.

Second, and consistent with Amato's arguments, effects of mother and father may be different for different developmental outcomes; and studies that include only a single parent may overestimate that parent's effects by not taking into consideration the possibility of effects shared by mother and father.

Third and finally, it should not be presumed, as most current research designs imply, that all children are affected in the same way by similar experiences. The fact of the matter is that some children, perhaps for genetic reasons, may be more susceptible to environmental influence than are others. If that is so, it may well be the case that most estimates of parent influences are both under- and overestimates, under for those most susceptible to influence and over for those least susceptible to influence.

ACKNOWLEDGMENT

Research reported in this chapter was supported by a grant from the National Institute of Mental Health to Jay Belsky and Keith Crnic (MH44604).

REFERENCES

Achenbach, T., Edelbrock, C., & Howell, C. (1987). Empirically-based assessment of the behavioral/emotional problems of 2–3-year-old children. *Journal of Abnormal Child Psychology, 15*, 629–650.

Arcus, D., Gardner, S., & Anderson, C. (1992, April). *Infant reactivity maternal style and the development of inhibited and uninhibited behavior profiles.* Paper presented at the Biennial Meetings of the International Society for Infant Studies, Miami.

Barber, B. L. (1994). Support and advice from married and divorced fathers: Linkages to adolescent adjustment. *Family Relations, 43,* 433–438.

Belsky, J. (1997). Variation in susceptibility to environmental influence: An evolutionary argument. *Psychological Inquiry, 8,* 182–186.

Belsky, J., Hsieh, K., & Crnic, K. (1996). Infant positive and negative emotionality: One dimension or two? *Developmental Psychology, 32,* 289–298.

Belsky, J., Woodworth, S., & Crnic, K. (1996a). Trouble in the second year: Three questions about family interaction. *Child Development, 67,* 556–578.

Belsky, J., Woodworth, S., & Crnic, K. (1996b). Troubled family interaction during toddlerhood. *Development and Psychopathology, 8,* 477–495.

Coleman, J. (1988). Social capital in the creation of human capital. *American Journal of Sociology, 94,* 95–120.

Coleman, J. (1990). *Foundations of social theory.* Cambridge, MA: Harvard University Press.

Deater-Deckard, K., & Dodge, K. (1997). Authors response. *Psychological Inquiry, 8,* 166–179.

Gable, S., Belsky, J., & Crnic, K. (1995). A descriptive account of coparenting during the child's second year. *Journal of Marriage and the Family, 57,* 609–616.

Kochanska, G. (1993). Toward a synthesis of parental socialization and child temperament in early development. *Child Development, 64,* 325–347.

Park, S., Belsky, J., Putnam, S., & Crnic, K. (1997). Infant emotionality, parenting, and 3-year inhibition. *Developmental Psychology, 33,* 218–227.

Simons, R., Whitbeck, L., Beaman, J., & Conger, R. (1994). The impact of mother's parenting, involvement of nonresidential fathers, and parental conflict on the adjustment of adolescent children. *Journal of Marriage and the Family, 56,* 356–374.

Seifer, R., Sameroff, A., Barrett, L., & Kratchuk, E. (1994). Infant temperament measured by multiple observations and mother report. *Child Development, 65,* 1487–1490.

Suomi, S. (1995). Influence of attachment theory on ethological studies of biobehavioral development in nonhuman primates. In S. Goldberg, R. Muir, & J. Kerr (Eds.), *Attachment theory: Social, developmental, and clinical perspectives* (pp. 185–202). Hillsdale, NJ: The Analytic Press.

Wachs, T., & Gandour, M. (1983). Temperament, environment and six-month cognitive-intellectual development: A test of the organismic-specificity hypothesis. *International Journal of Behavioral Development, 6,* 135–152.

Chapter 15

Social Capital and the Role of Fathers in the Family

Frank F. Furstenberg, Jr.
University of Pennsylvania

Just when I think that I am catching up on the literature in a research area on divorce, along comes Paul Amato with another meta-analysis. He has produced a fine chapter that greatly advances our knowledge about the effects of paternal involvement on children's well-being. Amato's conceptualization of different dimensions of paternal participation that might affect children's well-being, his careful effort to delineate theoretical links among these dimensions, and his judicious review of the state of empirical evidence leaves the commentator with relatively little about which to write. I want to suggest a few areas in which our understanding of the evidence is dim and that may require further theoretical elaboration. Then, I will conclude with a couple of remarks about the policy implications of Amato's chapter.

AMATO'S ARGUMENT ABOUT THE EFFECTS OF PATERNAL INVOLVEMENT

Amato observes that the special contributions of fathers can be organized into several general domains: (a) the resources the father brings to bear in the form of human capital and financial capital; (b) the investment that he makes directly in childrearing and mentoring; and (c) the social capital that his presence contributes over and above what is offered by the mother. Although some of these constructs have been explored extensively, others have been largely omitted in the existing literature on fatherhood.

1. The effects of human and financial capital have been well documented. Amato shows that strong evidence exists indicating that the father's presence adds resources in the form of material goods and income, as well as educational resources that offer advantages to children. In effect, these forms of capital are cumulative: The more the better.

2. We know less about the impact of paternal interaction and emotional involvement. A growing body of research indicates that fathers may supplement what the mother offers by filling in when she is not present (Presser, 1988) or by teaching, modeling, or mentoring in ways that may not necessarily be part of the mother's repertoire of skills. Thus, it seems that parents can complement one another, modeling different sorts of behaviors (Gadsden & Hall, 1995; Marsiglio, 1995; Parke, 1981).

3. Practically nothing is known about men's contribution to social capital. The notion that parents reenforce one another's values is hardly new. "Just wait until I tell your father" remains a phrase familiar to many children. The idea that one parent is able to resort symbolically to the moral authority of another has been central in the family literature for many decades, and especially so in the work done on family systems (Bossard & Boll, 1968; Bott, 1971; Coser, 1964; Minuchin, 1974; Reiss, 1981; Waller, 1938). Yet the novelty of the term *social capital* has attracted renewed attention to the need for empirical study of how families operate as social systems.

SOCIAL CAPITAL AND MEN'S INFLUENCE

The term *social capital* as used by Coleman (1988), Putnam (1995), and others (Furstenberg & Hughes, 1995; Sampson, 1992) points to the advantages for children of being embedded in a social system. Part of these advantages derive from the social ties and linkages that are created by social participation, but social capital also refers to the benefits of being a member of a system with common values that are socially reenforced by others. Family-based social capital—if it means anything at all—implies that parents construct a common culture into which their children are inculcated: values, habits, practices, rituals, and norms (see Furstenberg & Hughes, 1995).

Families can be conceived as tiny subcultures with styles of language, ritual practices, and shared understandings that are unique and particular, yet that draw on customs and culture distinctive to ethnic, class, religious, and national affiliations. Almost no work has been done on the ways that internal cultures of families are constructed and sustained over lifetimes and how they are passed on from one generation to the next (Gillis, 1996; Hess & Handel, 1959). Thus, there is a sociological feature of social capital that is irreducible because it only operates at a shared and collective level.

Amato uses the quality of the co-parenting relationship as an indicator of social capital. This is probably appropriate, but the concept of social capital is much broader than this single feature of parental collaboration. In his own study, Amato devises a different indicator of social capital by employing the retrospective reports of children of the level of support provided by each parent. He enters separate measures for each parent into a statistical model to capture additive amounts of social capital provided by the family. This approach treats the notion of social capital as a psychological property of the dyadic relationship between parent and child, not as a sociological property of the family as a collective social system with a set of social norms and cultural understandings. One way out of this reductionist trap is to consider the shared perceptions of multiple actors as a measure of social capital. This type of measure comes closer to tapping the shared features of the family as a social and cultural entity. Perhaps, he might look at families where both parents provide overlapping and joint support to the child. The redundancy created in families when both parents cooperate and back each other up—colluding in the best interests of the child—is a key element of social capital. Consequently, the influence of fathers calls for a multilevel perspective; to measure the effect of social capital may require a multilevel form of analysis. What is the added effect on children of having parents who share the same norms, values, models of discipline, and the like?

Incidentally, this theoretical and analytic approach need not be confined to the analysis of the added value created by a father's presence in generating social capital. We could ask what effect any additional parent (another mother, grandmother, uncle, stepparent, or much older sibling) offers when she or he reenforces the values and regulations of a single parent. Thus, fathers may or may not be distinctive in their ability to help generate social capital in the family. This is a question of both immense theoretical and policy importance.

Amato's longitudinal analysis creatively makes use of the measures at hand. Perhaps, there is room to push the analysis even further. For example, he might differentiate his sample by families in which value consensus was high or low as indicated by both marital disagreements, common values, and childrearing practices among parents. This requires a clinical or holistic account of how families are working as units—the sort of systems approach that Reiss (1981) and other researchers employed to consider how families behave as entities rather than as collections of individual members. We would expect to find substantial differences between families that may not appear when multivariate analytic techniques are used that do not take account of the aggregate organizational effect of the family as a social and cultural entity.

This sort of strategy may also help us understand better the inability of many stepfamilies to forge a strong family system. Structurally, stepfamilies cannot easily create an environment of mutual trust, shared values, and tight bonds—what Cooley (1956) referred to as a primary group best indicated by a sense of we-ness. Typically, children do not regard their stepparent as parents in the fullest sense of the word (Cherlin & Furstenberg, 1994; Furstenberg & Spanier, 1984). This may be so because a nonresidential parent may be contesting for authority, attention, or validation. In addition, stepparents do not have full legitimacy in our kinship system. They are in-laws, who must earn their stripes as parents rather than acquiring them ascriptively through a blood relationship (Furstenberg, 1981; Johnson, 1988; Schneider, 1980).

This is not to say that stepfamilies cannot generate a high level of social capital. They can and frequently do. Building social capital in stepfamilies is simply a less efficient and reliable process. Similarly, nonresidential parents face structural barriers to sustaining social capital. Their ability to reenforce and be reenforced is usually weakened by divorce and by separate residence. Their authority may be undermined by the other parent or her or his kin. The dissipation of social capital is a likely result. By contrast, the potential for extending financial and human capital is somewhat greater both in stepfamilies and among nonresidential fathers.

HOW TO MEASURE SOCIAL CAPITAL

All of this sensitizes us to the need for more direct measures of social capital. Parenthetically, I should say that it is not an easy task to develop measures of social capital at the family level, but it is a promising area for further research. Several studies that I am conducting in Philadelphia and Baltimore indicate that social capital may have important consequences for the welfare of children. Whether social capital is a product of the family, the community, or connections between the two represents an intriguing theoretical issue (Furstenberg, Eccles, Elder, Cook, & Sameroff, in press; Furstenberg & Hughes, 1995).

Amato concludes his chapter by arguing that we need more policy incentives that would encourage "a larger number of nonresident fathers [to] behave more like the good dads in two-parent households" (p. 272). A noble entreaty, but one that is a little short on specifics. We could as easily argue that we need to cultivate ways of creating collaboration between fathers and mothers in nuclear households as well. Many men and women do not parent successfully together. Now, it is true that Amato has shown that fathers are only slightly less likely to be invested in childrearing as reported by their offspring in retrospective measures of paternal support. Frankly, I find this hard to believe from observational studies, time diaries, and current accounts of parenting that ask children about the frequency of interaction with their fathers in such activities as diapering babies, taking children to the doctor, supervising homework, or chauffeuring children to after-school activities. After all, no one speaks of the "soccer parents," much less the "soccer dads." Of course, some dads are out there on the playing fields, but only a handful as compared to the mothers. Most fathers are still "part-timers." Accordingly, children may have lower expectations for their dads and apply a sliding scale, perhaps especially when assessing their behaviors retrospectively.

In many respects, men derive influence in the family through their wives. Historians tell us that this was not always the case. Men assumed a larger familial role in the patriarchal system, their influence waning with the advent of a job economy (Demos, 1982; Gillis, 1996; Griswold, 1993; Rotundo, 1985). At least for much of this century, men have relied on their wives to lend credibility to their role as decision makers, role-models, and disciplinarians. Elsewhere, I described the indirect influence of men as part of a "package deal" that comes with marriage. When marriage dissolves, this deal, as I indicated, typically breaks down. Men who do not live with their children appear to retain relatively thin levels of contact over the long term, and children, accordingly, reduce the level of exchange that they have with their fathers when they reside apart.

Can we measure the level of social capital that is lost by divorce? Perhaps, but only by conducting longitudinal research in which social capital is measured before and after a marital breakup. It is possible, then, that men who will subsequently leave marriages are not contributing significant amounts of social capital when they are still present in the home. As I have already said, family conflict usually undermines the level of family-based social capital, thereby reducing the child's commitment to parental standards. If it is true that less committed and capable fathers are more likely to migrate from marriage, then it may also be true that the dissolution of many marriages may do nothing more than turn the illusion of unity into the reality of disunity.

POLICY IMPLICATIONS

We must exercise some modesty and caution in offering policy recommendations to strengthen men's role in the family, for to do so, in my view, requires some confidence in our ability to increase the likelihood of creating and maintaining stable and collaborative partnerships between men and women. High on my list are ways of equipping fathers with the skills to assume a larger share of child care and crafting employment policies that encourage fathers to become more involved in domestic duties.

Consider the case of Norway, which provides a paid leave of absence to new fathers (in addition to mothers). It is offered to men on a "use it or lose it" basis. It is difficult to imagine such a policy being instituted in this country when we still lack a paid leave of absence for mothers. The gender gap in the 1996 election attests to the real distance between men and women on many issues involving governmental assistance to families.

Promoting greater involvement of fathers in child care might contribute to more stable unions for at least two different reasons. First, men who help out more tend to get better approval ratings by their wives and thus are more likely to maintain gratifying unions. Second, men are less likely to leave a decent, but not highly rewarding, marriage when they are highly invested in their children. There is not a great deal of research to back up the latter proposition, but it seems a plausible extrapolation from fragmentary evidence on how the presence of children affect the likelihood of divorce (Morgan, Lye, & Condran, 1988; Waite, Haggstrom, & Kanouse, 1985).

Having said this, time is the enemy of the quality of men and women's relationships. Currently, fathers and mothers are making difficult and often mutually unsatisfactory trade-offs between time and money. It may well be that as fathers build greater financial capital, they actually diminish the level of social capital provided to the family. That is yet another study, and we have to thank Paul Amato for the one that he has already completed. His chapter provides a hefty agenda for future research.

REFERENCES

Bossard, J. H. S. & Boll, E. S. (1968). *Family situations: An introduction to the study of child behavior.* New York: Greenwood Press.

Bott, E. (1971). *Family and social network* (2nd ed.). New York: The Free Press.

Cherlin, A. J. & Furstenberg, F. F., Jr. (1994). Stepfamilies in the United States: A reconsideration. *Annual Review of Sociology, 20,* 359–381.

Coleman, J. S. (1988). Social capital in the creation of human capital. *American Journal of Sociology, 94,* S95–S120.

Cooley, C. H. (1956). *Social organization: Human nature and the social order.* Glencoe, IL: The Free Press.

Coser, R. L. (Ed.). (1964). *The family: Its structure and functions.* New York: St. Martin's Press.

Demos, J. (1982). The changing faces of fatherhood: A new exploration in American family history. In S. H. Cath, A. R. Gurwitt, & J. M. Ross (Eds.), *Father and child: Developmental and clinical perspectives* (pp. 425–445). Boston: Little, Brown.

Furstenberg, F. F., Jr. (1981). Remarriage and intergenerational relations. In R. W. Fogel, E. Hatfield, S. B. Kiesler, & E. Shanas (Eds.), *Aging: Stability and change in the family* (pp. 115–142). New York: Academic Press.

Furstenberg, F. F., Jr., Eccles, J., Elder, G. H., Jr., Cook, T., & Sameroff, A. (in press). *Managing to make it: Urban families in high-risk neighborhoods.*

Furstenberg, F. F., Jr. & Hughes, M. E. (1995). Social capital and successful development among at-risk youth. *Journal of Marriage and the Family, 57*(3), 580–592.

Furstenberg, F. F., Jr. & Spanier, G. B. (1984). *Recycling the family: Remarriage after divorce.* Newbury Park, CA: Sage.

Gadsden, V. & Hall, M. (1995). *Intergenerational learning: A review of the literature.* Paper commissioned by the National Center for Fathers and Families, University of Pennsylvania.

Gillis, J. R. (1996). *A world of their own making: Myth, ritual, and the quest for family values.* New York: Basic Books.

Griswold, R. L. (1993). *Fatherhood in America: A history.* New York: Basic Books.

Hess, R. D. & Handel, G. (1959). *Family worlds: A psychosocial approach to family life.* Chicago: University of Chicago Press.

Johnson, C. L. (1988). *Ex familia: Grandparents, parents, and children adjust to divorce.* New Brunswick, NJ: Rutgers University Press.

Marsiglio, W. (Ed.). (1995). *Fatherhood: Contemporary theory, research, and social policy.* Thousand Oaks, CA: Sage.

Minuchin, S. (1974). *Families and family therapy.* Cambridge, MA: Harvard University Press.

Morgan, S. P., Lye, D. N., & Condran, G. A. (1988). Sons, daughters, and the risk of marital disruption. *American Journal of Sociology, 94,* 110–129.

Parke, R. D. (1981). *Fathers.* Cambridge, MA: Harvard University Press.

Presser, H. (1988). Shift work and child care among dual-earner American parents. *Journal of Marriage and the Family, 50,* 3–14.

Putnam, R. (1995). Bowling alone: America's declining social capital. *Journal of Democracy, 6,* 65–78.

Reiss, D. (1981). *The family's construction of reality.* Cambridge, MA: Harvard University Press.

Rotundo, E. A. (1985). American fatherhood: A historical perspective. *American Behavioral Scientist, 29*(1), 7–25.

Sampson, R. J. (1992). Family management and child development: Insights from social disorganization theory. In J. McCord (Ed.), *Advances in criminal theory, volume 3* (pp. 63–93). New Brunswick, NJ: Transaction.

Schneider, D. M. (1980). *American kinship: A cultural account* (2nd ed.). Chicago: University of Chicago Press.

Waite, L. J., Haggstrom, G. W., & Kanouse, D. E. (1985). The consequences of parenthood for the marital stability of young adults. *American Sociological Review, 50,* 850–857.

Waller, W. (1938). *The family: A dynamic interpretation.* New York: Cordon.

Chapter 16

Men's Contributions to Children and Social Policy

Judith A. Seltzer
University of Wisconsin–Madison

Paul Amato's chapter (chap. 13, this volume) evaluates the importance of fathers in children's lives. To do this, Amato reviews recent research on the effects of fathers on children, develops a conceptual model of paternal influence, and provides a new analysis of longitudinal data on parents and young adult offspring. These are ambitious tasks, the results of which may contribute to the formation of policies affecting fathers and their families. I consider three aspects of Amato's contribution. First, Amato makes modest claims about the importance of the question he poses about the effects of fathers on children. I argue that these claims are too modest, and I demonstrate that Amato contributes to a broad tradition of social theory and research. In doing this, I show how attempts by Amato and others to address theoretical debates in sociology also inform debate about policies for parents and children in divorced and nonmarital families. Second, I raise questions about the conceptualization of fathers' effects on children and about the analysis that Amato reports. I argue that because of problems in his analysis, Amato's results should be interpreted cautiously, particularly with regard to their implications for social theory and policies about fathers. Finally, I propose two avenues for future research on men's contributions to children.

FATHERS' CONTRIBUTIONS: THE BIG PICTURE

Amato's chapter raises three questions that are central to family sociology. These questions are not the tasks he explicitly defines; rather, the questions are implicit in his formulation of the research problem. Amato begins his chapter by asserting that American men used to know what it meant to be a father, but that now the rights and responsibilities of fatherhood are a matter of debate. This characterization of recent change in contemporary fatherhood reflects two important sociological questions: What is a father? And, what factors create or reduce ambiguity in social understanding about what it means to be a father? The third sociological question that Amato considers is the title for this section of the volume: How do fathers affect children? By his framing of the question, Amato challenges the assumption that fathers' involvement with children always benefits them. Amato questions this popular myth by asking when fathers help and when they harm children. I address each of these questions in turn.

What Is a Father?

Students of the family have a long history of asking, "who is a father?" and "what do fathers do in families?" Malinowski's (1964) distinction between social and biological paternity nearly 70 years ago is an early example of social scientists' preoccupation with men's contributions to children, men's role in childrearing, and men's responsibility for placing children in the social world. Note that Amato's title is about "men's" contributions to children, in principle leaving open the question of which men, and how these men are socially connected to the children.

Debates about the universal structure of marriage and the family center on the age-old problem of understanding societal continuity (Fortes, 1950; Gough, 1959; Murdock, 1962; Reiss, 1965). Concern with societal continuity is, by definition, also a concern with how best to raise children. Cross-cultural evidence shows wide variation in childrearing practices, and especially in who rears children (Cardoso, 1984; Page, 1989). Differences across societies in ideas about the physiological process of reproduction and rules of descent suggest that fatherhood is socially defined. Fathers need not be the physiological progenitors of their children.

The contemporary United States provides many examples of children who have social fathers who are not their biological fathers. Stepfathers, as Amato notes, are the most obvious example, but grandfathers, uncles, or important community figures may also play the role of father. That stepfathers sometimes contribute more resources to children than do their nonresident biological fathers shows that men may act as social fathers when they are not biological fathers, and men who are biological fathers may not be fatherlike in their behavior (Seltzer, 1994). Amato's concern with how men contribute to children's well-being is a politically important question now, or, as Furstenberg (1988) said elsewhere, "fatherhood is 'in vogue' " (p. 193). But the question has also been a long-standing, driving focus of social theory and research.

Institutionalization of Fatherhood

Amato's claim of cultural dissensus about what fathers should do points to ambiguity in how the rights and responsibilities of fatherhood are defined. Increases in mothers' labor-force participation, declines in employment opportunities for men with little education, and related increases in divorce and nonmarital childbearing alter the circumstances under which men become fathers and fulfill the responsibilities of fatherhood. How families respond to changes in the labor market and other social institutions is a central question in social-demographic research (Smith, 1989). This work points to individuals' perceptions of social rules and circumstances and to dyadic negotiations as the locus of new understandings about social roles, such as parenthood (Mason, 1991; Pollak & Watkins, 1993). Thus, Amato's work on contemporary fathers also contributes to social scientists' long-standing concern with the process by which the rights and responsibilities of family membership are defined.

The problem of institutionalization or the lack of shared understanding about the father role is particularly relevant to stepfathers (Cherlin, 1978) and to nonresident fathers, those who live apart from their children (Seltzer, 1991, 1994). For nonresident fathers, there are few clear expectations about how they should continue to care for their children. Public messages about the importance of nonresident fathers' child support contributions pose the potential for nonresident fatherhood to be defined solely by men's financial ties to children. Working against this is the recent emphasis on fathers' rights to access (visitation) and decision-making rights over children through joint legal custody.

One interpretation of recent findings that joint legal custody (decision-making rights) increases the amount of time nonresident fathers and children spend together is that the status of legal custodian reduces ambiguity in fathers' and mothers' expectations about nonresident fathers' rights and responsibilities to children (Seltzer, 1997; Gunnoe & Braver, 1996). By clarifying that divorced fathers are still *fathers*, parents may take for granted that the fathers and children will spend time together. Codifying the nonresident father's role is one aspect of institutionalization, which may reduce ambiguity, and possibly conflict, about nonresident fathers' access to children after divorce.

Effects of Fathers on Children Depend on the Father's Characteristics

Amato approaches a third sociological question by challenging the assumption in much contemporary commentary on fathers—that spending time with fathers is always good for children. Amato's observation that fathers' effects on children depend on the fathers' own characteristics is consistent with a long line of research, which shows that fathers' socioeconomic status affects children's health, values, progress in school, and extracurricular opportunities (Alwin 1984; Angel & Worobey, 1988; Fuchs, 1974; Gamoran & Mare, 1989; Heyns, 1978; Kohn, 1977; Medrich, Roizen, Rubin, & Buckley, 1983; Rubin, 1976; Sewell & Hauser, 1975). As Amato notes, when fathers have more resources, children benefit. When fathers have few resources, children suffer.

By placing his work in the context of this traditional sociological concern, Amato contributes to policy debates about fathers' effects on children. For instance, by recognizing that fathers can both benefit and harm children, Amato provides insight into possible unintended consequences of child support, custody, and visitation policies to increase nonresident fathers' contact with children. Improved child support enforcement may increase contact between parents who would otherwise prefer to avoid each other. Increased contact between parents who get along badly may harm children by exposing them to more conflict, at the same time that children benefit from their fathers' higher child support contributions. Preliminary evidence suggests that more rigorous enforcement of child support responsibilities may actually reduce conflict among previously married families, thereby enhancing children's welfare. But for children born outside of marriage, child support enforcement may increase their exposure to conflict and their problems in school (McLanahan, Seltzer, Hanson, & Thomson, 1994). Amato's investigation of both positive and negative effects of fathers on children is also consistent with concerns about universal adoption of joint custody, which may increase contact between abusive fathers and children (California Senate Task Force on Family Equity, 1987; Schulman & Pitt, 1982).

REASONS FOR CAUTION ABOUT THE ANSWERS THAT AMATO PROVIDES

On the matter of the "big picture," Amato's chapter addresses key problems in social theory and research. His modest statement of the tasks he pursues underrepresents the importance of his project for ongoing sociological and policy debates. Nevertheless, several issues in Amato's conceptualization of the problem and the results that he reports about the absolute and relative magnitude of the effects of fathers' and mothers' characteristics on children merit further attention before they are used to inform public policy. I consider Amato's treatment of social capital and then turn to specific aspects of his empirical work.

The Conceptual Model: The Role of Social Capital

Amato draws on Coleman (1988, 1990) to outline a conceptual model of parents' investment in children. Amato distinguishes among human, financial, and social capital. His decision to limit his focus to two aspects of social capital, the relationship between parents and the relationship between the parent and child, is a practical one, but it ignores that parents also provide children with social resources by acting as a bridge between the family and the broader community. For instance, when mothers have a strong help network, children are more likely to go on to college (Furstenberg & Hughes, 1995). Fathers may also help children by connecting them to social institutions outside the family, such as the world of paid employment.

Before drawing any general conclusions about the relative importance of fathers' and mothers' contributions to children through social capital, it is important to consider that social capital is multidimensional and that the benefits of diverse dimensions may vary across different aspects of child well-being (Furstenberg & Hughes, 1995; see also Baron & Hannon, 1994, on the concept of social capital). Why be cautious about the definition of social capital? First, if mothers and fathers invest different types of social capital, focusing only on a restricted number of dimensions may overrepresent those in which mothers (or fathers) specialize. Second, to make policy recommendations from research like Amato's and other studies in the same tradition, it is more useful to be specific about the particular family processes or social ties to the community that affect children's well-being, than to argue that children need more social capital. Being concrete about what studies measure informs policy debates, whereas references to abstract concepts about which there is little definitional consensus limits the value of social research for policymakers.

Many Variables, Many Arrows, Many Numbers, But Not Enough Information

Amato's chapter uses valuable longitudinal data with reports from both mothers and fathers as well as their young adult children to examine the effects of fathers on a variety of child outcomes. He uses path analysis to clarify the causal order of relationships in his theoretical model and uses confirmatory factor analysis to summarize multi-item indicators of the quality of parents' marital relationship and each parent's relationship with the child. Amato's attention to causal order and his attempt to develop reliable measures of family relationships are commendable. Despite these strengths, it is worth asking what is behind his analysis and whether it provides information useful for social policy and theory about paternal involvement.

Are the Variables the Right Ones? Amato treats both parents' incomes as
key variables predicting child outcomes. The financial resources that each
parent brings to the family are obviously important, but it also matters for
children how their parents acquire income. For the vast majority, income
comes from their parents' earnings. Amato's analysis reflects this by operationalizing financial capital as earnings. However, about 40% of the
mothers in Amato's analysis were not in the paid labor force. The number
of hours parents work, the type of work they do, and their patterns of
employment affect the quality of children's home environment and some
aspects of child well-being (Parcel & Menaghan, 1994). These important
omitted variables may help to explain the apparently different effects of
father's and mother's earnings on children's schooling. "Unpacking" the
earnings variables would also provide insight into how parents' participation in activities outside the household affect their children.

Do All Children Need the Same Thing? Amato's model assumes that the
processes determining children's education and social-psychological well-
being are the same for everyone. Yet recent findings from Harris and
Marmer's (1996) analysis of another longitudinal study suggest that fathers
may play a larger role than mothers in determining educational outcomes
for youths who were not poor, but that mothers play the larger role in
poor families. In his review of past work, Amato is sensitive to the question
of how context affects the relationship between fathers' contributions and
children's well-being. In his analysis, he also considers whether the processes of parents' investment work similarly for sons and daughters and
finds that the processes are the same, at least for marital discord and
child's perception of mother's and father's support. He does not, however,
consider socioeconomic variation in the effects of parents' characteristics
on children. This would be an important extension of the analysis, in light
of Harris and Marmer's findings. We need both more analysis and more
conceptual work about when fathers' and mothers' investments are likely
to matter and when one parent's investments may be more important than
the other's.

Is This the Right Way to Compare Effects of Fathers and Mothers? Amato
rightly notes that one cannot assess the importance of fathers in families
without also considering mothers. He adopts the strategy of comparing
fathers' and mothers' contributions by asking whether each parent's characteristic has a statistically significant effect on a child outcome. This strategy does not answer the question of how the effects on children of fathers'
characteristics compare to the effects of mothers' characteristics. Amato's
strategy only shows whether the effect (coefficient) for each variable is
significantly different from 0. Instead, what we want to know is whether

the effects (coefficients) for each parent's characteristics are equal to each other. For instance, it is quite possible for the effect of father's support on child's psychological distress to be significantly different from 0, and for the effect of mother's support on distress not to be significantly different from 0, but for the coefficients on mother's and father's support not to differ significantly. That is, even if one coefficient is significantly different from 0 and the other is not, it is possible that we would not be able to reject the hypothesis that the effects of mother's and of father's characteristics are the same. The approach that Amato uses does tell us whether father's characteristics have any net effect on child outcomes, but this is not the same thing as answering the question: What do fathers contribute compared to what mothers contribute? It is a straightforward test to constrain the effects on child outcomes of each parent's support or earnings —or any other characteristic—and to compare this to a model in which the effects of mother's and father's characteristics are allowed to differ. This is an important next step for analyses like the one Amato reports.

Is the "Effect" of Father Support on Psychological Distress a Real Effect? Amato sensibly criticizes past research for using contemporaneous measures of relationship quality and child outcomes obtained from a single source. The obvious ambiguity about the causal association between the independent and dependent variables and the potential reporting bias severely limit the value of this analytic strategy. By using longitudinal data from multiple sources, Amato improves on much past research. However, his conclusion that "paternal support has a modest beneficial effect" on young adults' psychological well-being ignores that information about paternal support comes from the adult child's retrospective reports obtained at the same time as the measures of psychological welfare. The likely reporting biases suggest that Amato's results overstate the effects of paternal support on young adult children.

Who Are More Important, Fathers or Mothers? Amato's Fig. 13.7 summarizes the relative explanatory value of fathers' and mothers' characteristics. This calculation of the proportion of variation explained has two problems for applying the results to social policy. The first of these has to do with the difference between variance explained and metric coefficients. Explained variation does not provide information about the magnitude of effects of fathers' and mothers' characteristics on child outcomes. The variance explained strategy ignores the metrics of the variables. Amato recognizes this in the text of his paper by reporting information about unstandardized partial coefficients, in which he describes how an increase of 1 year in father's education increases his child's education by about one fifth of a year. (Note that Amato does not, however, provide the same information about the effect of a change of 1 year in mother's education on child's schooling.) This information, which uses the real metric of variables, is what matters for anticipating the effects of policy changes, not variance explained. Policy interventions ask questions such as: If father's education were increased, how much better off would children be? Would children get more education if we increased father's earnings or if we increased father's education? Would increasing mother's education result in larger gains for children's schooling than increasing father's education? If we reduce children's exposure to conflict, how much would their self-esteem increase? The proportion of variation explained by father's characteristics does not show how important fathers are for children because variance explained does not indicate the magnitude of fathers' effects (Cain & Watts, 1970; on related points see Goldberger & Manski, 1995).

The second problem with using proportion of variance explained to inform policy stems from the importance of making policy recommendations based on generalizable research findings. The proportion of variance explained describes a specific sample, but is not an estimate of a population characteristic (Duncan, 1975). Metric coefficients, in contrast, are unbiased estimates of population characteristics (assuming the model is correct). The proportion of variation explained simply describes the correlation of independent and dependent variables in the sample. That the proportions explained are sample specific means that the results in Fig. 13.7 cannot be used to generalize about the relative explanatory power of fathers' characteristics beyond this particular sample. Thus, the analysis reported in Fig. 13.7 is of limited value to theoretical or policy debates.

IS IT MORE THAN MONEY?
WHERE DO WE GO FROM HERE?

Despite the emphasis in my research on child support contributions from nonresident fathers, I have never thought fathers were just important for their money. A finding in past research on nonresident fathers makes this point very clearly. A number of studies using data from a variety of sources show that a dollar of child support has a much bigger impact on children's well-being than a dollar of income from other sources (Beller & Graham, 1993; Graham, Beller, & Hernandez, 1994; Knox, 1996; Knox & Bane, 1994; McLanahan et al. 1994). This suggests that a dollar is not just a dollar when it comes as child support. Child support dollars may be worth more if they have symbolic importance to children, if parents in families with child support get along better than in families in which fathers do not pay child support, if fathers who pay support also have better relationships with their children—or, as Amato suggests, if mothers experience less anxiety about financial matters when fathers pay support (Seltzer, 1994).

Amato's chapter makes a good start on figuring out what fathers do in families where both parents live together. His use of longitudinal data is a step in the right direction toward uncovering how fathers and mothers provide for their children when they live together. I propose two avenues for new research, one at the microlevel and one a macro-oriented question.

There is a growing body of research on men who live with their children, men who live apart from their children, and men who live with other men's children. What we lack is a good description and understanding of the dynamics of the processes in families, in couples, and within individuals as they move from one of these family circumstances to another. For instance, we know little about how fluctuations in fathers' and mothers' incomes affect family dynamics and the process of relationship dissolution and reconstruction. We need information about family dynamics before parents decide to separate, to complement recent studies of families after parents file for divorce (Gunnoe & Braver, 1996; Maccoby & Mnookin, 1992). We should study relationships between unmarried men and women who have children together, whether or not they co-reside. Studies of cohabiting relationships speak to my concern, but, especially among African Americans, high rates of childbearing outside of a cohabiting union show the importance of studying relationships and families who live apart.

Notice that I refer to families, parents, and relationships. This is to emphasize that we must understand what men do in families in the context of what others—women—do in families. I am asking about relationships, not just about one person's perception or experience of the relationship. We cannot understand men without also understanding women. No one type of data can address my microlevel concerns. Certainly following families over time is essential for understanding family dynamics. Survey data provide insight into these processes, but are less appropriate for studying family processes and interactions, which may be better observed in laboratories or observations in natural settings.

Existing data can begin to address my second proposal. Arguments about the changing roles of men in families motivate a tremendous amount of public debate, and many of us invoke the claim of changing roles to justify our investigations of microlevel phenomena, such as the effect of divorce on child well-being. But few studies systematically link trends in demographic and economic phenomena, on one hand, and children's well-being, on the other hand. Reasonably long time series data exist on changes in family structure, declining family size, increasing education of parents, and changes in employment and earnings of men and women. By Amato's argument, these structural changes are a possible source of change in social understanding about men's roles. It is also possible to construct a parallel time series of child outcomes, including education and some aspects of social and psychological welfare (e.g., see Condran & Furstenberg, 1994; Furstenberg & Condran, 1988; Uhlenberg & Eggebeen, 1986; Zill & Rogers, 1988). The obvious question is whether changes in family structure and men's and women's economic opportunities translate into change over time in children's well-being. Previous attempts to address this question show little or no correspondence between aggregate trends in children's well-being and trends in mothers' labor force participation and family structure (Condran & Furstenberg, 1994). A more complete answer requires a consideration of such things as the extent to which divorce and nonmarital childbearing are countered by declines in family size and increasing education of parents (e.g., Condran & Furstenberg, 1994; Mare, 1996). Documenting an association between these dramatic social-demographic changes and child outcomes would go a long way toward substantiating the claim that change in men's roles matters for children.

ACKNOWLEDGMENTS

Preparation of this chapter was supported by a grant from the National Institute of Child Health and Human Development (HD24571). The author appreciates helpful comments from Robert D. Mare on a previous draft.

REFERENCES

Alwin, D. (1984). Trends in parental socialization values: Detroit, 1958–1983. *American Journal of Sociology, 90,* 359–382.

Angel, R., & Worobey, J. L. (1988). Single motherhood and children's health. *Journal of Health and Social Behavior, 29,* 38–52.

Baron, J. N., & Hannon, M. T. (1994). The impact of economics on contemporary sociology. *Journal of Economic Literature, 32,* 1111–1146.

Beller, A. H., & Graham, J. W. (1993). *The economics of child support.* New Haven, CT: Yale University Press.

Cain, G. G., & Watts, H. W. (1970). Problems in making policy inferences from the Coleman Report. *American Sociological Review, 35,* 228–242.

California Senate Task Force on Family Equity. (1987, June). *Final report.* Sacramento, CA: Author.

Cardoso, R. C. L. (1984). Creating kinship: The fostering of children in *Favela* families in Brazil (E. Hansen, Trans.). In R. T. Smith (Ed.), *Kinship ideology and practice in Latin America* (pp. 196–203). Chapel Hill, NC: University of North Carolina Press.

Cherlin, A. J. (1978). Remarriage as an incomplete institution. *American Journal of Sociology, 84,* 634–650.

Coleman, J. S. (1988). Social capital in the creation of human capital. *American Journal of Sociology, 94*(95), S95–S120.

Coleman, J. S. (1990). *Foundations of social theory.* Cambridge: Harvard University Press.

Condran, G. A., & Furstenberg, F. F., Jr. (1994, November). *Are trends in the well-being of children related to changes in the American family? Making a simple question more complex?* Paper prepared for the International Year of the Family Conference, Paris, France.

Duncan, O. D. (1975). *Introduction to structural equation models.* New York: Academic Press.

Fortes, M. (1950). Kinship and marriage among the Ashanti. In A. R. Radcliffe-Brown & D. Forde (Eds.), *African systems of kinship and marriage* (pp. 252–284). London: Oxford University Press.

Fuchs, V. R. (1974). *Who shall live? Health, economics and social choice.* New York: Basic Books.

Furstenberg, F. F., Jr. (1988). Good dads—bad dads: Two faces of fatherhood. In A. J. Cherlin (Ed.), *The changing American family and public policy* (pp. 193–218). Washington, DC: The Urban Institute.

Furstenberg, F. F., Jr., & Condran, G. A. (1988). Family change and adolescent well-being: A reexamination of U.S. trends. In A. J. Cherlin (Ed.), *The changing American family and public policy* (pp. 117–155). Washington, DC: The Urban Institute.

Furstenberg, F. F., Jr., & Hughes, M. E. (1995). Social capital and successful development among at-risk youth. *Journal of Marriage and the Family, 57,* 580–592.

Gamoran, A., & Mare, R. D. (1989). Secondary school tracking and educational inequality: Compensation, reinforcement, or neutrality. *American Journal of Sociology, 94,* 1146–1195.

Goldberger, A. S., & Manski, C. F. (1995). Review article: *The Bell Curve* by Hernstein and Murray. *Journal of Economic Literature, 33,* 762–776.

Gough, E. K. (1959). The Nayars and the definition of marriage. *The Journal of the Royal Anthropological Institute of Great Britain and Ireland, 89,* 23–34.

Graham, J. W., Beller, A. H., & Hernandez, P. M. (1994). The effects of child support on educational attainment. In I. Garfinkel, S. S. McLanahan, & P. K. Robins (Eds.), *Child support and child well-being* (pp. 317–354). Washington, DC: Urban Institute Press.

Gunnoe, M. L., & Braver, S. L. (1996). *The effects of joint legal custody on family functioning, controlling for factors that predispose a joint award.* Unpublished manuscript, Child Trends, Inc., Washington, DC.

Harris, K. M., & Marmer, J. K. (1996). Poverty, paternal involvement and adolescent well-being. *Journal of Family Issues, 17,* 614–640.

Heyns, B. (1978). *Summer learning and the effects of schooling.* New York: Academic Press.

Knox, V. W. (1996). The effects of child support payments on developmental outcomes for elementary school-age children. *Journal of Human Resources, 31,* 816–840.

Knox, V. W., & Bane, M. J. (1994). Child support and schooling. In I. Garfinkel, S. S. McLanahan, & P. K. Robins (Eds.), *Child support and child well-being* (pp. 285–316). Washington, DC: The Urban Institute.

Kohn, M. L. (1977). *Class and conformity: A study of values* (2nd ed.). Chicago: University of Chicago Press.

Maccoby, E. E., & Mnookin, R. H. (1992). *Dividing the child: Social and legal dilemmas of custody.* Cambridge: Harvard University Press.

Malinowski, B. (1964). Parenthood, the basis of social structure. In R. L. Coser (Ed.), *The family: Its structure and functions* (pp. 3–19). New York: St. Martin's Press. (Original work published 1930)

Mare, R. D. (1996). Changes in families and trends in schooling. In A. Booth & J. F. Dunn (Eds.), *Family-school links: How do they affect educational outcomes?* (pp. 175–184). Mahwah, NJ: Lawrence Erlbaum Associates.

Mason, K. O. (1991). Multilevel analysis in the study of social institutions and demographic change. In J. Huber (Ed.), *Macro–micro linkages in sociology* (pp. 223–230). Newbury Park, CA: Sage.

McLanahan, S. S., Seltzer, J. A., Hanson, T. L., & Thomson, E. (1994). Child support enforcement and child well-being: Greater security or greater conflict? In I. Garfinkel, S. S. McLanahan, & P. K. Robins (Eds.), *Child support and child well-being* (pp. 239–256). Washington, DC: Urban Institute Press.

Medrich, E. A., Roizen, J. A., Rubin, V., & Buckley, S. (1983). *The serious business of growing up: A study of children's lives outside of school.* Berkeley, CA: University of California Press.

Murdock, G. P. (1962). Structures and functions of the family. In R. F. Winch, R. McGinnis, & H. R. Barringer (Eds.), *Selected studies in marriage and the family*, revised edition (pp. 19–27). New York: Holt, Rinehart and Winston. (Original work published 1949)

Page, H. J. (1989). Childrearing versus childbearing: Coresidence of mother and child in Sub-Saharan Africa. In R. L. Lesthaeghe (Ed.), *Reproduction and social organization in Sub-Saharan Africa* (pp. 401–441). Berkeley, CA: University of California Press.

Parcel, T. L., & Menaghan, E. G. (1994). *Parents' jobs and children's lives.* New York: de Gruyter.

Pollak, R. A., & Watkins, S. C. (1993). Cultural and economic approaches to fertility: proper marriage or mesalliance? *Population and Development Review, 19,* 467–496.

Reiss, I. L. (1965). The universality of the family: A conceptual analysis. *Journal of Marriage and the Family, 27,* 443–453.

Rubin, L. B. (1976). *Worlds of pain: Life in the working-class family.* New York: Basic Books.

Schulman, J., & Pitt, V. (1982). Second thoughts on joint child custody: Analysis of legislation and its implications for women and children. *Golden Gate University Law Review, 12,* 539–577.

Seltzer, J. A. (1991). Relationships between fathers and children who live apart: The father's role after separation. *Journal of Marriage and the Family, 53,* 79–101.

Seltzer, J. A. (1994). Consequences of marital dissolution for children. *Annual Review of Sociology, 20,* 235–266.

Seltzer, J. A. (1997, February). *Father by law: Effects of joint legal custody on nonresident fathers' involvement with children.* National Survey of Families and Households (Working Paper No. 75). Center for Demography and Ecology, University of Wisconsin, Madison.

Sewell, W. H., & Hauser, R. M. (1975). *Education, occupation, and earnings: Achievement in the early career.* New York: Academic Press.

Smith, H. L. (1989). Integrating theory and research on the institutional determinants of fertility. *Demography, 26,* 171–184.

Uhlenberg, P., & Eggebeen, D. (1986). The declining well-being of American adolescents. *The Public Interest, 82,* 25–38.

Zill, N., & Rogers, C. C. (1988). Recent trends in the well-being of children in the United States and their implications for public policy. In A. J. Cherlin (Ed.), *The changing American family and public policy* (pp. 31–115). Washington, DC: The Urban Institute.

Chapter 17

Men in Families:
Looking Back, Looking Forward

Susan L. Brown
Matthew F. Bumpus
The Pennsylvania State University

The roles of fathers and husbands in families have come to the forefront as important issues. The increased focus on men is apparent in legislation aimed at deadbeat dads, social movements such as the Million Man March and Promise Keepers, in the development of advocacy groups, and in think-tanks. Contemporary research on men in family relationships has very mixed results. Some studies show small effects of fathers on child development and in preventing antisocial behavior. Others find no effects. Still other research indicates the primary importance of men in families is in their role as provider. Some suggest husbands and fathers do their most vital work following the transition to parenthood, whereas others indicate it is when offspring reach adolescence. This volume brings together scholars from a range of disciplines (including anthropology, clinical and developmental psychology, demography, history, and sociology) to try to define men's past and current family roles, as well as estimate what the future portends for fathers and husbands. Specifically, their remarks focus on two questions: What roles do men play in families? And, how involved are men in families, and what difference does this involvement make?

Here, we review the four lead chapters (chaps. 1, 5, 9, and 13), integrating discussants' comments and our own, in an effort to arrive at general conclusions about men in families. We begin with a historical perspective on men's familial roles to provide a background for the contemporary research described in the remaining three chapters. We discuss next the topic of men's marital relationships as well as their relations with their children and finally turn our attention to men's decisions to become parents and the effects of fathers on children's lives.

MEN IN FAMILIES: A HISTORICAL PERSPECTIVE

In his historical overview of men's familial roles, Mintz (chap. 1, this volume) provides (at least) three valuable lessons for students of the family. First, he documents variation in men's roles across time, proposing explanations (e.g., the organization of the economy or major historical events) for observed changes. Indeed, men's roles cannot be understood without some attention to the economic and cultural climate of the times. Second, he highlights the importance of variation in men's roles within a given time period by emphasizing the influences of race, class, and geography on fathers, husbands, and sons. Finally, Mintz traces the alterations in male authority within families across time. He convincingly demonstrates that male authority is, and has been historically, closely tied to the breadwinner role. Each of these three conclusions concerning men in families is now examined individually.

Perhaps the most important lesson of history is that the changes in men's familial roles over time have not been unilinear. Mintz refutes the popular notion that men's roles in U.S. families have shifted from patri-archal to egalitarian. This simplistic portrayal ignores the complexities that have characterized men's familial roles since the colonial period. For example, evidence exists to support two views on men's familial roles in colonial times. One view stresses intense male involvement in families. Work and home were not sharply differentiated, which meant that fathers likely spent most of their time at home among family members. Fathers were responsible for the educational and religious upbringing of their children and, in the case of separation or divorce, were most likely to receive custody of their children.

However, ample evidence also supports an alternative view that fathers' and husbands' roles in colonial times were very patriarchal. Fathers exercised strict control over their children's attainment of independence by monitoring courtship and withholding land. In exchange for bearing responsibility for their family members, men were entitled by colonial law to the earnings and property of their wives and offspring. Nevertheless, women performed roles that eventually became male-dominated, including trade and home manufacturing and estate supervision. Limitations on male authority were imposed by laws that, for example, forbade adultery and fornication and required men to assume responsibility for their dependents' debts and criminal behavior. Thus, the historical record indicates that during colonial times, men were involved in their families, although the substance of the involvement was in part symbolic and largely authoritarian in nature.

Part of the complexity involved in understanding men's roles in families over time has to do with variations in race, class, religion, and region. Again, looking at the colonial period, for instance, historical evidence indicates that the forms of men's involvement and the pervasiveness of patriarchal rule in families was anything but uniform. Demographic differences between northern and southern colonists resulted in striking economic and cultural variation in the roles of men in families in these contrasting contexts. The unbalanced sex ratio (6 men to 1 woman) and the high mortality rate that characterized the Chesapeake region into the 18th century weakened males' patriarchal authority to the extent that the establishment of stable, patriarchal families was difficult, if not impossible. High mortality rates meant that less than 50% of all marriages lasted 10 years. Consequently, extended kin networks were important for both survival and success. In contrast, the lower death rate and sex ratio in New England facilitated the establishment of the kind of patriarchal families just described.

The eventual demise of patriarchal authority in both north and south largely stemmed from changing generational relations. As the proliferation of nonagricultural jobs increased, and the size of land plots fathers had available to pass on to their sons decreased, paternal control of offspring declined. Marriage became a matter of personal choice for women, whose economic well-being was tightly linked to their selection of a mate. Clearly then, fathers' weakened control of their offspring resulted from changes in economic circumstances. Children were less dependent on their fathers financially and, simultaneously, fathers had less to offer their children, thereby decreasing paternal authority.

Although fathers' roles became less patriarchal, their position in the family was not significantly reduced. Instead, the ethos of romanticism so characteristic of the 19th century prescribed masculine involvement in the family. The separation of home and work yielded new variants on men's roles as moral overseers, providers, and protectors of their families. The instability of the economy, along with an increased standard of living, placed heavy burdens on men, particularly those in the working class who were unable to attain the middle class ideal of male as sole breadwinner. Working-class families were able to achieve this ideal only when the family wage gained popularity in the first decade of the 20th century.

The struggle of the working class to obtain the family wage exemplifies the importance of the breadwinner role to men's self-definitions and his position of authority in their families. Further evidence of the linkage between the male breadwinner role and male authority within the family is apparent in the high number of women who reported being deserted by their husbands during the Great Depression. In fact, the primary goal of the New Deal was to restore men's opportunities to provide materially for their families.

Throughout history, men's familial roles have been changing, largely in response to economic changes and major historical events. Mintz and discussants Burton and Snyder (chap. 2, this volume), Cherlin (chap. 3, this volume), and Lamb (chap. 4, this volume) all caution against drawing facile conclusions from the historical record, arguing that "the realization that fathers have filled and continue to fill a diverse variety of roles in their families and in society is an essential prerequisite for understanding contemporary debates about the meaning and nature of fatherhood" (Lamb, chap. 4, p. 49).

Indeed, even today we are confronted with two very different images of fathers: the involved, nurturing egalitarian father and the deadbeat dad. History suggests, as Cherlin points out, that effecting change in men's familial behaviors may be more difficult than anticipated, particularly because there is no traditional form of fatherhood, either today or in America's past. The contours of fatherhood, and men's roles in families more generally, have been in flux, responding to the economic and cultural climate of the times within the contexts of race and class.

But Burton and Snyder (chap. 2, this volume) challenge the assumption that men only react to societal forces. In fact, they argue that privileged men shape society and thus actively create realities for others. Marginalized men's lives are influenced by the lives of men in power. This theme underlies their comments on the importance of understanding the familial roles of non-White men from an historical perspective. For instance, White men who sired children with their Black female slaves complicated their own familial lives as well as those of Black men (and women) by blurring the lines of family. In such scenarios, White slaveholders had the power to impose their desires, whereas Black males could only react. Furthermore, Burton and Snyder argue that historical anchors are to some extent race-specific. The Reconstruction period following the Civil War, for example, presented unique obstacles for African Americans, including the difficulty of establishing familial and economic stability under Jim Crow.

The historical perspectives presented by Mintz and the discussants inform our approach to the study of men in families today. The variation in men's roles in families both within and across time cautions against expectations that such roles can be readily restructured. Instead, a more accurate view of men's familial roles acknowledges the interactions between larger societal forces and individual circumstances in shaping men's lives. We turn now to men's contemporary marital roles, focusing on those individual circumstances generating stability and satisfaction for husbands, wives, and their children.

MEN AND MARRIAGE

More than 90% of all American men marry at some point in their lives (Alhburg & DeVita, 1992). How do men behave in their marriages, and how important is their behavior for marital success? Gottman (chap. 9, this volume) contributes a wealth of information pertaining to men's and women's marital interactions and their implications for marital satisfaction and stability. Additionally, he explores the linkages between the marital relationship and the father–child relationship, demonstrating that the same skills underlie positive outcomes in both types of relationships. The discussions of Gottman's chapter, provided by three sociologists (Coltrane, Ferree & McQuillan, and Nock, chaps. 10, 11, and 12, respectively), call attention to the broader social and institutional contexts in which the marital relationship is played out. Following a brief description of Gottman's approach to the study of marriage and the major findings from his analyses, we draw on the discussants' comments to situate the microlevel results within a larger, macrolevel framework.

Gottman's research on marital interactions and relations is arguably the most intricate and extensive to date. Gottman employs a multimethod approach that includes not only questionnaires and interviews, but also videotapes of couple interactions in a laboratory setting and the collection of physiological data. Close study of newlyweds and couples in stable and unstable, happy and unhappy marriages, allowed Gottman to identify key ingredients for a successful, satisfying marriage. Grounding his hypotheses in the body of research that shows children are socialized differently according to their gender and boys are less likely than girls to accept the influence of someone of the opposite gender, Gottman posits that marriages work to the extent that husbands are able to accept influence from their wives. His analyses support his assertion; physically violent husbands are less likely to accept their wives' influence than are husbands in either nonviolent unhappy or nonviolent happy marriages. Additionally, he corroborates his hypothesis with a sample of newlyweds. Typically, wives initiate discussion of a marital problem. A husband's refusal to accept his wife's influence increases the wife's negative affect which, in turn, leads to withdrawal and stonewalling by the husband. This pattern of behavior is a strong predictor of divorce. On the other hand, stable, happy marriages are characterized by wives who employ a "softened startup" (p. 162) when introducing a negative topic of conversation and receive from their husbands in return acceptance and diffusion of negative affect. Positive affect during such exchanges further enhances the conflict resolution process. Indeed, the success of repair attempts hinges on Positive Sentiment Override (PSO), that is, the ability to perceive even negative affect from the spouse as neutral or positive. PSO is contingent on the ratio of positive to negative affect in routine, nonconflictual spousal interactions. Essentially, strategies for engaging in nonconflictual interaction parallel those which are used in conflictual situations. Gottman notes that the low (20% to 30%) long-term success rate of marital therapy may be partially due to inattention to the nature of everyday, nonconflictual spousal interaction.

Gottman not only portrays some critical dimensions of marital interaction and conflict that affect marital stability and satisfaction, he also illustrates the connections between the marital relationship and the father–child relationship. Men who are aware of, and express their emotions are better equipped to help their children effectively cope with their own feelings, promoting positive child development. It is not merely the presence of fathers that benefits children, but rather *how* fathers are present. Men's emotional engagement not only improves their children's lives, but also contributes to the maintenance of a healthy marriage. Men who deny or ignore their own and others' emotions are more likely to have poor marital satisfaction and to divorce than men who are willing to express their emotions and acknowledge the emotions of others.

Gottman's analyses provide us with a detailed portrait of marital interactions and reveal that husbands' willingness to accept their wives' influence is perhaps the key component to reducing marital conflict. More generally, men's emotional expressiveness fosters positive familial outcomes, specifically, a happy, stable marriage and well-adjusted offspring. Put another way, as suggested by Ferree and McQuillan (chap. 11, this volume), men who engage in behavior that is not stereotypically masculine are most successful in achieving picture-perfect family lives.

Which men are capable of accepting their wives' influence and acknowledging their own feelings? Ferree and McQuillan cogently assert that if childhood socialization were the sole explanatory factor, then Gottman's research would be unnecessary. Variability among men makes possible Gottman's conclusions that some men can accept influence whereas others cannot and that men's behaviors are better predictors of effective family functioning than women's behaviors (because there is much less variability among women). Ferree and McQuillan suggest that structural gender inequalities might explain some of the variation in men's willingness to accept the influence of their wives, but drawing on a sample of dual-earner couples they find just one predictor: Younger men are more willing to accept influence.

Men's acceptance of spousal influence, as well as their parenting styles, are likely contingent on social and cultural factors such as race or ethnicity, and social class. Coltrane (chap. 10, this volume) reminds us that although wives may most often introduce conflict, husbands still retain more power within marriage and derive more benefits from marriage. Even men who hold relatively little power nevertheless hold an amount sufficient to permit them to physically abuse their wives. For this reason, Coltrane is reluctant to endorse Gottman's finding that implies that wives' startup could influence their husbands' responses. He proposes that the content and history of the conflicts be examined. Spouses' sense of entitlement, feelings of obligation and gratitude toward one another serve as the context for their conflicts. Couples most often argue about money, children, and housework, all of which are gender and power issues. An understanding of the context in which marital conflict occurs would facilitate researchers' interpretations of marital interactions.

Coltrane and Ferree and McQuillan evaluate Gottman's work from a feminist, sociological perspective. Nock (chap. 12, this volume) focuses his remarks on the institutional context of marriage, arguing that marriage makes males men. One cannot truly be a man in U.S. society without being married, for masculinity is achieved through marriage. Nock shows that, for men, economic and occupational achievement increases with the transition to marriage. But surely there must be a wide range of definitions of masculinity among married men if Gottman's conclusions about variability in acceptance of wives' influence are true. This point brings us back to that of Ferree and McQuillan, which is what factors determine which husbands will accept their wives' influence and which will not. To the extent that marriage confers masculinity, but stereotypically male behavior, in turn, exacerbates marital conflict and instability, perhaps definitions of masculinity within marriage require closer scrutiny. That is, which definitions facilitate men's expression of emotions and acceptance of their wives' influence?

Gottman's work reveals aspects of the marital relationship that are crucial to its success, namely, a husband's willingness to accept influence from his wife. He also links the marital relationship to that of the parent–child, arguing that men's emotional expression has ameliorative effects on both types of relationships. We turn now to this issue of fatherhood.

MEN'S INVESTMENTS IN FERTILITY AND PARENTING

In modern industrial societies, more resources are available, and are used, than ever before. Why, then, is the fertility rate continuing to decline to unprecedented levels? This fundamental, yet eminently complicated question is the basis of the chapter by Kaplan, Lancaster, and Anderson (chap. 5, this volume). Kaplan et al. merge concepts from two theoretical approaches—life-history theory and economics—to address this question. The balance between fertility and parental investment, the authors assert, has evolved to the point where it can best be understood in modern economic terms.

Two conditions reflective of the changing fertility patterns motivated the search for alternative theoretical explanations. First, and most simply, reproduction patterns are not predicted by fitness maximization models; in virtually every industrial society, population reproduction levels are lower than would be estimated by virtually any model. Second, wealth does not predict greater reproductivity, as it did (and continues to do) in preindustrial societies. Such a shift suggests that in modern industrial societies, high levels of parental resources should be associated with greater parental investment in the quality of a small number of children, rather than higher numbers of children.

Economic Explanations

Two factors associated with modern competitive economies are effective at explaining why fertility rates are lower and are not positively associated with wealth in industrialized societies. The first factor suggests that an equilibrium between supply and demand exists—there is a point at which increased wages are beneficial for companies, as they attract workers who have the skills to increase the profit margin of the company. This concept can be applied to parental investment as well; parents with high levels of resources may be more willing to invest in their existing offspring rather than increase their fertility levels, as they realize that their investments will result in their offspring possessing more resources as adults. These improved circumstances for offspring equal or exceed any potential gain from having more children.

The second contributing factor involves the continuity of fertility rates among economic classes by implicating the types of skills most valued in industrial societies. Workers with the types of resources necessary to obtain and keep desirable jobs—mathematical, interpersonal, writing, and so on—will be better equipped to pass on to their children those attributes, which are also valuable in school achievement. Therefore, parents with more resources are able to invest in their children more efficiently and with more benefits to the children.

These ideas led to a number of empirically testable hypotheses regarding embodied capital, parental investment, and fertility. The predictions were tested using data derived from short and long interviews with a representative sample of New Mexico men who were recruited while receiving or renewing their drivers' license. Respondents during the short interview gave demographic information, including family structure, education, and income. The long interview involved obtaining detailed retrospective accounts of selected respondents' life histories.

For the most part, findings support the hypotheses; only a few will be discussed here. The level of education attained by the respondents is negatively related to fertility, although this relationship weakens with age such that after age 35 it is actually positive. However, the education level of respondents' mates is a more powerful predictor of delayed fertility. The effects of education on fertility vary by time period and ethnic class. For White Americans, education is negatively related to first reproduction regardless of time period. For Hispanics, education is unrelated to reproduction until the post-World War II Baby Boom, when the hypothesized relationship emerges. Men's total fertility over the time periods studied by Kaplan et al. has remained somewhat constant; however, marital fertility was much higher during the pre-Baby Boom years, whereas nonmarital fertility accounts for a higher percentage of births during the post-Baby Boom era.

One of the more intriguing findings involves fathers' monetary investments in their children: Although, not surprisingly, fathers invested the most money in genetically related offspring who were living with them, they also invested more in nongenetically related coresiding offspring than they did in their own genetically related children not residing with them. Findings also suggest that the paternal investment of time has implications for offspring outcomes. Respondents' children's education levels were positively predicted by paternal time involvement levels, income, and education (although, again, respondents' wives' education was a stronger predictor than the respondents' own educational attainment).

The explanations for shifts in fertility among industrialized societies are presented convincingly by Kaplan et al. Their marriage of biological and economic theories is an innovative approach to a perplexing problem. Data to test their model were obtained in unique, creative ways, resulting in a representative sample that included White American and Hispanic men, who are understudied in fertility research. Although Marsiglio (chap. 7, this volume) rightfully mentions in his commentary that analyses of retrospective, cross-sectional data should be interpreted cautiously, he acknowledges the low feasability of collecting such detailed data longitudinally and prospectively from a representative sample.

Kaplan et al. are rightfully critical of some of their measures, especially parental investment. For example, men were asked to recall how much time they spent with their children during their elementary school years. This method should raise concerns regarding the types of fathers who may overestimate time spent with children. For instance, high-achieving fathers might be more likely to exaggerate the time they spent with their children.

A somewhat different angle is presented by Surra (chap. 8, this volume) in her commentary. Relationships and decisions about fertility, she argues, are based less on external factors (such as education or income) and more on interpersonal factors. Surra details her methods of studying couples' courtship histories to determine the reasons why they make decisions about commitment to their relationship. Surra's discussion of her work is a reminder that relationship characteristics are not adequately represented in the model of Kaplan et al. For example, what role does marital satisfaction play in fertility decisions or the transmission of paternal resources to children? After all, there is evidence that happily married fathers are more involved with their offspring (Amato, chap. 13, this volume). Other studies (e.g., Starrels, 1994) have suggested that parents, especially fathers, may differentially invest in sons and daughters. As Marsiglio (chap. 7, this volume) points out, potential variability in men's behavior due to the gender of their offspring is an important consideration that is ignored for the most part by Kaplan et al.

Draper's (chap. 6, this volume) commentary asks a fundamental question that supplements those addressed by Kaplan, Lancaster, and Anderson. It appears that when fathers pass on human capital to their offspring, the benefits are numerous and substantial. Why, however, are fathers more variable than mothers in the extent to which they do so? Two possible explanations are offered by Draper. First, perhaps at certain points in the past, environments did not dictate that paternal investment in children be valued; those psychological tendencies, then, have been less likely to be selected in the evolutionary history of men. An alternative explanation is that such selection differences have occurred independent of environmental conditions: Men and women simply have different goals in terms of the fitness of their offspring, with men interested in quantity, and women in quality. Although such questions are difficult to answer empirically, theoretical models such as those proposed by Kaplan et al. provide insight into such issues.

Explaining the shifts in men's fertility patterns over time is the goal of Kaplan et al.; understanding the ways in which men can influence the lives of their children is of secondary importance. Little attention is paid to the nature of parent–child and marital relationships, and their potential impacts on children. Amato's (chap. 13, this volume) work picks up where Kaplan et al. leave off by more broadly defining, and then examining, the potential contributions of fathers to children's outcomes.

MEN'S CONTRIBUTIONS TO THEIR CHILDREN'S LIVES

Men are less likely than ever before to be exclusive heads of households—and yet are not to a large degree taking on increased caregiving and household responsibilities. Given these seemingly incongruous trends, what value do men in families have? Do fathers make any unique contributions to the development of their offspring? If so, what are they? These complex questions are addressed by Amato in his ambitious chapter. First, he lays out a framework for understanding potential father influences using Coleman's (1988) conceptualizations of human capital, social capital, and economic capital. Children are natural consumers; they use available resources as they develop. Presumably, the more resources parents are able to provide, the better off their children will be. Amato then evaluates the model by reviewing the relevant literature and supplementing the reviewed studies with results of his own longitudinal study.

Human Capital

The term *human capital* refers to skills, traits, and knowledge possessed by parents that facilitate achievement. The primary indicator of parents' human capital is their level of education. Well-educated parents are more likely to provide experiences that encourage academic achievement in their children. Amato presents the hypothesis that fathers' human capital, specifically their level of education, should be positively related to children's well-being. Indeed, in his conceptual model, he posits that fathers' human capital predicts economic capital, social capital, and child outcomes.

For the most part, previous research provides support for the idea that fathers' human capital is related to positive outcomes for children. Several studies have found that fathers' education positively predicts the educational levels of their sons and daughters; Kaplan et al. (chap. 5, this volume) obtained similar results, although maternal education was a more powerful predictor than paternal education.

Economic Capital

As its name suggests, *economic capital* includes income, and resources purchased with income, that are provided to children by their parents. As with human capital, Amato hypothesizes that fathers' economic capital—their income level—is positively associated with their children's development. In addition, the model proposes that economic capital is a predictor of social capital (the quality of marital and parent–child relationships).

Parental wealth may not necessarily help children; presumably, parents must "share" in order for children to reap the benefits of high-income levels. However, most of the studies reviewed support the proposed relationship. Especially clear is the negative effect of poverty on children's physical health, school achievement, and social development. However, Amato accurately points out two problems with studies on children and parents' economic capital. First, most studies do not distinguish between effects due to paternal versus maternal income. Amato assumes, however, that because men generally possess more earning power than women, income's effects on children are primarily due to fathers. The second problem is that economic capital (paternal income) is often confounded with human capital (paternal education); much research has failed to control for paternal education when looking for the effects of paternal income. The few studies that include appropriate controls, however, have found significant effects of paternal income on children's development.

Social Capital

Social capital is defined by Amato as familial and extrafamilial relations that are beneficial for children's development. Two areas of social capital, the marital relationship and the parent–child relationship, are discussed. Marital quality, according to the model, should be predictive of father–child relationship quality; both the quality of the marriage and the father–child relationship should also be linked directly to positive child outcomes.

The marital relationship can be helpful for children in several ways. First, children can learn dyadic skills, such as communication, listening, and conflict negotiation more easily when they can learn them from parental models. Second, a strong marital relationship can make parental authority more evident and effective. Finally, spouses who feel supported in their marital relationship are likely to transmit those positive feelings to their parenting, resulting in parent–child relations that are beneficial for children.

Several studies (e.g., Davies & Cummings, 1994) have found positive associations between marital quality and child outcomes. Specifically, it appears that fathers can have an impact on family relations through the extent to which they provide affection, warmth, and support to their wives. However, few researchers have been able to separate the effects of fathers' and mothers' perceptions of marital quality, and several studies that purport to do so employ only mothers' reports of their husbands' support.

The parent–child relationship has the potential to provide many important resources for children, especially, it appears, when parents provide appropriate levels of support and control. Amato, in his review of the father–child relationship literature, illustrates effectively the cautions that are often necessary when attempting to draw conclusions from existing research. Most of the studies uncovered were weakened by either a reliance on single-source data or a failure to control for maternal characteristics. Only four studies were found that included multiple data sources, controlled for maternal factors, and found significant father–child relationship effects.

Nonresident Fathers

One of the strengths of Amato's review is his summary of the research on the potential effects of the contributions of human capital, economic capital, and social capital from nonresidential fathers. Very few studies have examined the effects of absent fathers' human capital; those that have provide evidence that absent fathers' levels of education are not strongly related to children's educational attainment.

Nonresident fathers' social capital can have an impact on their children's development. A powerful predictor of children's functioning following a divorce is the nature of the relationship between the divorced parents (Buchanan, Maccoby, & Dornbusch, 1996). The evidence does not allow for consensus as readily, however, regarding the effect of the relationship between absent fathers and their children. As Amato points out, the nature of the nonresident father–child relationship is usually qualitatively different from that of residential fathers and their offspring; often nonresident fathers cease to fully function as parents, and the parent–child relationship may be of a more recreational nature. To some extent then, the ways in which researchers conceptualize nonresidential father involvement may explain some of the inconsistency in the results. When social capital is operationalized simply as frequency of contact, nonresident fathers who are primarily playmates may look similar to nonresident fathers who remain supportive, engaged parents, and any effects of such engagement may be obscured.

Perhaps the most pertinent question for those interested in policy issues is the effect of nonresident fathers' economic capital on the lives of their children. Does it matter if absent fathers pay child support? Several studies cited have found significant positive effects of child support payment, even when controlling for potential confounds such as paternal contact and conflict between parents. Although other studies have not found support for the effect of child support payments, Amato concludes that the majority of evidence supports the hypothesized relationship. However, the causal mechanisms linking child support payments to positive outcomes are unclear. Also, most studies have used children's academic achievement as the dependent variable; it is less clear whether child support payment is related to non-academic outcomes as well.

Findings from Amato's Own Work

Data presented by Amato came from the 1992 phase of the Marriage Over the Life Course study, which began in 1980 and focused on married persons and their offspring. The structure of the study allowed him to examine the impact of the three categories of paternal resources (human capital, economic capital, and social capital) on the well-being of young adult offspring.

Amato's model (chap. 13, this volume) estimating the effects of paternal human and economic capital shows that fathers' education and earnings are positively associated with the educational attainment of their offspring.

Offspring's level of education is in turn directly associated with the other measures of their well-being (e.g., ties to kin, close friends, overall life satisfaction, psychological distress, and self-esteem). These findings suggest that paternal human and economic capital affects young adults primarily by influencing their educational attainment. In this model, maternal education, but not maternal income, is a significant predictor of offspring educational attainment.

To assess social capital, Amato employs measures of spouses' marital problems, marital instability, and marital conflict, and then uses confirmatory factor analysis to create a latent variable, marital discord. Marital discord significantly predicts two outcomes, offspring life satisfaction and offspring self-esteem. In addition, marital discord negatively predicts paternal support, which, in turn, is associated with offspring psychological distress.

Reactions to the Amato Model

In their commentaries, Seltzer (chap. 16, this volume), Belsky (chap. 14, this volume), and Furstenberg (chap. 15, this volume) highlight several concerns with Amato's model. First, as Amato admits, social capital may be conceptualized too narrowly when it is limited to marital and parent–child relationships. Parents also connect their children to extrafamilial influences, such as peer groups, extracurricular activities, and neighborhood resources; the impact of such linkages are understudied at present. Furstenberg suggests as well that social capital is insufficiently operationalized by Amato; young adults retrospectively rated their mothers' and fathers' levels of support separately, meaning that parental support is conceptualized as something parents do independent from each other. What does it mean to have parents who are not only supportive of their children, but are supportive of each other?

Furstenberg additionally points out a potential flaw in Amato's measurement of parental support. Paternal and maternal support are reported at virtually identical levels by the young adult respondents; recollecting parental behaviors retrospectively, however, may result in young adults applying, in Furstenberg's words, a "sliding scale" (p. 299). This double standard may lead to the exaggeration of paternal involvement and the underestimation of maternal involvement.

No review can adequately cover every facet of every study discussed, although Amato comes close. Future reviews, however, would be strengthened by systematically discussing those studies that are weakened by small or unrepresentative samples. Another concern noted by Belsky is the lack of distinction between cross-sectional and longitudinal studies; it is difficult, therefore, to draw conclusions from the findings reported by Amato without full knowledge of relevant sampling and design issues.

In his summary, Amato accurately points to the dearth of research that attempts to disentangle the contributions of child effects beyond children's gender to observed associations between parental variables and child variables. Belsky's commentary summarizes his most recent research on infant temperament as a moderator of the effect of parenting on children's development. Toddlers' levels of inhibition and externalizing problems are more susceptible to parental influence when the toddlers are highly negatively emotional as infants. Work such as Belsky's serves as a reminder that reviews aimed at understanding father effects can be most useful when they indicate whether studies purporting to examine paternal effects on child development control for child effects.

In conclusion, Amato's model credibly estimates the potential fathers possess for influencing the lives of their children. However, questions remain unanswered. Although it is clear from the evidence provided by Amato that fathers can make a difference, less attention is paid to the question of when fathers are likely to get involved. What are the circumstances under which fathers are likely to be positive transmitters of social capital by developing nurturing relationships with their children? Such process-related questions can enhance further attempts to model paternal effects on the development of their offspring.

CONCLUSION

In our concluding remarks, we return to the two questions posed initially in the chapter: (a) what roles do men play in families and (b) how involved are men in families, and what difference does this make? These two issues link the four sets of papers, which provide a multifaceted, interdisciplinary understanding of men's familial roles and involvement. Nevertheless, important questions concerning men in families remain. Following a brief discussion of the two topics that structured the symposium, we present future directions for research in this area.

First, what roles do men play in families? Men's roles as fathers and husbands have varied both within and across time. Demographic factors such as race and class interact with larger sociocultural forces, resulting in unique contexts for individual lives. Men's roles cannot be easily prescribed; the diversity of their familial roles in the past suggests that alterations in contemporary men's roles could be difficult to achieve.

Second, how involved are men in families, and what difference does this involvement make? In their roles as husbands and fathers, men's behavior is crucial. A successful marriage depends primarily on the husband's willingness to accept influence from his wife. Additionally, men's emotional expressiveness enhances both marital and parent–child relationships. Paternal capital and investment have positive consequences for children's outcomes.

New Directions

For the most part, the research discussed in this volume examines fathers in two-parent, intact families. Attention to nontraditional fathers, including step-, nonresident, and cohabiting fathers, is needed to refine our understanding of both the heterogeneity in fathers' roles in contemporary families and the varying implications of these roles. More research on these types of fathers, as well as the significance of transitions across family statuses (e.g., married to divorced), should also provide insights on strategies for effective fathering in these increasingly common family forms.

Indeed, today's diversity of family forms and living arrangements make it imperative that we not only acknowledge the heterogeneity that characterizes men's roles and involvement in families, but that we also continue to explicitly incorporate it in our research. Failure to do so means that our knowledge of men in families will be necessarily circumscribed and generalizable to a shrinking segment of the population.

Future research would also benefit from increased attention to the reciprocal effects of fathers and children on each other. As noted by Belsky, researchers often conceptualize parenting as something parents "do to" children, ignoring the possibility that children's characteristics and behaviors influence the parenting they receive. Men's socioemotional development is thought to respond to their personal relationships, including fathering, and underscores the importance of studies that examine the implications of children for fathers' psychological well-being and personal development, as well as their parenting strategies and evaluations of their relationships with their children.

Taken together, these chapters provide ample evidence that men play significant roles in their families and that their involvement contributes to the success of marital and parent–child relationships and offspring well-being. For these reasons, fathers and husbands deserve greater research attention.

REFERENCES

Ahlburg, D. A., & DeVita, C. J. (1992). New realities of the American family. *Population Bulletin*, *47*, 1–52.

Buchanan, C. M., Maccoby, E. E., & Dornbusch, S. M. (1996). *Adolescents after divorce*. Cambridge, MA: Harvard University Press.

Coleman, J. (1988). Social capital in the creation of human capital. *American Journal of Sociology*, *94*, 95–120.

Davies, P. T., & Cummings, E. M. (1994). Marital conflict and child adjustment: An emotional security hypothesis. *Psychological Bulletin, 116,* 387–411.

Starrels, M. E. (1994). Gender differences in parent–child relations. *Journal of Family Issues, 15,* 148–165.

Author Index

333

Subject Index

A

African American men, 31–32
  roles of, *see Invisible Man* (Ellison)

B

Black men, *see* African American men

C

Capital, *see also* Fathers, capital of
  economic, 325–326
  human, 325
Childrearing, *see* Parenting
Children, *see also* Father–child relationships; Fathers; Parenting
  paternal investment in stepchildren, 103
  socialized into gender inequality, 205–206
Competitive labor market theory
  fertility and parental investment and, 65–77, 125
Co-parental relationship, *see* Parenting

D

Divorce among newlyweds
  prediction of, 155–162

E

Ecological variation
  mechanisms of responses to, 64–65

Economic capital, 325–326, *see also* Fathers, capital of
Economics, family
  life history theory and, 56–61
Education, *see* Fathers, education of; Fertility, male, education and

F

Families, *see also* Fatherhood; Marital interaction; Marriage; Men's family roles; Parenting
  changes in American, 177–179
  historical eras in, 37–38, *see also* Men's family roles, historical perspective on
  positive influence of feminism, 222–225
Family economics
  life history theory and, 56–61
Father–child relationships, *see also* Parenting
  child well-being influenced by, 254–258, 286–292
  nonresident fathers and, 256–257
  paternal influence and child well-being, 279–292
Fatherhood, *see also* Men; Men's family roles; Parenting
  flexibility of, 41–46
  flight from, 22
  institutionalization of, 305
  methodological research issues, 47–49, 279–282
Fathers, *see also* Men; Men's family roles; Parenting

343